HORROR VIDEO
GAMES

THE UNIVERSITY OF WINCHESTER

Martial Rose Library
Tel: 01962 827306

ILL

2 5 NOV 2016

3242330

ILL

2 9 NOV 2019

1485 03958

To be returned on or before the day marked above, subject to recall.

HORROR VIDEO GAMES

Essays on the Fusion of Fear and Play

Edited by Bernard Perron

FOREWORD BY CLIVE BARKER

McFarland & Company, Inc., Publishers
Jefferson, North Carolina, and London

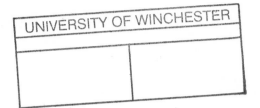

LIBRARY OF CONGRESS CATALOGUING-IN-PUBLICATION DATA

Horror video games : essays on the fusion of fear and play / edited
   by Bernard Perron ; foreword by Clive Barker.
        p.   cm.
      Includes bibliographical references and index.

      ISBN 978-0-7864-4197-6
      softcover : 50# alkaline paper ∞

      I. Video games—Psychological aspects.   2. Horror.   I. Perron,
   Bernard.   II. Barker, Clive.
   GV1469.34.P79H67   2009
   794.8 — dc22   2009026379

British Library cataloguing data are available

Cover art by Frédéric Côté.

Manufactured in the United States of America

*McFarland & Company, Inc., Publishers
   Box 611, Jefferson, North Carolina 28640
   www.mcfarlandpub.com*

Acknowledgments

First and foremost, I would like to thank all the contributors for having taken part in this dark and fun ride in the world of horror video games: Clive Barker (the master mind), Inger Ekman, Ewan Kirkland, Tanya Krzywinska, Petri Lankoski, Christian McCrea, Simon Niedenthal, Michael Nitsche, Martin Picard, Dan Pinchbeck, Richard Rouse III, Guillaume Roux-Girard, Laurie N. Taylor, Carl Therrien and Matthew Weise.

A big thank you to Shantal Robert and Léa Elisabeth Perron who, once again, let me spend all those sleepless nights in horrific worlds, and all those sleepy days recovering from my nightmarish visits.

To my parents, as always.

To Shanly Dixon who has helped me have and keep clearer thoughts all along the proofreading process.

To Kelly Boudreau who has taken a rigorous look at each and every essay.

To the "Ludiciné Strike Team" (Carl, Dominic, Guillaume and Martin) for its constant support, help and friendship.

Table of Contents

Foreword: A Little Light in the Darkness

Clive Barker

This is an important time for games, because they are being ignored.

Not, of course, by the millions of players who make gaming one of the most popular pastimes in the world, nor by the obsessive and hyper-critical individuals who play and review games for the plethora of glossy and heavily illustrated magazines dedicated to the subject. The people who are ignoring this significant phenomenon are the very people who should be most concerned with its power and its influence upon the predominantly young and therefore impressionable minds of our populace: the Zeitgeist-watchers, the professional commentators who make it their business to read the auguries of our culture in the entrails of pop phenomena. To them falls the very significant responsibility of creating a critical vocabulary which will need to be unique.

After all, whatever the shortcomings of games at their present state of development, they are shaping the imaginations, intellects and even the sexual development of the voting populace who will shape the world tomorrow.

> (Here, a short footnote. I realize that not all games are enjoyed by younger players. There are a lot more gamers over twenty who are having fun with what are essentially adolescent power trips. Second short footnote. There are many honorable exceptions to the generalization that these games are adolescent power trips, but this collection of essays focus on Horror Video Games, which by and large play into the primal of those initiation journeys.)

In an earlier time, this audience would have been satisfied with the wonders of Ray Harryhausen's wonderful stop-motion monsters and Raquel Welch's pneumatic breasts in "*One Million Years B.C.*" or had their gonads tickled by the stylized sex games of Comic Books (all those tight-fitting garments that reveal everything and show nothing; the vast array of phallic weapons and monstrous vaginal dimension breaches). Now the audiences that would have lapped up Raquel and her dinosaurs are immersed in far more murky territory and it is serious stuff.

1

Why? Because unlike the audiences for earlier adventure epics involving exquisitely beautiful women, abominable tortures, and fantastically grotesque monsters, these players are involved—*profoundly, intimately involved*—in the action. They do not sit, as I did, seven days in a row, watching every performance of *One Million Years B.C.* in my local cinema in Liverpool. They are locked away in their rooms with sugar and caffeine stoked energy drinks engaging in battles with Dark Forces. This is not remotely the same kind of experience that I had watching the Harryhausen's masterpiece. These players are defining their own kind of heroism, or, more perniciously being drawn into an identification with evil. Let us not dismiss the power of these stories too lightly. *They tell lies.* The most monstrous lie, of course, is the merciless contempt that they stir up for Otherness; the ease with which something other than the human is demonized, and reduced, and made fodder for the gun-wielding player who stands anonymously behind the screen.

Is this not very dangerous territory?

There are of course other, arguably less pernicious lies perpetrated by these ubiquitous fictions. That, for instance, physical beauty is likely to be an indication of moral purity. That, for instance, ugliness is almost certainly the sign of evil. That, for instance, Black Means Bad.

It is encouraging then that you have before you, elegantly edited by Bernard Perron, a collection of essays that treat the phenomenon of Horror Gaming with great seriousness. There were names here amongst the authors that I knew. Dan Pinchbeck, for instance, is a writer whose work is I believe the stuff of lucid visions, showing us the shapes the future may well take. But there are also many names here I did not know, and I was immensely impressed by the profound seriousness with which each of the authors approached this vital area of popular culture.

It's easy to dismiss the stuff which gives people pleasure. We are so often guilty of assuming that the experience which provides pleasure is likely to be benign.

The spectacles in the Coliseum were not benign.

They pandered to the cruelest, most callous, and most vicious part of our nature as animals who have found a way to ritualize their appetites. The sophistication of those rituals does not make the atrocities on view any the less vile; nor any the less dangerous if removed from a truly moral context.

I take it as a given that to dismiss the idea of a moral context is to despair of our species and of our planet.

With that thought, as the Cesar would have proclaimed:

"Let the games begin!"

Clive Barker
Los Angeles, 2009

Introduction:
Gaming After Dark
Bernard Perron

Evaluating Actual Resources

From the gothic novel to the stories of Edgar Allan Poe, Howard P. Lovecraft, Clive Barker and Stephen King, from the Hammer movies to the gore or slasher craze, horror literature and cinema have always elicited a strong interest in the academic community, surprisingly so considering their popular status. On the one hand, this can be explained by the simple fact that fear, as Lovecraft rightly underlines, is the oldest and strongest emotion experienced by humans. What's more, as the ethologist Irenäus Eibl-Eibesfeltd notes: "Perhaps man is one of the most fearful creatures, since added to the basic fear of predators and [above all should we say nowadays] hostile conspecifics come intellectually based existential fears" (quoted in LeDoux, 1996: 129). By exteriorizing doubts and anguish (of death, the body, the other, transgression, etc.), the horror genre helps us to understand and express these feelings. On the other hand, the genre is associated with well-known and easily recognized conventions. Acknowledging more or less flexible rules, the reader/viewer is playing at frightening himself. The mediation of horror has always supposed an important ludic dimension. While this description suits horror video games perfectly, no book has, thus far, been dedicated to the phenomenon. Yet, as Mark Hills asserts in the introduction of *The Pleasures of Horror*, video games go "beyond the critical hegemony of 'horror = films and novels'" (2005: 6).

Academic interest regarding video games has been constantly rising since 2000. Books with a broad and general theoretical approach of the phenomenon are now many: *The Medium of the Video Game* (2001), *The Video Game Theory Reader 1 and 2* (2003 and 2008), *Rules of Play: Game Design Fundamentals* (2003), *Half-Real: Video Games Between Real Rules and Fictional Worlds* (2005), *Tomb Raiders And Space Invaders: Videogame Forms & Contexts* (2006), *An Introduction to Game Studies: Games in Culture* (2008), just to name a few. But as Rune Klevjer points out in a hard core column for the Digital Games Research Association: "There is a gap on our field between general theory and analysis of particular games. [T]here are surprisingly few that direct their attention at the level of genre" (2006). This "genre blindness" is visible insofar as English books on video games studying a generic body of work are, to my knowledge, almost inexistent except maybe for massively multiplayer online role-playing games with titles like *Massively Multiplayer Online Role-Playing Games: The People, the Addiction and the Playing Experience* (2004) or the more focused *Digital Culture, Play, and Identity: A World of Warcraft Reader* (2008).

Apart from two Italian publications— Francesco Alinovi's *Resident Evil. Sopravvivere all'orrore* in 2004 and Bernard Perron's *Silent Hill: Il motore del terrore* in 2006, no study deals entirely with the horror genre in the video game. The few scholarly incursions into that world are to be found in conference proceedings, academic journals and various collections of essays. There is among others, the case of "'Evil Will Walk Once More': Phantasmagoria — The Stalker Film as Interactive Movie?" by Angela Ndalianis (1999), "Hands on Horror" by Tanya Krzywinska (2002), "Proliferating Horrors: Survival Horror and the *Resident Evil* Franchise" by Richard J. Hand (2004), "Sign of a Threat: The Effects of Warning Systems in Survival Horror Games" by Bernard Perron (2004), "Playing with Ourselves: A Psychoanalytic Investigation of *Resident Evil* and *Silent Hill*" by Marc C. Santos and Sarah E. White (2005), and "The Self-Reflexive Funhouse of *Silent Hill*" by Ewan Kirkland (2007). To address in length the issue of fear, terror, and horror in fiction, it is necessary to look in the direction of literature and cinema. One has to take into account past seminal contributions like Todorov's *The Fantastic. A Structural Approach to a Literary Genre* ([1970], 1973), Julia Kristeva's *Powers of Horror: An Essay on Abjection* ([1980], 1982), Carroll's *The Philosophy of Horror or Paradoxes of the Heart* (1990), and anthologies like Barry K. Grant's *Planks of Reason: Essays on the Horror Film* (1984) and Ken Gelder's *The Horror Reader* (2000). However, the many books published in the last few years leave no doubt about the academic vigor surrounding the study of horror. Besides, the genre is growing in popularity. According to Mort Castle: "In 1997, the horror field was emerging from a decade-long slump/disappearance. Today, horror is commercially viable once again, with horror imprint to be found at most major publishers of fiction, and horror a virtual 'sure sell' for youth-oriented films, television programs, and video games" (2006:1). When one knows that the average gamer is now 33 years old (according to the Entertainment Software Association), and that many undergraduates and graduates are now studying games in hundreds of academic programs that include video/computer/digital games in their titles, one realizes the validity and necessity of initiating the study of horror in the videoludic field of research.

A Short Historical Cut-Scene

The horror genre emerges relatively early in the history of the video game with the famous *Haunted House* (Atari, 1981). Of course, the available resources were very limited at the beginning of the eighties. To attract the potential gamer, the horrifying content was mainly evoked by the information on the box. With its 4-kilobyte ROM-based game cartridge (comparatively to the gigabytes of the contemporary home console video games DVD and Blu-ray), the games' capacity to propose a horrifying experience obviously seemed negligible. The forms were already a little clearer in the 1985 action game, *Chiller* (Mastertronic). Ironically, a text adventure game (i.e. that is almost exclusively generated from writing) which will mostly mark this decade: *The Lurking Horror* (Infocom, 1987).

Very quickly, the horror video game attempted to measure itself against literary and film canons. Slashers like John Carpenter's *Halloween* (1978 — game: Atari, 1983) and Sean S. Cunningham's *Friday the 13th* (1980 — game for the NES: LJN Toys, 1989) were adapted. *Project Firestart* (Dynamix, 1989) borrowed generously from the films *Alien* (Ridley Scott, 1979) and *Aliens* (James Cameron, 1986). The game presented the creatures, and other horrifying elements, through shot cut-scenes skillfully integrated into the gamer's playing time. Several third-person graphic adventure games, some with more detailed but static pictures, related themselves to the horror. One may recall, among others, *Call of Cthulhu: Shadow of the Comet* (Infogames, 1993) inspired by the myth created by H. P. Lovecraft. In this line, it was *Alone in the Dark* (1992) that obtained the greatest notoriety. The Infogrames' game simulated the variety of typical filmic shots and exploited the offscreen space so as to create effects of surprise. *Alone in the Dark* equally obtained its fame because it was associated with the birth of a specific horror video game genre: the survival horror; that is horror-based third-person action-adventure games. The game set up several of the generic conventions (inventory, limitation in ammo and health, maze-like world, etc.) of a genre series like *Resident Evil* (Capcom, 1996–2009) and *Silent Hill* (Konami, 1999–2008) which later became very popular. Indeed, the first games of these series are true video game classics, using all the audio-visual tricks of horror film (camera angles and movements, lighting, deadly silences, eerie music, scary monsters, etc.) and showing a wide spectrum of effects, from horror to terror and from the visceral to the psychological. Online specialized databases, such as those of *All Game Guide, Mobygames* or the ones on websites covering and reviewing games like *Gamespot*, although not as exhaustive and precise as one might wish, refer to hundreds of horror video games and denote how much the horror has taken root in the video game.

Looking at the Horror

Given that a great majority of video games are based on the need to stay alive (in front of mushrooms, soldiers, gangsters, cars, spaceships, etc.), survival horror might be the video game genre *par excellence* since it brings out this notion of survival and converts our fear of threats into dreadful monsters (other reasons also allow this statement, see Perron, 2006: 19–26). However, one should not limit the videoludic horror to the sole survival horror genre. The question of genre isn't answered anymore with an inclusive/exclusive approach. Sets of common elements (attitudes, characters, places, aesthetic traits, etc.) and sequences of events serve as constraints for both the production and the reception of an artwork. Genres certainly frame the way a novel, a film or a game is to be understood. Since genre boundaries have become more and more blurred, alternative questions like those of Tom Ryall are required: "'What genre or genres constitute an effective and pertinent context for the reading of this film [or game]?' or 'What is/are the world/worlds invoked by aspects of this film [or game] which will enable it to be situated and understood, its narrative trajectory anticipated, its characters to be constructed, and son on?'" (2000: 236). We can also ask: "What are the most effective effects aim by the games (or the films)?" In that perspective, horror games are mainly intended to scare the gamers. They are, borrowing the expression from Isabel Pinedo, a "bounded experience of fear" (1996: 25).

The video game raises a specific query pinpointed by Thomas Apperley in "Genre and Game Studies: Toward a Critical Approach to Video Game Genres": "It is by turning to the notion of 'interactivity' in particular, that new notions of video game genre are able to emerge from the domination or remediated genre categories" (2006: 19). The ergodic dimension of games extends the scope of the generic study. Take the lists of the top scariest games regularly published in video game magazines, on websites and even made into a series of clips that can be viewed on video sharing websites like You Tube. We find games like *Resident Evil* (Capcom, 1996), *Silent Hill* (Konami, 1999), *Silent Hill 2* (Konami, 2001), *Fatal Frame* (Tecmo, 2001), *Fatal Frame II: Crimson Butterfly* (Tecmo, 2003), *Eternal Darkness: Sanity's Requiem* (Silicon Knights, 2002), *Call of Cthulhu: Dark Corners of the Earth* (Bethesda, 2005), *DOOM* (id Software, 2003), *DOOM 3* (id Software, 2003), *Half-Life* (Valve, 1998) *System Shock 2* (Irrational Games/Looking Glass Studios, 1999). If the first six games are in the tradition of the survival horror, that is third-person action-adventure games where the vulnerability of the player character is played out through not so powerful weapons and limited ammo and health, *Call of Cthulhu: Dark Corners of the Earth* proposes an action-adventure from a first-person perspective. Starting with *DOOM*, the final three games are first-person shooters, relying on or centered on combat and shooting. On the top of their semantic elements and syntactic relationships, borrowed from fantastic, detective, and science-fiction genres in literature and film, those scary games also blurred the boundaries in relation to the gameplay. With the recent release of *Silent Hill: Origins* (Climax, 2007) for the Sony PlayStation Portable (or PSP), the adaptation of the first *Resident Evil* for the Nintendo DS, *Resident Evil: Deadly Silence* (Capcom, 2006), and the first-person shooter *Dementium: The Ward* (Renegade Kid, 2007) and rail-shooter *Touch of Dead* (DreamOn Studio, 2007) for the same DS, the videoludic horror is leaving, with effective results, the home for the handheld game consoles.

Moreover, the essence of the survival horror genre has recently been debated on blogs, online gaming discussion communities, and video game magazines. Leigh Alexander asks: "Does Survival Horror Really Still Exist?" (2008); Jim Sterling adds: "How survival horror evolved itself into extinction" (2008); and Sid Shuman and Patrick Shaw open their report of *Resident Evil 5* (Capcom, 2005) with: "Action or horror?" (2009:37). The possible vanishing of the genre is announced because of the increasing focus on action and the possible vanishing of the Japanese more thought-provoking way of dealing with the genre. Reacting to *Dead Space* (EA Redwood Shores, 2008), Alexander wonders: "So whatever happened to our imperfect, psychologically damaged heroes, our creepy little doll rooms, our feeble switchblades, our crawling dread? And why have they been replaced by gun-toting professionals and space marine types—as if gaming needed any more space marines?" (2008). In fact, with Capcom's *Resident Evil 4* (Capcom 2005), and certainly with the cooperative mode of *Resident Evil 5*, the survival horror game mechanics seems to have moved towards more heroic, tough and robust protagonists whose attacks are more centered on shooting, with more powerful firearms and more ammunition. And successful horror games such as *Condemned: Criminal Origins* (Monolith, 2005) and the Japanese-influenced *F.E.A.R.: First Encounter Assault Recon* (Monolith, 2005) are first-person shooters, the first one placing emphasis on melee combat game. No doubt that with better Artificial Intelligence, physics, rendering capacities and game controls, the videoludic horror is evolving. In the words of Chris Pruett: "Games are not created in a vacuum; game design is like DNA, combining and mutating with each generation" (2008). As a new "nightbreed" is coming, emphasizing again the importance of studying this genre, we need to immediately scrutinize the past and present ones.

Taking Two Strategic Approaches

Knuckling down to work and fill the gap in game studies, between general theory and analysis of particular genres and games, this collection of essays has been divided into two sections.

Approaching the Genre

The first section addresses the question of the horror genre in the video game.

Creative director and writer of *The Suffering* (Surreal Software, 2004) and its sequel, *The Suffering: Ties That Bind* (Surreal Software, 2004), Richard Rouse III begins this section with a great insider's appraisal in "Match Made in Hell: The Inevitable Success of the Horror Genre in Video Games." With practical considerations and references to game mechanics, he explains why horror stories work so effectively in video games. He shows that with their immersive and empowerment nature, video games can scare players in ways far beyond what other mediums have been able to attain. For Rouse, the future for horror games is bright.

As promising as the future of horror games may appear, Carl Therrien underlines in "Games of Fear: A Multi-Faceted Historical Account of the Horror Genre in Video Games" how the history of the genre, and of the video game in general, is far from being written. Non-linear, his historical account examines to what degree the horror genre has affected the many gameplay types it was associated with throughout the history of the medium. As he says, "understanding how horror video games integrated and modified pre-existing figures of interactivity, and which figures came to be associated with the genre, constitutes an interesting way to study the phenomenon." Closely relating to the matter broached in the previous section of this introduction, Therrien also considers the notion of genre and uses Tzvetan Todorov's theory of fantasy literature and its distinction between the uncanny and the marvelous.

Genre definitions are also at the core of Laurie N. Taylor's essay, "Gothic Bloodlines in Survival Horror Gaming." For Taylor, "survival horror," like any genre, is a loose category; it has been used to label games that are not always horror and are not always about survival. Consequently, to fully understand survival horror games and the creation and function of horror in games, Taylor traces the history and influence of other important factors, like the Gothic. Her essay defines the Gothic in prior media and covers the conventions established in Gothic literature, especially in terms of process and materiality. It explains how the Gothic transfers and changes within video games, as well as how those changes impact gaming overall and especially gaming's ability to create horror. Taylor uses the term ludic-gothic to refer to games that may be generically classified as horror or Gothic, but which are dependent on the boundary crossing that is definitional to the Gothic in other forms.

Ewan Kirkland's "Storytelling in Survival Horror Videogames" explores the use of storytelling as an organizing element of horror videogames, the methods of narration they employ, and the relationship between storytelling and horror affect. The essay deals with narrative's role as it facilitates game-play, aids player progress and enriches the gaming experience. As cut-scenes are prominent in survival horror, Kirkland also examines the ways different media are employed to situate gameplay in narrative context and to imply past or future narrative events (newspaper articles, lab reports, photographs, diaries, audio cassettes, painted portraits and computer logs). He also ana-lyzes the various ways the game space and the gameplay contribute to narra-tive processes, from the virtual camera cuts and the pre-determined events triggered by the avatar's movement to the requirement to pick up and cor-rectly use narratively-loaded objects and the very narrow ideal route the gamer has to take.

In "Shock, Horror: First-Person Gaming, Horror, and the Art of Ludic Manipulation," Dan Pinchbeck concentrates on first-person shooters (FPS). He is revealing the ubiquity of horror in the genre. Pinchbeck investigates the pervasion of horror themes and imagery in FPS from the base definition of computer games as systems of affective manipulation and the use of psy-chological constructs. By offering readings of key FPS titles and demonstrat-ing how in-game content contributes to the manipulation of expectations, behavior and affect, Pinchbeck demonstrates that a psychological approach to understanding the functional nature of horror themes, images, devices and schema in FPS games increases the understanding of why such a hallowed relationship exists.

Considering that many survival horror classics have been made in Japan, Martin Picard takes a look at Japanese horror video games in "Haunting Back-grounds: Transnationality and Intermediality in Japanese Survival Horror Video Games." Picard's point of view definitely remains transnational and intermedial, in order to interrogate the "Japaneseness" of the games and to disclose their intriguing mix of Japanese and Western themes and audiovi-sual aesthetics. The essay calls into question the Orientalist and essentialist functions of Japanese icons in survival horror games for the Japanese video game industry. It also analyses how some games revive and revitalize significant cultural figures such as the ghosts and spiritual beings found in the Japanese myths and legends of classical literature and art, and how they explicitly borrow the singular "atmospheric" aesthetic of Japanese visual arts, from the first paintings of the Nara period to the recent trends in Japanese horror movies.

The horror film is defined as a "body genre" because its bodily and ecstatic excess is causing the body of the spectator to be caught up in an invol-untary mimicry of the emotion or sensation of the body on the screen. Inso-far as the gamer is not only caught up in this involuntary mimicry, but is also urged to act and feel through its presence, agency and embodiment in the fictional world, the survival horror genre extends those bodily sensations.

Bernard Perron's "The Survival Horror: The Extended Body Genre" studies these corporealized responses in relation to the three different bodies engaged in the videoludic horror experience: the body of the monster, the body of the player character and the body of the gamer.

ENCOUNTERING THE GAMES

Each contribution to the second section of the collection adopts its own perspective or concentrates on a specific topic in order to take a closer look at some of the key horror video games.

In "Plunged Alone into Darkness: Evolution in the Staging of Fear in the *Alone in the Dark* Series," Guillaume Roux-Girard takes a formalist approach to analyze the *Alone in the Dark* (Infogrames, 1992) series, in which the first installment of the game is considered to be the "godfather of survival horror. Therefore, he shows how the series has continuously evolved to intensify the gamer's emotional dread. For each game, Roux-Girard takes into consideration the narrative, the aesthetics and the gameplay, pointing along the way to the role that the games played in the development of the genre and the innovations they pioneered.

The experience of playing a survival horror game is marked by a sense of vulnerability and an ongoing effort to adapt to unfolding events and environments. These qualities and tasks can be better understood by exploring the similarities between this genre of games and gothic literature, in which obscurity plays an important role in achieving the desired effect. In "Patterns of Obscurity: Gothic Setting and Light in *Resident Evil 4* and *Silent Hill 2*," Simon Niedenthal concentrates on the design and illumination of survival horror environments, such as those found in *Resident Evil 4* (Capcom, 2005) and *Silent Hill 2* (Konami, 2001). According to Niedenthal, those elements are key to achieving obscurity, and contemporary eyetracking technologies can help differentiate the different types of obscurity provided by occlusion, atmosphere or darkness, leading us to begin to grasp how these elements are used to inflect fear.

Inger Ekman and Petri Lankoski's essay, "Hair-Raising Entertainment: Emotions, Sound, and Structure in *Silent Hill 2* and *Fatal Frame*," examines the construction of emotion in games. Ekman and Lankoski combine various theories such as narrative comprehension, goal-oriented evaluations, and the representation of player character to explain the emotional reactions to the video game. Since horror relies a great deal on the audio for creating and supporting the emotions it elicits, they are very attentive to sound, its functional role, its extension into space and its feedback for gameplay. Ekman and Lankoski analyze *Silent Hill 2* (Konami, 2001) and *Fatal Frame* (Tecmo, 2001) to expose the tricks and treats of the survival horror emotional design. In both game worlds where sounds are omnipresent and crucial to survival, they place the threatening monsters or ghosts and the goals of the two player characters at the center of those scary experiences.

The use of a magic camera as a weapon to exorcise powers and to destroy the otherwise immaterial ghost spirits through the act of photographing them being the most original feature of the *Fatal Frame* series (Tecmo, 2001–2008), Michael Nitsche focuses his attention on this device, its use and the concept of spirit photography in the game. The main argument of "Complete Horror in *Fatal Frame*" is that *Fatal Frame* utilizes the ambiguity of the photographic image as both a document and a manipulation to evoke terror. Almost as a mirror to the mediating effect of the photograph, the avatar of the games is interpreted as a kind of medium itself: one that uses the axis of agency and interaction with the game world to transcend the horror from the virtual out to the real world and to ultimately situate the gamer in a horrific situation in both the game space and the real world.

As there is no concept of the dead without one of the trappings of memory, no present with the past, Christian McCrea refers to Jacques Derrida's notion of "hauntology" to study the anachronistic reflections in the horror video game. His essay "Gaming's Hauntology: Dead Media in *Dead Rising*, *Siren* and *Michigan: Report from Hell*" carries on the theme of Nitsche's essay as it observes technologies of representation and video game's own ghosts. The search through static for television channels to tune in to and the VHS aesthetic of the sightjacking of system in *Siren* (SCE Japan Studio, 2004), the photograph taking in *Dead Rising* (Capcom, 2006), and the action seen through the viewfinder of a digital video camera in *Michigan: Report from Hell* (Grasshopper Manufacture, 2004) make the literal connection between the specters of the dead and the specters of media visible.

Matthew Weise introduces in "The Rules of Horror: Procedural Adaptation in *Clock Tower*, *Resident Evil*, and *Dead Rising*" the concept of procedural adaptation to explain the operation of taking a text from another medium and modeling it as a computer simulation. For Weise, procedural adaptation encapsulates what video games do when they codify the conventions of horror texts. To expose the ins and outs of this process, Weise discusses two horror subgenres: the stalker film and the zombie film. He demonstrates how *Clock Tower* (Human Entertainment, 1995), and *Clock Tower 2* (Human Entertainment, 1997) both use the recurring components of the stalker film identified by Carol J. Clover (the Killer, the Weapon(s), the Terrible Place, the Victims, and the Final Girl) and the character behaviors to stimulate the subgenre. As Weise says: "The core transmedial pleasure lies in the player getting to step into the Final Girl's role and discover the emergent dynamics of her iconic peril for themselves." Dealing with the behaviors of the zombie itself, and the dynamics of dwindling safety which are a common dilemma of zombie film protagonists, he then exposes the zombie simulation found in *Resident Evil* (Capcom, 1996), *Resident Evil 2* (Capcom, 1998), and *Dead Rising* (Capcom, 2006).

Tanya Krzywinska also takes us on a journey through the gamescape of adaptation. "Reanimating H.P. Lovecraft: The Ludic Paradox of *Call of Cthulhu: Dark Corners of the Earth*" appraises the aforementioned game released by Bethesda in 2005, a direct adaptation of several short stories written by H.P. Lovecraft. Krzywinska shows how the core characteristics of the "Cthulhu" brand are treated within the terms of video game media and through the design choices along with the ways in which aesthetic values related to the brand and genre are bounded by commercial imperatives as well as to their relation to the way games commonly offer an experience where orchestration is woven with the ludic and participatory. Her essay also takes us through some aspects of both video game history and the horror genre while eventually opening up some questions about the nature of the video game industry, its markets, and what might be said to constitute good or bad design.

The reading through of each one of the exciting essays in this collection remains a great front door to the world of horror video games. So, to anyone who has been gaming after dark, it is time to be thinking after dark.

Works Cited

Alexander, Leigh (2008), "Does Survival Horror Really Still Exist?," *Kotaku.com*, September 29, available online at <http://kotaku.com/5056008/does-survival-horror-really-still-exist>.

Alinovi, Francesco (2004), *Resident Evil. Sopravvivere all'orrore*, Milan: Unicopli.

Apperley, Thomas (2006), "Genre and Game Studies: Toward a Critical Approach to Video Game Genres," *Simulation & Gaming*, Vol. 37, No. 1, pp. 6–23.

Carroll, Noël (1990), *The Philosophy of Horror or Paradoxes of the Heart*, New York: Routledge.

Castle, Mort (ed.) (2006), *On Writing Horror: A Handbook by the Horror Writers of America*, Cincinnati: Writer Digest Books.

Corneliussen, Hilde G., and Jill Walker Rettberg (eds.) (2008), *Digital Culture, Play, and Identity: A World of Warcraft Reader*, Cambridge, MA: MIT Press.

Gelder, Ken (ed.) (2000), *The Horror Reader*, London: Routledge.

Grant, Barry K. (ed.) (1984), *Planks of Reason: Essays on the Horror Film*, Metuchen, NJ: Scarecrow Press.

Hand, Richard J. (2004), "Proliferating Horrors: Survival Horror and the *Resident Evil* Franchise," in Steffen Hantke (ed.), *Horror Film: Creating and Marketing Fear*, Jackson: University Press of Mississippi, pp. 117–134.

Hills, Matt (2005), *The Pleasures of Horror*, Londres: Continuum.

Juul, Jesper (2005), *Half-Real: Video Games between Real Rules and Fictional Worlds*, Cambridge, MA: MIT Press.

Kelly, Richard V. (2004), *Massively Multiplayer Online Role-Playing Games: The People, the Addiction and the Playing Experience*, Jefferson, NC: McFarland.

King, Geoff and Tanya Krzywinska (eds.) (2006), *Tomb Raiders and Space Invaders: Videogame Forms & Contexts*, London: I.B. Tauris.

Kirkland, Ewan (2007), "The Self-Reflexive Funhouse of *Silent Hill*," *Convergence: The International Journal of Research into New Media Technologies*, Vol. 13, No. 4, pp. 403–415.

Klevjer, Rune (2006), "Genre Blindness," Hard Core Columns, *Digital Games Research Association*, November 1, available online at <http://www.digra.org/hardcore/hc11>.

Kristeva, Julia (1982), *Powers of Horror: An Essay on Abjection* (1980) (translated from French by Leon S. Roudiez), New York: Columbia University Press.

Krzywinska, Tanya (2002), "Hands on Horror," in Geoff King and Tanya Krzywinska (eds.), *ScreenPlay: cinema/video games/interfaces*, London and New York: Wallflower, pp. 206–23.

LeDoux, Joseph (1996), *The Emotional Brain. The Mysterious Underpinnings of Emotional Life*, New York: Simon & Schuster.

Lovecraft, Howard Phillips (1973), *Supernatural Horror in Literature* (1927), New York: Dover Publications.

Mäyrä, Frans (2008), *Introduction to Game Studies: Games in Culture*, London and New York: Sage Publications.

Ndalianis, Angela (1999), "'Evil Will Walk Once More': Phantasmagoria — The Stalker Film as Interactive Movie?," in Greg M. Smith (ed.), *On a Silver Platter. CD-ROMs and the Promises of a New Technology*, New York: New York University Press, pp. 87–112.

Perron, Bernard (2004), "Sign of a Threat: The Effects of Warning Systems in Survival Horror Games," *COSIGN 2004 Proceedings*, Art Academy, University of Split, pp. 132–141, available online at <http://www.aestheticsofplay.org/perron.php>.

_____ (2006), *Silent Hill: Il motore del terrore*, Milan: Costa & Nolan.

_____, and Mark J. P. Wolf (eds.) (2008), *The Video Game Theory Reader 2*, New York: Routledge.

Pinedo, Isabel (1996), "Recreational Terror: Postmodern Elements of the Contemporary Horror Film," *Journal of Film and Video*, Vol. 44, No 1–2, Spring-Summer, pp. 17–31.

Pruett, Chris (2008a), "Is Action the Death of Horror?," *dreamdawn.com*, November 22, available online at <http://www.dreamdawn.com/sh/post_view.php?index=7141#comments>

Ryall, Tom (2000), "Genre and Hollywood," in John Hill and Pam Church Gibson (eds.), *The Oxford Guide to Film Studies*, Oxford: Oxford University Press, pp. 327–338.

Salen, Katie, and Eric Zimmerman (2003), *Rules of Play: Game Design Fundamentals*, Cambridge, MA: MIT Press.

Santos, Marc C., and Sarah E. White (2005), "Playing with Ourselves: A Psychoanalytic Investigation of *Resident Evil* and *Silent Hill*," in Nate Garrelts (ed.), *Digital Gameplay: Essays on the Nexus of Game and Gamer*, Jefferson, NC: McFarland, pp. 69–79.

Shuman, Sid, and Patrick Shaw (2009), "Running on Evil," *Gamepro*, No. 244, January, pp. 36–46.

Sterling, Jim (2008), "How Survival Horror evolved itself into extinction," *destructoid.com*, December 8, available online at <http://www.destructoid.com/how-survival-horror-evolved-itself-into-extinction-114022.phtml>.

Todorov, Tzvetan (1973), *The Fantastic. A Structural Approach to a Literary Genre* (1970) (translated from the French by Richard Howard), Ithaca: Cornell University Press.

Wolf, Mark J. P. (ed.) (2001), *The Medium of the Video Game*, Austin: University of Texas Press.

_____, and Bernard Perron (eds.) (2003), *The Video Game Theory Reader*, New York: Routledge.

APPROACHING THE GENRE

Match Made in Hell:
The Inevitable Success of the
Horror Genre in Video Games
Richard Rouse III

Games have inhabited the horror genre for almost as long as they've been in existence. Going back to the text-only interactive fiction game *Zork* (Marc Blank and Dave Lebling, 1980) (which, granted, most would call a fantasy game, not a horror game), a significant portion of the game involved players stumbling around in a dark cave system, hideously afraid of being eaten by a Grue, a terrifying situation no player had ever experience before. Indeed, this was a new type of horror, because death would no longer be something happening to someone else, but instead to you, the player. Any chance of redemption and eventual success would involve you facing down death again and again and somehow, finally, emerging victorious.

The horror games kept going from there, from one of the first graphical adventures *Mystery House* (Roberta Williams and Ken Williams, 1980), to the more overt horror of Infocom's *The Lurking Horror* (Dave Lebling, 1987), to the horror parody of *Maniac Mansion* (Ron Gilbert, 1987), to *Alone in the Dark* (Frédérick Raynal, 1992), to *Resident Evil* (Shinji Mikami, 1996), to *Silent Hill* (Keiichiro Toyama, 1999), to *F.E.A.R.: First Encounter Assault Recon* (Craig Hubbard, 2005), to *Dead Space* (Brett Robbins, 2008). It isn't by accident that so many games have found success in the horror setting. The goals of video games and the goals of horror fiction directly overlap, making them ideal bedfellows. Indeed, when I started out designing and writing the action horror game *The Suffering* (2004), I didn't yet realize just how useful the conventions of horror could be to the inherently constrained and un-realistic world of a video game. By the end of development on the first game and through production of the game's sequel, *The Suffering: Ties That Bind* (2005), we pulled out every horror trope we could that also matched our game design goals, while avoiding techniques that were too cinematic or fundamentally non-interactive.

The horror genre embraces disturbing content and twisted subject matter. This material inherently limits the potential audience, as the mass-market gamers who pick up the squeaky-clean space opera of *Halo: Combat Evolved* (Jason Jones, 2001) or the amusing, virtual dollhouse of *The Sims* (Will Wright, 2000) don't want anything to do with warped nightmares or wading through lakes of blood. Yes the marriage of horror and games just seems too perfect for designers to avoid. And still, there's also a lot of room to continue to evolve the horror game, to move it away from just emulating horror in other media, and instead, to employ the genre to explore the dark corners of humanity in ways that no other medium can.

Practical Considerations

Suspense-driven horror films have long focused on life and death struggles against a world gone mad, with protagonists facing powerful adversaries who are purely evil. One need only look at film examples from *Nosferatu* (F.W. Murnau, 1922), *The Thing from Another World* (Christian Nyby and Howard Hawks, 1951), *Night of the Living Dead* (George A. Romero, 1968), *Alien* (Ridley Scott, 1979) and *Ringu* (Hideo Nakata, 1998) to observe this dynamic at work. These are not films where the evil presence is explained extensively, if at all. Through its actions, this antagonistic force shows itself to be so thoroughly inhuman that no audience member would fault the hero for killing the evil as an act of self-defense. This exactly maps to the experience most action-oriented designers want to create, going all the way back to *Space Invaders*; the player is thrown into a dangerous situation with a clear, undeniable "kill to survive" motivation. The evil forces are numerous and all deserve to die. Hence horror games are a natural fit. Indeed, many games that few would describe as "horror" use variations on those same horror tropes to justify the action in their world (among the many examples, see *DOOM* [Sandy Peterson, John Romero and Tom Hall, 1993], *System Shock* [Doug Church, 1994], and *Half-Life* [Gabe Newell et al., 1998]).

Game storytelling works best when the plot is fairly simple. A lot of nuance can be worked into the environment and the characters the player meets, but the plot is something that needs to be immediately understood and which propels the player through the whole game experience, motivating the actions and choices they're making. Since horror works best the less that is explained and the more that is left up to the imagination, it maps well to game storytelling. In *The Suffering*, I wanted to keep the cut-scenes to a minimum to keep the player in the game as much as possible. With a minimum of "forced" storytelling moments, we had to keep our high level plot understandable without much exposition. As a result, we buried a lot of our back-story in subtle storytelling sections involving dialog played over game-play, graffiti written on walls, very quick semi-animated flashbacks, and cryptic journal entries the player could unlock. This enabled us to keep the story mysterious enough that the player would still be left with numerous unanswered questions. My hope was that the player would fill in the blanks with his own imagination (see Rouse, 2004). One need only look at horror films like *The Birds* (Alfred Hitchcock, 1963), *The Shining* (Stanley Kubrick, 1980), and *The Blair Witch Project* (Daniel Myrick and Eduardo Sánchez, 1999) or some of the best horror writing by Lovecraft or Poe to see that the plot of these works is quite simple, the explanation minimal, and what does happen is barely explained, if explained at all. In horror, the way the audience fills in the blanks will be far more disturbing than anything a writer could possibly come up with. Thus, minimalist game storytelling fits perfectly in the horror genre.

Horror is also ideal for games because it presents a familiar world but with enough of a twist to make it seem fantastic and special. Horror stories are typically set in highly recognizable locations that players can identify but which have been invaded by some evil force. This force has often altered the rules of the world in some way. Thus, horror can be used to introduce unique gameplay mechanics based on this altered reality. Military shooters or open world crime games, set in very recognizable spaces, will always feel pretty similar to each other purely on the level of mechanics, due to the realistic enemy combatants and weaponry at the player's disposal. A horror game can introduce a supernatural element which justifies why the player has unique abilities, why he is hearing the thoughts of others, why bizarre enemies can materialize out of nowhere, and so forth. Yet the familiar setting of horror fiction keeps the player grounded. This is in contrast to the fantasy and science fiction settings popular in so many games. These more fantastic settings allow for unique mechanics but only let them exist in worlds which are inherently foreign to players. One game that both succeeded and failed on this front was the horror-influenced *Half-Life*. Set in the recognizable Black Mesa research facility for the majority of the game, the player spends his time fighting bizarre creatures in this familiar space; it's a very tense and fictionally cohesive experience. In the last quarter of the game, the player travels to the home-world of the aliens, a bizarre space unlike anything the player has seen before. It was at this point that most players felt the game went a bit off the rails and lost the delicate balance of the familiar and the alien that had been present in the beginning of the game.

Even the best simulated game never comes close to feeling like the real world. Even *Grand Theft Auto IV* (Leslie Benzies et al., 2008) and *Assassin's Creed* (Patrice Désilets, 2007), which have arguably come the closest to making the player feel like they are in a true "living, breathing" world, fall short of feeling all that real as soon as one stops to look at them. It's pretty obvious that characters are running on artificial intelligence (AI), no matter how sophisticated. Indeed, the more realistic their behavior and appearance become, the more the perilous "uncanny valley" takes over the experience. This sort of "slightly off" world is ideally suited to the uneasiness of a horror setting. Often people joke that games feel like they're populated by zombies, so why not embrace that? *Dead Rising* (Yoshinori Kawano, 2006) had an excellent simulation of a world filled with zombies, probably indistinguishable from a real shopping mall filled with the undead. The more "human" characters found in *Call of Cthulhu: Dark Corners of the Earth* (Christopher Gray and Simon Woodroffe, 2005) feel zombie-like, but that AI limitation is understandable, given that the town of Innsmouth is supposed to be in the thrall of The Green Sticky Spawn of the Stars. The weird artificiality of game worlds plays directly into the brand of creepiness that the horror genre thrives on.

Finally, it is also convenient that horror tends to draw a younger and more male audience than other fictional settings. Historically, the people who are most interested in the horror setting are also the people who spend a lot of time playing video games. This simple market reality helps keep the horror genre financially viable and subsequent horror games inevitable.

Game Mechanics

A popular game design device is to give players some information about their surroundings, while leaving a lot out. This again is a natural fit for the horror genre. Protagonists in slasher films are never sure where an enemy is or when the next attack is going to come. Being completely blind-sided isn't a lot of fun though, so a number of horror games have used limited information techniques to keep the player apprised that danger is imminent without "giving away" too much. In *Silent Hill 2* (Masashi Tsuboyama, 2001), the player finds a radio which generates static whenever a creature is near. This doesn't tell where exactly it is or what type of enemy it might be, but serves to warn the player and helps build tension in the process. The film *Aliens* (James Cameron, 1986) was famous for its use of the motion detector, which provided a bit more information than the *Silent Hill 2* radio static. This device naturally showed up in the *Aliens vs. Predator* (various) games, and before that in Bungie's first-person shooter *Marathon* (Jason Jones, 1994) (which itself featured a number of levels that felt distinctly horror-inspired). This device only shows enemies that are currently moving, and has the disadvantage of not communicating where they are vertically. With a sufficiently complex "over and under" environment (as was found in *Marathon*) this forces the player to both carefully monitor the detector but also to make choices based on erratic information, creating a much more tense experience in the process.

Much classic horror fiction deals with a fear of the dark. Darkness is great for technologically constrained games, because a lot of darkness means the game doesn't have to render everything for great distances in all directions. Stephen King's story *The Mist* (1980) and John Carpenter's film *The Fog* (1980) are ideal set-ups for a game, particularly when one considers how much cheaper rendering fog is than showing a long, detailed vista. The fog or mist means the player cannot see very far and also allows creatures to get up really close to him before attacking while tidily providing a fictional justification for where they're coming from. And of course this very device was used in numerous *Silent Hill* games. Interestingly, as game graphics have become higher fidelity, what designers can do with them has become more limited. For instance, look at the original *DOOM* games. The games were capable of rendering large areas filled with many enemies (which were all sprites in a 3D world, hence fairly cheap to put on the screen). For the more modern *DOOM 3* (Tim Willits, 2005), the engine technology had come much farther and was capable of rendering highly detailed characters with complex lighting. The drawback was that it wasn't capable of showing that many of them and the advanced lighting was expensive enough that it forced more limited play spaces. Hence, the game took a significantly more horror direction, with fewer, tougher enemies leaping out of nearby shadows, instead of the giant battlefields packed with zillions of creatures. The horror theme was a perfect match for these new mechanics and the new technology.

Various horror scenarios are also ideal for limiting where the player can go. When using a real world environment, it's nice to have a good reason why someone can't just leave town or run to the police, beyond just saying "you can't do that." It can be quite convenient if the player has some sort of psychic disorder that prevents them from leaving. This is easily done in a horror setting, as is the handy thick mist which has descended around the town, filled with tentacled beasties sure to rip a player limb from limb if they enter into this mist. Mysterious "voices" in the player's head can also provide the player with direction or just deliver back-story in an inexpensive fashion. *Silent Hill 4: The Room* (Suguru Murakoshi, 2004), which contains perhaps the most confining primary space ever seen in a narrative video game, places mysterious chains on the door with only the shadiest of justifications. If the player tries to open one of the windows, it is explained that his nightmares have made him fearful of opening them. The player would never buy this in a military or crime game, but in a horror setting it is immediately accepted.

Emotional Response

Beyond the practical benefits of the horror genre for game designers, the horror genre manipulates certain key emotions, which happen to be the same emotional responses games specialize in. For the February 2001 issue of *SIGGRAPH Computer Graphics* I wrote an essay, titled "Games on the Verge of a Nervous Breakdown: Emotional Content in Computer Games," where I noted that games are good at eliciting certain emotions and less effective at others. I encouraged game designers to exploit this potential as much as possible, instead of trying to mimic other genres and the emotions they do well. As it happens, many of those key "game" emotions are also ones ideally suited to the horror genre.

Two of the most obvious of these emotions, in both games and films, are tension and fear. Games provoke these better than other media because there's actually something at stake for the player. In any non-interactive media, the audience is seeing unfortunate events or life-threatening occurrences happen for another person, and the audience's own tension is only possible through empathy with that character's plight. In an immersive game, the player actually projects himself into the experience. The most extreme example of this is a near-miss projectile in a first-person shooter, which may actually cause someone to shift to one side in their seat while they play. With the player fully immersing himself in the world, fear becomes much more intense. Furthermore, in games one can fail, often through their avatar dying. Death means the player will have to replay a section of the game in order to progress, giving death real stakes, unlike a movie, where the plot will keep going no matter who dies.

Another key emotional response that games are good at evoking is pride. This is an emotion other media can't really muster at all. Though there's some bragging rights to be had by saying "I survived a viewing of *The Texas Chain Saw Massacre*," few would argue that it's the same as emerging victorious in a game. In a horror setting, where the player is typically ill equipped and facing nearly-insurmountable and profoundly evil challenges, surviving the situation is all the more meaningful. There's also something about helping other people in the world that makes it a common theme in horror games. When someone asks you directly for help and you are able to solve their problem while saving them from certain death, a very real sense of accomplishment follows. Certainly, no other media provides that sort of direct satisfaction to the audience.

Games are also great at allowing players to experience taboo subject matter in a safe environment. Audiences go to see thrillers for a reason: their lives typically aren't that thrilling or perilous, and movies give them a vicarious thrill. The thrill in a game is less vicarious and more direct, though of course the player is still ultimately safe. The adversaries in a horror game can be dark and twisted, in the best cases evoking real-world horrors that most players would typically not think about, further emphasizing the horror of the experience. For instance, in *The Suffering* games, I deliberately themed all of the enemy creatures after different methods of human execution, because capital punishment is inherently creepy and unsettling, and because most people, even those who are pro death penalty, prefer not to think of the specific realities of execution techniques (figures 1 and 2). Emphasizing this taboo topic forced players to face it, without actually making them attend an execution.

Top, figure 1: In ***The Suffering*** (Richard Rouse III, 2004), Torque is fighting some Slayers in the third-person perspective. ***Bottom, figure 2:*** An Infernas viewed in the first-person perspective in ***The Suffering*** (Richard Rouse III, 2004).

Immersion and Empowerment

One of the biggest advantages games have over other media is how immersive a gaming experience can be. Since players are, to some extent, able to determine the actions of the main character, while playing a game they project themselves into the main character much more than in any other medium. This is especially true in first-person games, where immersion is undeniably one of the primary goals. But even in third-person camera games, players will put themselves in the player character's shoes significantly more than they might in any book or film. *The Blair Witch Project* may be one of the most immersive horror films ever made; however, the audience still feels distanced from the film's characters, pulled along by their dubious choices— whether they agree with them or not. Though no game offers players infinite freedom, even the relatively limited choices presented in a linear point-and-click adventure game makes players feel empowered and thus immersed. Few genres benefit from this immersion as much as horror; but at the same time, some common horror film techniques may actually work against immersion.

A supernatural horror setting allows designers to throw all sorts of bizarre happenings at the player. These may have tremendous game mechanics benefits (as discussed earlier) and can easily be made to fit within the fiction. The challenge for horror game designers is to not go too far with this, to the point where the player starts feeling that he has lost any control over the situation. Despite a supernatural setting, designers must make their world consistent and rules-based, giving the player a fair chance at success. Even in horror, the game player needs a consistent world where the choices he makes will have consistent results that are predictable and will allow him to plan his next move with a reasonable hope of success.

For example, the back-story of *The Suffering* was such that we could materialize a creature out of thin air if we wanted. However, if enemies constantly popped out at the player character, we might have gotten some good scares out of it, but the player would quickly have felt he had no chance of success. Consequently, we worked hard to give characters different "tells," in order to alert the player to the enemies' arrival without completely telegraphing it. For example, the Slayer creatures crawled along the ceiling and could pounce down on the player at inopportune times. After a few encounters with Slayers, the player would learn that whenever they walked into a room they should look up to have a chance of seeing the Slayers on the ceiling before it was too late. Similarly, the Mainliner creatures always emerged from puddles of fluid on the ground (water, blood, et cetera). These puddles were challenging to see ahead of time, but not impossible. Burrower creatures could tunnel through the ground, but left a trail of dirt behind them so players could see where they were coming from. Thus, the astute player could get away from the burrowers by jumping out of the path of the dirt trails. Again, if we had enemies who sprung literally from anywhere, it would have been frightening and plausible fictionally, but far more frustrating; and as soon as a player finds the experience to be excessively unfair their immersion is broken.

Another trap for game designers who are looking to horror films for inspiration is to map the weakness of the main character too much, to the point where the player feels cheated by the ineptness of the character they are controlling. Horror fiction is almost always about a power imbalance of some kind, where the forces of evil are vastly more powerful than those of the hero, making the eventual victory or survival of the hero all the more impressive. However, it's important to keep in mind that almost all narrative video games are power fantasies of one kind or another. If too much of the player's feeling of power is taken away, in comparison to what they're accustomed to experiencing in other games, they're going to feel frustrated and hence pulled out of the experience. Although it may heighten terror in a film, when a protagonist trips over a root while fleeing through the woods from a homicidal maniac wearing a hockey mask, in a game that exact same experience would be infinitely frustrating.

The early *Resident Evil* games featured fixed camera angles that forced players into some pretty terrifying experiences. The fixed camera angles allowed the games to use pre-rendered backgrounds, which made the games look significantly better than their contemporaries who often relied on much lower fidelity real-time 3D environments. This allowed the games to pull off some uniquely "cinematic" scare moments, such as walking down a dark hallway toward the camera and thereby not seeing what was ahead. The fixed camera view also necessitated non-camera relative controls, which could be pretty confusing when a dog burst through a window next to the player. However, as that graphic dominance became less and less of a factor, the games moved away from the fixed camera angles and towards more player empowerment. For instance, look at the evolution from the first *Resident Evil* to *Resident Evil 4* (Shinji Mikami, 2005). The latter allowed the player much more control over where they were looking and featured far more intuitive shooting controls. Yet *Resident Evil 4* remained a scary experience. Instead of featuring a purely "cinematic" feel, the game featured game systems and mechanics that empowered the player while still leaving them at a distinct disadvantage in relation to the zombies. Though the amount of freedom of movement, control, and sheer agency present in *Resident Evil 4* is much less than one might find in a first-person shooter, it was enough to keep the player more immersed in the game than they had been in previous installments.

Of course, relatively few games, horror or otherwise, have done away with that most cinematic device, the cut-scene, surely one of the most jarring immersion breakers in a game's toolbox. Though a cut-scene can perfectly recreate a horror moment from a movie (since it is a movie), it tends to pull players out of the experience. Players instinctively know that the game would never kill them off during a cut scene. Thus a game's most immersive device, the constant fear of death and setback that keep players supremely focused on the moment, is not at all present during a cut-scene. Consider the introduction of Pyramid Head in *Silent Hill 2*. Trapped in a closet, the player is forced to watch this bizarre enemy up close for the first time without being able to do anything to stop him. The creature design is brilliant and as a movie scene it's plenty scary, but in the end it's just a cut-scene. As soon as a cut-scene starts, the player's level of engagement in the game drops, and many players will put the controller down entirely, almost completely disengaging from the game.

Similar creature introductions, in a cut-scene free game like *Half-Life*, may place the player in just as little jeopardy (none), but since the player is in control the entire time they can't be sure they're ever completely safe. Without actually killing the player, the game can very effectively present the illusion of true jeopardy. The player has no way of knowing if the hideous creature may finally break through the glass, creating a situation where they'll need to immediately do something to fight back. Games like *Half-Life* and the recent *Left 4 Dead* (Mike Booth, 2008) give players a good number of choices about how they play, yet are still highly scripted experiences that funnel the player through spaces that give the illusion of being open, but which are typically quite linear. AI-driven events are mixed with highly scripted encounters. But with the same amount of linearity and scripting, a game that leaves the player in control of the camera feels more immersive than one where the camera control is constantly taken away. The perfect framing of a shot may be lost, and even with the most meticulous planning, there's always the chance a player may be looking away at the wrong time and miss a critical event. But what's gained in immersion and the feeling of potential threat more than makes up for these shortcomings, transforming what could have been simply a well-implemented cinematic moment into a still-compelling and distinctly interactivity-focused moment.

Despite some exceptions (notably Square Soft games), the trend over the last decade has been to add shorter and more seamless cut-scenes, with some games such as *Half-Life*, *BioShock* (Ken Levine, 2007) and *Dead Space* eschewing them almost entirely. *Resident Evil 4* introduced the notion of keeping the player immersed in the cut-scenes by adding very limited interaction to them. At key moments, players would need to hit a button to make their character swing a knife at just the right instant to stop a potentially fatal attack. Though this minimal interaction kept players on edge, it did nothing to make them feel truly empowered, creating a *Space Ace* (Rick Dyer and Don Bluth, 1994)-esque experience which had the potential to be frustrating in its own right. However, these barely-interactive cut-scenes were very well executed and quite thrilling, thus representing an interesting evolution of the cut-scene.

In *The Suffering*, we had a specific story to convey, but we didn't want storytelling to get in the way of our core game experience with excessive cut-scenes. With immersion as a core design principle, we had a rule of thumb that cut-scenes were to be used exclusively for short, pivotal story points or for intensely scary scenes. Furthermore, we wanted to keep the player character (Torque)'s actions fairly neutral during these scenes to avoid negating the player's feeling that they were fully in control of Torque at all times. As I mentioned earlier, this meant we kept our plot quite simple, and integrated a lot of our storytelling into the game-world itself.

The Bright Future of the Blackest Night

With all the ways in which games are the ideal medium for the horror genre, it seems we gamers will be playing them for a while to come. But what form will they take in the future? I've never been one to make far reaching predictions, but it seems there is ample room for growth. A lot of the non-game horror examples I've referenced in this essay have been examples from movies, which makes sense since most horror games have taken films as their primary source of inspiration. But as horror games continue to evolve, I suspect they will become more and more distinct from horror films, in the same way horror films have progressed beyond being straight adaptations of horror prose. In my opinion that is a good thing. Consider the interesting case of H.P. Lovecraft adaptations. One might conclude that his work has fared better as games than it ever has on film. This is true for the classic pen and paper game *Call of Cthulhu* (Sandy Peterson, 1981) and the recent *Dark Corners of the Earth* console game, as well as the Cthulhu-inspired *Eternal Darkness: Sanity's Requiem* (Denis Dyack, 2002). It would seem that Lovecraft's unique brand of unease, insanity, and slow paced terror works better in an interactive space than it ever can as a movie. As the horror game keeps evolving, more such cases will emerge, to the point where games that borrow too much from films will start to look dated. The future for horror games is bright indeed, and the sooner developers embrace what makes them unique, the better.

Works Cited

Rouse, Richard III (2004), "Postmortem: The Game Design of Surreal's *The Suffering*," *Gamasutra.com*, June 9, available online at <http://www.gamasutra.com/features/20040609/rouse_pfv.htm>.

_____ (2001), "Games on the Verge of a Nervous Breakdown: Emotional Content in Computer Games," *ACM SIGGRAPH Computer Graphics*, Vol. 35, No 1, February, pp. 6–10, available online at <http://delivery.acm.org/10.1145/380000/377032/p6-rouse.pdf?key1=377032&key2=9495221321&coll=&dl=acm&CFID=17246211&CFTOKEN=13109303>.

Games of Fear:
A Multi-Faceted Historical
Account of the Horror Genre
in Video Games
Carl Therrien

Long before the introduction of the gothic novel, the playful evocation of fear and dread in the audience had been a central component in a great variety of legends and folktales. Succubus, incubus, imps, and harpies populate medieval imaginary; an impressive bestiary permeates literature, the visual arts, and reality to a large extent. As reason theoretically superseded those "dark ages," the Enlightenment saw the rise of the phantasmagoria show, delighting audiences with a variety of effects (building on magic lantern expertise) that sought to represent otherworldly apparitions. Cultural artifacts associated with horror fiction, from the gothic masterpieces of Shelley and Stoker, the stories of Maupassant, to the contemporary *slasher* movie series, have received a lot of academic attention. Still lacking from these accounts, however, is the contribution of a medium that, like the horror genre itself, has been seen mostly as popular fare: video games. This essay proposes to shed light on the contribution of gaming culture through a general historical overview of horror games. Faced with the necessity of delineating a historical corpus, the lingering problem of genre definition naturally emerges. Scholars frequently disagree on the constitutive features of horror literature and cinema; the interactive medium adds a whole layer of structural elements that can potentially be integrated in genre definitions, adding to the confusion in many ways. Rather than producing another attempt at refining the existing definitions, this essay puts forth the various conceptions of horror fiction and presents examples of video games that correspond to each of these conceptions. Rereading the evolution of the genre from thematic specifications to presentation and gameplay mechanics, it seeks to pave up the way for a multi-faceted, non-linear historical account of the phenomenon.

The History of Video Games

In spite of the vigorous wake of video game studies in the past ten years, the history of the medium is still a field in emergence at best. Clear equivalents of film conservation institutions are just starting to emerge, and accessibility issues are rampant.[1] Most history books are journalistic efforts that focus on the development of the industry and the creation of landmark games. Steven L. Kent's *The Ultimate History of Video Games* (2001) was constructed from a previous account by Leonard Herman (*Phoenix: The Fall & Rise of Videogames*, 1994) and 500 interviews with major figures in the industry. Van Burnham's account (*Supercade: A Visual History of the Videogame Age 1971– 1984*, 2003) focuses on the "classic" period of video game history that is said to end with the crash of 1983. For every year under examination, the book proposes visual documents and short descriptions of major consoles and games. Kent's focus on the game creators and the industrial context — the "source" of games in a very limited sense of causality — and Burnham's "objective" chronological periodization and accumulation of "facts" are both reminiscent of the blind empiricism associated with positivist methodology, and represent the reality of the medium and its evolution in a superficial way. Moreover, the constant development of imaging techniques, processing power, and interactive devices favors a teleological view of video game history. A constant onslaught of seemingly perfected yet constantly perfectible machines has been associated with the medium. This ongoing technological evolution generates an overarching narrative which defines the ideal stage of the medium in terms of immediacy (Bolter and Grusin),[2] feeding on actual techno-military devices (complex simulations, virtual reality interfaces) as much as fantasized versions of these experiments (the Star Trek Holodeck). Consequently, historical accounts have a tendency to give particular attention or significance to the hardware and games that represent a technological breakthrough.[3] On top of the obvious industry landmarks, the timelines integrated in history books focus, to a great extent, on the first occurrences of specific technological aspects. The launch of major consoles and computer systems are listed along important games, and generations of hardware often serve as historical period markers.[4]

Many defining aspects of the video game experience are likely to be obscured by such progress-laden, technology-focused means of organization. It is certainly possible to reintegrate technical aspects into broader concepts that encompass design rationales as well as specify modes of reception, and thus understand more accurately video games and their evolution as a cultural phenomenon. For reasons that will become progressively obvious throughout this essay, the study of genres from a historical perspective represents a step in the right direction. Yet, surprisingly few efforts have been made in that area. *The Video Game Explosion* (2007) proposes only a few chapters on specific genres ("Adventure Games," "Interactive Movies"). At the time of writing this contribution, the history of horror video games is primarily being developed by the gamer community itself; amateur and journalistic resources do exist. "Chris' Survival Horror Quest" proposes a database dedicated to the horror genre with what appears to be very large inclusion criteria (horror themes, and a clear intention to scare), yet with somewhat arbitrary restrictions designed to keep this amateur endeavor manageable (no PC, handheld or lightgun games).[5] Both *Gamespot.com* (Todd, 2001) and *IGN.com* (Barraza, 2008) have proposed features on the history of the genre; both simply list a few landmark games. Clearly, genuine academic research on the history of horror video games has limited foundations to build on. By exploring the various conceptions of horror fiction and their relevant ludic manifestations, this contribution aims to present a broad account of the phenomenon in the hope of triggering further historical investigations on the genre.

Defining the Horror Genre

Considering its multidimensional nature, the concept of genre can be rather confusing. As Tzvetan Todorov pointed out, following Russian formalists, the concept has been used to theorize many traits of the literary (and by extension artistic) manifestation, in a spectrum ranging from the most formal aspects to the thematic content; "we may already accept that genres exist at different levels of generality, and that the content of this notion is defined by the point of view we have chosen" (1973: 5). Gérard Genette has demonstrated how one of the most abstract uses of the concept, stemming from Aristotle's *Poetics*, has generated centuries of confusion. The common distinction between the lyrical, narrative, and dramatic modes of representation have not only been falsely attributed to the great thinker, but the defining aspects of the typology have been reinterpreted countless times from the classical to the post–romantic eras (Genette, 1979). Genres can be defined as a mix of formal and thematic traits. Aristotle proposed a system where the mode of imitation (narrative or dramatic) combines with the quality of human beings portrayed (superior or inferior to "us"), resulting in four classical genres: tragedy and comedy for the dramatic mode, epic and parody for the narrative mode.[6] At the other end of the spectrum, the concept of genre can also refer solely to the type of content to be found in a fictional world: romance novels are saturated with courteous love and similar themes, whodunits and film noirs revolve around an investigation, westerns are concerned with the frontier and the conflicts that arose during this phase of American expansion, etc. The type of content is commonly conceptualized as the "thematic specification" of a broader genre (Genette), or through a biological metaphor (the detective novel being a "species" of the genre known as the novel). Needless to say, horror fiction has been thoroughly discussed at the thematic level. Elements such as scary animals, supernatural beings and otherworldly manifestations are put forth, most often hinting at a clear intention to incite fear in the user.[7]

H. P. Lovecraft has notoriously insisted on the fearful experience of the reader in order to define horror and fantastic literature (Todorov, 1973: 34). Many contemporary commentators would agree with Isabel Pinedo that horror fiction, at its core, is a "bounded experience of fear" (Perron, 2005). However, Todorov rejected this point of view most clearly: if the feeling of fear becomes a defining criterion, then "we should have to conclude that a work's genre depends on the *sang-froid* of its reader" (1973: 35). The author acknowledges the primary function of the fantastic elements in this type of literature: to incite fear, horror, or curiosity in the reader, in a specific way that can't be reproduced by other genres (1973: 92). However, in his conception still influenced by structuralism, literature is an autonomous system closed on itself; the actual reader of the text and the emotions experienced are not the object of literary studies. Nonetheless, the reader, understood as a mere function of the text, is central to Todorov's definition:

> ... in the universe evoked by the text, an event — an action — occurs which proceeds from the supernatural (or from the pseudo-supernatural); this action then provokes a reaction in the implicit reader (and generally in the hero of the story). It is this reaction which we describe as "hesitation," and the texts which generate it, as fantastic [1973: 103].

Through narration, fantastic literature constantly stresses a hesitation between two potential explanations: a naturalistic one, and a supernatural one. The genre appears to be staging the real-world fear associated with the unknown. Evoking a psychological response from the reader is certainly not as problematic today as it would have been when Todorov wrote his seminal essay. The hesitation of the implicit reader most likely translates into a diffuse apprehension — the least intense level of fear on Robert Plutchik's scale of fear — for the actual reader.[8] It also evokes the slower build up of tension that Will Rockett labeled "terror" in a study about the "cinema of cruelty"; the author clearly opposes horror and terror based on the actual perception of a threatening element (horror) versus the anticipation of such an encounter and the lingering anxiety that it supposes (referred in Perron, 2004).

Todorov locates fantastic literature in the middle of a continuum of genres ranging from the purely uncanny — where exceptional events can still be explained through common laws — and the purely marvelous — where the supernatural elements have become accepted as natural. Horror in its most striking form, for the author, clearly falls on the side of the uncanny (1973:

47); he evokes the stories of Ambrose Bierce, renowned for their gruesome depiction of war. The source of dread is striking yet completely rational, thus minimal doubt or hesitation arises. This association is consistent with *slasher* movies such as the original *Friday the 13th* (Cunningham, 1980) and *The Texas Chain Saw Massacre* (Hooper, 1974). However, it seems to contradict the common association between horror and "supernatural" evil creatures. The very existence of monstrous figures—werewolves, vampires, zombies, aliens, etc.—or the reality of supernatural manifestations can be clearly acknowledged early on in many stories deemed horrific in nature. The potential vivid imagination of a protagonist or a trickery of the senses are not brought up in *Alien* (Scott, 1979) or *Village of the Damned* (Carpenter, 1995); no hesitation arises about the extraordinary events, and thus this type of horror would fall under the "marvelous" category for Todorov. By contrast, Noël Carroll's seminal work on horror fiction (*The Philosophy of Horror or Paradoxes of the Heart*, 1990) focuses entirely on the theme of monstrosity to define horror fiction, and in doing so, excludes the previous examples relating to the purely uncanny. There is obvious common ground between Todorov's connection with the uncanny and Carroll's insistence on monstrosity: both appear to associate horror with revulsion. But to complicate matters even more, fictions that don't integrate repulsive elements but instead rely on hesitation — the defining criterion of fantastic literature — to instigate fear have also been labeled "horror" (*The Blair Witch Project*, Myrick & Sánchez, 1999).

It is now obvious that disagreements on the thematic elements that define horror fiction and its effects generate a great deal of confusion. The same confusion exists in the realm of video games: many famous games can be associated with the uncanny, marvelous and fantastic versions of horror. It is unclear just how supernatural the bats and tarantulas of *Haunted House* (Atari, 1981) really are — the proportions at this early stage of visual development being impossible to read — but at least one element of this alleged first horror game puts it under the "marvelous" category. The back-cover of the retail box clears-up any potential ambiguity about the white collection of pixels moving on the screen: "*Ghosts*. Bats. Tarantulas. One-Player Game" (emphasis mine). In *The Lurking Horror* (Infocom, 1987), a seminal text-adventure game, one of the first otherworldly manifestations occurs when the player reaches the higher structure of the great dome in the aeronautic engineering building: "[a] single, bright-blue eye opens in the squishy mass, and the tentacle *(for that's what it is)* retracts" (emphasis mine). Similarly, no hesitation arises in the *Castlevania* series (Konami) or in *Diablo* (Blizzard, 1997), where dozens of different hell minions hinder players on their quest to destruct the ultimate source of evil.[9] The three Edgar Allan Poe stories adapted in *The Dark Eye* (Inscape, 1995) focus on sordid tales of murder and malevolence.[10] Much like its source material, the game falls into the category of the uncanny. The same could be observed about the *Jack the Ripper* games (St. Bride's School, 1987; Intergalactic Development, 1994; Galiléa, 2004), based on the famous unsolved murder mystery. Even though most publications simply labeled them "adventure games," further inspection of the promotional material and editorial reviews indicate the horror connection.[11] The original *Clock Tower* (Human Entertainment, 1995, Super Famicom) is clearly inspired by the *slasher* movie breed of uncanny, while some supernatural elements permeate later games in the series.

As is true for horror cinema, games that rely on the fantastic effect until the end are few and far between. In *Phantasmagoria* (Sierra On-Line, 1995), many plot devices and themes seek to instigate a sense of doubt about what might really be happening. Since moving into a new luxurious mansion with her loving husband, Adrienne has been experiencing a series of horrific nightmares. This classic framing device can trigger a skeptical attitude (for it could be only a dream)[12] and points towards the potential psychological instability of the protagonist. The couple's new house once belonged to a famous magician, Zoltan Carnovasch (Carno), and many other elements are related to the trickery of the senses (not the least of which is the title of the game). However, as her husband becomes increasingly aggressive, and as ghostly apparitions multiply, the supernatural explanation clearly prevails. At various points in *Condemned: Criminal Origins* (Monolith, 2005), indistinctively during interactive segments or cut-scenes, the protagonist is subjected to nightmarish visions that appear to be hallucinations. At the beginning of chapter five, the introductory cut-scene shows Ethan Thomas alone in public transit; when he is attacked by a strange creature, Ethan "wakes up" and ponders "Maybe I've gone crazy." Similar devices have been used in the *Gabriel Knight* series (Sierra On-Line) and in *Dark Seed* (Cyberdreams, 1992). The *Silent Hill* series (Konami) is probably the most relevant example of the fantastic effect in the realm of video games. Even though the creatures you encounter in town can kill your avatar, leading to an actual "game over" screen, the reality of the events depicted is not clearly established. Without warning or explanations, the player is frequently transported to a nightmarish version of the locales. Protagonists sometimes express disbelief; after the first visit to this darker realm, Harry (the avatar in the first game) wakes up in a café and wonders out loud "Was I dreaming?" As the player completely uncovers the background story of James Sunderland at the end of *Silent Hill 2* (Konami, 2001), it appears that the character has been caught in some sort of psychological hell. Yet the continuity of the setting from one game to the next seems to indicate that Silent Hill could be a very real place where lost souls go to wander.

Todorov's typology of genres has been used as a pretext to dive in the world of horror video games. One could argue, however, that generic models designed to study literature or cinema are not completely relevant in understanding the medium. In "Genre and Game Studies: Toward a Critical Approach to Video Game Genres," Thomas Apperley has made a strong case against the remediation of existing generic labels and urged researchers to focus on interactivity to develop video game genre studies.[13] Generic labels referring specifically to gameplay elements do exist, and it is interesting to note that horror-themed games have emerged in a great variety of ludic genres: side-scrolling action games (*Castlevania* and *Akumajo Dracula X: Chi No Rondo*, Konami, 1986/1993; *Alien Storm*, Sega, 1990; the *Splatterhouse* series, Namco); shooting galleries (The *House of the Dead* series, Sega; *Space Gun*, Taito, 1990; *Corpse Killer*, Digital Pictures, 1994) and first-person shooters (*Blood*, Monolith, 1997; *Clive Barker's Undying*, Dreamworks Interactive, 2001); fighting games (the *Mortal Kombat* series, Midway); text-adventures (*The Lurking Horror*) and point-and-click adventure games (*I Have No Mouth and I Must Scream*, Cyberdreams, 1994; *Call of Cthulhu: Shadow of the Comet*, Chaosium, 1993); role-playing games (*Diablo*; *Parasite Eve*, Square, 1998) and at least one MMORPG (*Requiem: Bloodymare*, Gravity, 2007); even some racing/vehicular combat games (*Carmageddon*, Stainless Software, 1997; *Twisted Metal Black*, Incognito, 2001) and strategy games (the *Dungeon Keeper* series by Bullfrog) make use of horror themes. However, when Capcom released *Resident Evil* in 1996, a new generic label was quickly embraced by the gaming community; the infamous intro screen read: "Welcome to the world of survival horror."

In the context of video game studies, where broad theoretical efforts are still far more common than specific studies of games or genres, survival horror games have clearly attracted more attention than other genres (if one excludes the sociological focus on MMORPGs). Since the label emerged specifically to describe a type of video game, it might seem paradoxical that its definitions rely heavily on formal traits which actually restrict the typical gameplay experience. Bernard Perron observed that "the survival horror genre might be the game genre most often compared to film" (2005). In another contribution, he studied how scare tactics in these games often build on cinematographic expertise: point of view restrictions (third-person perspective, fixed camera angles) and editing effects (rapid change of camera angles) seek to accentuate startle effects (2004). Similarly, Jay McRoy declares that survival horror games "are 'viewed' primarily from a third-person perspective framed in high-angle long shots intended to intensify the sensation of vulnerability, isolation, and, in certain 'key' moments, shock" (2006). McRoy also underlines the importance of cut-scenes in the genre, following an extensive study by Tanya Krzywinska. For Krzywinska, the succession of gameplay segments and non-interactive cut-scenes, between self-determination and pre-determination, is particularly suited to the experience of horror, for it "ties into and consolidates formally a theme often found in horror, in which supernatural forces act on, and regularly threaten, the sphere of human agency" (2002: 207).

Video game creators' fascination for cinema has played a decisive role in shaping the general evolution of the medium, yet the connection does seem even more palpable in the case of horror games. It goes much beyond the simple commercial synergy one can already observe in the adaptations of classics such as *The Texas Chain Saw Massacre, Halloween* (both by VSS, 1983) or *Friday the 13th* (Domark, 1985). After just a few generations of hardware, horror video games tried to recreate the same visceral revulsion, subtle moods, and other strategies that cinema had achieved. When one of your friends is about to be brutally murdered in *Friday the 13th*, a gloomy piece of music forewarns of the upcoming tragedy. In order to maximize the startle effect when the actual murder occurs, the game will display a gruesome image —

provided the player is close enough to the scene (figure 1); it also produces a horrendous scream whose overly synthetic nature only adds to the shocking effect. Similarly, in *Project Firestart* (Dynamix, 1989), horrific elements are presented through short cut-scenes as the player approaches; more detailed than the typically distant point of view of 2D action games, these gruesome depictions also sought to create startle effects (figure 1).

The representational economy of the graphical adventure genre always favored detailed visuals over fast manipulation of the assets and as such became an ideal format to develop the repulsive aspect of horror; notable examples include *Shadow of the Comet* and *Prisoner*

Figure 1: Gruesome images in *Friday the 13th* (Domark, 1985) and *Project Firestart* (Dynamix, 1989). These short cut-scenes, which also include shocking audio elements, are inserted in the middle of a play session in order to accentuate startle effects.

of Ice (Chaosium, 1995), both inspired by the Cthulhu mythology created by H. P. Lovecraft. Building on this economy, *Alone in the Dark* (Infogrames, 1992) used a mix of hand-drawn backgrounds and real-time 3D characters to mimic the analytical editing of mainstream cinema. Along with *Doctor Hauser* (River Hill, 1994), the *Alone in the Dark* series influenced the look and pacing of *Resident Evil* to a great extent.

Despite being the only game genre to be defined with such obvious cinematographic references, survival horror also supposes specific gameplay mechanics. However, the confusion we exposed regarding the horror genre also exists with this new label. *Cahiers du Cinéma*'s description is somewhat hazy:

> The player progresses alone in a worrisome universe. In the shadows one can feel the presence of strange creatures that can be heard before being seen; soon, zombies and other monsters will strike. Initially an adventure game located in the world of a horror movie, Survival Horror — as the name implies, it's mainly about not dying — has slowly become a genre in itself [2002: 82, freely translated].

Bernard Perron also identifies the adventure game connection: "At the action level, in a third-person perspective, the gamer has to find clues, gather objects (you cannot do without keys) and solve puzzles" (2004). On top of the inventory system and linear puzzle-driven progression inherited from adventure games, the genre incorporates a combat element whose paradoxical nature has been underlined many times: "in the world of Survival Horror, given the limited ammunition at one's disposal and the less than marksman-like aim of the player's character, 'discretion' is frequently 'the better part of valor'" (McRoy, 2006). If one actually brings to scrutiny these associations, however, it becomes clear that many defining features are often restricted to a specific game series and not relevant to the corpus as a whole. The first *Resident Evil* game indeed limits the resources such as ammunition and healing plants, but by the time the Capcom franchise reached its fourth installment, the amount of weapon-related action exceeded any big budget action blockbuster. Moreover, a skilled player in *Silent Hill* can accumulate a lot of ammunition and health packs.[14] This second landmark series is associated most clearly with the relative "ordinariness" of the protagonists — an aspect that McRoy wrongfully links to a lack of shooting skills; although the same observation could be made about other games such as the *Clock Tower* and *Fatal Frame* series, it is not relevant in the case of *Resident Evil*, where players impersonate highly trained members of special military units. Even some first-person shooters or brawlers, such as the *Condemned* games by Monolith and *DOOM 3* (Id Software, 2004), have been associated with survival horror.[15] In a gesture that is highly controversial from a historical point of view, some publications even retrospectively attributed the label to older games: *Gameinnovation.org* declares *Sweet Home* (Capcom, 1989)[16] to be the first of the genre, and *Haunted House* possesses all of its characteristics according to *Gamespy.com*.[17] Recently, Leigh Alexander — the news director for *Gamasutra*—wrote a feature entitled "Does Survival Horror Really Still Exist?"[18] After this brief inspection of the games, one could go even further and ask: what exactly was survival horror to begin with?

The answer will not come as a surprise to anyone familiar with genre studies: as any other genre, survival horror is a concept caught up in time. The historical — more specifically, evolving — nature of genres has been acknowledged even when the urge to define stable structures still prevailed. Todorov observed that in natural sciences, the concept of genre is not fundamentally altered when a new specimen is born; evolution occurs at such a slow pace that it can be neglected more easily. In the realm of artistic practices, by contrast, "evolution operates with an altogether different rhythm: *every* work modifies the sum of possible works, each new example alters the species" (1973: 6). In spite of the various attempts to restrict horror to one or a combination of the three dimensions of the uncanny, the marvelous, and the fantastic, and to define survival horror according to very specific aspects, it appears that these labels have a tendency to become more inclusive than exclusive. One could say that the academic efforts to clearly define these objects actually go against the natural fluctuations of concepts that are often put forward by the production pole — as in the case of survival horror — and reappropriated by a community of receptors that range from critics to casual players. In this exchange, which is not always concerned with the clarity of generic definitions, it is likely that any novel, movie or game that evokes a strong experience of fear or related emotional states (apprehension, anxiety, alarm, terror, despair) will become associated with the horror or survival horror genre.[19] Is the only purpose of genre studies to refine definitions and "canonize" specific traits in order to clear-up "wrong" genre associations? Instead of perpetuating what Hans Robert Jauss has called the substantialist approach (1986), whose rigid definitions only serve classificatory purposes at best, genre studies should strive to develop analytic tools that can account for the evolution of the concepts it seeks to understand.

Caught Up in History

Designing comparative tools to better understand the evolution of a genre is a complex endeavor. For instance, such tools became a preoccupation during Bernard Perron's funded research project on interactive cinema. The *Ludiciné* online database (www.ludicine.ca), conceived in the course of this project, integrated a complex taxonomy in order to categorize all the relevant objects through a systematic terminology, pertaining to various dimensions ranging from technical aspects to interactive design. Developing a simple, yet precise descriptor system to account for the gameplay experience was one of the biggest challenges faced by the Ludiciné team. It became obvious early on that relying on existing generic labels would not allow a clear description of the interactive encounter. As we have seen, genre labels can be loosely defined and information about a specific game can vary greatly from one database to the next.[20] Even if such a stable genre typology existed, many games stray from acknowledged formulas by integrating gameplay elements from other genres or by simplifying typical game mechanics. It was decided to define gameplay components based on the imaginary represented actions performed by the player in the virtual world; these components are referred to as "figures of interactivity." Interactive cinema, which encompasses experiments in theatres, artistic works on various formats (installations, CD-ROM), and video games integrating live-action video, share many figures of interactivity with the later form such as "conversation," "spatial exploration" and "shooting." The research also uncovered very specific figures such as mediated forms of editing — spatial, temporal, and rhythmic (see Perron & Therrien, 2007, and Perron, Arsenault, Picard and Therrien, 2008). Similarly, understanding how horror video games integrated and modified pre-existing figures of interactivity, and which figures came to be associated with the genre, constitutes an interesting way to study the phenomenon.

Even though many survival horror games involve combat, the first *Resident Evil* clearly directed players to adopt a new attitude towards confrontation: "Be smart! Fighting foes is not the only way to survive this horror" reads an introductory screen before the self-running demo. Indeed, if players empty their pistol clip on the first zombie they encounter instead of fleeing, their chances of survival is quite limited considering the scarcity of ammunition to be found early on. For all the incongruities and arbitrary conventions of the game, it is at least consistent in that players can even flee some boss encounters. It is interesting to note that "flight" is actually quite a prevalent action in many horror-themed games. In *The Lurking Horror*, the only way to survive an onslaught of rats in the steam tunnels underneath the aeronautic engineering building is to flee back and break a pipe to chase the vermin with steam. In the second stage of *Akumajo Dracula X: Chi No Rondo*, a behemoth suddenly bursts in and starts chasing the player's avatar, Richter Belmont (figure 2). One of the most terrifying moments in *Fatal Frame II: Crimson Butterfly* (Tecmo, 2003) comes when Mio looses the camera obscura, her only weapon against the spectral apparitions; for a good part of chapter 7, players have no choice but to flee from Sae, a particularly deadly ghost. *Call of Cthulhu: Dark Corners of the Earth* (Headfirst, 2005) proposes many lengthy, obstacle-laden chase sequences in the troubled Lovecraftian little town of Innsmouth. *Parasite Eve* (1998) comes from the same team that brought us *Final Fantasy VII* (1997) at Square Soft — a franchise and a company that became emblematic of Japanese role playing games and turn-based, menu-driven combat; for this sci-fi horror RPG, the team privileged a hybrid combat system that puts a lot of emphasis on dodging the minions' attacks (figure 2). Last but not least, escaping the scissor man in *Clock Tower* is one of the major components of the game; Jennifer has to run from room to room, where few hiding spots will actually fool the stalker.

The scarcity of offensive resources is interconnected with another common figure in horror video games: management. In a context where ammunition is hard to find, players are more

Figure 2: Fleeing the behemoth in *Akumajo Dracula X* (Konami, 1993); Dodging attacks in *Parasite Eve* (Square Soft, 1997).

likely to use these resources very carefully, take the time to aim properly, and salvage more powerful weapons for the most terrifying encounters. In *Condemned: Criminal Origins*, it is impossible to carry more than one weapon at any given time, and firearms are hard to come by; once they put their hands on a .45 pistol or a sawed-off shotgun, players can either empty their charger immediately and then rely on melee weapons, or use the firearm itself as a melee weapon in order to save ammunition. The scarcity of resources thus favors a potentially more methodical attitude with regards to fighting or shooting mechanics. However, "management" takes on a very literal meaning in games where the avatar can gather resources in an "inventory" whose space is restricted. In the first *Resident Evil*, each weapon, ammunition clip, healing herb and puzzle-related item takes up one square in an inventory system that comprise no more than six or eight, depending on the avatar selected at the beginning of the game. In 1981, *Haunted House* already proposed a restrictive inventory system. Even *The Lurking Horror*, a text-adventure game, made inventory management an integral part of the experience. In a world were many useless objects could be gathered, the nameless G.U.E Tech student that players guide can only carry so much; the amount that can be carried actually depends on an implicit strength attribute that the player can restore by drinking cola.

In some horror games, actions such as combat and flight are integrated in a broader system pertaining to the sanity of the protagonist, who is typically defined by a health capital in most action games. A variety of meters and signs indicate this relative sanity, thus having players adopt an attitude of "psychological monitoring." In *Friday the 13th*, the expression of your avatar — which is constantly shown in close-up at the bottom of the screen — becomes progressively aggravated as Jason kills your friends one by one. The failing sanity of your avatar, however, doesn't have any real implications or consequences on the gameplay. The original *Clock Tower* on Super Famicom proposes a similar meter at the bottom of the screen where the strength of the protagonist, Jennifer, is color-coded from blue (maximum strength) to red (minimum strength). Strength in this case is directly linked to a psychological aspect: it will deplete when Jennifer is faced with stressful situations (such as a confrontation with the scissor man). Once the meter reaches red, the avatar is more likely to lack the physical/psychological strength to escape danger, no matter how fast the player taps on the "panic" button (figure 3). It is Silicon Knights' *Eternal Darkness. Sanity's Requiem* (2002) that thoroughly developed the concept of psychological well-being in a game. Here the sanity meter is a purely conventional green line that will deplete when any of the twelve characters to be controlled by the player faces a frightening element, most notably the many skeletons and zombies that populate each of the game's settings. Before the player can regain sanity, typically by finishing off the wounded monsters, the game will introduce a series of increasingly disturbing effects that can hinder gameplay in many ways: camera angles become more oblique; sound effects are covered by lingering low tones, frightened whispers and sobbing; sudden decapitation of the protagonists and modification of rooms' proportions are revealed to be hallucinatory sequences; etc. *Call of Cthulhu: Dark Corners of the Earth* seeks to create similar effects in first-person mode: when players gaze on horrific elements or when they are chased by an angry mob, intrusive trailing and blurring effects will permeate the point of view; if the threatening situation is not escaped in due time, the protagonist might go as far as to commit suicide! On top of the rhythmic "simon-says" segments, *Indigo Prophecy* (Quantic Dream, 2005) makes sanity a decisive factor to progress in the game: if the meter is depleted, its game over (figure 3).

In the realm of horror games, the study of specific figures of interactivity is faced with a challenge that didn't surface as clearly for the study of interactive cinema. Whereas the integration of live-action video favored simple interactive design throughout the corpus, horror video games range from the early days to the most complex contemporary productions (*Dead Space*, EA Redwood Shores, 2008) and consequently,

Figure 3: Stressful situations have a direct impact on Jennifer's psychological well being in *Clock Tower* (Human Entertainment, 1995); In *Indigo Prophecy* (Quantic Dream, 2005), the sanity of your avatar is a decisive element to progress in the game.

the complexity of control methods vary greatly from game to game. "Flight" is really not experienced in the same way in a lateral 2D game (*Clock Tower*) as it is in a first-person "square-by-square" exploration game (*Waxworks*, HorrorSoft, 1992); similar observations could be made about fighting and shooting experiences. Are there gameplay design choices that clearly differentiate these figures and others such as "stealth," "puzzle" and "management of resources" from their integration in non horror games? To address this issue would require a methodical descriptive tool that is precise enough to account for the great variety of interactive encounters, yet abstract enough to avoid listing all the actual manipulations on the various control devices and their effects in the game on a case-by-case scenario. This tool should encompass game design as a whole, since the representation of space, the relative complexity of the rules associated with the avatar's physical and psychological integrity, and the relative complexity of the simulated world (A.I., physics) all have an impact on the overall balance of the game and the player's agency. "Spatial exploration" could be carried out in first- or third-person perspective, by lateral scrolling, square-by-square, or on the depth axis through illusory depth cues and interpolation of 2D objects, or in a fully realized 3D world; the world to be explored could be opened in many directions, organized linearly, or even circularly. The monitoring of vital resources might involve basic physical and/or psychological integrity, or each of these categories could be affected by many other variables (as in the AD&D-inspired RPGs that include stats on endurance, strength, dexterity, intelligence, wisdom, charisma, etc.); players might be able to accumulate some capital for each variable, and the variation of these variables might affect gameplay in a binary fashion (life/death), through various distinct stages, or in a progressive manner.

Commenting on the evolving nature of genre, Jauss declares:

> If we replace the substantialist concept of genre [...] with the historical concept of continuity [...], the relationship of a unique text with the series of texts that constitutes the genre is revealed as a process of creation and constant modification of a horizon. The new text conjures up for the reader (the listener) the horizon of an expectation and of rules that he knows thanks to previous texts, and that are immediately subjected to variations, rectifications, modifications or that are simply repeated [1986: 48–49, freely translated].

Jauss' aesthetic of reception is not only a plea for the exhaustive study of the interaction between art and its audience, but a very strong case for the reformation of literary and art history. Genre studies, incidentally, appear to be a good starting point for this reformation, since generic constructs play a major role in the interaction between the creative and receptive poles. In order to define and understand the evolution of the "horizons of expectations" specific to an epoch and culture, Jauss listed three relevant areas of investigation: preliminary experience with the norms of artistic forms/genres; relationship of the work with other works in the reception context; comparison between the poetic and pragmatic uses of language (1982). Applying Jauss' recommendations to the study of video game genres and their evolution supposes a colossal amount of work. Such research necessitates the elaboration of detailed comparative tools that can account for the great disparity of audiovisual and procedural design on many levels: between games associated with the same generic label; between the whole spectrum of video game genres; between games and relevant daily life experiences such as learning and pragmatic uses of computer-mediated interaction; etc.

Needless to say, the tentative comparative system that was briefly introduced in the context of this essay on the historical study of horror games represents but one humble, yet necessary step to develop a conception of video game history that can give the interactive encounter and its evolution at least as much importance as the techno-industrial accounts. This proposition clearly echoes the methodological reformation of cinema history triggered by the Brighton conference in 1978; historians sought to evacuate teleology, underlining the partial nature of previous efforts "written and theorized under the hegemony of narrative films" (Gunning, 1990: 56), and developing accounts that integrate design rationales, specify modes of reception, and position the medium in larger cultural series. Tom Gunning suggested that "[e]very change in film history implies a change in its address to the spectator, and each period constructs its spectator in a new way" (1990: 61). In order to investigate horizons of expectations and define prevalent "modes of address" at any given time, video game studies would benefit from an extensive historical account of gameplay mechanics. By restricting the focus on a corpus whose defining features are constantly modified, genre studies constitute a good opportunity to attract attention to this evolution.

One might suppose that horror games typically integrate the most dysphoric of gameplay combinations; the development of "flight" sequences are a good point in case and the prolongation of the whimsical puzzle tradition inherited from the adventure genre can certainly put the player in a state of "aporia" (Aarseth, 1997) quite frequently. A closer investigation, however, might reveal that the evolution of the horror genre runs parallel to the evolution of the medium as a whole, whose "mode of address" seems progressively geared towards player gratification. The puzzles in *Resident Evil 4* are much simpler than those of the first episode; a typical first-person shooter demands better shooting skills than survival horror games; death in the first *Silent Hill* is not only easily erased through a save system that is restricted solely by the actual space on the memory card, but tips and tricks are displayed to make sure that players are aware of the better strategies to progress in the game. The notorious difficulty of early titles such as *Donkey Kong* (Nintendo, 1981) and *Pac-Man* (Midway, 1980) encouraged a highly competitive environment where the display of proficiency in arcade parlors became an attraction in itself. As the industry progresses from this highly competitive model, where technological attractions are presented in the context of an arcade parlor in order to maximize the potential "attraction of the self," to the domination of home-based entertainment geared towards the gratification of casual gamers, we might have witnessed already a major change in video games' mode of address that is echoed by the evolution of the industry as a whole. Incidentally, the study of learning curves, manipulation complexity, satisfactory performance intervals, tutorials, in-game aids, save systems and check points, from a historical perspective, could flesh out this proposition, eventually resulting in a functional historical conceptualization. Although the amount of comparative work needed to refine these tentative propositions is quite substantial, genre studies are clearly a good starting point to advance, fearlessly, in this investigation.

Notes

1. If one excludes the web databases that collect virtual copies of the games, the closest approximation of such an essential resource has been the itinerant Videotopia exhibit. However, some decisive efforts are being made: the Library of Congress announced it would preserve a "game canon" formed of the ten "most significant" titles (Chaplin, 2007), and academics from Nottingham Trent University, in collaboration with the National Media Museum in Bradford, has created the U.K.'s first official National Videogame Archive in November of 2008 (Pigna, 2008).

2. *Immediacy* refers to the logic whereby media is made to disappear and become transparent as much as possible (Bolter and Grusin, 1999: 21).

3. *The Video Game Explosion* (Wolf, 2007), the first truly academic effort on the subject, also exemplifies this focus on technology to conceptualize the history of the medium; games are thematically organized in accordance to a technical aspect in many instances ("Vector Games," Laserdisc Games," "CD-ROM Games," "Handheld Video Game Systems," "Online Role-Playing Games," etc.).

4. On the Wikipedia account of video game history, generations play a major role; from the Magnavox Odyssey to the PlayStation 3, seven major generations have been outlined. In his 2001 account, Kent dedicates two chapters to "The 'Next' Generation" (the mid 1990s competition between the Sony PlayStation, Sega Saturn and Nintendo 64), and underlines the relative nature of this "next" phase furthermore in "And The Cycle Continues." One of *The Video Game Explosion*'s major period distinction is entitled "Advancing to the Next Level (1995-Present)"; Wolf notes that by the end of 1994, "[t]he industry was booming again, providing the revenue to invest in new technological advances, like 32-bit home game systems, that were just around the corner" (Wolf, 2007:107).

5. <http://www.dreamdawn.com/sh/index.php>

6. As a matter of fact, subsequent distortions often resulted from a misunderstanding of these associations made by Aristotle; "the romantic and post-romantic division envisions the lyric, epic and dramatic not as simple modes of enunciation, but as genuine genres, whose definition inevitably integrates a thematic element, vague as it may be" (Genette, 1986: 140, freely translated).

7. For an overview of the different thematic elements associated with horror and fantastic literature, see Todorov (1973: 100–102).

8. The model developed by Robert Plutchik includes height basic emotions, organized in a circle in order to represent the relative semantic opposition of the emotional tags. The four antinomic pairs are: anticipation/surprise, joy/sadness, trust/disgust, fear/anger (1980). Plutchik refined his model by introducing different intensity levels for each of the basic emotions. Fear is then located in the middle of a scale going from apprehension to terror. According to Plutchik, the combination of two of these basic affective components can account for more complex emotions. Fear thus becomes a central component in many emotional "dyads":

with trust, it becomes submission; with surprise, it creates a sense of alarm; with joy, it corresponds to guilt; with sadness, it causes despair; with anticipation, it turns into anxiety.

9. *Diablo*'s inside box cover reads: "Experience the horror of a world held in the grasp of the lord of terror."

10. The three stories are: *The Tell-Tale Heart*, *The Cask of Amantillado* and *Berenice*.

11. The 1987 text adventure game contained a few gory depictions of murder victims, and received a restrictive 18+ rating from the British Board of Film Censorship. The cover art of the 2004 game reads "From Out of the Shadows the Legendary Terror Returns"; the review on GamerHell underlines the horrific elements (Berntsen, 2004).

12. The box cover actually reads: "Pray it's only a nightmare."

13. "I suggest that the primary problem with conventional video games genres is that rather than being a general description of the style of ergodic interaction that takes place within the game, it is instead loose aesthetic clusters based around video games' aesthetic linkages to prior media forms" (Apperley, 2006: 7).

14. In the third installment in the series, more ammunition can be added in the various locales in order to help players who didn't find enough clips on their way.

15. For example, *UGO* has included *Condemned 2: Bloodshot* in their top 11 survival horror games list (Thor Jensen, 2008). *DOOM 3* and *F.E.A.R: First Encounter Assault Recon* (Monolith, 2003) are featured in *IGN.com Australia*'s "The Evolution of the Survival Horror Genre" (Barraza, 2008).

16. <http://www.gameinnovation.org/>. In a previous, open-contribution version of database, the first survival horror game was said to be *Aliens: The Computer Game* (Activision, 1986).

17. <http://www.gamespy.com/articles/490/490366p1.html>.

18. Writing about the upcoming *Resident Evil 5*, Alexander (2008) observes: "When you watch Chris Redfield (who over the years has apparently been lifting a lot of weights) charge through an open village with the camera over his brawny shoulder, toting heavy arms with his tough-sexy partner Sheva by his side, it ought to make you thrill with anticipation for what could be the next great action game. But it also ought to make you wonder — is this really survival horror?"

19. Incidentally, many online publications offer their own list of the "scariest games" of all time. *IGN.com* has repeated the feature on multiple occasions, typically on the 31st of October of each year; on top of the classic titles such as *Silent Hill* and *Fatal Frame* (Tecmo), it is interesting to note that less obvious games such as *Half-Life* (Valve, 1999) and *X-COM: UFO Defense* (a turned-based strategy game from Mythos, 1994) occasionally made the list. *Gametrailers.com* has also produced a top ten list in 2006.

20. Mobygames lists 8 genres, including "action," "educational," while distinguishing "racing/driving" and "sports." Additionally, it includes 27 sports and 42 non-sports "themes" that can specify the type of fictional world ("Cyberpunk/Dark Sci-Fi," "Naval") or refer more or less directly to gameplay elements ("Puzzle-Solving," "Shooter"). KLOV lists 35 genres ranging from "Card" and "Trivia" to classic arcade genres such as "Shoot'em up" and "Scrolling Fighter."

Works Cited

Aarseth, Espen J. (1997), *Cybertext. Perspectives on Ergodic Literature*, Baltimore: The Johns Hopkins University Press.

Alexander, Leigh (2008), "Does Survival Horror Really Still Exist?," *Kotaku.com*, September 29, available online at <http://kotaku.com/5056008/does-survival-horror-really-still-exist>.

Apperley, Thomas (2006), "Genre and game studies: Toward a critical approach to video game genres," *Simulation and Gaming*, Vol. 37, No. 1 (March), pp. 6–23.

Barraza, Clara (2008), "The Evolution of the Survival Horror Genre," *IGN.com*, September 1st, available online at <http://pc.ign.com/articles/906/906852p1.html>.

Berntsen, Andreas Misund (2004), "Jack The Ripper Review," *GamersHell.com*, January 31st, available online at <http://www.gamershell.com/pc/jack_the_ripper/review.html>.

Bolter, Jay David, and Richard Grusin (1999), *Remediation. Understanding New Media*, Cambridge, MA: The MIT Press.

Burnham, Van (2003), *Supercade. A Visual history of the Videogame age 1971–1984*, Cambridge, MA: The MIT Press.

Carroll, Noël (1990), *The Philosophy of Horror or Paradoxes of the Heart*, New York: Routledge.

Chaplin, Heather (2007), "Is That Just Some Game? No, It's a Cultural Artifact," *New York Times*, March 12, available online at <http://www.nytimes.com/2007/03/12/arts/design/12vide.html>.

Collective (2002), *Cahiers du Cinéma*, Special Issue on Video Games, September.

Genette, Gérard (1986), "Introduction à l'architexte" (1979), in Gérard Genette and Tzvetan Todorov (eds.), *Théorie des genres*, Paris: Seuil, pp. 89–160.

Gunning, Tom (1990), "The Cinema of Attractions. Early Film, Its Spectator and the Avant-Garde," in Tom Elsaesser (ed.), *Early Cinema: Space-Frame-Narrative*, London: BFI, pp. 56–62.

Jauss, Hans Robert (1986), "Littérature médiévale et théorie des genres" (1970), in Gérard Genette and Tzvetan Todorov (eds.), *Théorie des genres*, Paris: Seuil, pp. 9–36.

_____ (1982), *Toward an Aesthetic of Reception*, Minneapolis: University of Minnesota Press.

Juul, Jesper (2005), *Half-Real. Videogames Between Real Rules and Fictional Worlds*, Cambridge, MA: the MIT Press.

Kent, Steven L. (2001), *The Ultimate History of Video Games*, New York: Three Rivers Press.

Krzywinska, Tanya (2002), "Hands-On Horror," in Geoff King and Tania Krzywinska (eds.) *ScreenPlay. Cinema/Videogames/Interfaces*, London: Wallflower Press, pp. 206–223.

McRoy, Jay (2006), "The Horror Is Alive. Immersion, Spectatorship, and the Cinematics of Fear in the Survival Horror Genre," *Reconstruction*, Vol. 6, No. 1, available online at <http://reconstruction.eserver.org/061/mcroy.shtml>.

Perron, Bernard (2005), "Coming to Play at Frightening Yourself: Welcome to the World of Horror Games," *Aesthetics of Play. A Conference on Computer Game Aesthetics*, University of Bergen, available online at <http://www.aestheticsofplay.org/perron.php>

_____ (2006b), "The Heuristic Circle of Gameplay: The Case of Survival Horror," in M. Santorineos (ed.), *Gaming Realities: A Challenge of Digital Culture*, Fournos: Athens, pp. 62–69, available online at <http://www.ludicine.ca/sites/ludicine.ca/files/Perron — Heuristic Circle of Gameplay — Mediaterra 2006.pdf>.

_____ (2004), "Sign of a Threat: The Effects of Warning Systems in Survival Horror Games," *COSIGN 2004 Proceedings*, Art Academy, University of Split, pp. 132–141, available online at <http://www.ludicine.ca/sites/ludicine.ca/files/Perron_Cosign_2004.pdf>.

_____ (2006a), *Silent Hill: Il motore del terrore*, Milan: Costa & Nolan.

_____, and Carl Therrien (2007), "»Pointez-et-cliquez ici« Les figures d'interactivité dans le cinéma interactif des premiers temps," *Film Style*, Udine: Forum, pp. 395–403, available online at <http://www.ludicine.ca/sites/ludicine.ca/files/Perron & Therrien — Pointez et cliquez ici.pdf>.

_____, Dominic Arsenault, Martin Picard and Carl Therrien (2008), "Methodological Questions in Interactive Film Studies," in *New Review of Film and Television Studies*, Vol. 6, No. 3, December, pp. 233–252.

Pigna, Kris (2008), "U.K. Launches First Official National Videogame Archive," *1up.com*, available online at <http://www.1up.com/do/newsStory?cId=3170366>.

Plutchik, Robert (1980), *Emotion, a Psychoevolutionary Synthesis*, New York: Harper & Row.

_____ (1994), *The Psychology and Biology of Emotion*, New York: HarperCollins.

Poole, Steven (2000), *Trigger Happy. Videogames and the Entertainment Revolution*, New York: Arcade Publishing.

Schaeffer, Jean-Marie (1986), "Du texte au genre" (1983), in Gérard Genette and Tzvetan Todorov (eds.), *Théorie des genres*, Paris: Seuil, pp. 179–205.

Scholes, Robert (1986), "Les modes de la fiction" (1974), in Gérard Genette and Tzvetan Todorov (eds.), *Théorie des genres*, Paris: Seuil, pp. 77–88.

Stempel, Wolf Dieter (1986), "Aspects génériques de la réception" (1979), in Gérard Genette and Tzvetan Todorov (eds.), *Théorie des genres*, Paris: Seuil, pp. 161–178.

Therrien, Carl (2007), "Graphics in Video Games," in, Mark J. P. Wolf (ed.), *The Video Game Explosion. A History from PONG to PlayStation and Beyond*, Westport: Greenwood Press, pp. 239–50.

Thor Jensen, K. (2008), "Survival Horror Video Games Top 11," *UGO.com*, available online at <http://www.ugo.com/games/survival-horror-games-top-11/>.

Todorov, Tzvetan (1973), *The Fantastic. A Structural Approach to a Literary Genre* (1970) (translated from the French by Richard Howard), Ithaca: Cornell University Press.

Tood, Brett (2001), "Ghouls, Ghosts, and Long-Legged Beasts. A Modern History of Horror Games Part 1," *Gamespot.com*, July 6th, available online at <http://uk.gamespot.com/gamespot/features/pc/history_horror_pt1/index.html>.

Wolf, Mark J. P. (ed.) (2007), *The Video Game Explosion. A History from PONG to PlayStation and Beyond*, Westport: Greenwood Press.

Gothic Bloodlines in
Survival Horror Gaming
Laurie N. Taylor

Introduction

Like many other avid video game players, *Resident Evil* (Capcom, 1996) presented me with something unfamiliar. My first experience with the *Resident Evil* series was playing *Resident Evil 2* (Capcom, 1998). As a player, the opening sequence required me to run past enemies and to avoid fighting. After so many years spent perfecting button sequences and learning new fighting skills, running was not an option. Playing the opening sequence again and again, the thought of running simply did not exist as an alternative, or at least not as an acceptable option. Learning to run, or unlearning to always fight, accompanied other processes of learning and unlearning. Mastering — or perhaps mastering how to cope with — the alternative gameplay mechanics presented by *Resident Evil 2* made me rethink my understanding of games and gameplay. The linear progression of video games as a form — with improvements and expansions that relied on exploiting technical advances and demanded ever-improving player skill — had forked. *Resident Evil 2* is not the first or the last game to present an alternate path to traditional game development. However, it was the first of the games I had encountered that I now describe as ludic-gothic, which has also been labeled survival horror.

Games labeled survival horror, however, are not always horror (as with the *Dino Crisis* games that game producer Capcom attempted to classify as "panic horror") and are not always about survival, as with the light-gun *Resident Evil: Survivor* (Capcom, 2000). As with other genres, survival horror is the child of many other genres, notably adventure, but also including action, horror (without the survival component), and the Gothic. Survival horror games earned their genre title because of their use of horror elements and because of their gameplay emphasis on surviving instead of thriving. Like most genre definitions, survival horror is a loose category and one unevenly applied by players, journalists, designers, and scholars. Its origin is generally traced back to *Alone in the Dark* (Infogrames, 1992) and then its exemplification and subsequent expansion in *Resident Evil.*[1] *Alone in the Dark*'s game designers drew from H. P. Lovecraft's horror writing, elements of horror and Gothic fiction and film, and added an unusual gameplay format. These elements allowed *Alone in the Dark* to give birth to a "new" type of horror genre, but a genre that had not taken its first breath. *Resident Evil* sounded survival horror's first cry, drawing from horror, science-fiction, the Gothic, and many other genres as they operate in non-gaming media yet, it subverted typical gaming genres and conventions.

The *Resident Evil* series was foundational for the establishment of the *survival horror* genre and for the definitions of its boundaries. The survival horror genre definition was quickly stressed to contain the many games labeled by it, especially with the release of *Resident Evil 4* (Capcom, 2005). Any discussion of genre works risks formalizing and limiting the genre, instead of simply creating a loose definition for use in analysis. As Lawrence Alloway contends, "One of the dangers of genre theory is that the categories may be taken rigidly. When that happens they lose their descriptive usefulness and assume a normative function" (1971: 53). The same descriptive usefulness, weighed against the dangers of over normalization, can be said of video games as well as video game genres. Marie-Laure Ryan notes that Wittgenstein's arguments from *Philosophical Investigations* can be used to show that games as a medium have a complicated network of similarities and details, which sometimes overlap and sometimes do not. From Ryan's perspective, Wittgenstein argues that particular forms are best characterized by "family resemblance" because they overlap and criss-cross without forming an exact structure (2001: 177). Consequently, video game genres, like larger media structures, are constituted by systems of family resemblances that cannot be strictly delimited. Ryan further states, "What constitutes a family, however, is not resemblance but kinship relations. The set of games may be fuzzy, which means that there is no set of necessary and sufficient conditions for an activity to be covered by the word game" (2001: 177). While Ryan is addressing how to classify games as a general category, the same "kinship relations" apply to game genres. The individual games may or may not share specific resemblances with each other, but they will share kinship relations in terms of their formal and functional elements. As genres, survival horror, horror, and Gothic influenced games, share many family traits as they exist in other media. However, tracing the Gothic's influence on gaming is particularly important because of the Gothic's obsession with boundary crossing.

This essay examines the Gothic in video games, games which I term ludic-gothic, to show how the process of boundary transgression is transformed by the video game medium to create horror. I use the term ludic-gothic to refer to games that may be generically classified as horror or Gothic, but which are dependent on the boundary crossing that is definitional to the Gothic in other forms. In the process of ludic-gothic gaming's transgression, boundaries move and shift, changing available methods and manners for transgression, further changing genre definitions and canonical classifications for gaming. Because of their reliance on boundary transgression, ludic-gothic games aid in defining many video game conventions as well as many of the conventions for related genres, like horror. Tracing the Gothic, one of survival horror's parents, as it is feeds into the development of survival horror or its ludic-gothic sibling I examine the Gothic influence and impact on video games. The ludic-gothic is created when the Gothic is transformed by the video game medium, and is a kindred genre to survival horror. By differentiating the Gothic into the aesthetically Gothic and the ludic-gothic, I explain how the Gothic transfers into and changes within video games, and how those changes impact gaming overall and especially gaming's ability to generate horror. In doing so, I also explain the significance of ludic-gothic and horror games to define video games as a cultural form and their canonical works by which to derive new concepts and definitions.

(Survival) Horror & the Gothic

Video game genre definitions are more problematic than the already fluid genre definitions for most other media forms because video game genres rely on existing genres—from art and literature — and then add genre conventions related to gameplay. Genres like survival horror are named in relation to their narrative and aesthetic qualities, which relate to horror, and their gameplay qualities, where the game goal is survival. While survival horror may seem like an ideal genre classification because it embraces narrative, aesthetic, and gameplay elements, the survival horror label has also been applied to games that are based on survival (e.g.; games with limited ammunition) even when those games were not horror games. Survival horror is sometimes inaccurately applied to games that draw on the aesthetics of horror and limited ammunition, as with light-gun horror games like *The House of the Dead* (Sega, 1996, arcade) or the aesthetics of horror and heightened difficulty levels as with the *Devil May Cry* games (Capcom, 2001–2008).[2] Richard J. Hand describes survival horror as "generally understood to be a game in which the player leads an individual character through an uncanny and hostile environment where the odds are weighed heavily against the avatar" (2004, 17). However, this focuses on the gameworld's general conceptualization and the difficulty level rather than the actual operations of gameplay. Similarly, the typical canon of survival horror games—*Alone in the Dark, Resident Evil, Silent Hill, Fatal Frame*—draws from multiple narrative and aesthetic genres including horror and the Gothic. Horror games existed prior to the development of the survival horror genre. However, the games within the horror genre were often classified inappropriately because classifications were based on aesthetic or narrative qualities rather than the ability to generate horror.

Hand rightly argues that survival horror predates gaming, yet he misapprehends the fundamental differences between narrativized and played event, collapsing story and game without considering process or affect; "'survival horror' in literature or film presupposes a narrative in which the reader/spectator follows (rather than 'plays') the journey of a protagonist (not avatar) through the eerie and horrific" (2004: 122). Gaming draws from prior media; however, gaming is played. And survival horror in particular is defined — even if loosely or problematically — on playability. Playability itself is determined by the narrative, game design and play structures, the operations of those structures in terms of play processes, and the affect of gameplay. While Hand's explanation of survival horror could suffice for horror alone, it does not address the way in which horror is elicited nor the significance of gameplay. Clarifying part of the equation, Noël Carroll defines horror in relation to affect. Carroll states that horror and the Gothic share a close relationship, but that horror "is essentially that linked with a particular affect [...] horror" (1990: 4–5, 15). Horror can be represented and invoked through aesthetic and narrative conventions established in various media forms as well as through the younger conventions of gameplay. In "Hands-on Horror," Tanya Krzywinska studied the increased levels of horror as contingent upon the players' ability to control or to loss of control in gameplay (2002), and Jay McRoy followed; describing horror games as augmenting traditional horror texts through the addition of play (2006). As a genre, horror can continue to function similarly across media forms— novels, cinema, and games— but can be intensified by the appearance of control and then its loss. Yet, that alone does not encompass what survival horror has come to mean nor does it reflect the related influence of the Gothic, whose reliance on process necessitates further changes for its translation into gaming.

Unlike horror, which is defined by affect, the Gothic is best defined by its processes,[3] and, in particular, by subversion or transgression of boundaries, especially those boundaries that define the normative power structures (e.g.; family, law, and society). Horror often transgresses boundaries in order to generate fear; however, Gothic texts transgress boundaries to question, define, and redefine them. While horror and the Gothic may rely on the same elements and boundaries, their purposes and processes differ. The Gothic is defined by the process of transgressing boundaries, which may generate fear;

and horror is defined by the process of generating fear, which may be accomplished by the transgression of boundaries. The Gothic and horror genres are thus defined by their processes. The *survival* component of survival horror similarly relies on a process— here the process in gameplay of surviving rather than thriving.

Tracing survival horror's lineage thus includes the Gothic, as defined by the transgression of borders and boundaries: horror, as defined by the bounded experience of fear; and terror, defined as beginning at the ends of horror where the experience of fear escapes all bounds. Under these general and always mutable definitions, horror and terror genres are defined in relation to fear, to engender a particular affect; whereas, the Gothic is one defined the boundaries and their operations— specifically their transgressions or subversions— within a given text. Hence, horror may rely on the Gothic to create the situation necessary for fear, and the Gothic may create horror in designing its boundaries and their illicit crossings.

The Gothic requires material and formal elements as well as the process of becoming Gothic through the transgression of boundaries. Because of its emphasis on process, the video-ludic Gothic is tied to gameplay, especially as technology shapes and alters gameplay. The process of adaptation in survival horror is thus "procedural rhetoric," defined by Ian Bogost as the underlying method that structures and informs the game world (2007: 2–3). Survival horror's procedural rhetoric, prior to and including *Resident Evil 4*, has been the subversion of gameplay norms. However, this subversion is not present in all games currently classified as survival horror. For games utilizing the procedural rhetoric of subversion taken from the Gothic, along with aesthetic and thematic concerns from the Gothic and horror, ludic-gothic becomes a more analytically productive classification.

Survival Horror Is Born

Survival horror games began with the release of *Alone in the Dark* in 1992 on multiple gaming platforms. The first *Alone in the Dark* followed several rules, which would come to found part of the rubric defining survival horror; for example limited ammunition and the need to run from enemies, forced backtracking over the same areas in new game contexts, and limited carrying space. While *Alone in the Dark* was the first game to be dubbed "survival horror," *Resident Evil*, released in 1996 to widespread acclaim, immediately defined the emerging genre.[4] At the same time as *Resident Evil* was exploring the popular arena of survival horror, winning several awards and being mass-marketed, *Silent Hill* was released in 1999 (Konami Team Silent). It also helped to define the survival horror genre because it further exploited the technical limitations of the PlayStation platform to present a truly horrific gaming experience. From these early genre-defining works, many other pivotal works for the genre have sprung, such as *Fatal Frame* (Tecmo, 2001) and *Fatal Frame 2: Crimson Butterfly* (Tecmo, 2003),[5] in addition to less genre-defining works like *Silent Hill 2* (Konami Team Silent, 2001) and *Silent Hill 3* (Konami Team Silent, 2003), along with survival horror derivatives like the *Onimusha: Warlords* (Capcom, 2001) and the *Dino Crisis* series (Capcom, 2000). Because the survival horror genre label is insufficiently defined, these works are only sometimes termed survival horror by journalists, scholars, developers, and players. The differing inclusion or exclusion of particular games is often based on the particular writer's consideration of the importance of certain formal and functional characteristics for the genre.

Because survival horror began in 1992 and became immensely popular in 1996, and started largely on console platforms, as opposed to the faster processing power offered by home computers, survival horror began as a genre bound with and by technical limitations.[6] The technical limitations actually led to many of the formal and the functional elements of survival horror. Perhaps the most immediately recognizable characteristic of survival horror was the limited visual scope. The early *Alone in the Dark* and *Resident Evil* games were all actually two-dimensional games with the game areas sutured together like a series of photographs, and then each individual segment could only be viewed through one fixed point so that the movement over the flat photograph-plane appeared to be movement on a three-dimensional plane. The three-dimensional effect was supported through the use of three-dimensional character models that moved across the two-dimensional space. These games used the two-dimensional presentation because the games were too large to be adequately created or played otherwise because the three-dimensional presentation could not fit on the game discs and would slow the game consoles to unacceptable levels for gameplay. Even *Alone in the Dark: The New Nightmare* (Infogrames, 2001) continued the use of the two-dimensional pre-rendered space although they augmented the game engine to allow for accurate lighting and shadows cast by the three-dimensional player character's flashlight. This formal characteristic of the creation of a three-dimensional appearance through the use of fixed views over two-dimensional plane increments led to functional characteristics. One of these functional characteristics was that players most often could not see anything outside of the immediate playing screen except for one flat area and that players even had limited visibility within a single playing screen because scenery and other objects could obstruct the view. A subsequent formal characteristic comprised of constrained camera views for any playing screen, which was necessary to maintain the appearance of a three-dimensional world using two-dimensional graphics.

Because of the two-dimensional display, survival horror games often rely on a relative control structure within the stitched-together game spaces. While this developed in response to technical limitations, it also led to a gameplay style where players cannot master the controls because the controls change based on the location in the game. David Smith explains the "classic issues with games like this is movement colliding with the shifting camera... when the camera shifts to show a new scene, the definitions of right, left, and forward suddenly change" (2002: para. 10–11).[7] The prevention of mastery subverts the typical gaming apparatus because most gaming interfaces are presented as mere extensions of the gamer, to be learned and acclimated. However many games, particularly horror games, use the interface as part of the overall gaming experience. For example, many action games have game controllers which can be set to "rumble" or vibrate to complement gaming activity. Unlike those complementary sequences, horror games often use the interface to contradict normal play. For instance, the *Resident Evil* series regularly uses the rumble functions to thump mimicking a human heart beat. This thumping is done to increase tension during gameplay. Similarly, *Eternal Darkness: Sanity's Requiem* (Silicon Knights, 2002) uses an insanity factor when the player encounters too many enemies. The insanity factor causes the internal game representations to blur and slide and allow enemies that are not actually there to be displayed. Such insanity factors even affect the interface itself. These include messages stating that the game controller is unplugged, that all of the saved game information is being erased, and so forth. These uses of the gaming interface question the relationship of the gamer to the game, and of the gaming interface as a mediator in that relationship. The majority of games use the interface as a functional means of allowing for gameplay to occur; survival horror games often use the interface to subvert typical play and to challenge conceptions of game interface design and game design, questioning the materiality of the text itself. The process of play prevents mastery of the game controls, and prevents full vision. As Gothic texts repeatedly obscure vision or show vision to be unreliable, so too do the visual interfaces of Gothic and horror games. Where most games try to ease players into a level of mastery or control over the avatar — so that the game becomes more immersive — survival horror games attempt to prevent mastery following the traditions of the Gothic to increase the power of horror.

As a genre born of technological limitations that required non-traditional solutions, survival horror adapted to technical limitations. The methods of adaptation were selected to increase the power of horror, but as I have just said, they also followed traditions established by the Gothic. Like the paranormal sciences of communication in Shirley Jackson's *The Haunting of Hill House* (1959) and the vague letter in Henry James's *The Turn of the Screw*

(1898) which show the disjunction between communication systems and communication, survival horror games selected textual fragments to indicate the larger gameworld and narrative in which the games took place. Survival horror games followed Gothic texts by drawing on technologies of communication to illustrate cycles of miscommunication while also repeatedly emphasizing the importance of written texts, textual materiality, and its processing.

In Gothic literature, lost histories are often uncovered through the castle or haunted house in which the narrative takes place, with frequent remarks on the past inhabitants through decorations, paintings, and other elements. In survival horror games—which are most often set in haunted houses, castles, or science-fiction or cyberpunk Gothic settings like space ships and island-based laboratories—the same elements remain. The frequent use of books, paintings, pictures, vases, sculptures, and other elements populate the game world to show that it is already inhabited by the past. [8] Like Gothic literature's use of lost letters and hidden stories, games drawing on the Gothic tradition rely on the same elements for the game narratives and then extend those elements into the gameplay as with *Silent Hill 2,* which begins with the main character James receiving a letter from his dead wife. The letter begins the game's narrative, but James finds other documents throughout the game — which allow the player to solve puzzles and progress through the game. Richard J. Hand notes that each game in the *Resident Evil* series expands this process even further, with every game release containing more "documents, characters, and back-stories that fulfill a complex interpolative function intended to enrich the *Resident Evil* history and narrative further" (2004: 127). Even the use of anachronistic technology, so prevalent in survival horror, follows the Gothic tradition of creating rupture by using fragments to uncover the past and unravel the horrors of the present. The *Silent Hill* series' radios only broadcast static, growing louder based on the proximity of monsters thereby alerting players to nearby enemies. The radios serve as a sort of sonar with the visual landscape in the *Silent Hill* series games obscured by a blanket of deep fog. [9] The *Fatal Frame* series' similarly use technology to connect to other worldly beings through spirit radios which players can use to listen to the past and through cameras for spirit photography. The *Resident Evil* series' use of typewriters for saving gameplay is conjoined with systems of communication and miscommunication with forgotten letters and journals from the now-dead that players read to reconstruct the past to solve gameplay puzzles. The use of often anachronistic technology and their focus on language and textuality returns the games to their Gothic roots—roots repeatedly alluded to throughout the games, which expand the spaces that these game narratives reference.

In addition to the changes in the presentation and gameplay, survival horror games also increased replay value by adding additional playable characters and shifting between playable characters. In the *Resident Evil* games, players can choose among different playable characters. In the *Fatal Frame* games, players can play as different characters for different parts of the games although often playing within the same game areas. And in lesser known games like *ObsCure* (Hydravision, 2005), players can choose among several characters. The additional playable character required few additional technical resources (in terms of game design time or game memory space), and it increased marketability with expanded gameplay. However, it required changes to the narrative. Those narrative changes included the use of multiple characters, normally a man and a woman who are presented as equally strong for gameplay and as visually equivalent, a rarity in gaming and other media.[10] The additional characters brought the need for a narrative connection, and thereby opened the door for the family narratives of the Gothic to intrude. The Gothic has often subverted social and cultural systems in order to present empowered women characters, whereas survival horror games' adaptations to technical constraints subverted the normal trajectory of gaming from visual representation, narrative, and thematic cultural constructs. Thus, while survival horror games have been defined by aesthetic, narrative, and gameplay elements, many of the games termed survival horror follow the Gothic in their reliance on the process of subversion. The limits of the more narrowly understood survival horror genre are perhaps clearest when understood within the long history of the *Resident Evil* series as it defined and redefined the genre.

Learning to Run; And Later, Not to Walk Away

As many reviewers and game players have noted, *Resident Evil 4* is and is not survival horror.[11] *Resident Evil 4* is not a formulaic survival horror game because it allows players nearly unrestricted ammunition, allows for convenient saving, and the visual presentation is actually three-dimensional. The new world design accompanies new play mechanics with smarter and more enterprising enemies that can climb ladders, break down doors, and use tools against players. While becoming a more normal action game, *Resident Evil 4* still breaks with video game convention by requiring action during cinematic sequences, and it breaks with its own tradition by changing the rules it helped create. *Resident Evil 4* continues to follow the traditions of the Gothic with a rich abundance of textual materials, multiple characters in play, a fixation with the monstrous, and the continued subversion of convention. Viewing *Resident Evil 4* as ludic-gothic allows it to be placed within its historical context and within the future trajectory for the genre. Similarly, approaching the current survival horror genre in terms of horror, survival, and ludic-gothic — with each operating as game genres as well as drawing from their related narrative and aesthetic genres — allows for a clearer approach to game design, gameplay, and gaming conventions.

As a result, ludic-gothic can only appropriately apply to those games that exemplify the poetics of the Gothic, emphasizing a process of transgression for the game design including the game narrative and gameplay. Defined in this manner, ludic-gothic games may or may not have activist components to their countergaming play styles, but they would utilize an established poetics of gaming and then subvert that process throughout gameplay.[12] Ludic-gothic games are narrowly defined in relation to their processes and the operations of those processes in contrast to survival horror games which are based on horror and survival — meaning focused on affect and on running instead of fighting for gameplay. Survival horror thus continues to encompass games like *Clock Tower 3* (Capcom, 2003). In *Clock Tower 3*, players generally cannot fight and must instead flee and hide from enemies. *Clock Tower 3* includes many horror and Gothic narrative and aesthetic elements, yet the gameplay mechanics are a simple exchange of fighting for running. Many of the major survival horror games — games from each of the *Alone in the Dark, Resident Evil, Fatal Frame, Silent Hill* series — can be classed as ludic-gothic, yet the minor related games are in some ways more useful in showing the borders of survival horror and the ludic-gothic. For instance, while gaming procedural rhetorics normally include a gameplay mechanism for adding difficulty or complexity, increasing that difficulty does not uproot learned conventions and is not, on its own, sufficient to subvert typical gaming poetics.[13] With most difficulty level mechanics as inappropriate indicators of gameplay poetics, *Devil May Cry* would not be considered ludic-gothic and could be more appropriately reframed within other aesthetic, narrative, and gameplay genres and histories. Viewing the ludic-gothic as a genre based on the game's procedural rhetoric clarifies the otherwise ill-defined lines of descent from aesthetic, narrative, and gameplay elements. In contrast, Richard J. Hand (2004: 119) connects survival horror to the *Snakes and Ladders* board game and to early horror video games like Atari's *Haunted House* (1981). This is productive only at the aesthetic and narrative levels. Other anomalous games could also be better studied in terms of the significance of their anomalies. For instance, where most multiplayer games include voice chat, the online mode of *Resident Evil: Outbreak* chose not to do so because including voice chat — while taking advantage of gaming technology — would not follow the series' procedural rhetoric.[14] Using the ludic-gothic as a genre for the game's procedural rhetoric still allows for additional affect-based descriptions rather than "survival" which does not differentiate between gameplay mechanics and the level of difficulty. Devendra Varma in *The Gothic Flame* famously described the difference between terror and horror as the "awful apprehension and sickening realization: between the smell of death and stumbling against a corpse" (1966, 130). This sort of distinction is necessary for gaming, especially for horror games because of the need to analyze emotion.

Bloodlines, Canons (Curses and Cures)

Survival horror as a term may be of limited use, but the popularity of the term and of games bearing its classification points to the significance of the ludic-gothic procedural rhetoric and of the ability of horror to elicit emotion. The significance of horror and ludic-gothic games is only increased by the current cultural moment for gaming. As a form, video games are still in their infancy and a game canon has not been established. Like genres, canons can be restrictive and problematic; however, canons are also productive conceptual categories that list canonical works based on which works typify, exemplify, or change a particular media form. In *Unit Operations,* Ian Bogost explains games as relying on unit operations which are "modes of meaning-making that privilege discrete, disconnected actions over deterministic, progressive systems" (2006: 3) and that these "privilege function over context, instances over longevity" (2006: 4). Like the units within an individual game that give rise to the game's operations, game genres function as units within the emerging game canon, defining current methods, expected trajectories, and unexpected errors or collisions. Game genres function as collections of components or units, rather than deterministic, progressive systems. But both the procedural components and the individual units aid in defining genres as well as more discrete game styles and the more general significance to gaming as a whole.

Gaming's canon is being formally developed through the International Game Developers Association after first being proposed in the conference presentation "Ten Games You Need to Play: The Digital Game Canon" by Henry Lowood, Steve Meretzky, Warren Spector, Matteo Bittanti and Christopher Grant. For their first proposed list of canonical games, Heather Chaplin writes, "Almost all of the games on the Lowood list represent the beginning of a genre still vital in the video game industry" (2007), which shows the current relevance of genres to establishing and updating the gaming canon. Films exemplifying cut, montage, and character studies such as *Citizen Kane* (Orson Welles, 1941), and those deconstructing other genres such as *Chinatown* (Roman Polanski, 1974) in regards to film noir, are canonical for what they are and what they are not. Canonical films show the possibilities for the medium just as horror and the ludic-gothic illustrate and continue to expand the possibilities for gaming.

For continued rapid growth as a field, game studies requires the full articulation of methodologies for investigating games. The development of an official game canon as well as Mia Consalvo and Nathan Dutton's call for the development of a methodological toolkit for the qualitative study of games (2006) speak to the need for the articulation of additional game genre definitions, their histories, and their kinship relations. In any examination of gaming, each different critical methodology and apparatus can allow for a more accurate or more fully developed perspective. To that end, game studies research continues to develop and define different areas for inclusion. For instance, Bernard Perron (2005) has advocated the examination of emotion in terms of states and processes, as actions and actionable, and this is essential in any study of horror gaming as well as to the development of methodologies for studying games and other related forms. Similarly, the history of the Gothic as it relates to gaming especially in terms of its processes is particularly beneficial for game studies. The Gothic's influence on gaming extends far beyond ludic-gothic games and narrative and aesthetic styles, to genre and canonical definitions for gaming. The Gothic is of particular relevance because, as David Punter and Glennis Byron explain, the Gothic's "focus on the contemporary world does not mean that Gothic relinquishes its interest in the past. At the same time as it is appropriated to represent new social problems, it also offers a space in which the past can persist in modified form" (2004: 29). The past's modified form for the present can be seen in the *Resident Evil* series' transition to the terrorist in *Resident Evil 4.* Where the zombies of the earlier games are more traditional monsters, the terrorist figure reflects current cultural concerns. As an outsider, the terrorist figure still embodies the monstrosities of the past, however, the terrorist reconfigures past monstrosity to bear more directly on the present.[15] Similarly, as video games transform and expand into augmented or alternative reality games and as massively multiplayer online games continue to develop, the need to define gaming history as it bears on the present increases.

Video games foreground aspects of the Gothic, including its relying on existing structures and, from this reliance, the continual need to subvert new structures lest they be allowed to operate transparently or be allowed to dominate. Ludic-gothic games show how borders and boundaries can be erected using cutting-edge technology while also being subsumed into a process that undermines the transparency and hierarchy that technology brings. As a form founded on instability, the Gothic has repeatedly focused on the removal or transgression of boundaries. As Kelly Hurley suggests; "Gothic in particular has been theorized as an instrumental genre, reemerging cyclically, at periods of cultural stress, to negotiate the anxieties that accompany social and epistemological transformations and crises" (1996: 5). Anne Williams explains the Gothic even more succinctly as a category that "systematically represents 'otherness,' which is, of course, always a relative term" (1995: 18). Continuing the Gothic's lineage, ludic-gothic games complicate definitions of gaming and gameplay and notions of progress, particularly in relation to technology and globalization, to the transmittal of transnational concerns,[16] and to the boundaries between technology and its users. Ludic-gothic games recapitulate the transgression of the Gothic, blurring and reaffirming certain genres. Newer genres like the ludic-gothic, born of aesthetics, narrative, gameplay, and affect aid in defining the fundamental elements of the gaming medium and in defining gaming's relationships to other forms and to the cultural moments in which the games operate.

As Ruth E. Burke reminds us in her study of the play within riddles and poems, "In order to break the spell woven by the poet, the reader must know the rules of the game [...] and be initiated into the society of those who understand the significance and the interpretation of the symbols" (1994: 15); so too must game players know the rules in order to play and study games. As video games continue to develop rapidly and continue to develop stronger ties to existing media,[17] conventions and their subversion demand attention within the context of a particular media ecology and within gaming as a whole. By addressing the significant influence of horror and the Gothic on games, we can more effectively articulate definitions of gaming, game genres, studies of game genres, their ancestry, and game studies as a whole.

Notes

1. Capcom's *Sweet Home* (1989) for the original Nintendo Entertainment System is now referred to as the first true survival horror game, but this is a reclaimed history found much later because *Sweet Home* was not widely known outside o f Japan for many years. Other games also compete for their place in the history of survival horror, but *Alone in the Dark* and *Resident Evil* are the best known and the earliest defining games within gaming culture. See Chris Pruett's "The Prehistory of Survival Horror" (2007) for more on the earlier history being reclaimed.

2. Blurring components used to create the circumstances for the affect of horror with the horror genre itself, *Devil May Cry* producer Hiroyuki Kobayashi explains in an interview with *Play Magazine* that *Devil May Cry* was not focused on horror so "we've removed stuff like the item box and ink ribbons— things that aren't really necessary for or don't fit in with the gameplay" (2005: 21).

3. For film, Misha Kavka explains, "there is no established genre called Gothic cinema or Gothic film. There are Gothic images and Gothic plots and Gothic characters and even Gothic styles within film, all useful to describe bits and pieces of films that usually fall into the broader category of horror, but there is no delimited or demonstrable genre specific to film called the Gothic" (2002: 209).

4. The series quickly grew with additional games: *Resident Evil 2* in 1997, *Resident Evil 3: Nemesis* (also named *Biohazard* in Japan) in 1999, *Resident Evil — Code: Veronica*— in 2000, *Resident Evil: 0* in 2002, *Resident Evil: Outbreak* in 2004, *Resident Evil 4* in 2005, and other games not within the main series like *Resident Evil: Gaiden* in 2002, *Resident Evil: Survivor* in 2003, and others including the re-releases of the games on multiple console platforms (Capcom).

5. See Miguel Lopez's review defining *Fatal Frame* as an "alternative" survival horror game like *Illbleed* (Crazy Games, 2001) with the traditional survival horror elements "specifically formulaic, repetitive puzzles and more backtracking than you can stand" (2004: para. 1).

6. Brett Todd notes that the technology led to many adventure-style game design choices: "Technology at the time was a serious limitation.... But perhaps the most important trend introduced by Resident Evil was that gamers would accept, and even flock to, cross-genre efforts" (2004).

7. See also Laurie N. Taylor's "Compromised Divisions: Thresholds in Comic Books and Video Games" (Spring 2004).

8. For more on the Gothic and textuality, see Dani Cavallaro's *The Gothic Vision: Three Centuries of Horror, Terror and Fear* (2002) and Anne Williams' *Art of Darkness: A Poetics of Gothic* (1995).

9. For a discussion of sound in survival horror, see Zach Whalen's "Play Along — An Approach to Videogame Music" (2004).

10. Most women video game characters are hyperbolically sexualized, as with Lara Croft's breasts, but the women in Gothic and horror games — while depicted as attractive and fit — are not overly sexualized. This follows in the trajectory identified by Carol J. Clover in her study of the "Final Girl" in horror films (1992). However, Gothic and horror games continue this trajectory by using the game's control and world structures to subvert dominant western — and masculine — modes of representation and play.

11. See Brady Fletcher "Review of *Resident Evil 4:* Survival Horror Reborn," *Play Magazine,* January 2005.

12. See Alexander Galloway's *Gaming: Essays on Algorithmic Culture* (2006).

13. A notable recent exception has been the Nintendo Wii and many articles speak to a backlash by "hardcore games" against the "easier" actual movement for playing Nintendo Wii games. Underlying these claims is a disagreement over video game interface development and the lack of desire by some players to adapt to the new controls or, in my case, both a lack of desire to use the Wii's controls and a disappointment that additional interface and control designs aren't developing as quickly.

14. Chris Hoffman notes, "Though there's no voice chat — Capcom doesn't want the tension-filled atmosphere ruined" (2003: 32).

15. As David Punter reminds us, "two figures which haunt the Gothic, the monster and the terrorist" (1998: 204). Both are similar, yet "where the monster presents us, and presents the world, with a seemingly irreducible body which is none the less doomed to extinction, the terrorist confronts us with an excess of control" (1998: 204).

16. Technology and language are conjoined in games, as they are in Gothic literature's narratives, to act as a conduit for transfer. The transnational transfer of games allowed for games to transfer cultural views and national histories. For instance, *Fatal Frame* focuses on the Meiji Era of Japanese history, allowing players to play in Japan's real and mythologized past and allowing the transfer of real and cultural histories through the games and their embedded ghosts and texts.

17. Video games continue to impact other media, as with the film *Stay Alive* (William Brent Bell, 2006) which draws heavily from horror video games.

Works Cited

Alloway, Lawrence (1971), *Violent America: The Movies 1946–1964,* New York: MOMA.
Bogost, Ian (2007), *Persuasive Games: The Expressive Power of Videogames,* Cambridge, MA: MIT Press.
_____ (2006), *Unit Operations: An Approach to Videogame Criticism,* Cambridge, MA: MIT Press.

Burke, Ruth E. (1994), *The Games of Poetics: Ludic Criticism and Postmodern Fiction*, New York: Peter Lang.

Carroll, Noël (1990), *The Philosophy of Horror or Paradoxes of the Heart*, New York and London: Routledge.

Cavallaro, Dani (2002), *The Gothic Vision: Three Centuries of Horror, Terror and Fear*, New York: Continuum.

Chaplin, Heather (2007), "Is That Just Some Game? No, It's a Cultural Artifact," *New York Times*, 12 March, available online at <http://www.nytimes.com/2007/03/12/arts/design/12vide.html?ex=1184904000&en=ddcec8145483e87c&ei=5070>.

Clover, Carol J. (1992), *Men, Women, and Chain Saws: Gender in the Modern Horror Film*, Princeton, NJ: Princeton University Press.

Consalvo, Mia and Nathan Dutton (2006), "Game Analysis: Developing a Methodological Toolkit for the Qualitative Study of Games," *Game Studies: the International Journal of Computer Game Research*, Vol. 6, No. 1, December, available online at <http://gamestudies.org/0601/articles/consalvo_dutton>.

Fletcher, Brady (2005), "Review of *Resident Evil 4*: Survival Horror Reborn," *Play Magazine*, Issue 37, January, pp. 18–20.

Galloway, Alexander (2006), *Gaming: Essays on Algorithmic Culture*, Minneapolis: University of Minnesota Press.

Hand, Richard J. (2004), "Proliferating Horrors: Survival Horror and the *Resident Evil* Franchise," in Steffen Hantke (ed.), *Horror Film: Creating and Marketing Fear*, Jackson, MS: University Press of Mississippi, pp. 117–134.

Hoffman, Chris (2003), "Preview of *Resident Evil: Outbreak*, a New Type of Fear," *Play Magazine*, pp. 32.

Hurley, Kelly (1996), *The Gothic Body: Sexuality, Materialism, and Degeneration at the fin de siècle*, Cambridge: Cambridge University Press.

Jackson, Shirley (1959), *The Haunting of Hill House*, New York: Viking Press.

James, Henry (1999), *Turn of the Screw* (1898), New York: W. W. Norton.

Kavka, Misha (2002), "The Gothic on Screen," Jerrold E. Hogle (ed.), *The Cambridge Companion to Gothic Fiction*, Cambridge: Cambridge University Press, pp. 209–228.

Krzywinska, Tanya (2002), "Hands-on Horror," in Geoff King and Tanya Krzywinska (eds.), *ScreenPlay. Cinema/videogames/interfaces*, London: Wallflower Press, pp. 206–223.

Lopez, Miguel (2004), "Review of *Fatal Frame*," *Gamespot*, March 8, available online at <http://www.gamespot.com/ps2/action/fatalframe/review.html>.

Lowood, Henry, Steve Meretzky, Warren Spector, Matteo Bittanti, and Christopher Grant (2007), "Ten Games You Need to Play: The Digital Game Canon," *IGDA Conference Panel Presentation*, 8 March.

McRoy, Jay (2006), "The Horror Is Alive. Immersion, Spectatorship, and the Cinematics of Fear in the Survival Horror Genre," *Reconstruction*, Vol. 6, No. 1, available online at <http://reconstruction.eserver.org/061/mcroy.shtml>.

Perron, Bernard (2005), "A Cognitive Psychological Approach to Gameplay Emotions," *Changing Views: Worlds in Play. Proceedings of DiGRA 2005 Conference*, Vancouver, available online at <http://www.digra.org/dl/db/06276.58345.pdf>.

Play Magazine (2005), "Interview with Hiroyuki Kobayashi," *Play Magazine*, No. 37, January, pp. 21–26.

Pruett, Chris (2007), "The Prehistory of Survival Horror," *Chris' Survival Horror Quest*, available online at <http://www.dreamdawn.com/sh/features/prehistoryofhorror.php>.

Punter, David (1998), *Gothic Pathologies: The Text, the Body and the Law*, New York: St. Martin's Press.

_____, and Glennis Byron (2004), *The Gothic*, Malden, MA: Blackwell.

Ryan, Marie-Laure (2001), *Narrative as Virtual Reality: Immersion and Interactivity in Literature and Electronic Media*, Baltimore, MD: Johns Hopkins University Press.

Seif El-Nasr, Magy, Simon Niedenthal, Igor Knez, Priya Almeida, and Joseph Zupko (August 2007), "Dynamic Lighting for Tension in Games," *Game Studies: The International Jour-*

nal of Computer Game Research, Vol. 7, No. 1, available online at <http://gamestudies. org/0701/articles/elnasr_niedenthal_knez_almeida_zupko>.

Smith, David (2002), "Review of *Fatal Frame*," *IGN*, March 5, available online at <http://ps 2.ign.com/articles/354/354927p1.html?fromint=1>.

Taylor, Laurie N. (2004), "Compromised Divisions: Thresholds in Comic Books and Video Games," *ImageTexT: Interdisciplinary Comics Studies*, Vol. 1, No 1, Spring, available on line at <http://www.english.ufl.edu/imagetext/archives/v1_1/taylor/>.

Todd, Brett (2001), "Ghouls, Ghosts, and Long-Legged Beasts: A Modern History of Horror Games, Part I," *Gamespot*, available online at <http://www.gamespot.com/gamespot/features/pc/history_horror_pt1/index.html>.

Varma, Devendra P. (1966), *The Gothic Flame*, New York: Russell & Russell.

Whalen, Zach (2004), "Play Along — An Approach to Videogame Music," *Game Studies: The International Journal of Computer Game Research*, Vol. 4, No. 1, November, available online at <http://www.gamestudies.org/0401/whalen/>.

Williams, Anne (1995), *Art of Darkness: A Poetics of Gothic*, Chicago: University of Chicago Press.

Storytelling in Survival
Horror Video Games
Ewan Kirkland

"This is your life, but you'll play by my rules."
— Prince of the Red Crayon Aristocrats, *Rule of Rose*

"We're nothing but pawns in all of this?"
— Jill, *Resident Evil 3: Nemesis*

"You killed Mary again?"
— Maria, *Silent Hill 2*

Survival horror has an intrinsic relationship with story and storytelling media. The horror video game, as Bernard Perron (2006) observes, is a largely story-driven genre; Tanya Krzywinska noting that *Resident Evil 2*'s opening challenge — "Can you survive the horror?" — situates survival horror's founding series within the rhetoric of horror cinema (2002: 207); while the textuality of survival horror video games mobilizes a broad range of narrative media technologies (Kirkland, 2009). Defined by Egenfeldt-Nielsen, Smith and Tosca as games in which "the player controls a *character* who has to get out of some *enclosed place solving puzzles* and *destroying horrific monsters* along the way" (2008: 184, emphasis mine), survival horror is a genre whose very labeling suggests aspects of narrative and story. *Horror*, as employed by such titles as *Resident Evil* (Capcom, 1996), *Silent Hill* (Konami, 1999), *Fatal Frame* (Tecmo, 2001), *Eternal Darkness: Sanity's Requiem* (Silicon Knights, 2002), *Clock Tower 3* (Sunsoft, 2003), *Forbidden Siren* (SCE Japan, 2003), *The Suffering* (Surreal Software, 2004), *Haunting Ground* (Capcom, 2005), *Rule of Rose* (Punchline, 2006) and *Alone in the Dark* (Hydravision, 2008, Wii), involves a range of visual and audio iconography self-consciously drawn from horror narrative culture. *Survival* entails a narrative situation including *existents* in the form of central protagonist ("character"), adversaries ("horrific monsters"), location ("enclosed place"); and *events*, the process of "solving puzzles" and "destroying" — which more problematically implies successful player interaction. This might involve guiding a condemned criminal through a ghost infested prison, a lost girl through a deserted airship ruled by sadistic children, or a sulky teenager through a monster filled shopping mall. From the opening cut-scene, gameplay is invested with a strong, even overwhelming, sense of narrative. Reduced to their basic formal or ludological bones, these tests in maze navigation, puzzle solution, evasion, and target practice, are devoid of either horror or any notable sense of survival. It is through aspects of narrative, representation, and characterization that gameplay acquires the "edges, meaning and motivation" which constituted the "definition and substance" of the genre (Atkins and Krzywinska, 2008: 6). These games' debt to horror narratives is frequently acknowledged, either through the prominent presence of literature by Poe, Lovecraft and Blake within the game diegesis, by the naming of streets after American horror and suspense authors, or in the self-conscious situation of play within a past-tense storybook.

This essay looks at survival horror's relationship with narrative and narration. It examines the ways different media are employed to situate gameplay in narrative context and to imply past or future narrative events; the use of video game space in storytelling; and the ways game structure is organized to produce story through play. While it is beyond the scope of this essay to recount in detail the debate surrounding narrative and games, a consideration of survival horror's relationship with narrative reflects many arguments which accompanied the emergence of game studies as an academic field. Examples of survival horror are "adventure games dressed up as stories" (Crawford, 2003: 259), the "so-called adventure game" (Aarseth, 2004: 51), or what Klevjer (2002) ironically refers to as "rhetorical-ludological bastards." These games do not primarily model behavior in the manner of Gonzalo Frasca's (2003) flight simulation, tending instead towards narrative and representation. Simulational aspects may be evident in the controlling of the avatar, the reaction of zombies and monsters to player actions, emulation of safes, number locks, cash registers and other puzzle-based devices, or the complex formula which decide the final cut-scene upon completion of *Silent Hill 2* or *The Suffering*. But the artificial intelligence (AI) design of survival horror adversaries, even in boss battles, frequently appears less important than the creatures' visual design, and puzzles are largely stand-alone set pieces rather than overarching simulations, self-contained brainteasers which often occupy a zone outside normal interactions. Successful survival undoubtedly involves learning the broad rules of the game: mixing herbs or medallions in the right combination, matching weapons to adversaries, conserving and distributing ammunition wisely. But winning these games is more a case of figuring out what one-off actions must be performed to open *this* door, solve *this* puzzle, evade *this* trap, before moving on to the next challenge.

Survival horror games unfold in static game spaces. They do not so much "create an environment for experimentation" (Frasca, 2003: 225) as present a world where the single solution to individual puzzles must be discovered. Survival horror is closer to *ludus* than *paidia*, characterized by closed systems, limited participation, dichotomized worlds divided between good and evil, a sense of centralized authorship, and moral certainties. Embodying the very definition of ludic video gaming, in survival horror, "you must do X in order to reach Y and therefore become the winner" (230). Sharing the characteristics of narrative Frasca contrasts with simulation, these games are binary, not dynamic systems; they work with information, not rules. The player of a survival horror video game is internal-exploratory, rather than external-ontological (Ryan, 2001). He is tasked with guiding a hapless character through a fictional world, rather than being privileged with the god-like ability to build and influence the world itself. Survival horror video games contain only "prefabricated scriptons," the signs generated by the game program. There are no "completed scriptons"—those produced through a combination of player and game—as outlined in Eskelinen's development of Aarseth's typography of cybernetic semiotics. Characterized by static interpretation, not dynamic manipulation, survival horror games contain "ready-made relations not to be tampered with" (Eskelinen, 2001). There is no modding in the genre, beyond dressing Fiona as a cowgirl or Travis as a butcher, both of which merely entail selecting from pre-defined avatars. Players are not permitted to re-design the station of *Resident Evil*'s Raccoon City Police Department, redecorate *Fatal Frame*'s Himuro Mansion, or level up Harry Mason's combat skills in *Silent Hill*. In this lies an important aspect of these games' impact: The sense of helplessness, entrapment and pre-determination that they generate would be compromised if such potential interactivity were allowed. Players move around the game space, but their actions cannot change the shape of game-world history, past or future, or impact in any significant way upon their surroundings. Comparing the interactive possibilities, and the audiovisual richness, of Racoon City or the eponymous Silent Hill with *Grand Theft Auto*'s Vice City illustrates the extent to which survival horror rejects simulational complexity for narrative and representational detail.

That such titles are located in an overarching narrative framework is evident to anyone who has ever browsed a game sleeve or picked up a joypad and engaged with one of the examples listed above. The purpose of this essay is not to debate whether survival horror video games are a "narrative thing," but, like Eric Zimmerman, to examine in what ways they might be considered so (2004: 157). How is narrative integrated into these interactive texts, how do storytelling functions impact upon game design, and how is the interactive experience bounded by narrative dictates while maintaining a sense of player control. Given the centrality of story to survival horror, exploring the genre in this way allows an overview of work on video games and narrative which is grounded in a range of specific contemporary game texts, thereby revisiting debates which in many ways characterized games studies' early years. Gameplay and narrative are regarded by many as incompatible. Temporality is considered to problematize video games' relationship with narrative (Juul: 2001), while other authors have seen interactivity and immersion as in some ways antithetical (Van Looy, 2003). One of the main problems, as Marie-Laure Ryan (2001) points out, is that of the three elements of narrative — setting, character and action — the third is left in the hands of the player, whose actions may not accord with those of a prescribed story. Game designers can provide the horror, but survival is up to you. The ways in which survival horror video games deal with these problematics— by locating narratives in the past, by restricting interactivity, and by constructing play as a process of storytelling — reveal what James Newman observes as the "curious and sometimes seemingly antagonistic relations between narrative and play" (2004: 100), a relationship which this essay sets out to unpick.

> "What the hell was that? It was like a video in my mind..."
> — Heather Mason, *Silent Hill 3*

Remediation in Survival Horror

While appreciative of the limitations in applying film theory to games, King and Krzywinska argue video game narratives share some similarities with academic models of cinema storytelling (2006: 121), and there are many parallels between classical Hollywood narrative and the structuring components of survival horror games. These might include: the construction of the avatar as a psychologically-motivated character, the establishment of clear goals, objectives and obstacles which must be overcome, and a cause and effect logic whereby each problem or puzzle overcome leads logically to the next set of challenges. As if to emphasize this affinity, virtually every survival horror video game uses the conventions of narrative cinema in its introductory sequence to communicate characterization, situation, and location. Cutscenes' remediation (Bolter and Grusin, 2001) of cinema's audiovisual style is further evoked in games such as *Fatal Frame*, *Forbidden Siren* and *Silent Hill Origins* (Climax, 2007) which switch to monochrome or emulate scratched celluloid aesthetics throughout such sequences. Like the letterbox format discussed by Juul (2004: 136), such signifiers of the cinematic cue players to read these scenes according to conventions of film rather than of gaming. This might include the medium's non-participatory form of engagement, its director/author origin, and narrative tradition. Within gameplay, reproducing the aesthetic and modality of a medium synonymous with storytelling permits a momentary violation of in-play spatial and temporal unity normally bound by real-time player/avatar action. This allows the depiction of events from the past, those taking place in distant locations, and the interrogation of game space in a more explicit manner than otherwise possible.

The prominence of cut-scenes in survival horror is notable, frequently punctuating gameplay, fleshing out moments of playable character movement, actions, and interaction with non-playable characters. In some games and game levels, such as the Gloomy House in *Clock Tower 3*'s second chapter, player movement seems perpetually interrupted by cinematic moments. In their consideration of the cut-scene, the functions Egenfeldt-Nielsen et al. identify predominantly relate to narrative: the creation of narrative tension, the shaping of narrative, compensation for absent game narrative (2008: 176–7). Far from tinsel, gift wrapping, or any other metaphor indicating an aesthetically pleasing yet shallow superfluity, cut-scenes serve to locate gameplay within a certain narrative frame, upon which the survival horror genre is reliant for its affect. As Klevjer (2002) argues, cut-scenes serve to strengthen the analogy between the player and the avatar body in fictional video game space, and the process by which ludic actions assume a symbolic, metaphorical or representational resonance. Cut-scenes drawing on horror film narratives inflect the player's future actions with generic meaning, important in games which "depend on our familiarity with the roles and goals of genre entertainment to orient us to the action" (Jenkins, 2004: 119). Moreover, in remediating a cinematic sense of being narrated to by a text, rather than interacting with a game, cut-scenes also produce what Krzywinska (2002: 211) sees as a generically-specific oscillation between control and loosing it, and of being subjected to the influence of higher occult powers. This is certainly the frustrating experience of navigating the Gloomy House, where play is constantly being suspended for unwelcome cut-scenes, introducing supernatural elements into the game space and depicting tragic past events over which the player has no influence. This sense of play being stiflingly constrained by a non-interactive narrative medium is most profoundly felt in titles like *Eternal Darkness: Sanity's Requiem* or *Rule of Rose* where the experience is framed as a story book, one held by the main character throughout the game. In the latter example, actions within the game are narrated in the past tense, a feature which underlines the inescapability of the protagonist's ordeal.

As this example suggests, cut-scenes, with their remediation of popular film, constitute only one of many narrative media employed in survival horror. Indeed, while *Resident Evil 2*'s (Capcom, 1998) opening challenge may situate the series in terms of horror cinema, the words "survival horror" first appeared on screen as typed letters, locating the genre within more literary narrative forms. Given the potentially chronoclasmic consequences of interactive flashbacks, Juul points to the ways game designers create in-game artifacts which reveal to players past events (2004: 136). Consequently, the spaces of Racoon City, Himuro Mansion and *The Suffering*'s Abbott State Penitentiary are littered with narrative fragments in the form of newspaper articles, lab reports, photographs, diaries, audio cassettes, painted portraits and computer logs, accessible through both game-space and what Aylish Wood labels "info-space" (2007: 127). In survival horror, everyone, it seems— research assistants, academics, mercenaries— keeps a journal. As Ryan notes, such techniques produce two narratives running in parallel: "the story to be discovered, and the story of their discovery" (2008: 16); going some way to reconcile Juul's (2001) insistence on the temporal incompatibility of narrative and interactivity. Many of these documents constitute the definition of "a narrative situation" which Eskelinen (2001) considers absent in actual video game play, one involving a clear sense of previous events being recounted from narrator to narrate/s. These texts tell of the development of the T virus, of the cult of the ropes, and of the Rooders and their history. Like the RPGs' typed dialogue which Newman discusses in relation to the fan culture videogames generate (2008: 48), *Resident Evil*'s virtual documents bearing witness to zombie mutation, attack and siege, emphasizing the games' narrative and characterization, undoubtedly encouraging the kind of fanfiction Newman observes as emerging from the *Final Fantasy* franchise. Marvin's Report from *Resident Evil 3: Nemesis* (Capcon, 1999) detailing the theft of two jewels from the Town Hall clock also foreshadows a challenge players will subsequently face. While solving the puzzle would be a little harder without this document, it functions to situate the ludic task in narrative context communicated through a more traditional non-participatory medium. Marvin's back-story provides verisimilitude, instilling Racoon City with an authentic and generic sense of place, without which players' actions in *Resident Evil 3: Nemesis* might feel more like interaction with an abstract game space. If, as Mark J. P. Wolf argues, a tension has historically existed between video game abstraction and representation (2007: 193), both horror and its survival entail a strong sense of the latter. Narrative context delivered through these remediated forms undoubtedly works in conjunction with such techniques as photorealistic graphics and simulated camera angles to enhance these video games' representational dimensions.

In their psychoanalytic reading of the *Resident Evil* and *Silent Hill* series, Santos and White discuss the "hermeneutic pleasure" of horror video game play as the correct reading of such documents. As "champions of the symbolic order," players are tasked with imposing narrative structure onto the texts and files found throughout the game, thereby giving ontological meaning to the movements of the avatar, psychoanalyzing their fractured, false and repressed memories, "ordering an infinite amount of events into a seemingly coherent unity, or in simplest terms, supplying the story with a plot"

(2005: 74). Hermeneutic pleasure involves constructing a consistent linear narrative from the potential chaos of the game. The sanatorium level of *Silent Hill: Origins*, a game which is part of a series not without specific psychoanalytic resonance, illustrates the extent to which players are required to read multimedia texts, and place them in narrative order pertaining to the protagonist's past and psychology. Employing the method information redundancy which Jenkins discusses as an element of video games narration (2004: 126), throughout this section, various fragments tell of a woman incarcerated in the medical institution after attempting to take her son's life, her failure to recover, and the boy's subsequent attempt to visit his mother. A doctor's note detailing a patient's obsession with a "mirror world," a police report telling of a woman's attempted gassing of her son, a recorded therapy session heard as ghostly voiceover, and a message scrawled in blood on the wall of the women's restroom showers are encountered throughout the player's journey through Cedar Grove Sanatorium. Collectively, they tell a story of Silent Hill's past in which the game protagonist, Travis Grady, is heavily implicated. Written documents, an audio file, graffiti, all contribute to the foreshadowing of the level's conclusion. When, upon reaching the final door, players are told by a supporting character "You KNOW who's in there!" everything is present for attentive players—cued by these audio, printed and written media texts— to read this moment as the climactic culmination of narrative information. The conclusion — that the woman referenced in these texts, the person behind the door, the level's boss monster, and Travis' mother are one and the same — is a particularly chilling one. These collective remediations serve to fix the protagonist and the player in a story over which they have no control. The unalterable past, and a fatalistic destiny-driven present collide, communicated in this level's penultimate scene through a scratchy black and white cut-scene of a young Travis entering his mother's room, only to snap back into the present, as the player begins battle with a monstrous manifestation of the protagonist's memory.

"There must be some clue in this old mansion revealing what happened." (Alexandra Roivas, *Eternal Darkness: Sanity's Requiem*)

Narrative Architecture and Spatial Storytelling

The design of spaces in survival horror games and the manner in which players are encouraged or permitted to interact within them are central to the genre's management of the interactive experience to fit a determined narrative pattern. Along with cut-scenes, survival horror video games also remediate cinema in their depiction of interactive space. "Predetermined framing" as found in *Dino Crisis* (Capcon, 1999) or, *Resident Evil* (King and Krzywinska, 2006: 118) and countless subsequent survival horror games employs a visual structure whereby action is viewed through a series of fixed camera points, cutting from one to the next according to the players' movement. This creates a generically-appropriate experience of entrapment and claustrophobia, surveillance, and subordination. The dissection of game space in this directed manner also channels survival horror gameplay in a particular direction. Just as cut-scenes remediate narrative film, and in-game documents remediate print media, virtual camera cuts during game play function to cue certain spaces and objects as important in the manner of cinema and television storytelling. For example, in *Silent Hill*, the majority of houses are closed off to players. Attempts to use their doors produce either no response, or messages indicating their broken or inactive status. Those few houses open to the player are signaled by a dramatic change in camera perspective, a cut from tracking just behind the avatar's shoulder, to a static long shot overtly emphasizing the building available for entry. The conventions of narrative cinema's continuity editing, whereby audience attention is directed through similar grammatical devices, are used to communicate ludic information. If such moments constitute a kind of "interactive cinema," it is a form of gameplay remediating the directed narrative nature of the cinematic medium, the cut of the cinematic-style camera implying authorial orchestration for storytelling purposes. The player is invited to participate by leading the avatar through a path which produces the most satisfying cinematic experience, entering the house, examining the desk drawer, or pulling the switch as indicated by the virtual cut. Similarly, the practice whereby playable protagonists turn their head in the direction of important objects, non-playable characters or architectural features— ammunition, bloodstains on the tarmac, a body bearing useful supplies—constructs the avatar as a character who has knowledge and intentions beyond those of the player. The most productive gameplay strategy involves correctly reading these grammatical and visual cues, completing the actions being foreshadowed, and producing an audiovisual experience which ideally approximates that of narrative cinema.

Game objects and adversaries in survival horror video games often react to character movement in a scripted manner, as part of a pre-determined series of events requiring the player's participation. The dog leaping through the window which so startles first-time players of *Resident Evil* is triggered by the avatar's movement along the corridor; while an entire building falling apart in the recent *Alone in the Dark* reacts more to player progress across its façade than seismic activity. In the action-orientated *Cold Fear* (Ubisoft, 2005), the familiar technique by which zombies suddenly come to life, or burning canines crash through walls is elevated to new heights. Elaborate action sequences have previously-dormant corpses staggering to their feet, bursting through floorboards and appearing out of nowhere, all cued by the player's movements. According to action movie conventions, a well-placed fire extinguisher or explosive barrel often allows a preferably more ammunition-conscious solution to such onslaughts, and the more spectacularly cinematic narrative experience. Sometimes such scripted events function in the manner of cut-scenes, to indicate the player's preferred route through the game's environment. *The Suffering* use spectral figures in this manner. During his journey through Abbott State Pen, Torque encounters many "micronarratives" (Jenkins, 2004: 125) from the institution's tortured history, together with members of his dead family, frequently indicating the direction the player should move. In *Eternal Darkness: Sanity's Requiem*, Alex sees an apparition of Dr. Maximillian Roivas, a character the player is yet to play, going through a door which no longer exists in her grandfather's mansion, which subsequently becomes an entrance to be uncovered by the player in the final stages of the game. Similarly, the ghosts of *Fatal Frame* contribute to the story of Himuro Mansion, while showing players the presence of doors and objects otherwise obscured. Given the tendency for survival horror narrative to be structured around past events, such apparitions serve as temporal bridges. They simultaneously function as an intra-diegetic afterimage of past narratives, and as an extra-diegetic prefiguring of players' future movements in accordance with the game's determined path. Like the cut-scenes discussed by Klevjer (2002), these in-game apparitions constitute a "narrative of pre-telling" which serves the purpose of "strengthening the diegetic, rhetorical dimension of the event to come." *Fatal Frame*'s camera serves a similar purpose. Throughout the game, pictures taken of locked doors reveal the photograph which players must take in order to break the seal blocking progress. The ghostly image is a spectral premonition of player future action.

Henry Jenkins emphasizes the ways in which spatial design can tell stories. The notion of "embedded narrative" (2004: 126), already explored in relation to narrative texts scattered throughout the game environment, also applies to the broad visual elements, or *mise-en-scène*, of survival horror game spaces. Interiors in *Resident Evil* are testimony to the narrative power of such storytelling techniques. The boarded up windows, overturned desks, mutilated corpses and spilled documents which make up Racoon City's municipal buildings testify to a zombie invasion fought and lost. From bloodstained reception areas bearing witness to grizzly events, to book-filled libraries and laboratories suggesting unnatural scientific activity, to the cells and torture chambers which exhibit the stains of long-departed prisoners, survival horror space suggest story. *Silent Hill 4: The Room*'s (Konami, 2004) Apartment World represents an exemplary case of characterization through interior decor. South Ashfield Heights is home to a nurse, a peeping tom, a gun fanatic, and a video game enthusiast, all evident through the objects contained in their rooms and pictured in portraits found in a painter's apartment. Each room in the block functions as an otherwise-absent character to be read by the player, many of whom are implicated in a multi-stranded story involving a love triangle, a dead cat, and a violent act of humiliation. To use Ryan's terminology, in survival horror video games spaces constitute the material signs or discourse through which the player mentally constructs the game's story (2008: 9). Yet such spaces also operate according to certain limitations. A feature of Jenkins' "environmental storytelling" (2004), rather than telling unique and self-sufficient stories, survival horror games tend to be located in already-familiar narrative spaces, like the themed zones of an amusement park: the mad scientist's laboratory, the haunted mansion, the spooky castle, or the mist-shrouded ghost town. Moreover, just as narrative and interaction are seen as incompatible, Stuart Moulthrop (2004) suggests narrative immersion is at odds with video game engagement. Similar to Jan Van Looy's (2003) identification of a perceived antipathy between interaction and immersion, Moulthrop argues traditional techniques of media transparency evident in popular film and television — in which absorption in the story world is produced by encouraging spectators to forget the presence of the camera — rest uneasily with the kind of configurative practices characterizing the video game medium. Yet the horror of survival horror would seem to depend upon the kinds of immersion Moulthrop and Van Looy find so problematic, a reliance which impacts upon the genre's interactive potential. If survival horror spaces are designed to encourage a sense of situation within a believable location, producing an immersive verisimilitude dependent on richly detailed photorealistic graphics, a necessary technical and aesthetic consequence of such a strategy is the absence of interaction with survival horror game spaces. While survival horror games present players with many impressively detailed and atmospheric locations, macabre scenes of carnage, unsettling interiors seen through disorientating camera perspectives, for all such complexities these spaces function largely as static tableaux for players to move through. The comment Aarseth makes about *Myst* (Cyan Worlds, 1993)— "Nice video graphics, shame about the game" (2004: 51)— might reasonably be applied to many of the game spaces in *Clock Tower 3*, *Haunting Ground* or *Resident Evil 2*. Bookshelves lined with leather bound volumes, decapitated corpses, burning cars, twisted metal ruins, desks spilling with documents, invite engagement, yet upon examination produce the deadpan response: "Nothing especially strange here." If these spaces have any relationship with stories, they are firmly embedded in the past, closed off to player involvement, suggesting further the difficult relationship between narrative and interactivity.

"There's only one road, you can't miss it."
(Angela Orosco, *Silent Hill 2*)

Play as Story

The participatory nature of video games, the active, real time role of the player in the generation of the audiovisual signs of the game, poses particular problems in identifying the process of video game play as one of narrative. Given the range and unpredictability of player engagement, and the diversity of potential meaning and experience inherent in the interactivity of its form, notions of narrative reliant upon an ordered series of specific events unfolding over a fixed period of time, seem inapplicable. In this respect video games, survival horror or otherwise, differ from older media in which the author has almost total control over sequentiality, action and pace. As if to underline this point, many of the different methods of narrative discussed so far have largely entailed static media: the non-participatory cut-scene, the unalterable typed document, the interaction-proofed game space tableaux. At the same time, another form of storytelling has also been implied, one which uses various techniques to invite or conscript the player into the narrative process. This collaborative storytelling might involve the retrieval of documents in a particular order, interacting with doors and objects as cued by camera edits, or the activation of event-triggering hotspots. In such situations the survival horror game constitutes not so much narrative-free interactivity punctuated by a series of isolated story fragments—a mode dismissively described by Crawford as "games alternating with stories" (2003: 260)—but rather a story text reliant for its complete unfolding upon players performing in a particular way, with much of the game organized around eliciting particular actions over others.

Various writers have considered the ways video game storytelling might involve the player in this manner. In mapping structures of ludic gameplay onto structures of narrative, Frasca (1999) writes of the adventure game's one "'correct' path" involving a series of functions which the player performs leading to "the triumphal denouement of the adventure's 'story.'" Barry Atkins discusses video games as presenting "a form of narrative storytelling where the production of story is the end result of play" (2003: 7); Egenfeldt-Nielsen et al. consider video game narrative as "a scripted succession of events that the player has to perform in a specific order" (2008: 172); while Newman similarly argues playing video games constitute not an act of reading a story but of "producing — in a real sense — narrative *sequences as a consequence of* play" (2004: 104, emphasis in original). Jenkins discusses games which "enable players to perform or witness narrative events," and while the latter might relate to the non-participatory media found within survival horror, the game as a narrative "pushed forward by the character's movement across the map" (2004: 124) more fully incorporates the player into the process. This form of storytelling is driven by players' curiosity for the game's narrative to unfold, but also the more ludic desire to encounter fresh spaces, experience new visuals, puzzles and weapons, master new modes of interaction, and enjoy a more complete engagement with the video game in which they have invested both time and money. Adventure games characteristically refuse player progression until certain actions have been completed in a particular order. The "implied designer," the author in the text as considered by Klevjer (2002), embeds an ideal pathway which can be followed through a process of ideal play; Juul (2001) observing that many contemporary computer games contain such an "ideal sequence" which players can follow to complete the game. The many instructive walkthroughs available on YouTube illustrate the extent to which such perfect performances constitute the exemplary video game experience, and the degree to which such an ideal game resembles a traditional story, albeit one bereft of ellipses. Admittedly, beyond the realms of such honed displays of game mastery, this perfect playing is far removed from the messiness of common gaming experiences. Just as a reader or viewer might not necessarily interpret their respective texts in accordance with the ideal interpretation, so players are unlikely to complete a video game in its initial play. Nevertheless, as a component of game design discernable through analysis, this theoretical performance or pathway serves as a means of distinguishing "ergodically significant" (Eskelinen, 2001) elements from the insignificant, quantifying the potentially polysemic — or poly-ludic — nature of the video game experience into a series of essential components.

In survival horror, the necessary actions which make up the "ideal sequence" of play are imbued with narrative significance: through the design and organization of avatars, spaces, puzzles, objects, adversaries, and the scattering of info space documents. Games elicit a story produced through gameplay by requiring that certain narratively-loaded objects be picked up and correctly used, elaborate yet causally motivated series of tasks performed, or psychologically-resonant enemies defeated. Such elements are constructed as representational rather than abstract. A crank in *The Suffering* opens prison cells, a switch stops electrical charge passing through a pool of water blocking the player's path, a button opens a passageway. Ludic tasks are given narrative meaning relating to the game environment and the story of Torque's attempts to survive it, just as the game's horrific monsters reflect the methods of execution and the pain of those executed in the fictional penitentiary. Evading the adversaries in *Haunting Ground* involves placing the avatar beside an architectural feature which could conceivably function as a hiding place in the story of Fiona's escape from Castle Belli and its deranged residents. The videotape in *Silent Hill 2*'s Lakeview Hotel is not just a counter which must be placed in a square on the board, but an item literally — or virtually — inscribed with narrative content, revealing the answer to the mystery surrounding Mary's death, and instrumental in the story of James' realization of his complicity in her demise. Traveling through the game levels of *Clock Tower 3* demands players acquire certain key objects: a photograph revealing a hidden doorway, a security card, a stone compass. These can only be found by putting to rest the ghosts who wander the game worlds by matching these spectres to other respective significant objects, which include: an engagement ring, a letter, a pair of glasses. Such tasks involve correctly recognizing from environmental clues the narrative history of the corpse each spirit circulates. But players do not just read the story from the game, a more static form of narrative embed in past events; players also produce the story in real time by reacting to these game cues and performing appropriately. Successful progress consequently involves the player fulfilling the destiny of the central character in releasing these spirits from their restless wandering. Such actions gain greater significance in the game's wider context, as each level ends with players defeating the murderous creatures which caused the character's death. The story of *Clock Tower 3*, of Alessa's realization of her powers as a Rooder, and subsequent defeat of the evil Subordinates is not just a narrative of cut-scenes, documents and spaces, but one into which player participation is fully incorporated.

Of course, many games have such ideal paths. What makes survival horror distinct is not only the existence of a preferred path to play, and the narrative contextualization of objects and objectives through which this path is realized, but the extent to which in the majority of titles this ideal route is extremely narrow. If survival horror games are engines for telling stories, in any meaningful understanding of the term, there is really only one story that can be told, albeit with different endings. The rigid nature of the genre is emphasized in Diane Carr's discussion of the "tense, sparse and linear" structure of the original *Silent Hill*. Underlining the sequential nature of this spatial progression, Carr notes: "the clues, keys and puzzles all lead the player in a particular direction: forward" (2006: 60). This maze-like linearity, in contrast to the more unstructured multi-branching rhizome, is considered to be a fundamental element of the game's ability to scare. Directed, unalterable, claustrophobic gameplay produces a generic experience of tension and fright (Carr, 2006: 60–2). Similarly, Krzywinska argues such determining structures relate to broader aspects of the horror genre, whereby: "The operation of the game's infrastructure invokes for the player an experience of being subject to a pre-determined, extrinsic, and thereby, Othered force" (2002: 208). If survival horror video games are dominated by a sense of narrative determination and restriction which limits their interactive possibilities and underlines the incompatibility of narrative and interactivity, this is an intrinsic quality of the horror genre. The sense in which players perform a linear pre-defined narrative dictated by the game structure is often reflected in the narrative which they perform, protagonists being subjected to the same controlling supernatural authorities as the player who follows the path determined by the god-like game designer. In *Clock Tower 3*, despite the agency of the player and the protagonist, Alessa is simply fulfilling her Rooder destiny. As Jill in *Resident Evil 3: Nemesis* observes, all her actions have been orchestrated to cover the tracks of the evil Umbrella Corporation. Despite the illusion of character and player free will, Harry, Heather and Henry are merely pawns of the higher forces presiding over the *Silent Hill* universe. *Rule of Rose* has a similar sense of melancholic pre-determination, exemplified by the story book presented to the central character at the game's beginning, itself endemic of the generic function of narrative in survival horror games. In telling the story of the game's hapless protagonist, a tale still unfolding as a traditional non-interactive print media text, the agency and interactive role of the player is blatantly dismissed.

Conclusion

Exploring survival horror in terms of narrative reveals much about the nature of the genre. As Santos and White (2005) observe, the survival horror player more often than not assumes the role of detective, sifting through fragments of diaries, masonry, bodies, in order to find out what happened to this town/ship/school/prison. How did everyone become zombified, what is the origin of the deadly "fissures," who put the dead cat in apartment 102's refrigerator? Storytelling in survival horror, in common with many qualities of video game narrative, is a process of uncovering not narrating (Grieb, 2003: 166), solution rather than creation (Egenfeldt-Nielsen et al., 2008: 182). This is why so many games—*Haunting Ground, Rule of Rose, Alone in the Dark, Silent Hill 2, 3, Origins* and *Homecoming* (Double Helix, 2009)—feature protagonists suffering from amnesia. Play involves uncovering repressed memories which are as new to the player as to the game protagonist. A range of media texts—printed documents, photographs, computer files—aid players in this quest. As records of the past uncovered in real-time present, these snippets of narrative allow the unfolding of a story according to the temporal specificities of the video game medium. Architecture is a recurring metaphor used to understand video games, and in survival horror buildings and spaces tell stories, much like the documents which litter them. They serve as the location of extraordinary or horrific past events which can be read in the bloodstains on the walls, the wooden planks on the windows, the disemboweled prison guards crawling across the floor. The fact these detailed environments offer limited opportunities for disruptive interaction indicates the trade off between prescriptive story telling and player participation. Survival horror video games also present players with a potential story of performance inherent in successful progress through the game itself, a tightly bound linear path entailing the retrieval of these storytelling scraps, navigation of these malignant spaces, and the completion of certain narratively-coded objectives. If the question introducing *Resident Evil 2* is to be answered in the affirmative and the player has survived the horror created by the game, they would have followed a fixed sequence of tasks as defined by the game design. The play experienced by that player, and its preferred organization as evident in the text of the game, might represent the clearest sense of video game narrative in survival horror.

The argument, forcefully and repeatedly well made, that video games are not stories, that they should not be interpreted simply as stories, and that if they use narrative it is in a radically different way to traditional media, has been appreciated throughout this essay. As Egenfeldt-Nielsen et al. conclude: "fiction in video games does not work according to the same parameters as it does in representational media" (2008: 203), and many of the forms of storytelling examined in this essay are specific to the medium. Survival horror, which depends for its generic operation and effect upon various narrative and representational elements, illustrates ways in which the video game medium is developing new forms of storytelling, by combining modes and media, through *mise-en-scène* and spatial design, and in the structuring of the player's pathway through the game maze. This essay has also illustrated the impact such elements have on the kinds of interactive play permitted within the genre. In many respects, survival horror video games bear out Aarseth's claim that, in its traditional form, "narration and ... gameplay, like oil and water, are not easily mixed" (2004: 51). But the fact horror video games provide a pleasure, even if it is a masochistic one, suggests that in the area of interactive digital entertainment a desire remains for users' control to be compromised by a narrative experience which leads the player down a dark and twisty, yet fundamentally linear, path. Survival horror play entails a narrative contract between player and game-text. In exchange for channeling their interactive energies along the defined route, the game promises the player this pathway will produce an experience which is thrilling, exhilarating and terrifying in varying pleasurable and un-pleasurable measures. Play in survival horror involves playing along.

Because as Carr (2006) and Krzywinska (2002) suggest the lack of interactivity which comes with a sense of linearity and pre-determination fortifies the generic impact of such games, the single pathway enhances fear and tension, just as the inability to significantly impact upon events intensifies the impression of supernatural forces orchestrating the game universe. Often storytelling elements serve to emphasize players' lack of control, be it the non-participatory cut-scene which precedes the zombie siege, the bloodstained diary detailing a mercenary's untimely demise, walls etched with the claws of monstrous entities, or the feeling gameplay evokes of retracing the steps of the protagonist towards some psychologically-scarring event from the past. The creepy sensation of play existing within a narrative matrix, where fragments of long-dead researchers litter your path, where apocalyptic creatures leave their claw-marks on shattered furniture, where every footstep might trigger a life-threatening cut-scene of scripted zombie animation, intensify the experience of imperilment to a nauseating degree. A feeling of being manipulated and orchestrated by unseen forces is produced by the camera cut which reveals the only open doorway. A sense of fate-like preordination builds as the solutions to puzzles are revealed in newspaper clippings, photographs, and archived hospital notes. These games elicit an experience of obsessive compulsion as successful play involves the repetition of psychologically destructive actions protagonists have already performed. All induce the vertiginous sensation of not really being in control, no matter how expertly one might manipulate the controller. The ultimate horror of survival horror is the suggestion that, despite our strongest feelings to the contrary, we are not the masters of our own fate.

If the archetypal horror cinema moment involves an ill-equipped protagonist entering a room we know she should not, audiences well aware of the serial killer lurking within but unable to warn the heroine; survival horror video games insist that, despite possessing the same generically-informed knowledge, we actively aid the protagonist, not only in opening the door, but in solving the puzzle to get the password to find the key to unlock the door. We do indeed KNOW who's in there, but we direct our avatar to enter the room nonetheless. Upon which the screen fades to black and the inevitable cut-scene of uncontrollable horror.

Works Cited

Aarseth, Espen (2004), "Genre Trouble: Narrativism and the Art of Simulation," in Noah Wardrip-Fruin, and Pat Harrigan (eds.), *First Person: New Media as Story, Performance, and Game*, Cambridge, MA and London: The MIT Press, pp. 45–55.

Atkins, Barry (2003), *More Than a Game: The Computer Game as Fictional Form*, Manchester and New York: Manchester University Press.

_____, and Tanya Krzywinska (2008), *Videogame, Player, Text*, Manchester and New York: Manchester University Press.

Bolter, Jay David, and Richard Grusin (2001), *Remediation: Understanding New Media*, Cambridge, MA: MIT Press.

Carr, Diane (2006), "Space, Navigation and Affect," in Diane Carr, David Buckingham, Andrew Burn, and Gareth Schott (eds.), *Computer Games: Text, Narrative and Play*, Cambridge: Polity, pp. 59–71.

Crawford, Chris (2003), "Interactive Storytelling," in Mark J. P. Wolf and Bernard Perron (eds.), *The Video Game Theory Reader*, New York and London: Routledge, pp. 259–73.

Egenfeldt-Nielsen, Simon, Jonas Heide Smith, and Susana Pajares Tosca (2008), *Understanding Video Games: The Essential Introduction*, New York and London: Routledge.

Eskelinen, Markku (2001), "The Gaming Situation," *Game Studies*, Vol. 1, No 1, available online at <http://www.gamestudies.org/0101/eskelinen/>.

Frasca, Gonzalo (1999), "Ludology Meets Narratology: Similitude and Difference Between (Video)games and Narrative," available online at <http://www.ludology.org/articles/ludology.htm>.

_____ (2003), "Simulation versus Narrative: Introduction to Ludology," in Mark J. P. Wolf and Bernard Perron (eds.), *The Video Game Theory Reader*, New York and London: Routledge, pp. 221–235.

Grieb, Margit (2002), "Run Lara Run," in Geoff King and Tanya Krzywinska (eds.), *Screenplay: cinema/video games/interfaces*, London and New York: Wallflower Press, pp. 157–70.

Jenkins, Henry (2004), "Game Design as Narrative Architecture," in Noah Wardrip-Fruin, and Pat Harrigan (eds.), *First Person: New Media as Story, Performance, and Game*, Cambridge, MA and London: The MIT Press, pp. 118–30.

Juul, Jesper (2001), "Games Telling Stories? A Brief Note on Games and Narrative," *Game Studies*, Vol. 1, No 1, available online at <http://www.gamestudies.org/0101/juul-gts/>.

_____ (2004), "Introduction to Game Time," in Noah Wardrip-Fruin, and Pat Harrigan (eds.), *First Person: New Media as Story, Performance, and Game*, Cambridge, MA and London: The MIT Press, pp. 131–42.

King, Geoff, and Tanya Krzywinska (2006), "Film Studies and Digital Games," in Jason Rutter and Jo Bryce (eds.), *Understanding Digital Games*, London, Thousand Oaks and New Delhi: Sage.

Kirkland, Ewan (2009), "*Resident Evil*'s Typewriter: Survival Horror and its Remediations," *Games and Culture*, Vol. 4, No. 2, April.

Klevjer, Rune (2002), "In Defence of Cutscenes," in Frans Mäyrä (ed.), *Computer Games and Digital Cultures Conference Proceedings*, Tampere: Tampere University Press, available online at <http://www.digra.org/dl/db/05164.50328>

Krzywinska, Tanya (2002), "Hands on horror," in Geoff King and Tanya Krzywinska (eds.), *ScreenPlay: cinema/video games/interfaces*. London and New York: Wallflower, pp. 206–23.

Moulthrop, Stuart (2004), "From Work to Play: Molecular Culture in the Time of Deadly Games," in Noah Wardrip-Fruin, and Pat Harrigan (eds.), *First Person: New Media as Story, Performance, and Game*, Cambridge, MA and London: The MIT Press, pp. 56–69.

Newman, James (2008), *Playing with Videogames*, London and New York: Routledge.

_____ (2004), *Videogames*, London: Routledge.

Perron, Bernard (2006), "Coming to Play at Frightening Yourself: Welcome to the World of Horror Video Games," *Aesthetics of Play Conference Proceedings*, Berger, Norway, available online at <http://www.aestheticsofplay.org/perron.php>.

Ryan, Marie-Laure (2008), "Beyond *Ludus*: Narrative, Videogames and the Split Condition of Digital Textuality," in Barry Atkins and Tanya Krzywinska (eds.), *Videogame, Player, Text*, Manchester and New York: Manchester University Press, pp. 8–28.

_____ (2001), "Beyond Myth and Metaphor: The Case of Narrative in Digital Media," *Game Studies*, Vol. 1, No 1, available online at <http://www.gamestudies.org/0101/ryan/>.

Santo, Marc C., and Sarah E. White (2005), "Playing with Ourselves: A Psychoanalytic Investigation of *Resident Evil* and *Silent Hill*," in Nate Garrelts (ed.), *Digital Gameplay: Essays on the Nexus of Game and Gamer*, Jefferson, North Carolina: McFarland, pp. 69–79.

Van Looy, Jan (2003), "Uneasy Lies the Head That Wears a Crown: Interactivity and Signification in *Head Over Heals*," in *Game Studies*, Vol. 3, No. 2, available online at <http://www.gamestudies.org/0302/vanlooy/>.

Wolf, Mark J. P. (2007), "On the Future of Video Games," in Paul Messaris and Lee Humphreys (eds.), *Digital Media: Transformations in Human Communication* Oxford: Peter Lang, pp. 187–95.

Wood, Aylish (2007), *Digital Encounters*, London and New York: Routledge.

Zimmerman, Eric (2004), "Narrative, Interactivity, Play, and Games: Four Naughty Concepts in Need of Discipline," in Noah Wardrip-Fruin, and Pat Harrigan (eds.), *First Person: New Media as Story, Performance, and Game*, Cambridge, Mass and London: The MIT Press, pp. 154–64.

Shock, Horror: First-Person Gaming, Horror, and the Art of Ludic Manipulation

Dan Pinchbeck

This essay explores the use of horror imagery and devices in first-person games, normally known as First-Person Shooters (FPS). Unlike their survival horror counterparts, the core ludic interface of these games means that conventional, structural devices often used in third-person perspective gaming are not available to the developer. The most obvious of these is the lack of system control over the camera, with its impact upon the ability of the player to freely visually examine the presented environment. Forced camera angles are extensively used in survival horror to limit this ability, directly manipulating tension and creating moments of shock where action occurs just beyond the capacity of the player to see. Then, first-person games, especially more contemporary examples of the genre, have a far greater lack of cut-scenes than survival horror ones, demonstrating a consistent drive to keeping action both flowing and within the control of the free perceptual exploration of the player. As Krzywinska notes of *Clive Barker's Undying* (DreamWorks Interactive, 2001), the "freedom to look and explore ... marks a departure from the way horror films use editing and framing to create tension and claustrophobia. By contrast, the third-person shooter mode of *Resident Evil* (Capcom, 1996) is closer to film..." (2003: 209). Similarly, the relative lack of visualized avatars in FPS games has been argued to enable a greater and more direct relationship between the player and the system (Calleja, 2007). Whether this is accurate or not (in fact most FPS games expend considerable effort ensuring that there is a clear division between avatar and player), what can be stated confidently is that there is a direct, if reduced, perceptual mapping between avatar and player in FPS games and this has the potential to reduce the emotional distance between world and player. This argument can be supported by the clear shift across the genre to move epistemological and orientating devices within the presented diegesis, rather than relying upon heterodiegetic, system level, information (such as save screens, quad damage, pop-up instructions). This, alongside the atrophy of the use of cut-scenes, is highly suggestive of a drive within the genre towards an unbroken, highly immersive experience. Thus, we should examine gameplay devices and representational strategies in terms of their potential contribution towards this type of idealized experience.

Evident from the shifts in structures of contemporary FPS games, this experience is nevertheless predicated upon the act of removing agents from the presented environment, symbolically represented as high intensity action and combat. This, on the surface, appears to push the genre away from the horror experience. There is a very different relationship between the avatar and the world in FPS games as opposed to horror scenarios. In the former, the micro-goal/reward structure — Bungie's famous "30 seconds of fun" repeated over and over again — is based around being the most powerful agent in the given environment. Since the avatar is meant to be kept alive in survival horror games, this is clearly not the relationship most horror scenarios are based upon. However, there is clear and frequent use of horror themes in First-Person Shooters. Devices and the co-option of the experiential qualities of a horror experience are also visible right across the genre. It is thus pertinent to consider both why this might be and how horror is deployed and managed by a genre unable to resort to normal structural devices to aid its successful application.

We will argue in this essay that player experience is the result of managed schemata, established and handled by the system to initiate particular readings and forms of behavior, including expectation, affect and reaction on the part of the player. We will also show how horror provides some very specific and powerful means of setting and adjusting the parameters of this process. Thus, even though many of the games within the FPS genre are ostensibly more science-fiction than true horror in terms of the presented diegesis, there is extensive adoption from images and structures likely to fall within the player's established cultural schema of horror to support a diversity of play experience and specifically manage the constraints and requirements of the system to deliver a predetermined experience. Horror can be understood as a gameplay device.

Schema and Horror: If It Looks Like a Zombie and Barks Like a Zombie...

On the crudest level, we have horror themes: in *Painkiller* (People Can Fly, 2004), *DOOM* 3 (id Software, 2003), and *Hellgate: London* (Flagship,

2007), we are set against the very forces of Hell itself; *Call of Cthulhu: Dark Corners of the Earth* (Headfirst Productions, 2005) and *Clive Barker's Undying* substitute Hell for equivalent mythoi. This is the explicit stuff of horror we are well aware of from Stoker, Lovecraft and King as well as a plethora of movies and TV shows; it is explicit horror *by reference*. Indeed, it's hard to find a game where the undead don't feature, which is perhaps not surprising as zombies and ghosts have power particularly because they twist the normal in a way which is profoundly recognizable and wrong in equal measure — they are classically interstitial monsters. In other games, we find the contemporary Frankenstein's genetic laboratory, producing monsters and cyborgs that nevertheless also have their historical and literary roots back in the golem and the undead. *Quake 4*'s Strogg (Raven Software, 2005) bolt together parts of dead marines and build cyborg/zombie fighting machines; *Far Cry's* (Crytek, 2004) Trigens were once men and monkeys but are now monsters; *Bioshock*'s ("K Games, 2007) population has reduced itself to Adam-riddled subhuman predators. However, as Carroll notes, the appearance of monsters is not, in itself, necessarily indicative of the horror genre. It is the relationship between reader, viewer and player and these monsters — the particular affective state that is generated — that is the crucial factor (1990: 16–24). The Strogg are horrible, but is *Quake 4* a horror game? How about *Half-Life* (Valve, 1998)? *Painkiller* makes extensive use of demonic monks and nuns; spectral soldiers; witches and undead lunatics, but it is entirely questionable whether on an affective level, it can be defined as more of a horror game than the (superficially) straightforward science-fiction of *System Shock 2* (Irrational Games/Looking Glass Studios, 1999).

As well as this explicitly *referential level*, where we are expected to find the subject matter horrific because we already know it is supposed to be, games work hard on the *representational level* to make the images and objects of FPS games horrific. *DOOM 3*'s zombies shuffle about with missing jaws, intestines and heads, groaning painfully into the dark; *Bioshock*'s splicers are twisted, unpleasant distortions of the human form and *Resistance: Fall of Man*'s Chimera (Insomniac Games, 2007) aren't going to win any beauty contests. This is backed-up with a gamut of screams, screeches, moans, and roars designed and selected to sound as nasty and frightening as possible. The deployment of these devices — their orchestration constitutes a third level — further influences the way in which we respond to the objects. The word "zombie" has a level of horror about it by reference; a bloodied corpse mounted by a grossly organic and pseudosexual headcrab that screams "Help me! Help me!" has an additional one, but both are amplified hugely by the zombie in question suddenly lurching out of near pitch-black after five minutes of tense build-up and when we only have four bullets left in the chamber. The *orchestrational level* of horror thus refers primarily to the manipulation of the context of the deployment of the referential and representational objects, including the baseline, background mood-manipulators that may not necessarily be tied to any explicit object or event. The comparative devices from film are scores, camera angles, timing, and architecture and it is here that FPS games lose the split between avatar and player perception (or camera positioning) as a key tool. Perron, in particular, has focused upon the relationship between horror and gameplay (2004, 2005), and we will compliment his explorations here by placing them within an overall framework for the use of diegetic elements to manipulate the player, and extend his field of inquiry to the FPS genre.

Lindley has argued that we should understand gameplay as the learning, recognition, and activation of a particular gestalt (2002: 209). Alternatively, we can describe gameplay as the generation and application of media schema (IJsselsteijn, 2003). Schemata are generalized mental structures relating to stereotypical patterns of activity, similar in essence to Schank and Abelson's scripts (1977). They argue that we develop a large number of scripts, dealing with common occurrences that reduce cognitive workload by streamlining possible behavioral response according to this mental template. Thus, in the restaurant script (ibid: 42–46), our template would determine that we will have to pay for our food, and we should not do so until we have eaten it, that the people moving between the tables are staff, not diners (particularly if wearing aprons), and so on. Unless there is deviation from this template, they argue, we do not need to give it full attention, particularly in relation to temporal sequencing. This is the same basic argument as made by Bartlett, in his study of how Western subjects re-interpreted the Inuit story *The War of the Ghosts* to fit a Western narrative template (1932: 64–94).

Both gestalts and schemata, when applied to gameplay, suggest that play is based around the generation of templates for input-output relationships between system and player. There is a commonsense aspect to this: we learn how to operate our consoles, we develop skills and modify our behavior to succeed and progress. On the other side of the equation, we find presence and flow (Csikszentmihalyi, 1991), both of which have been the subject of recent inquiry by games scholars (Ermi and Mayra, 2005; Sweetser and Wyeth, 2005; Adams and Rollings, 2006; Calleja, 2007; and Lemay, 2007). Essentially, in this context, flow represents an optimum psychological state of play, where activity is seamless, highly engaging and highly rewarding. Likewise, presence suggests the player is focused upon the contents of a representational system, rather than the system itself (they are worrying about fighting the Flood, not about which button to press next, or the fact that a car alarm is going off outside the house, and so on). Both presence and flow states are characterized by a lowering of the significance of the world outside the experience; less attention being paid to the structural act of engaging with a mediated experience and more paid to engagement occurring at an affective or psychological level with its content. Emotion has been proposed as being core to presence (Huang and Alessi 1999), although the exact determination of presence as either a physiological or psychological condition, or both, remains somewhat contentious. There is thus a natural conceptual relationship between schema, which essentially semi-automate part of the cognitive process, and presence/flow, which require a shift of attention from the mechanics of performing an action, towards its effect (just as when we are steering a car, we rarely think "move left arm up a bit, down a bit, down a bit more" and so on).

Similar to schemata are Minsky's frames (1974). Rather than being explicitly temporal, frames nevertheless hold stereotypical information about common contexts. A house frame would contain a generalized set of nested frames: we would expect to find a kitchen, bathroom, at least one bedroom and so on. These nested frames contain a further level; in a kitchen we would expect a cooker, a sink. This final level of frames contains generalized information about the objects in question, so a cooker has a box that heats up, plus hobs, perhaps an extractor fan, and so on. The information at this primary level relates to the *affordances* of the object — what it lets us do. So, once again, a cooker frame contains information that infers a purpose, it affords the activity of heating (food). In other words, frames present a stereotypical object that, once identified, allows use without recourse to determining function from scratch; we do not, on encountering each new variation of a cooker, have to learn what it does, as it fits a pre-existing frame with associated affordances. This is, of course, closely related to object recognition in general, particularly the prototype theory of categorization. In layman's terms, when we perceive an object, we access already existing information about it (classically termed *percepts* in the psychological literature), including how it functions, which is dependent upon both its perceived characteristics and its context.

If schema and frames exist for restaurants, cookers, driving, and playing games, there is no reason to deny their existence in relation to specific genre. Indeed, Wes Craven's *Scream* (1996) is famously a rather overextended joke about the highly formal conventions of the horror movie — it only succeeds because we, as viewers, have an established horror-movie schema. In more conventional horror films (amongst other genres), one of the key means of manipulating the audience is the subversion of expectations— of schema, in other words. Stingers, the synchronization of high-impact music with moments of high drama or tension, are common techniques implemented in film, and subverting a stinger (building to a false climax, then having the monster jump from the closet at the same moment the audience realizes they've been duped and let out their breath) is equally common in horror films. Likewise, films—and games—co-opt existing schema and frames, in the form of cultural assumptions or tacit knowledge, as well as genre and medium specific expectations. This is essentially the referential level of horror we described above. Thus, when we see a zombie on screen, in a film or a game, prior understanding of zombies, what they do, how they act, and how we should react to them, not only become available, but influence our responses to them. Incoming signals, when close enough to the prototypical object or situation, cross a threshold and fire the respective schema, in essence establishing a framework for further expectation and response. Further, as Neisser has noted, this process is dynamic (1976); exploration and investigation informs and alters schema, altering the properties by which they are triggered and applied.

Gameplay in general is comprised of a fit of the player's activities to the affordances defined by the game; in return for which, the system confers an affective experience within a predetermined range. In other words, there are only certain, vastly simplified, actions available to the player, as defined by the system. At this point, we can posit, gameplay schema swings into effect: if it looks, sounds, and feels enough like a game, and we know how to play games, we do not have to learn the system all over again, our expectations about what affordances are supported, are, to an extent, automated. When we boot up *Painkiller*, note the lack of an intervening avatar, note the gun at the bottom of the screen and the sudden appearance of multiple agents, if we know FPS games—we have a developed schema—we do not have to attend to the systemic level of rules. In other words, we know that we are required to line up objects with the vanishing point and press the appropriate button, we have movement along the horizontal plane as standard, we can't walk or shoot through walls, most things in the environment are hostile, we will probably have a depreciating ammunition count, and so on. The idea of describing gameplay according to a schematic or cognitive model is, of course, not new. Perron (2006) describes gameplay as a "heuristic cycle," explicitly basing this upon Neisser's cycle, noting for example that the schema not only defines expectations, but is a template for action. It is not simply a case of understanding what might occur, but what our side of the bargain is, what types of activity (perceptual, interpretative, and actual) we need to undertake in order to close the circle.

As suggested above, however, these schema are not necessarily limited to the system, we can also extend cultural frames beyond the domestic and into the horrific. As Carroll notes, horror is really to be defined by a specific reaction to its contents—and the referential level, combined with our understanding of frames and schema, certainly relates to this. There are two potential levels of affect. In the first, there may be a natural, or tacit, reaction to certain stimuli that have their roots as much in evolutionary psychology as culture: we tend to have an instinctive negative reaction to deformity, decay and certainly operate with underlying schema regarding to threat and danger. In addition to this, many horrific creatures and situations are predicated upon a lack of understanding, control, or breakdown of normal categorization (Cavallaro, 2002: 173 and Carroll, 1990: 32–35). Darkness limits our perception, creating space for tension and doubt to flourish. Death is not a positive outcome.

On the second level, we generally arrive at horror with a set of schema and frames already established. Most of us know from childhood that trolls and ogres are frightening, evil creatures and have seen countless images of them. Equally, Halloween helps to formalize our understandings and categorizations of vampires, ghosts, ghouls, devils, and zombies. By the time we pick up a copy of *DOOM 3*, it is highly unlikely that we will not already know what a zombie or demon is, or have an established set of expectations for their behavior

These two levels of schema map more or less directly across to the representational and referential levels of horror respectively. When we see a zombie in *DOOM 3*, our cultural knowledge about zombies kicks straight in, defining a template of expectations about its actions, and our responses. This is reinforced by the representational level, the engagement of our natural reaction to a pallid, shuffling, moaning humanoid dragging its entrails along behind it. Finally, supporting this, the orchestrational knowledge also operates upon the first schema type, reducing our field of vision, projecting sounds behind us and so on. Horror in games co-opts existing schema to function effectively, and this is hardly a radical position to take. However, what we can move onto is how these schema work backwards in terms of being gameplay devices; in other words, what are the benefits to a system of using horror specifically?

Co-opting Schema as a Gameplay Device: The Advantages of Horror in Systems Terms

Let's start with the simplest advantage of using horror schema in gameplay: agents. We have previously argued that when it comes to agents, the fundamentally important issue is not necessarily AI but rather the attribution of agency to action: the interpretation of agents as intelligent by the player (Pinchbeck, 2008). The vast majority of FPS agents are anthropomorphic, humanoid in both appearance and projected behavior. This is a direct co-option of tacit schema — we can see which way they are facing, we can adopt the intentional stance towards them and project motive and contextual understanding of the environment onto them.

This contextual understanding is particularly important, as it has a direct bearing upon the AI required to create a convincing agent. The affordances attached to an agent must enable it to act appropriately in its environment, thus human beings in a normal space should operate in a way that appears natural. When the player finds R. George hiding in a cupboard towards the beginning of *Resurrection of Evil* (Nerve Software, 2006), it is a beautifully valid and empathisable response to the sudden appearance of demonic monsters. Smart civilians run away; soldiers radio for help if outnumbered, and so on. Therefore, the placing of agents in an unfamiliar environment is a powerful means of cutting them off from such highly expectable actions; the common drive to survive. However, such actions, which also include having intelligent or even just contextually appropriate conversations with the avatar and others, are a tough AI challenge, and the breakdown of such appropriate behaviors is hugely problematic for an immersive diegesis. Examples of this are common—failure of agents to take cover when being shot at, or to assess threatening situations and take appropriate actions. FPS games, with their high orientation around combat, have made great strides in AI regarding tactical behavior in gunfights, with AI teams capable of flanking, finding cover, using grenades to flush the avatar out and so on. But it is striking that, even in a game such as *S.T.A.L.K.E.R.: Shadow of Chernobyl* (GSC Gameworld, 2007) that attempts to create a self-sustaining world where agents sleep, chat, and play guitar, there is little evidence of the types of activity one might expect from groups: factions are semi-permanently "on duty" and tellingly, rarely run away from a fight.

Monsters, however, are a quick and easy means of bypassing some of this pressure to behave with ecological validity. Zombies are, according to our cultural schema, profoundly stupid and unaware of their surroundings. Demons and other more monstrous forms *do not belong in the world*; they have no interest in human surroundings. Thus, the semantic characteristics of monstrous agents almost de facto reduce the need for complicated ecological behavior; however, keeping them anthropomorphized enables a basic project of intentionality onto them. *DOOM 3*'s Imps are monstrous demons, who do not belong in the world. Whilst they look human enough to be able to apply some prediction to their behavior — and their proximity to prototypical monsters imports expectations such as "they are here to harm humans," and "they are dangerous"— they retain the interstitiality necessary to be creatures of horror and, critically, they do not have to interact intelligently with the environment in any real depth in order to be convincing beings. In other words, they can have a vastly simplified relationship with their environments, reducing the AI load. In system terms, monsters are cheap.

It is therefore not surprising to find such powerful devices in a large number of titles spanning the FPS genre, and whether "true" horror titles or science-fiction titles using horror imagery: *Half-Life, System Shock 2, Return to Castle Wolfenstein* (Gray Matter Software, 2001), *Clive Barker's Undying, Thief: Deadly Shadows* (Ion Storm, 2004), *DOOM 3, Quake 4, Halo: Combat Evolved* (Bungie, 2002), *Painkiller, Prey* (Humanhead Studios, 2006), *S.T.A.L.K.E.R.: Shadow of Chernobyl,* and *Hellgate: London* all contain zombies and monsters. In addition to this, *Far Cry, Deus Ex* (Ion Storm, 2000), *F.E.A.R: First Encounter Assault Recon* (Monolith, 2005), *Condemned: Criminal Origins* (Monolith, 2005), *Bioshock, Blacksite* (Midway Austin, 2007), and *Resistance: Fall of Man* all use interstitial creatures whose semantic characterization justifies a reduced relationship with the environment. *Bioshock's* splicers are mentally deranged; *Deadly Shadows* supplements its undead, Rat-men and Kurshok with living statues; *Far Cry* has hairless mutant apes and *Resistance: Fall of Man's* Chimeras are virus-ridden ex-humans. Put simply, monstrous characteristics, imported directly from horror schema control expectations of intentionality. If it looks like a zombie, sounds like a zombie and moves like a zombie, then the zombie schema fire, and the game's designer can use this diegetic wrapping to reduce the system load of the agents.

Similarly, there is an advantage to co-opting many of the schemas associated with horror in relation to the environments which are presented. Horror is predicated upon a breakdown in knowledge or understanding, a realization of the boundaries of the rational and controllable, and a recognition that these boundaries have been transgressed. Likewise, many FPS games, certainly all those that have no pretense to historical accuracy, swiftly move beyond normality, introducing elements that explicitly undermine the controllable, known reality of the avatar. This disruption moves beyond the simple crisis-to-resolution model of narrative, and is delivered in a way, with a particular relation between transformation and avatar, which is indicative of an underlying horror theme. Once again, we can turn to Carroll's definition of horror and note that he requires both impurity and dangerousness as constitutional elements; thus when we see a transgression of reality, we should be looking for these quite specific devices (1999: 42).

Prey offers a great prototypical scenario, even though it is, broadly speaking, a science-fiction work. The alien vessel that abducts Tommy, Enisi, and Jen is profoundly organic, interstitial and disgusting. It is resplendent with orifices, fleshy obtrusions, vomit, exploding turd-like eggs, phallic tentacles, all interwoven and interbred with more recognizable walkways, doors, and gratings. Not only is it referentially repulsive—crawling around the intestines of another organism is acceptedly culturally transgressive after all—but the representational level is specifically designed to illicit this response, and in case it doesn't, Tommy's monologue reminds the player periodically how gross the whole situation is. Likewise, as *DOOM 3's* Mars Base succumbs to demonic invasion, it begins to manifest similar features; large intestinal bodies twist through the walls, blocking progress. *System Shock 2* features an entire level set within the Body of the Many, essentially traversing and sabotaging a giant stomach, complete with nerve endings and internalized molars. *Call of Cthulhu: Dark Corners of the Earth* not only includes the city of the Deep Ones and then the journey deeper into the subterranean world (with its implications of moving backwards to a past even more inhuman and stellar in scale) to the lair of the Polyps and Hydra's temple, but the occupation of the real world by the monstrous Shoggoth. Even *Halo: Combat Evolved*, perhaps the most classic space-opera of the genre, features in its sequels movement through spaces infected with Gravemind, once again a category transgressing a blend of organic and non-organic spaces. In fact, most FPS games, whilst not creating space as directly impure as these, contain large quantities of gore and disturbing scenes (in *Bioshock*, Steinman's medical experiments, Cohen's "artworks"), recognizably Gothic architectures (*Clive Barker's Undying*'s monastery and large, dark mansion; *Hellgate: London*'s Ancient Blood halls), or strange transformations of the normal world (*S.T.A.L.K.E.R.: Shadow of Chernobyl*'s anomalies and blowouts).

The transformation of the known, or its invasion by unknown elements, once again works to reduce the requirements of the system, by manipulating the player's expectation and knowledge of the environments. At its most base level, this is a creation of a liminoid space, where normal rules are altered, suspended and reduced, diegetically justifying a formalized set of behaviors that are defined by the system, not the player. *F.E.A.R: First Encounter Assault Recon* blurs the line between real, imagined, and supernatural by embedding visions of other spaces and times, ghosts who appear and disappear at will and exert their will upon normality. Alma causes fires, deaths, and explosions but remains profoundly insubstantial, an intruding, inexplicable and unpredictable presence. Together with the visions of Jankowski, Fettel, and the Point Man's own birth, this establishes a super-natural world, infringing upon the real, operating according to a physics and logic which is sinister and, critically, uncontrollable. This sends a message to the player: you are not in control, and it is impossible to predict what is around the next corner. When overlaid upon a highly predictable gameplay format — move along, kill some agents, move along again, kill some more agents, perhaps find a key to open a door, etc.— this is a powerful device, it breaks the repetitive flow of events by inferring an unpredictability of intrusion, of change. The ghosts of *System Shock 2*, *Clive Barker's Undying* and, to a more uneven extent, *Bioshock* fulfill a similar function. In all cases, the danger comes not from hostile agents, whose ubiquity and highly formalized affordance relationships with the player rob them of any deeper emotional resonance, but from forces whose motives are less easy to define, and who cannot be dealt with by the limited normal capacity of the avatar (shooting at them until they are removed from play).

The orchestrational level is supported by diegeses which enable this kind of destabilization of expectation, as it frees affective manipulation from the rules of the real. In *DOOM 3*, an agent can teleport in at any point, magically arriving from Hell, which increases the potential significance of all triggered sound cues. This, in turn, directly influences the attentional resources of the player, as does the diegetic device of power failures (enabling large portions of the game to occur in the dark). The effectiveness of these devices over a long period in *DOOM 3* remains questionable, as the player very swiftly learns the cues of agents about to teleport in; but at a local level, the combination of a dark environment (perception is directly reduced and controlled by the system) with an ambiguous, un-locatable, threatening sound has been established as a pan-genre device of huge importance in gaming. What is important to note is that these orchestrational devices can be helped or hampered by diegetics, and this fundamentally relates to control over the player's expectations of knowledge about the environment. The combination of interstitiality and unpredictability in the world is thus a potent tool in assisting this process.

Behind the transgressive environments, and crucial to much horror, is an unknown powerful agent with a direct motive relating to the action. The semi-deified manipulator is a common character in horror fiction; with attributes and intellect outstripping that of the protagonist. Indeed, in a ludic space that is predicated upon the avatar (and player) becoming the most physically powerful agent in the game, but one with extremely limited capacity to engage with the world in any complex way, a space is created for a nemesis with just these characteristics. Besides which, there is a profound difference between an unknowable motive and no motive; the latter makes tension exponentially more difficult to sustain.

Interestingly, the majority of nemeses are not represented in games as final Boss battles, which lends support to the idea that they are serving a different function to direct combat challenge. Thus, in *Quake 4*, Kane ultimately faces the Makron, but the Makron is never presented elsewhere in the game as a character. Likewise, the Nihilanth in *Half-Life* is not a running, developed figure in the game's narrative; Lucifer has no part to play in what little there is in the way of story in *Painkiller*; and Betruger is reinvented in *Resurrection of Evil* as the Maledict, but does not feature in any meaningful way in the narrative until the boss battle at the end. At the other end of the scale, *Half-Life 2* (Valve, 2004) presents Breen as a nemesis figure, but does not use him in a boss showdown at the end of the game. Interestingly, the same is true for Betruger in *DOOM 3* and Krone in *Timeshift* (Saber Interactive, 2007). Nor is *Condemned: Criminal Origins*'s nemesis figure, Serial Killer X, the boss battle at the end of the game. Although Paxton Fettel is established as the nemesis figure in *F.E.A.R: First Encounter Assault Recon*, this position is undermined as the story progresses in favor of the far less corporeal threat of Alma (and the conspiracy headed by Wade and Aristide). *Clive Barker's Undying's* family members, together with Keisinger, are used as bosses during gameplay, but the final battle is saved for the Undying King, once again, not a featured non-player character (NPC). Likewise, *Call of Cthulhu: Dark Corners of the Earth's* boss encounters are the Deep One gods, Mother Hydra and Father Dagon, yet the final cut-scene sets up the Flying Polyps as the real arch villains and there remains a highly ambiguous relationship between all of the mythos factions and races (including Cthulhu himself). In fact, *Prey* is comparatively rare in its use of Mother as an ongoing nemesis figure that results in a boss battle.

This may relate once again to the potential problems of retaining tension in a game that is profoundly based upon dominance of the presented space. The level of threat in an FPS game needs to shift dynamically to match the increase in power of the avatar, itself linked to the established system of power-up based rewards. One means of doing this is to increase the potency of agents set against the avatar or, more crudely, their numbers, but this in itself requires some diegetic management to convince the player (unless the game in question is *Painkiller*, which although dispensing with basically any notion of a coherent diegesis, nevertheless, and interestingly, still feels the need to place the action in a wider, semi-coherent context). Nemesis figures with godlike abilities are extremely potent and forgiving devices to anchor this to. Such characters, able to exert influence upon the world through powers that remain manifestly super-natural, provide a means for the game to transgress what is physically possible (*DOOM 3's* teleporting agents); alter the diegesis without warning (*F.E.A.R: First Encounter Assault Recon's* visions, *Call of Cthulhu: Dark Corners of the Earth's* Shoggoth), and communicate unpredictably with the player (Mother's voice in *Prey*). In other words, they are diegetic justifications for severing the links between design and reality, an immensely powerful gameplay tool.

Not only this, but their ambiguous motives, inhuman intellects and desires, and pervasive influence frees them from requiring full explanation of their actions and their influences upon the world. This adds a general capacity for plot management that can be deployed without warning or explanation. Whilst human nemeses, such as Breen in *Half-Life 2*, or Doyle in *Far Cry*, are constrained by the limits of physics and understandable motive, S.H.O.D.A.N., Aaron Covenant, Mother, Alma, Mother Hydra, Betruger, Lucifer and Gravemind, are all interstitial, demigod villains, who not only have powers to affect the world in mysterious ways, but whose motives are not required to be explicitly available or understandable. This fulfills two functions: firstly, it establishes a power relation with the avatar that does not conflict with their mastery over the ludic space and secondly, it places a greater power for plot manipulation with the system's designers, as the cosmic scale and ineffability of their plans dilutes the need for the ongoing action to make sense. If the avatar is really just a pawn in a grand, supernatural game, they are not required to understand why such things are occurring, merely to accept that *someone does*. This is a frequent device in Lovecraft's fiction, where protagonists end up with little more than a glimpse of the motives and plans of the Elder Gods and Old Ones and, indeed, those FPS games tending more towards classic horror offer only partial resolutions of their plots: *Clive Barker's Undying* leaves the avatar Patrick Galloway essentially in hiding, waiting for the next summons to engage with the supernatural world he has discovered; Jack Walters' suicide at the end of *Call of Cthulhu: Dark Corners of the Earth* is a result of experiencing the inhuman scale of the Old One's influence upon the world; at the climax of *F.E.A.R: First Encounter Assault Recon*, the true nature of the conspiracy is only just beginning to unfold and Alma is still at large; *Condemned: Criminal Origins*'s final cut-scene shows Agent Thomas infected with The Hate, the demonic force apparently, but unexplainably, behind the games' events.

Given all this, it is perhaps unsurprising that nemeses are not often found as boss battles, as it would reduce the powers they have been given in order to enable these far-ranging devices of diegetic and gameplay manipulation and justification to a level that can be dealt with by the very prosaic capacities of the avatar (not forgetting that Dracula himself was finally dispatched by a bowie knife to the heart). Instead, like transgressive realities and interstitial monsters, they shift the expectations of knowledge on the part of the player, thus assisting the manipulation that underpins gameplay.

In all of these cases, what is important is that the player is co-opted into colluding with this management system, and it is here that horror schema really come into play. Agents that fit the representational schema for creatures already known from horror trigger a set of behavioral expectations; sinister and ineffable nemeses are plot devices we recognize, and support a breakdown in the real, in itself a means of covering the limitations of the environment by reducing player knowledge; transgressed environments not only provide visual rewards and affective manipulation but also operate upon expectation, proposing that deviations and limitations from the normal are properties of the diegesis, not the failures and constraints of the system. Finally, because a model for what is happening and how it may develop is established, the player's attentional resources can be directed away from this issue, encouraging a more passive relationship with such questions and increasing focus upon the affective experience, a key factor in inducing presence and flow.

Conclusion

We started this essay by noting two things: firstly that FPS games cannot use some key structural techniques of the filmic horror genre such as defining perceptual boundaries, and secondly, that their nature may enable a greater degree of immersion within the presented diegesis. We have also noted the extensive co-option of existing schema as a means of orientating the player to the game, both in terms of ludic, structural schema, and referential, cultural ones. The use of such schema enables a game to utilize prior knowledge and understanding, but they require careful management, as there is the potential for the generation of expectations that are beyond the capacity of the game system to fulfill. Horror, as much as it is characterized by Carroll's twin poles of fear and disgust, is fundamentally driven by a breakdown in knowledge, through interstitial creatures and situations: boundaries are not only transgressed, but trust in the understanding of where these boundaries actually lie is undermined. Thus, the schema associated with horror frequently operate along these fault lines, often subtly co-opting the reader, viewer, or player into a more passive relationship with the media system. In this instance, a split between what should normally occur and what is to be specifically expected is established. And this split is a hugely beneficial underlying feature for gameplay. Not only can horror schema be appropriated for quite specific purposes— both the engineering of a particular affective outcome, and the support for limitations in AI, draw distances and architectures— but it acts upon the level of expected knowledge and power the player brings with them to the game. Protagonists in horror may be heroes, but they are frequently, simultaneously, victims, responding to situations that are outside their ability to control, or fully understand. Grand plans operate behind the scenes, with only glimpses of their full import; reality begins to fray, or is invaded, or destabilized; things are not as they should be. Thus, horror schema operate alongside the base schematic proposal of FPS games: you can move, look and interact with this world using your skills and knowledge of the real one (allowing attentional resources to be focused upon the experience, not its structural requirements), but you must realize, early, that these rules can and will be broken, manipulated and controlled externally. This is essentially establishing a critical power relationship between player and system and, indeed, it may be that the submission to a manipulating system is part of the draw of horror games, as with films (we want to be scared and for our experience to be, to an extent, unpredictable).

Whilst it is rare to find genuine horror FPS games, that are both referentially absolutely situated in the tradition, and that increase the threat from the world by reducing the potency of the avatar as a combat device (such as *Call of Cthulhu: Dark Corners of the Earth* or Frictional Games' 2007–2008 series *Penumbra*), the ubiquity of horror in the genre is striking. Partially, this does relate to the surface-level rewards, the grisly delight in the eviscerated bodies, shattered worlds, and noises in the dark; the orchestra of affect. But there is also a deeper psychological power of horror that is directly beneficial to defining a specific type of gameplay experience, with particular emphasis upon the manipulation of attention and expectation. By destabilizing our normal conceptual boundaries, encouraging us to enter into a position of reduced power relative to the system, where we surrender a degree of expectational control and accept that things are more sinister and less controllable than they seem, horror helps us forget the boundaries of the screen and plunge into the diegesis, into the dark.

Works Cited

Adams, Ernest, and Adam Rollings (2006), *Fundamentals of Game Design*, London: Prentice Hall.

Bartlett, Frederick (1932), *Remembering: A Study in Experimental and Social Psychology*, Cambridge: Cambridge University Press.

Calleja, Gordon (2007), "Revising Immersion," *Situated Play: Proceedings of DiGRA 2007 Conference*, Tokyo, available online at <http://www.digra.org/dl/db/07312.10496.pdf>.

Carroll, Noël (1990), *The Philosophy of Horror or Paradoxes of the Heart*, London: Routledge.

Cavallaro, Dani (2002), *The Gothic Vision: Three Centuries of Horror, Terror and Fear*, London: Continuum.

Csikszentmihalyi, Mikhail (1991), *Flow: The Psychology of Optimal Experience*, New York: Harper Collins.

Ermi, Laura, and Frans Mayra (2005), "Fundamental Components of the Game Play Experience: Analysing Immersion," *Changing Views: Worlds in Play. Proceedings of DiGRA 2005 Conference*, Vancouver, available online at <http://www.digra.org/dl/db/06276.41516.pdf>.

Huang, Milton, P. Norman, and E. Alessi (1999), "Presence as an Emotional Experience," in J.D. Westwood, R.M. Hoffman, R.A. Robb and H.L. Pick (eds.), *Medicine meets Virtual Reality: The Convergence of Physical and Informational Technologies: Options for a New Era in Healthcare*. Amsterdam: IOS Press, pp. 148–153.

IJsselsteijn, Wijand (2003), "Presence in the Past: What Can We Learn from Media History?," in G. Riva, F. Davide and W. IJsselsteijn (eds.), *Being There — Concepts, Effects and Measurements of User Presence in Synthetic Environments*, Amsterdam: IOS Press, pp. 17–39.

Krzywinska, Tanya (2002), "Hands-on Horror," in G. King and T. Krzywinska (eds.), *ScreenPlay. Cinema/videogames/interfaces*, London: Wallflower Press, pp. 206–233.

Lemay, Philippe (2007), "Developing a pattern language for flow experiences in video games," *Situated Play: Proceedings of DiGRA 2007*, Tokyo, available online at <http://www.digra.org/dl/db/07311.53582.pdf>.

Lindley, Craig (2002), "The Gameplay Gestalt, Narrative, and Interactive Storytelling," *Proceedings of Computer Games and Digital Cultures Conference*, Tampere, available online at <http://www.tii.se/zerogame/pdfs/CGDClindley.pdf>.

Minsky, Marvin (1974), "A Framework for Representing Knowledge," in P. Winston (ed.), *The Psychology of Computer Vision*, New York: McGraw-Hill, pp. 211–217.

Neisser, Ulric (1976), *Cognition and Reality: Principles and Implications of Cognitive Psychology*, Reading: W.H. Freeman.

Perron, Bernard (2005), "A Cognitive Psychological Approach to Gameplay Emotions,"

Changing Views: Worlds in Play. Proceedings of DiGRA 2005 Conference, Vancouver, available online at <http://www.digra.org/dl/db/06276.58345.pdf>.

_____ (2006), "The Heuristic Circle of Gameplay: The Case of Survival Horror," in M. Santorineos (ed.), *Gaming Realities: A Challenge of Digital Culture*, Fournos: Athens, pp. 62–69, available online at <http://www.ludicine.ca/sites/ludicine.ca/files/Perron — Heuristic Circle of Gameplay — Mediaterra 2006.pdf>.

_____ (2004), "Sign of a Threat: The Effects of Warning Systems in Survival Horror Games," *COSIGN 2004 Proceedings*, Split, available online at <http://www.cosignconference. org/downloads/papers/perron_cosign_2004.pdf >.

Pinchbeck, Dan (2008), "Trigens Can't Swim: Intelligence and Intentionality in First Person Game Worlds," in S. Gunzel, M. Liebe and D. Mersch (eds.), *The Philosophy of Computer Games 2008 Proceedings*, Potsdam: Potsdam University Press.

Schank, Roger C., and Robert P. Abelson (1977), *Scripts, Plans, Goals and Understanding*, Hillsdale: Lawrence Erlbaum Associates.

Sweetser, Penelope, and Peta Wyeth (2005), "GameFlow: a Model for Evaluating Player Enjoyment in Games," *Computers in Entertainment (CIE)*. Vol. 3, No. 3, pp. 1–24.

Haunting Backgrounds:
Transnationality and
Intermediality in Japanese
Survival Horror Video Games
Martin Picard

Someone looking at the American channel G4TV will notice particular segments of programs such as *Attack of the Show* ("What's Up in Japan?") and *X-Play* ("Made in Japan") presenting some Japanese "eccentricities" and their "strange" or "crazy" games. Alongside this kind of media coverage of Japanese culture from the West, part of a common approach in Japanese studies has been to put emphasis on cultural Japanese characteristics within art and fiction, which has often lead to an Orientalist vision of Japan. Acknowledged as truly reflecting the Japanese culture, this approach has been used to define the essence of Japan, commonly referred to as "Japaneseness." Studies on Japanese horror fiction do not differ. Jay McRoy (2005 and 2007) and Colette Balmain (2008) for films and Chris Pruett for video games (2005a, 2005b, 2006)[1] have described the specificity of Japanese horror in the light of the influence of traditional Japanese culture.

In such studies, mainly based on cinema, Japanese horror has been characterized as a unique type of horror. We usually stumble across arguments like this:

> Speaking of horror in Japan signify to refer to a set of long standing mythological and literary traditions, deeply rooted in the Japanese imaginary. A wide range of Shinto or Buddhist tropes and motifs, linked to the territory of the arcane, the demonic, the possession, the fantasies, the deaths and the avenging spirits, is part of many works of the Japanese literary and theatrical tradition and constitute a repertory on which cinema will then seize in order to appropriate the themes and figures [Gomarasca, 2002: 135; freely translated].

Pruett insists on the strangeness of Japanese horror and culture in an attempt to understand it: "So what is it about Japanese horror that we find so attractive? What has kept it comprehensible and accessible to mainstream Western audiences? What is with all the freaky women wearing white with their hair covering their face?" (Pruett, 2006). A part of his task is to "...explain how Japanese horror works within the context of Japanese culture and how this approach is [*sic*] differs from the type of horror that Americans are used to" (Pruett, 2006). Differences between American or Western cultures are essential to all the aforementioned examinations of Japanese horror and culture.[2]

Still, some believe that to capture the specificity of "the new wave of horror stories that swept the Japanese culture in recent years, it may be more useful to start from the tradition of Western popular culture (which has a major weight on these stories, or at least equal to that derived from indigenous horror) and the criticism related to this genre" (Gomarasca, 2002: 135; freely translated). Taken together, the studies of McRoy, Pruett and Hand have revealed, in one way or another, the influence of the American — and Japanese horror cinema — on Japanese horror games. As Hand underlined:

> The opening video sequence to the samurai survival horror *Onimusha Warlords* (Capcom, 2001) is like Akira Kurosawa's *Ran* (1985) crossed with Romero, and the subsequent gameplay presents a feudal Japan populated by the undead and teeming with the supernatural [Hand 2004: 123].

An approach of the specificity of Japanese horror games that would be lying uniquely on Japanese characteristics is inappropriate when we look at the diversity inside the genre. Almost all of the biggest Japanese video game companies have made horror games, and they all seem to have their own particularities. Amongst these companies, two or three stand out: Capcom with the *Resident Evil* series (1996–2009), *Onimusha* series (2001–2006), *Clock Tower 3* (2003) and *Haunting Ground* (2005); Konami with the *Silent Hill* series (1999–2008); and Tecmo with the *Fatal Frame* series (2001–2008).

Critics have typically drawn upon two very different games as the most representative of the survival horror genre, *Resident Evil* (Capcom, 1996) and *Silent Hill* (Konami, 1999) These two opposing horror games have helped to define survival horror and what Bernard Perron called "survival terror" (2006):

> Although both titles wished to have a cinematic horror feel, the references were not the same. *Resident Evil* has always been compared to *Night of the Living Dead* (George A. Romero, 1968) and *Silent Hill* to *The Exorcist* (William Friedkin, 1973). Those narrative frameworks finally gave birth to two different games. *Resident Evil* is known to be more action-oriented, more about quick thrill, jump scares and gory images. *Silent Hill* is considered to be more psychological, more about characters and atmosphere, and more about giving a sense of dread, anxiety and helplessness [Perron, 2006: 7–8].

Despite their horrific differences, and despite being Japanese in origin, the two series are rooted in America. Silent Hill is an American city and the characters that populate it are Americans. Alongside *The Exorcist*, Konami has always acknowledged the American and Western influences on the series, mainly American cinema with films such as *Jacob's Ladder* (Adrian Lyne, 1990) or David Lynch' films (see Perron, 2006). The design team at Konami wanted to make "modern American horror through Japanese eyes" (Pruett, 2005b). The *Resident Evil* series is even more imbued with American themes and topics. The beginning of *Resident Evil* is filled with American action movie stereotypes: STARS' (Special Tactics and Rescue Squad) Alpha and Bravo teams are assigned by helicopters to Raccoon City, a peaceful town located in the Mid-West of the United States. The economic stability of this community relies on the multinational pharmaceutical Umbrella Corporation, whose tests on humans have had disastrous consequences on the population that the American soldiers will have to face. However, just like Capcom's other successful horror series *Onimusha*, the *Resident Evil* series will slowly open up to internationalism. While the first iterations of the series are set in America, the last two are set abroad: a rural Spain in *Resident Evil 4* (Capcom, 2005), and a sunny Africa in *Resident Evil 5* (Capcom, 2009).

At the other end of the spectrum, Tecmo's *Fatal Frame* series is set in feudal Japan. This series is known for being strongly influenced by traditional Japanese culture. The most common reference to that effect, which is characteristic of typical Japanese horror in general, is the figure of the vengeful ghost, as we will see later. But as a series it is substantially different from the two paradigmatic games which define the realm of survival horror, it may be an example that is more the exception than the rule. As a result, rather than asserting that survival horror video games are truly Japanese, it may be more appropriate to consider them in light of their transnationality and intermediality. Even when placing the problematic topic of "Japaneseness" aside, it seems difficult to analyze purely Japanese characteristics in survival horror games, especially since the vast majority are heavily influenced by American and European media and culture. Following the work already done by McRoy and Pruett, amongst others, my essay will begin with the presentation of the intriguing mix of Japanese and Western themes and audiovisual aesthetics in series like *Silent Hill*, *Resident Evil*, *Fatal Frame*, and *Onimusha*. I will discuss these games from a transnational and intermedial point of view. I will also be considering some of the most apparent traditional Japanese characteristics in survival horror games, such as ghosts and demons, borrowed from Japanese folklore. Attempting to situate myself in a more materialist than idealist perspective,[3] I will then conclude this essay by calling into question in greater detail the Orientalist and essentialist functions of Japanese icons in survival horror games for the Japanese video game industry; hoping to show how the study of Japanese horror video games is more complex than it seems at first glance, requiring a nuanced and critical perspective.

Transnational Games

The survival horror genre is characterized by numerous influences and borrowings, both from their own culture, media, and art forms, and from Western popular culture, primarily American. Figure 1 shows the multiple connections of the Japanese horror video game, making such a genre a "media mix" *par excellence.* For Mizuko Ito, the "media mix" is a native industry term useful to describe the video game media in Japan, which "needs to be understood as one component of a broader media ecology that includes anime, manga, trading card games, toys and character merchandise" (Ito, 2006). In order to explore the concepts of transnationality and intermediality in greater depth, I wish to broaden Ito's notion of "media mix" to include all the remediations[4] and transnational — even transgeneric — influences on Japanese horror video games.

For Hand (2004), Pruett (2005b; 2005c) and others, even if consumed only by Western gamers, survival horror games have a distinct and specific nature (mostly aesthetic and thematic) which characterize them as "Japanese." At the very least, this is the common view conveyed by the industry, reviewers, and fans. Expanding upon the work of Henry Jenkins and Mary Fuller in "Nintendo® and New World Travel Writing: A Dialogue," we need to ask an important question:

> What exactly is the cultural status of a Nintendo® game, based partially on American generic traditions or adopted from specific Western texts, drawing some of its most compelling iconography from Japanese graphic art, licensed by Japanese corporations, manufactured and designed by corporations in both the Americas and Asia, and for sale to both Japanese and American marketplaces? [Fuller and Jenkins, 1995].

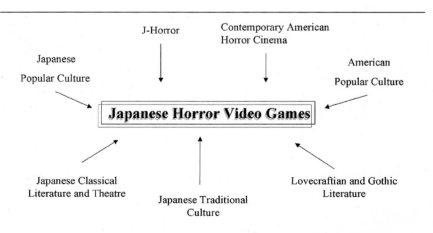

Figure 1: Multiple influences on Japanese horror video games.

We could easily replace the term "Nintendo" with "Japanese horror." Japanese horror games are works created and produced, but not necessarily distributed, by Japanese companies or designers, whether the targeted market is in Japan, America, or elsewhere. This underlines the new global economy of popular cultural goods, as much as any of the relatively recent concepts which have surfaced as a result; one of which is the notion of "transnationality."

Transnationality refers to the global ways in which cultural goods are created, produced, and distributed internationally. As explained in the introduction of *Transnational Cinema: The Film Reader* (where we could easily replace "films" with "video games"):

> In its simplest guise, the transnational can be understood as the global forces that link people or institutions across nations. Key to transnationalism is the recognition of the decline of national sovereignty as a regulatory force in global coexistence. The global circulation of money, commodities, information, and human beings is giving rise to films whose aesthetic and narrative dynamics, and even the modes of emotional identification they elicit, reflect the impact of advanced capitalism and new media technologies as components of an increasingly interconnected world-system. The concept of transnationalism enables us to better understand the changing ways in which the contemporary world is being imagined ... as a global system rather than as a collection of more or less autonomous nations [Ezra and Rowden, 2006: 1].

There are many occurrences of these transnational manifestations within the industry.

Firstly, many games are created by American studios but outsourced to Asia and then distributed worldwide (see Winterhalter, 2008). Secondly, there are also Japanese games developed in the West under a Japanese corporation and distributed worldwide for Japanese consoles, but marketed for the Western market; *Silent Hill: Homecoming* (Konami, 2008) is a good example. The latest iteration of this popular survival horror series was developed in the U.S. by Foundation 9 studio, Double Helix Games (formerly The Collective) and released on Sony PlayStation 3 and Microsoft Xbox 360. This was also the case for the prequel *Silent Hill: Origins*, developed by Climax Studios for Sony PlayStation Portable (PSP) in 2007 and then on PlayStation 2 in 2008. The original concept of the game was developed by the now-defunct Los Angeles office of the U.K.–based developer, but it was so badly received by the press (for resembling *Resident Evil 4*, more in look and feel, than *Silent Hill* Series), that the rest of the production returned to the England-based team (Bettenhausen, 2007: 77).

Finally, a Japanese game development company was hired by an American corporation to create "Japanese" games on an American console, which were then marketed to Japanese gamers. Indeed, Microsoft hired Square Enix to create Japanese Role Playing Games (JRPG) on their console (Xbox 360) for Japanese audiences in order to capture a part of the market in Japan. Surprisingly, their strategy was successful. The console was the biggest seller in Japan when some of these Square Enix games (*Infinite Undiscovery* and *The Last Remnant*) were released in the fall of 2008.

As a result, Japanese games are increasingly marketed for Western audiences, especially since the Japanese visual style is strongly linked to American popular culture. While demonstrating the influence of the American animation aesthetic, it becomes a selling point for Western fans of anime and manga[5]; the same of which could be said about survival horror games. Similarly to the way in which anime are Americanized Japanese animation, survival horror games are Americanized Japanese horror products, both in their themes and characterizations, as well as in their visual aspects. Thus, they are easily exportable. There is no doubt that the *Resident Evil* series was not only marketed for a Japanese audience, but for a global one.

The notion of transnationalism underpins other related concepts such as nationalism, Orientalism, and globalization. The advent of a transnational economy and popular culture made some old disputes emerge again — but in a new way — around essentialist theories surrounding the Japanese culture.

Nationalism (and Japaneseness)

From the time that Western scholars initially began to study Japan, the country has been consistently perceived as being very nationalistic. Classic writings on Japanese history slowly constructed the image of a specific nation characterized by precise elements such as Japanese ghosts, demons, and other cultural icons. For the majority of its history, Japan has been an isolated island, closed to exchange with other countries.[6]

In 1867, after pressure from the Americans, the Japanese finally opened their gates, which coincides with the beginning of a new era (Meiji era — 1868–1912). The Meiji restoration could be seen as the first step towards transnationalization since many American and European artists, scholars, and historians began taking interest in the unique Japanese culture. It was also the beginning of an Orientalism which still remains strong in American and European popular culture today.

The wavered overture of Japan to other countries led to a strong nationalist fever among Japanese intellectuals and politicians (who wanted a re-closure), which helps to explain the imperialist attitude of Japan during the World War II era. Another major step in transnationalization came after Japan was defeated in 1945 by the Americans, who occupied the country from 1945 to 1952. An alleged "Americanization" of Japanese culture have been the result, characterized by a rapid industrialization of the society and an integration (imposed as well as welcomed) of American culture and values.[7]

To this day, people outside Japan maintain a great interest in its culture, specificity, and originality. Since the early twentieth century, both Westerners and Japanese scholars have tried to define this specificity, in order to characterize what they called the "Japaneseness." This concept continues to be valued by people interested in Japanese (popular) culture. It is this idea that brings many video game fans and critics to talk about true "Japanese" video games or films (as for JRPG and J-Horror) and to be inclined to think that game designers can create a game "Japanese-style"—even if the game has been created by a Western studio (like the aforementioned example of *Silent Hill: Homecoming*). Part of this characterization came from the alleged originality or "uniqueness" of the Japanese culture. This culture has been marked with a specific visual art style, which has been disseminated in a variety of art forms and media.[8] Also, it has been distinguished by various themes, topics, and imageries displayed in arts and media, such as the "avengeful spirits" mainly depicted by uncanny female ghosts. This has led to a specific perception of a cultural and national Japanese identity. As McRoy pointed out, "[m]odern, and pre-modern, perceptions of cultural and national identity in Japan" have constructed a fundamental belief in seeing "the Japanese social body as an imagined wholeness" (McRoy, 2008: 93). Marilyn Ivy noted that the Japanese social body is a hybrid social entity that frequently denies the complex amalgamations that constitute it:

> The hybrid realities of Japan today—of multiple border crossings and transnational interchanges in the worlds of trade, aesthetics, and sciences—are contained within dominant discourses on cultural purity and nondifference, and in nostalgic appeals to premodernity: what makes the Japanese so different from everybody else makes them identical to each other; what threatens the self-sameness is often marked temporally as the intrusively modern, spatially as foreign. Although those discourses are being altered by the effects of advanced capitalism, they have proved remarkably resilient as they haunt the possibilities of a postnationalist consciousness in contemporary Japan [Ivy, 1995: 9].

As McRoy has already observed, Ivy's haunting motif is attractive here since "it represents, and contributes to, a discourse of a returning repressed" (McRoy, 2008: 93). Applied to a game such as *Fatal Frame* (Tecmo, 2001), the ghosts of the game come to haunt the characters and gamers, as well as the whole franchise. Consequently, the series is comprised as a—hybrid but still national—cultural product.

Orientalism

The notion of "Japaneseness" has been primarily promoted by Westerners, leading to a deep form of Orientalism, but was also supported by Japanese intellectuals themselves in studies known as *nihonjinron* (Japanese

essentialist discourse).[9] Japanese artists and filmmakers such as Akira Kurosawa and Kenji Mizoguchi were prompt to recycle worn-out clichés of traditional Japanese culture such as samurai, harakiri, kamikaze, Mont Fuji, and
geisha, just to name a few. Even today, but this time to question the underlying Orientalism, the internationally acclaimed Japanese filmmaker Takeshi
Kitano uses Japanese clichés in his work (Davis, 2001).

Orientalism is a complex notion that needs to be approached with pre-
caution, especially in a complex global world. One can nevertheless understand Elmer Tucker when he claims that an Orientalist perspective is still
prevalent in video games "both in the Western consumption of Japanese
games and in Japanese games depictions of Japanese-ness in the games"
(Tucker, 2006). As a media based mainly on the use of common places and
popular culture's myths and formulas, it is not surprising to observe a form
of Orientalism at work in video games, especially horror ones. A form of Orientalism which is frequently found in Japanese horror video games is the
"East's internalization of the Orientalist's fetish and its own production of
Orientalism" (Tucker, 2006). As Tucker further argues:

> Essentially, Orientalism acts as a two-way relationship in which the West con-
> sumes a fetishized version of the East and in which the East internalizes that
> fetishization and markets it to the West. Because the Oriental subject is founded
> on the exploitation of Otherness, the Oriental subject in turn allows an auto-
> exoticizing Japan to use cultural tropes and stereotyped icons to market them-
> selves to a Western audience and to enforce a culturally imperialistic policy for
> Asia. Japan's continuance of the commodification of Japanese icons, specifically
> seen with the Samurai and Ninja figures, reveals the use of Orientalist perspec-
> tive in selling games such as *Onimusha* and *Tenchu* that rely on distinctly Japa-
> nese archetypes [Tucker, 2008].

Ghosts and other Japanese folklore icons presented in *Fatal Frame*, *Onimusha
3: Demon Siege* (Capcom, 2004), *Kuon* (Agetec, 2004), *Siren* (Sony Computer
Entertainment Japan, 2004) or *Clock Tower 3* are indeed recycled in an Orientalist fashion. Orientalism is essentially displayed due to the fact that horror video games are cultural goods belonging to a global economy.

Globalization

As a product of a techno-capitalist global economy, the video game market and industry rely on international distributions for their products. The
functioning of the production studios fits inside this global economy, where
a part of the production process is often crafted outside the country of the
production facilities, a process known as outsourcing (which may be called
more appropriately "offshoring").

For the Japanese cultural industries, the international distribution of video games, as well as any popular cultural products such as films, anime, and manga has been a key economic strategy to promote their culture to the world. However, an essential strategy for helping their products to be accepted and consumed in other countries (especially the United States) has been the localization of the product. Since the American distributors, and even the Japanese ones, believe that their native customers would have difficulty understanding the context behind the cultural product — a belief based on an Orientalist view of Japan as a strange and eccentric culture, they feel obliged to tailor the product according to the cultural context of reception.

The internationally famous video game franchise *Pokemon* (1996–2008) is a good example of this "glocalization."[10] Survival horror video games undergo the same marketing strategy, particularly by companies like Capcom, as reflected by the *Resident Evil* games' increase of action moments (that is Americanization). The international contextualization of their settings (United States, Spain and Africa) becomes a key factor in their transnationalization. Nevertheless, the nature of survival horror games doesn't lie solely on their transnationality, but also on their "intermediality."

Intermediality

Intermediality, spawning from film studies, is a term derived from intertextuality, but applied to media. Livia Monnet defined it in this manner:

> ... [the] notion of intermediality ... can account simultaneously for the interactions, mutual remediations or transformations, and the conceptual convergence between various media in a particular medium or (media) culture, as well as for the mutations in the discursive, representational and cultural practices produced by such (inter)media relations [Monnet, 2002: 225].

As Bolter and Grusin said about the remediation process in new media, the video game is a medium that strongly encourages remediations from other media, especially cinema (1999: 88–103). Survival horror video games are no exception to this rule as their iconographies rely both on Western and Japanese traditions and cultures, and their aesthetics draw on many popular medias, such as J-Horror cinema. Games like *Fatal Frame* or *Onimusha* are exemplary cases of this unique "media mix" with their hybridized, transnational, and intermedial qualities.

Haunting Backgrounds

It is important to be careful not to advocate essentialism and Orientalism when analyzing video games, as will be demonstrated in the conclusion of this essay. However, if there is a specificity in survival horror games that many scholars and aficionados have rightly emphasized, it can be found in these games exemplified by the traditional Japanese ghosts (and other folk creatures). This motif is complicatedly interconnected with other influences in Japanese games, creating a singular horror form. Before taking a closer look at the consequences of this complex mix, I will explain these mixed influences and examine their interconnections in the *Fatal Frame* and *Onimusha* series. It should also be noted that there are other games that could have been considered such as *Clock Tower 3, Kuon, Siren, The Ring: Terror's Realm* (Infogrames, 2000), or even the sci-fi first-person adventure game based on ghost stories *Echo Night: Beyond* (From Software/Agetec, 2004), as well as some Japan-exclusive games such as *Hungry Ghosts* (SCEI, 2003) or *Phase Paradox* (SCEI, 2001).[11]

The first obvious influence on the themes and characters of many Japanese horror games come from the Japanese culture itself. Japanese mythology and folklore, itself bearing on Shinto and Buddhism — the two major religions of the country — have always had a strong influence on literature and popular arts and this influence remains powerful. Mainstream Japanese myths are based on Japan's oldest works of the seventh and eighth century A.D., mainly the *Kojiki* (*Records of Ancient Matters*), the *Nihonshoki* (*The Chronicles of Japan*) and a few other complementary books. The folklore of Japan involves several bizarre and humorous characters and situations including an assortment of supernatural beings such as *bodhisattva* and *kami* (venerated gods and spirits), *yokai* (monsters and supernatural spirits such as *oni, kappa* and *tengu*), *yūrei* (ghosts), dragons, and animals with supernatural powers such as the *kitsune* (fox), the *tanuki* (a mixture of dog and raccoon), the *mujina* (badger), and *bakeneko* (cats which are able to transform).

Beliefs and superstitions were already transnational in the Japanese traditional literature. As Kiej'e said in his book *Japanese Grotesqueries*: "Japanese traditions of the supernatural depicted in literature and art combine Chinese ideas of demons, Indian notions of the transmigration of souls, and the native Shinto belief in nature and animal spirits" (Kiej'e, 1973: 7). Since the rise of Japanese culture, belief in ghosts and demons have had a powerful effect on the people. And this merging of various beliefs from Asian cultures "has yielded a rich assortment of grotesque creatures, all of them odd, bizarre, and contrary to human notions of what is normal" (Kiej'e, 1973: 6).

By far, the figure of the ghost has most widely represented people's imaginings of menacing creatures. This figure is, for the most part, what defined the specificity of Japanese horror culture. As Kiej'e indicates: "Japanese ghosts, ghost-gods, and demons appear in the traditional art and literature in an abundance unequalled in any other culture" (Kiej'e, 1973: 7). The spirit world of Japanese tradition "provides the raw material for grotesqueries in art and literature" (Kiej'e, 1973: 21), and then continues to spread within contemporary popular culture, but in a revitalized way.

Japanese ghosts and spiritual beings fall into various classes, but the most popular are the spirits of dead persons (usually resentful and full of envy for the living); the most dangerous ones are stillborn children and frustrated women. The "avengeful spirit" (called *onryô*) or the wronged women coming back to haunt those who have betrayed them are the most common ones. The "physical" appearance of ghosts is diverse, but some characteristics have come to be expected: invisibility (ghosts of dead persons); silver patches (where the eyebrows should be); usually missing legs; bodies which tend to "taper to a narrow wavering end and cast no shadow" (Kiej'e 1973:14); haggard and pale faces; hair falling loosely over the face and shoulders; hands which are raised to the breast (fingers drooping downwards); and finally, the clothing, which is usually white.

For the Japanese, the female ghosts (typically with no eyes or just one, or a wavering head extending out from the body on a snakelike neck) are among the truly terrifying ghosts: "They are dreaded by living men, their wives, and paramours, as a deceased wife with a grudge can return to haunt the living and drive them to distraction, suicide, or murder, in the mad frenzy of fear that the apparition inspires" (Kiej'e 1973: 14–15). The most famous of these female ghosts is the *yūrei*, which has existed in Japanese art for centuries, especially in Japanese classical theatre.[12] Her image has been brought to Western popular culture thanks to the success of the 1998 film *Ring* (Hideo Nakata, 1998)[13] — which started the transnational genre of J-Horror.

Similarly to other Japanese folklore creatures, *yūrei* has a traditional appearance and follows a certain set of formal rules which have been perpetuated in visual arts, Japanese classical theatre, and then Japanese horror cinema. The "dead wet girls" (Kalat 2007; McRoy 2008) of today have not changed much over time: generally female, wearing white clothing, which is the color of funeral garb in Japan; they have long, often unkempt black hair, which comes from Kabuki theatre where each character has a particular type of wig that identifies them to the audience.

The *yūrei*, with other traditional motifs, followed the cultural history of Japan, from the indigenous beliefs to contemporary horror cinema through classical literature and theatre. Japanese traditional literature, particularly Japanese classical theatre such as Noh, Kabuki, and Bunraku (puppet theatre), have drawn most of their stories from myths and folklore (ghost) tales which have been constructed by the Japanese culture over centuries (mostly from the Nara period [710–794] to the Meiji Restoration). Continuing the tradition, Noh and Kabuki practices are central precursors for some of Japanese horror cinema's most prevalent narrative arc stories and iconographic images. Richard J. Hand (2005) has underlined some examples, such as the trope of the "demonic woman" (the *kyojo-mono* or *shunen-mono* in Noh theatre, or the *akuba* or *akujo* [evil woman] in Kabuki plays) or the graphic and stylized presentations of gory scenes. Hand locates antecedents in the traditional theatrical *keren*, likened to contemporary special effects, a Kabuki "stage tricks [designed to] startle the audience with moments of irrational displays, which find modern-day equivalents in the spectacle of Sadako crawling out of the television set in *Ringu...*" (Hand, 2005: 23) (see figure 2).

The better known Japanese ghost story, *Yotsuya Kaidan* (*Ghost Story of Yotsuya*) is a kabuki play written in 1825 by Tsuruya Nanboku IV. This tale of betrayal, murder, and ghostly revenge has been adapted to film more than thirty times—the most famous one by the master of Japanese horror Nobuo Nakagawa (1959)—and continues to exert its influence on the Japanese horror today mainly through its depiction of *onryô*. Another essential work for this portrayal, this time in literature, is Lafcadio Hearn's *Kwaidan: Stories and Studies of Strange Things* (often abbreviated to *Kwaidan*) written in 1904, which features several short ghost stories that were translated by the author from old Japanese texts. Some of these stories were the basis of the film *Kwaidan* by Masaki Kobayashi in 1965.

Edo Gothic Cinema

Another major influence on Japanese horror games is classical Japanese cinema and horror films. The Orientalist recycling of the Edo period (1603–1868) has been especially popularized by films from the fifties and the sixties, which many consider masterpieces of cinema (the films of Akira Kurosawa, Kenji Mizoguchi, Masaki Kobayashi, Teinosuke Kinugasa, Keisuke Kinoshita, etc.). As evidenced in these period films of the Golden Age of Japanese cinema, essentially about samurai struggles in a genre called "chanbara," the Edo period represents the quintessence of Japanese culture. This era contains the fundamental cultural foundations of "Japaneseness." In the late nineteenth century and early twentieth century, the Orientalism towards Japan derived mainly from the iconography of that time (Mt. Fuji, samurai, geisha, ghosts, demons, and so on) which was filtered by Western (and even Japanese) artists, writers, intellectuals, historians, sociologists.[14]

Japanese horror cinema of the fifties and sixties has its origins in traditional Japanese horror derived from the Edo period, a particular film genre that Balmain called "Edo Gothic" (Balmain, 2008: 50–69). As soon as the Edison's Kinetoscope and Lumière Brothers' Cinématographe made their entrance in 1896 in Japan, the strong presence of horrific themes in the Japanese folklore had a direct influence on cinema in Japan, particularly the *Kaidan* films (or films about ghosts).[15] As McRoy suggests:

> [*Kaidan* films kept] drawing on a multiplicity of religious traditions, from Shintoism to Christianity, as well as the plot devices from traditional folklore, literature and theatre (including *Noh's theatre's shunen-* [revenge] and *shura-mono* [ghost plays], and *Kabuki* theatre's tales of the supernatural). [They habitually depict] the incursion of supernatural forces into the realm of the ordinary, largely for the purposes of exacting revenge [McRoy, 2005: 3].

Of course, the ghosts are associated with the features of the *onryô*, including long black hair and wide staring eyes. Throughout the history of Japanese horror cinema, ghosts (for the most part), demons, and monsters have populated the imaginary. Some filmmakers, such as Nobuo Nakagawa (*The Ghost Story of Yatsuya* [1959], *Jigoku* [1960]) or Masaki Kobayashi (*Kwaidan*), have made their reputation on filmic adaptations of legends and ghost stories. In 1998, *Ring*, which borrowed again, along with the *yūrei*, some of the myths already discussed, experienced a huge popularity to the point of creating a genre whose name is now used when talking about any Japanese horror films: J-Horror. Based on the 1991 novel by Koji Suzuki, *Ring* merges the conventions of urban legend with the classic *kaidan eiga* tradition of the long-haired, pale-faced lady spectre through the tale of a videotape curse. The film is a transnational hybrid at its best, initiating a wave of reinvigorating ghost stories whose most obvious tropes are well known among fans of J-Horror:

> ... vengeful ghosts, long stringy black hair, impossible physical gymnastics, meowing little ghost boys, cursed videos (or cell phones or computers), old rotted buildings and corpses, moldy books and newspapers, elliptical storylines (or a total abandonment of logic), creepy sound design, and creepy cinematography. Then there're the bizarrely happy endings and, lest we forget, the saccharine pop songs [Rucka, 2005].

Moreover, Japanese folklore, ghost stories, supernatural myths, along with tales of honor and loyalty combined with the anxiety and unease of the Japanese society, and Japanese concerns about mass media have had an impact on contemporary Japanese horror films. J-Horror became a horror subgenre in itself, with common themes and images. As Tom Vick said:

> The term *J-Horror*, a marketing moniker invented in the West, refers to a particular type of Japanese horror movie that eschews blood splatter for deep psychological creepiness, movies in which the glimpse of a figure out of the corner of the eye can give more nightmares than any ax murderer, where just about any piece of technology, from appliances to telephones to videotapes, can be haunted, and where it's not even safe under the covers: the ghosts are hiding there too [Vick, 2007: 74].

Usually compared to European or American horror cinema, J-Horror is now known for its specific themes and its conventional treatment of the horror genre. Above all, it has also been recognized for its atmospheric works. It tends to focus on the psychological horror and dramatic tension and anticipation.

When "J" (-horror) is referred to, it is because those films particularly involve ghosts, most often the *yūrei*.

Ghostly Games

The cultural characteristics and influences of Japanese horror cinema were transposed into the Japanese horror video games, especially the survival horror games. During the Game Developer Conference (GDC), *Silent Hill*'s composer and producer Akira Yamaoka talked about characteristics of Japanese-style horror and how they were implemented in the *Silent Hill* series (Yamaoka, 2005). He highlighted this particular style as being marked by unseen enemies, vengeance or hatred, and usually a sad story. As Pruett has explained, Yamaoka insisted on "the Japanese concept of *onnen*, which is a grudge or need for vengeance that might be manifested even after the person's death." This demanding attention may be "because Japan has a rich history of horror folklore, and whether they realize it or not, everybody who grows up in Japan today is exposed throughout their lives to these traditional concepts" (Pruett, 2005c).

Video games rapidly became a suitable platform for perpetuating the pleasures of horror. The inspiration, especially for Japanese horror games such as *Resident Evil*, *The House of the Dead* (Sega, 1996) and *Silent Hill*, is drawn both from traditional British gothic and Lovecraftian themes as well as from horror in Japanese popular culture. Horror manga (Japanese comics) and anime (Japanese animation) have had an appreciable imprint on Japanese cinema in the eighties and nineties, with such success as *Vampire Hunter D* (1985) and *Blood: the Last Vampire* (2000) (Jones, 2005: 124). These two works have been adapted to video games: the survival horror game *Vampire Hunter D* (Jaleco, 2000) on the PlayStation, and Japan-exclusive graphical adventure games based on the *Blood: The Last Vampire* franchise on the PlayStation 2 and PlayStation Portable (PSP) in 2000 and 2006 respectively.

As in the West, the horror genre is very popular in Japan, proliferating on every platform of popular culture where they all act upon each other. Similar to contemporary Japanese horror cinema, such "cultural cross-fertilisation" (McRoy, 2008: 2) in Japanese horror games must be taken into account to explain the popularity of Japanese horror games internationally. As Krzywinska argued: "[t]he range and popularity of games based on horror suggests there are aesthetic and marketing advantages in the remediations of cinematic horror in interactive media" (Krzywinska, 2002: 208). In that sense, it is not surprising that some Japanese developers have eagerly picked up the "Edo Gothic" for their horror video games. *Kuon* and *Onimusha* set their actions in those ancient times,[16] while *Fatal Frame* or *Siren* simply evokes them. The renewed interest in traditional ghosts in Japanese horror cinema has led to their recuperation by Japanese horror games and series.

The inspiration for *Fatal Frame* (known in Europe under the name *Project Zero*, and under *Zero* in Japan — "Zero" is also a pun because the character normally reads as "*rei*" which means ghost) comes from a Japanese urban legend. The goal of the game is to solve a mystery which is linked to Japanese folklore. The premise of the story is that a girl goes in search of her missing brother in a mansion which appears to be a haunted house full of ghosts. Shinto rituals, exorcisms, and typically Japanese ghosts are reappearing elements throughout the course of the game. Ghosts are the enemy figures of the game, some are friendly, but most are not. The only defense against them is the use of a camera which allows the gamer to exorcise ghosts by taking a picture of them thus imprisoning their spirit in the film. The use of a camera for capturing the spirit of the ghost is interesting, since cameras were long forbidden in Japan for superstitious reasons. For Kiej'e, the wide use of cameras in Japan today is proof of a change in attitude as people are becoming less superstitious: "No people [than Japanese] have more cameras, yet the old-fashioned folk of earlier Japan believed a camera to be dangerous to the soul of the sitter" (Kiej'e 1973: 9). Here, it is the soul of the ghost which is endangered by the camera. The sequels of the series also contain their share of traditional Japanese ghosts. *Fatal Frame II: Crimson Butterfly* (Tecmo, 2003) contains a scene, early in the game, where a ghost creeps to the ground in a typical manner which is strangely reminiscent of the crawling out of the well by the ghost of the young Sadako in *Ring* (figure 2).

The *Onimusha* series, created by Capcom, exploits historical figures of Japan by retelling their stories with additional supernatural elements. The title "Onimusha" refers to "Oni Warrior" which literally means "Demon Warrior." The *oni* are Japanese folklore creatures. They include demons, devils, ogres, and trolls. These characters have populated the imagination of the Japanese people through art, literature, and Japanese theatre (especially Kabuki). The game mechanics are very similar to the *Resident Evil* series, although *Onimusha* is more action-oriented (samurai swordsmen slaying demons) through "hack and slash." It is probably the similarities with *Resident Evil* and the presence of demonic creatures in the game world that has resulted in *Onimusha*'s classification as survival horror. However, because the games are not based on the idea of scaring the gamer, or generating a sense of terror, and do not explicitly and intentionally evoke fear as *object*, we can question the relevance of designating the series as belonging to the genre. Nevertheless, through their reference to the horrific themes of Japanese mythology and folklore, the games certainly can be included here.

The setting of the *Onimusha* series is based on historical figures and facts of feudal Japan. The games feature the samurai Hidemitsu Samanosuke

Akechi[17] (modeled after motion captures of the actor Takeshi Kaneshiro) who must save Princess Yuki from the Saito clan and defeat Nobunaga Oda.[18] *Onimusha 3: Demon Siege* (2004) is the most interesting iteration of the series because of its transnational borrowings. The game takes place in 1582, when Japan was immersed in an era of feudal war between competing provinces. The heroes of the game are transported back and forth to different places and epochs through time portals, from the Japan of the end of the sixteenth century to the Paris of 2004. Samanosuke Akechi will meet Jacques Blanc (modeled on the actor Jean Reno) and together they will fight Genma demons. True to the vision of a transnational character, Akechi wears a mix of a traditional samurai costume with red armor based on Western chain mail.[19]

Several stereotyped places or icons of Japan (traditional Japanese temples, shrines and castles; the town of Sakai, Lake Biwa, Mt. Hiei) and

France (Arc de Triomphe, Notre Dame Cathedral, The Eiffel Tower, Mont Saint-Michel, the Bois de Boulogne) are used for the game settings. Several historical heroes and folkloric creatures of Japan have been reinvented for the game[20]: Oni (especially oni warrior [demoniac samurai]), Tengu (Ako, the little girl who assists Jacques and Samanosuke), demons (the Gajimaro, who claim to be children or dolls), Ouija (spellcasting Genma), several demonic animals (dragons, spiders, worms, grizzlies), and even zombies. Obviously, the zombies— and other living dead in Japanese horror games, made famous by *Resident Evil*— are inspired by popular American culture, mostly contemporary horror cinema.

Figure 2: The "Woman in Box" in *Fatal Frame II: Crimson Butterfly* (Tecmo, 2003); and Sadako coming out of the TV in *Ring* (Hideo Nakata, 1998).

As I have noted at the beginning of this essay, Capcom's action-oriented horror is very different from Konami (*Silent Hill*), Tecmo (*Fatal Frame*) or Agetec (*Kuon*). These latter games qualify as psychological horror, a type of horror akin to Japanese horror, as evidenced by the J-Horror phenomenon. For example, in *Silent Hill*, the fog and the harrowing sounds of the radio announcing unseen enemies create a terrifying atmosphere. In order to build tension, psychological horror relies on the characters' fear, guilt, beliefs, and emotional instability, as is the case with James Sunderland in *Silent Hill 2* (Konami, 2001),

Figure 3: The samurai costume of Samanosuke Akechi and Jean Reno as Jacques Blanc in *Onimusha 3: Demon Siege* (Capcom, 2004).

where his sanity is put into question during the entirety of the game. Psychological horror is terrifying to gamers due to the tension built up around the story and characters' actions. It creates discomfort by exposing common and universal psychological fears, such as the fear of the unknown (or the unseen in the case of ghosts), or of the hidden self which is most often repressed or denied, as illustrated by the ghastly creatures of the *Silent Hill* series. In a sense, psychological horror is based on the atmosphere created in the games. For instance, in *Fatal Frame*, the darkness, the creepy settings, and the way ghosts come out of nowhere produce a strong sense of psychological fear. The director of the series Makoto Shibata has called this subtle approach "subtracting horror":

> I believed that our method to invoke the fear in the player's own imagination maximizes the recipient's fear. We do not simply show scary things, but provide fragmental information and create a situation that forces the player to imagine these horrors. I personally call it, "Subtracting horror" [Stuart, 2006].

He explicitly wanted to create a horror experience that was different from the experience in *Resident Evil* and *Silent Hill*. The long periods of quiet between ghost attacks were designed to both differentiate *Fatal Frame* games from other survival horror games and to create a more "Japanese" horror experience. According to Stuart, the games are the condensed essence of Japanese horror:

> In Japanese horror, fear is not simply generated through surprise; the silence and suspense in-between the action is important too. This silence makes the player's fear build in his or her mind. Japanese horror is always designed this way [Stuart, 2006].

However, *Resident Evil* and *Silent Hill* are still Japanese games, but of a different nature. They require us to be cautious when it comes time to investigate their ambiguous nature, especially in regards to their marketing.

Survival Horror and the Japanese Video Game Industry

As I have demonstrated, survival horror represents a complex intertwining of media (cinema, anime, manga, video game genres), national (Japan, America, Europe), and cultural influences (traditional, modern and popular ones). The transnational and intermedial nature of the games complicates the characterization of the genre to a point where it becomes unavoidable but to further elucidate the claimed Japaneseness of these games.

Revisiting the questions raised by Davis in his article about the complexities surrounding a national cinema in Japan, one could ask:

> Has national distinctiveness always been no more than a marketing ploy? Is "Japaneseness" something Japanese [video games] should slowly outgrow? Have representations of what is commonly recognized as "Japanese" outlived their usefulness? If not, then to whom are they useful? Or are they re-imagined in new and innovative ways? With the pace of global compression (of data, access, space, and so on), how has [the video game industry] come to terms with questions of nationality within transnational circuits? [Davis, 2001: 56].

If we look at the American video game (and cultural) industry, we know that it is renown for recuperating anything from the popular and cultural themes and icons to the formal and aesthetics structures of any media and art forms to sell their games. American games are exemplary cases of globalization since they do not offer transparent representations of, or even permit much space for, the expression of national cultures. However, the Japanese video game industry seems to work in the opposite direction, or rather, in a more complicated manner. Since the last decade, Japanese corporations have slowly understood that their culture gains attention through "contemporary networks of globalization" (Davis, 2001: 61). Through anime, manga, horror films, and now video games— though this is still in its infancy, except for the biggest video game companies— they try to sell their culture to other countries. For Davis, the "'traveling cultures' require national cultures as a kind of prop or background, both spatially and temporally, before which they take definition and come to life" (Davis, 2001: 57). *Fatal Frame* and *Onimusha* are both examples of an insertion of traditional and cinematographic Japanese iconographies into a global marketplace for Japanese horror video games. In these games, many national cultural icons serve as background, for instance, feudal Japan, legends and folktales, ghosts, monsters, and film stars. However, far from purely representing a nation, this marketing device is used to sell products and they need the "Japanese signature" to sell well, in Japan or abroad.[21] Since the golden age of arcade games, the Japanese video game industry has had its market well established in the global economy of Japan (see Kohler, 2005). Some popular games and series made their way outside of Japan by way of localization — depending on the potential capacity of the receiving country to be able to understand the "alien" game — proving that it is not so much the cultural "Japaneseness" that foreign markets want,[22] but rather the brilliance and efficiency of their design and gameplay (see Carless, 2008).

For the gaming industry, the nationality of Japanese horror games can be both an advantage and a disadvantage. Many games cannot be exported because of their intense regionalism (as Pruett, 2005a has noted, these games might be seen as "bizarre" or "crazy" by distributors who are under the impression that regionalisms would not be understood). That is the case for *The Onee Chanbara* series (Tamsoft Corporation, 2004–2008), which is similar to the *Onimusha* series, except that the gamer is controlling a Japanese cowgirl dressed in a bikini, wearing a scarf, wielding a katana in order to slay hordes of zombies and other horrific creatures in a gory way.[23] On the other hand, many gamers are fond of Japanese video games precisely for their Japaneseness. The worldwide Japanophilia probably being at its highest level ever, the popularity of Japanese horror video games is not proportional to the economical health of the Japanese video game industry — which is, according to many, in a crisis (see Edge, 2008; Barnett, 2008; Sheffield 2008, and Various, 2008).

Horror video games— as a product of a cultural industry — often encourage contradictory contents. Similarly to effective advertisements or any capitalist commodities, the video game industry plays up different parts of its multidimensional nature for different audiences.

> Technological, commercial, and political imperatives helped produce and constitute "Japaneseness" in tandem with specific national needs. Cultural stereotypes took on use-value as pictorial and narrative representations. Theses stereotypes were useful for Japanese as well as non–Japanese purposes, but to different ends [Davis, 2001: 61].

However, culture is a limited and indirect explanation of style. Style is a "product of choices" made by producers, designers, distributors and even gamers, "all working within the intertextual [intermedial and transnational] norms available at a given historical moment" (Davis, 2001: 64). As a result, Japanese ghosts and other horrific artifacts, after being remediated during the entire course of the Japanese art history, are mainly aesthetic and thematic devices useful to entertain gamers (locally or internationally).

Ghost stories and other Japanese stereotypes are measured in accordance to their use-value; for instance, *Ring* has been a phenomenal success, which resulted in the spread of the *yūrei* and other Japanese ghosts throughout popular media. The figure of the zombie has brought success in the horror game genre (especially since the first *Resident Evil*), after which zombies have appeared in most horror games. It could also be suggested that the gameplay mechanic of the hugely popular *Resident Evil 4* has inspired actual survival horror games (and probably will inspire others in the near future) to be more action-oriented. Nowadays, Japanese games are gradually beginning to be developed in America or Europe, as a consequence of the technical skills and tools available for game development in those countries. This is in opposition to the situation which is occurring in Japan because the technological level of the American and European developers is difficult to match (Ashcraft, 2008). The example of *Silent Hill: Homecoming* demonstrates that Americans and Europeans are now creating "Japanese games." As Akira Yamaoka famously said: "...the original *Silent Hill* was our attempt at making classic American horror through a Japanese filter ... and now with *SH5* [*Homecoming*], it's an American take on a Japanese-filtered American horror" (Bettenhausen, 2007: 73).

These trends are simultaneously praised and criticized by gamers. Many have tried to explain the actual Japanese game industry crisis—where revenues have been declining for a few years[24]—by blaming their lack of innovation, aesthetically, and technologically, and their excessive serialization and merchandising of clones.[25] Japanese horror games may appear to be unique national products characterized by specific elements defining a country like Japan, but they are primarily defined by hybridizations and convergences.

The circulation of national artifacts has accelerated with globalization. Survival horror games and national cultures seem to blend into one another, producing a contaminated product. They are becoming more difficult to categorize as binary differences: east versus west; cinema versus video games; or action versus atmosphere. They are increasingly transnational and intermedial, exemplifying a syncretism specific of our global times.

A horror game like Capcom's *Onimusha 3: Demon Siege* cleverly inserts itself into a transnationality that suits the global form of the video game industry worldwide. The *Onimusha* series remediates other media forms (cinema), cultures (Japan, France), historical moments (Sengoku period, contemporary world), or local and international celebrities (motion captures of film actors Jean Reno and Takeshi Kaneshiro). Especially, it mixes video game genres such as "hack-and-slash" action games with horror game elements.

However, globalization is often associated with Americanization. As Davis said:

> New technologies of globalization provide instantaneous transmission of market information, blanketing the globe with American-style popular entertainment, news, food, and fashions. An incessant transplantation of communities, commodities, and corporate activities across national borders is the object and consequence of this global information explosion, resulting in new varieties of exploitation and alienation, as well as emerging identities [Davis, 2001: 66–67].

Transnationalism can reinsert national specificities in a global world, in which "national specificities jostle, catalyze, and 'thicken' without eclipsing or canceling [*sic*] one another out and without synthesizing into some new postnational order" (Davis, 2001: 65–66).

Japanese iconographies in survival horror games are useful as objects of cultural export as well as ornamentation and packaging for a more enjoyable gaming experience. But selling Japanese culture in games "requires adjustments for global tastes" (Davis 2001: 73), such as localization —for global market distributions— remediations of icons and hackneyed representations of other countries (as in *Onimusha 3: Demon Siege*), and adding gaming trends popular with American gamers into the recipe (as in *Resident Evil 4* and the *Onimusha* series).

Of course, one cannot say that there is nothing Japanese about Japanese horror video games. Nor that the experience of playing a Japanese horror game is the same as playing an American one. However, series such as Capcom's *Resident Evil* and *Onimusha* must be placed into their global context before claiming the Japaneseness of their contents. Asserting the total absence of Japaneseness in Japanese survival horror games is as problematic as arguing for their absolute presence, as the genre is filled with very different and even opposing products. As I said in the beginning of this essay, the *Fatal Frame* series appear to be the most "Japanese" ones, while the *Resident Evil* series is predominantly Americanized and the *Silent Hill* ones seems to strategically place itself between the two. One thing is certain, Japanese survival horror games allow us to live a truly special video ludic experience.

Notes

1. Chris Pruett has a video game website devoted to this task, and everything related to horror in video games: "Chris' Survival Horror Quest" at <http://www.dreamdawn.com /sh/>.

2. Mitsuhiro Yoshimoto (2000) criticizes the Western and Eurocentric approaches to the study of Japanese cinema. According to him, the attention to the differences between Japa-

nese and Western cinemas is an Orientalist approach that confirms Western stereotypes about the difference and exoticism of Japan.

3. Following the classical materialism-idealism distinction, the materialist approach is relevant for understanding the complex manifestations of horror in Japanese horror games because it foregrounds the reality or the materiality of the industry within economic, ideological, and historical contexts. From a materialist perspective, any particular stylistic and thematic content is determined not by any national or aesthetic essentialism, but by competing and historically contingent aesthetic and thematic conventions, media developments and economic and social forces.

4. In their groundbreaking book *Remediation: Understanding New Media*, Bolter and Grusin used the term remediation in order to describe "the formal logic by which new media refashions prior media forms" (Bolter and Grusin, 1999: 273).

5. Since the seventies, anime have been very popular in France, Italy, Canada and United States, offering an original look that has been qualified as truly Japanese. Nevertheless, many anime specialists have observed that this style is not "Japanese" per se while some characters' traits do not resemble real people's traits, such as the big round eyes instead of the slant eyes. This— non Japanese —look is clearly a consequence of the Western influences on Japanese animation, especially by Disney's animation which has inspired the father of manga and anime: Osamu Tezuka. It was an aesthetic strategy clearly aimed towards distributing their works for Western audiences (see Napier, 2005: 22–27 and Kelts, 2007). The same can be said about many Japanese video game franchises, especially *Pokemon* (see Tobin, 2004, especially 53–79).

6. Except in their old ages for their importation of Chinese culture through Korea. Also, Japan was doing business with some European countries (mainly Netherlands) in the early eighteenth century.

7. Although Iwabuchi (2002) has already put into question this paradigm.

8. For example, the Japanese visual style has been characterized first and foremost by its "flatness" (see Ehrlich and Desser, 2000). Japanese artist Takashi Murakami has further developed this concept for contemporary works in a style that he called "superflat" (see Azuma, 2001). Surman has applied this latter notion to videogames (2008).

9. The Japanese essentialist discourse is made of theories and discussions about the *Japanese* identity. It refers to a large number of texts, ranging over such varied fields as sociology, psychology, history, linguistics, philosophy and even science. These texts are predominantly published in Japan by the Japanese, though noted examples of the genre have also been penned by foreign scholars, journalists and residents.

10. *Pokemon* is considered to be the most successful global franchise in the video game industry. Following the huge success of the Game Boy cartridges in 1996, Nintendo partners with many Japanese and American companies to create a set of interrelated products such as comic books, television shows, movies, trading cards, stickers, small toys, and diverse ancillary products. From 1996 to 2001, *Pokemon* conquered North America, Europe, Latin America, East Asia, Australia, New Zealand, Israel, and the Philippines. In order to establish itself abroad, the franchise "gets rid of some of its "cultural odor" as part of its "glocalization" for markets in Asia and the West" (Tobin, 2004: 11). For more details on this issue, see Tobin, 2004: 53–107, and Masuyama, 2002.

11. The typical Japanese ghost was even picked up in the American game *F.E.A.R. First Encounter Assault Recon* (Monolith, 2005), a first-person shooter game clearly inspired by Japanese horror.

12. For more detailed accounts of the *yūrei*, and other traditional Japanese ghosts, see Screech, 1994; and Pruett, 2006.

13. Since the film has been released in Japan as *Ring* (like the title of Koji Suzuki's novel), I prefer to use, like Kalat (2007: 25), *Ring* instead of *Ringu*. The title *Ringu* was chosen by Dreamworks Pictures to distinguish the 1998 Japanese version DVD from the American remake of 2002, titled *The Ring* (Gore Verbinski). The word "Ringu" doesn't exist in Japanese.

14. Firstly, by painters such as Gauguin, Matisse, and Van Gogh in a movement known as "Japonisme," secondly through the Japanese popular cinema in international film festivals, and thirdly by the anime and manga, which bring a more (post) modern Japan, particularly by the "cyberpunk" genre. This genre has been created by an Orientalist vision of a futuristic Tokyo in William Gibson's *Neuromancer* (1984), and two years before in Ridley Scott's *Blade Runner* (a transnational vision of a city that looks both as Tokyo and as a futuristic Los Angeles). The cyberpunk genre has been perpetuated in Japan by anime which led to the "Japanese craze" in North America, namely *Akira* (Otomo, 1988) and *Ghost in the Shell* (Oshii, 1996).

15. See Lovgren, 2004; Pruett, 2006; Rucka, 2005; McRoy, 2005 and Kalat, 2007.

16. Whether it is exactly during the Edo period or another, the *Onimusha* series is partly set just before the beginning of the Edo era while *Kuon*, based on *Kaidan* (ancient Japanese ghost stories), takes place during the Heian period (794–1185), which is recognized as the period when Confucianism and Chinese influences were at their highest levels. It is also seen as the peak of the Japanese imperial court where art became a major element of Japanese culture, especially poetry and literature. The setting is a horrifying mansion in Kyoto (the capital of Japan at the time). The enemies in the game are not so much ghosts as mutant creatures who are lurking in dark corners of the mansion.[0]

17. Samanosuke is the nephew of Akechi Mitsuhide, a *shogun* (warlord) which is known historically for having betrayed and led Nobunaga Oda to commit *harakiri*.

18. Nobunaga Oda was a *daimyo* (feudal governor) during the Sengoku period (the Warring States period in Japan that lasted roughly from the middle of the 15th century to the beginning of the 17th century). This historical character, like several others in the history of feudal Japan, was extensively used as a reference for classical Japanese theatre, literature, film and now video games. In addition to the *Onimusha* series (where he is perceived as a villain), he appears as a hero in video game series such as *Kessen* (Koei, 2000–2005), *Samurai Warriors* (Koei, 2004–2008), *Nobunaga's Ambition* (Koei, 1988–2009), among others.

19. After beating the game once, the gamer can unlock a new Western outfit (a cowboy costume from the American pioneer age) for Samanosuke.

20. For visuals, see *The Art of Onimusha* (Birlew, 2004).

21. Even if a video game is targeted only for Japan, which is the case for almost the majority of Japanese games, Japanese cultural stereotypes are often used for aesthetic and narrative purposes only, and/or to please Japanese audiences, in a form of self–Orientalism as already described.

22. Unlike successful Japanese films in the international festival circuit or from the young manga and anime fans from Americas, Europe or other Asian countries. Those fans, or *otaku*, are often the ones who treat Japanese video games as unique Japanese cultural works of art and even subtitle Japanese video games that have not been released outside Japan or have been badly translated. On the fansubbing phenomenon, see Rusch, 2009.

23. However, announcing a deeper shift, Yoshiro Katsuoka, planning director for Marvelous Entertainment, one of Japan's most active anime and video game producers, says: "It's America that has changed, not Japan.... Japanese companies no longer need to localize their pop culture products, at least not to the same extent that they have in the past, to appeal to American audiences. Even the manga that is translated into English today retains certain Japanese phrases and writing in the native characters—undecipherable and illegible to most U.S. readers, but still considered cool" (Kelts, 2006: 24). This may partially explain why more and more "odd" Japanese games are exported, which would have been previously unthinkable due to the nature of their content. Indeed, even though most of the hundred titles of *The Onee Chanbara* series are Japan-exclusives, some have been released in Europe, under the name of *Zombie Zone* or *Zombie Hunters*, and are getting released in the United States under the name of *Bikini Samurai Squad* and *Bikini Zombie Slayers* with a slowly growing cult interest. American G4TV show's *X-Play* has made reference to this series in their "Made in Japan" segment.

24. See the *Gamasutra* website (gamasutra.com) for figures and news about the Japanese market.

25. We must not deceive ourselves here. Even if games like *Katamari Damacy* (Namco, 2004) or *LocoRoco* (Sony Computer Entertainment Japan, 2006) seem to reinforce the idea that Japanese video games are "original" and "unique," we have to be aware that these are exceptions rather than the norm in Japan (see Barnett 2008).

Works Cited

Alexander, Leigh (2008), "Does Survival Horror Really Still Exist?," *Kotaku.com*, September 29, available online at <http://kotaku.com/5056008/does-survival-horror-really-still-exist>.

Ashcraft, Brian (2008), "Western Games Are More Advanced Than Japanese," *Kotaku.com*, September 10, available online at <http://kotaku.com/5047749/western-games-are-more-advanced-than-japanese>.

Azuma, Hiroki (2001), "Superflat Japanese Postmodernity," lecture given at the *MOCA* gallery at the Pacific design Center, West Hollywood, April 5, available online at <http://www.hirokiazuma.com/en/texts/superflat_en1.html>.

Balmain, Colette (2008), *Introduction to Japanese Horror Film*, Edinburgh: Edinburgh University Press.

Barnett, J.C. (2008), "J-Dev Confidential," *Japanmanship*, October 23, available online at <http://japanmanship.blogspot.com/search/label/JDEV%20Confidential>.

Bettenhausen, Shane (2007), "American Gothic," in *Electronic Gaming Monthly*, No. 220, October 2007, pp. 73–80.

Birlew, Dan (2004), Onimusha 3: Demon Siege *Limited Edition Strategy Guide*, Indianapolis: Brady Games and Capcom.

Bolter, Jay David, and Richard Grusin (1999), *Remediation. Understanding New Media*, Cambridge, MA: The MIT Press.

Carless, Simon (2004), "Gamasutra — Lost in Translation — Japanese and American Gaming's Culture Clash," *Gamasutra.com*, January 21, available online at <http://www.gamasutra.com/view/feature/2024/lost_in_translationjapanese_and_.php?page=2>.

Davis, Darrell William (2001), "Reigniting Japanese Tradition with Hana-Bi," *Cinema Journal*, Vol. 40, No. 4, pp. 55–80.

Edge Staff (2008), "Is Japan Becoming Marginalized?," *Edge Online*, September 28th, available online at <http://www.edge-online.com/magazine/is-japan-becoming-marginalized>.

Ehrlich, Linda C., and David Desser (2000), *Cinematic Landscapes: Observations on the Visual Arts and Cinema of China and Japan*, Austin: University of Texas Press.

Ezra, Elizabeth, and Terry Rowden (eds.) (2006), *Transnational Cinema: The Film Reader*, London: Routledge.

Fuller, Mary, and Henry Jenkins (1995), "Nintendo® and New World Travel Writing: A Dialogue," in Steven G. Jones (ed.), *Cybersociety: Computer-Mediated Communication and Community*, Thousand Oaks: Sage Publications, pp. 57–72, available online at <http://www.stanford.edu/class/history34q/readings/Cyberspace/FullerJenkins_Nintendo.html>.

Gomarasca, Alessandro (2002), "Cauchemars roses: le boom multimédia de l'horreur," in Alessandro Gomarasca (ed.), *Poupées, robots: la culture pop japonaise*, Paris: Éditions Autrement, pp. 134–149.

Hand, Richard J. (2006), "Aesthetics of Cruelty: Traditional Japanese Theatre and the Horror Film," in Jay McRoy (ed.), *Japanese Horror Cinema*, Edinburgh: Edinburgh University Press, pp. 18–28.

_____ (2004), "Proliferating Horrors: Survival Horror and the *Resident Evil* Franchise," in Steffen Hantke (ed.), *Horror Film: Creating and Marketing Fear*, Jackson: University Press of Mississippi, pp. 117–134.

Ito, Mizuko (2006), "The Gender Dynamics of the Japanese Media Mix," *Girls 'n' Games Workshop and Conference*, May 8–9, Los Angeles: University of California, available online at <http://www.itofisher.com/mito/publications/the_gender_dyna_1.html>.

Ivy, Marilyn (1995), *Discourses of the Vanishing: Modernity, Phantasm, Japan*, Chicago: The University of Chicago Press.

Iwabuchi, Koichi (2002), *Recentering Globalization: Popular Culture and Japanese Transnationalism*, Durham: Duke University Press.

Kalat, David (2007), *J-Horror: The Definitive Guide to* The Ring, The Grudge *and Beyond*, New York: Vertical.

Kelts, Roland (2007), *Japanamerica: How Japanese Pop Culture Has Invaded the U.S.*, New York: Palgrave Macmillan.

Kiej'e, Nikolas (1973), *Japanese Grotesqueries*, Tokyo: Charles E. Tuttle.

Kohler, Chris (2004), *Power-Up: How Japanese Video Games Gave the World an Extra Life*, Indianapolis: Brady Games.

Krzywinska, Tanya (2002), "Hands-On Horror," in Geoff King and Tania Krzywinska (eds.), *ScreenPlay. Cinema/Videogames/Interfaces*, London: Wallflower Press, pp. 206–223.

Masuyama (2002), "Pokemon as Japanese Culture?" in Lucien King (ed.), *Game On: The History and Culture of Videogames*, New York: Universe Publishing.

McRoy, Jay (2006), "The Horror Is Alive. Immersion, Spectatorship, and the Cinematics of Fear in the Survival Horror Genre," *Reconstruction*, Vol. 6, No. 1, available online at <http://reconstruction.eserver.org/061/mcroy.shtml>.

_____ (ed.) (2005), *Japanese Horror Cinema*, Edinburgh: Edinburgh University Press.

_____ (2007), *Nightmare Japan: Contemporary Japanese Horror Cinema*, New York: Rodopi.

Monnet, Livia (2002), "Towards the feminine sublime, or the story of 'a twinkling monad, shape-shifting across dimension': intermediality, fantasy and special effects in cyberpunk film and animation," *Japan Forum*, Vol. 14, No. 2, pp. 225–268.

Napier, Susan J. (2005), *Anime From Akira to Howl's Moving Castle: Experiencing Contemporary Japanese Animation*, New York: Palgrave.

Perron, Bernard (2006), *Silent Hill: Il Motore del Terrore*, Milano: Costa and Nolan (translated version by the author).

Pruett, Christopher (2006), "Chris' Guide to Understanding Japanese Horror," *dreamdawn.com*, available online at <http://www.dreamdawn.com/sh/features/japanese_horror.php>.

_____ (2005b), "Culture-Conscious Nightmares," *Interface*, Vol. 5, No. 2, March, available online at <http://bcis.pacificu.edu/journal/2005/02/pruett.php>.

_____ (2005c), "GDC: Akira Yamaoka and the Atmosphere of *Silent Hill*," *dreamdawn.com*, available online at <http://www.dreamdawn.com/sh/post_view.php?index=1715#comments>.

_____ (2005a), "The Role of Culture in Video Game Characters," *Interface*, Vol. 5, No. 1, February, available online at <http://bcis.pacificu.edu/journal/2005/01/pruett.php>.

Rucka, Nicholas (2005), "The Death of J-Horror?," *Midnight Eye*, December 22, available online at <http://www.midnighteye.com/features/death-of-j-horror.shtml>.

Rusch, Adam (2009), "Otaku Collaboration: How Anime Fans Create New Media," *Kinephanos*, Vol. 1, No. 1, forthcoming online at <http://www.kinephanos.ca>.

Screech, Tim (1994), "Japanese Ghosts," in *Mangajin*, No. 40, November, pp. 14–19 (available online at <http://www.mangajin.com/mangajin/samplemj/ghosts/ghosts.htm>).

Sheffield, Brandon (2008), "PlatinumGames' Inaba: 'Japan Needs to Be More Creative,'" *Gamasutra.com*, September 10, available online at <http://www.gamasutra.com/php-bin/news_index.php?story=19941>.

Sterling, Jim (2008), "How Survival Horror Evolved Itself into Extinction," *destructoid.com*, December 8, available online at <http://www.destructoid.com/how-survival-horror-evolved-itself-into-extinction-114022.phtml>.

Stuart, Keith (2006), "'I call it, "Subtracting horror."' Project Zero creator speaks...," *Guardian.co.uk*, February 7, available online at <http://www.guardian.co.uk/technology/gamesblog/2006/feb/07/post13>.

Surman, David (2008), "Notes on SuperFlat and Its Expression in Videogames," *Refractory: A Journal of Entertainment Media*, Vol. 13 (Games and Metamateriality), May 23, available online at <http://blogs.arts.unimelb.edu.au/refractory/2008/05/23/notes-on-superflat-and-its-expression-in-videogames-david-surman/>.

Tobin, Joseph (ed.) (2004), *Pikachu's Global Adventure: The Rise and Fall of Pokemon*, Durham: Duke University Press.

Tucker, Elmer (2006), "The Orientalist Perspective: Cultural Imperialism in Gaming," *Proceedings of the 2nd Annual University of Florida Game Studies Conference: Video Games and the Alien Other*, Gainesville, available online at <http://www.gameology.org/alien_other/orientalist_perspective>.

Various (2008), "Japan Special," *Electronic Gaming Monthly*, No. 232, September, pp. 16–70.

Vick, Tom (2007), *Asian Cinema: A Field Guide*, New York: Harper Collins.

Winterhalter, Ryan (2008), "Gamasutra — Made In Japan: Western Perspectives on Japanese Game Development," *Gamasutra.com*, November 24, available online at <http://www.gamasutra.com/view/feature/1561/made_in_japan_western_.php>.

Yamaoka, Akira (2005), "Gripping Game Design: The Mood and Ambience of *Silent Hill*," *Proceedings GDC 2005*, slides of his PowerPoint presentation available online at <https://www.cmpevents.com/Sessions/GD/GrippingGameDesign.ppt>.

Yoshimoto, Mitsuhiro (2000), *Kurosawa: Film Studies and Japanese Cinema*, Durham: Duke University Press.

The Survival Horror:
The Extended Body Genre
Bernard Perron

Since the spectator is unable to take action during a film, Ed S. Tan uses in *Emotion and the Structure of Narrative Film. Film as an Emotion Machine* what he calls a "slightly grisly metaphor" to define the viewer's position in the fictional world: "the subject in fiction is actually a head without a body, which is placed on a cart by an obliging assistant [the "editorial intelligence" behind the narration that can manipulate the viewer] and wheeled — or even flown — around through the time and space of the fictional world" (1996: 241). The "ordinary man of cinema" would indeed be this disembodied eye (and ear), as for Jean Louis Schefer, not only is the body of the viewer not the center of the visual activity, but the point where this body is placed has been calculated so that it disappears completely (1980: 147–148).

A head without a body. Bringing into play a "grisly metaphor" is certainly a good way to start an essay on horror, and it should frighten the reader — at least a little bit; unless, as a keen horror aficionado, the reader has already noticed the strings of the trick and read its sub-text. Because, if I claim from the outset that cinema removes the body from the viewer — I will qualify this statement below, it is to better underline the operation performed by the video game, an operation which returns a virtual body to the viewer, now transformed into a gamer. If I was to push the grisliness of this introduction a little bit further, I would draw upon one of the most spine-tingling moments in the recent history of the third-person horror games associated with what has been called the survival horror genre and admit that in the end, one of the important aims of the horror video game is to cut the head from the gamer's specular body, just like the chainsaw maniac, masked with a potato sack, who chops off Leon's — the player character — head in *Resident Evil 4* (Capcom, 2005) (figure 1).

Bodies in Front of a Screen: Coming to Grips with Embodied Experiences

The concept of embodiment has grown into an important one in modern cognitive science. Contrary to Cartesian dualism that separated the immaterial and rational mind from the physical and irrational body, the role of the material part of a human being in cognition and emotion has been increasingly recognized. Remarking that "[a] body is not just something that we own, it is something that we are," Raymond W. Gibbs claims in *Embodiment and Cognitive Science*: "the regularities in people's kinesthetic-tactile experience not only constitute the core of the self-conceptions as persons, but form the foundation for higher-order cognition" ([2005] 2007: 15). Through the synthesis of a large corpus of studies, Gibbs shows how perception is linked to bodily action; to what extent cognitive processes are composed of internal processes and physical manipulation of objects in real-world environments; to what degree the body influences communication and language; in which ways imagery, memory and reasoning are related to sensorimotor simulations; and how consciousness and emotion partly arise from and are expressed in actions of the body. Emotion being a key component in the apprehension of a horrific event, it is rich in significance to note that "[e]motions arise as we become displaced or dislocated to another position in adaptive response to some situation. One way of characterizing the felt dimension of emotional experience is in terms of "affective space," or the space we move through as we experience distinct emotion" (Gibbs, [2005] 2007: 244). Etymologically speaking, the word *emotion* refers to the idea of "*moving* out." Feeling scared indeed drives us away from others, especially from monsters, as we will see. On the other hand, we hesitate to advance when we are worried. If there are emotions that really seize both our mind and body, it is certainly the fear, shock, or disgust associated with the horror genre.

Figure 1: The chainsaw maniac, masked with a potato sack, is chopping off Leon's head in ***Resident Evil 4*** (Capcom, 2005).

Insofar as perception, cognition and emotion are grounded in the body and its dynamical interactions with the environment, it becomes both difficult to subscribe to a conception of the film viewer — and gamers— as a disembodied eye and necessary to turn to the lived body in front of the screen. One has to read Vivian Sobchack's semio-phenomenological account of the film experience to reassert the cognitive science notion of embodiment. In her essay entitled "What My Fingers Knew: The Cinesthetic Subject, or Vision in the Flesh," Sobchack underlines the fact that contemporary film theory has by and large elided the cinema's sensual address and the viewer's body. But for Sobchack, echoing Gibbs' previously quoted remark, "film experience is meaningful *not to the side of our bodies but because of our bodies*" (2004: 60, italics in original). To advocate an embodied vision and the "carnal thoughts" provoked by movies, Sobchack recounts the way she experienced the first shot of Jane Campion's film *The Piano* (1993), how "her fingers knew" before her eyes that she was looking at fingers through the blurred subjective point of view of the female main character. This kind of prereflective bodily responsiveness to films, still linked to the mind one would say, is not unusual for Sobchack.

> Thus I would argue that my experience of *The Piano* was a heightened instance of our common sensuous experience of the movies: the way we are in some carnal modality able to touch and be touched by the substance and texture of images; to feel a visual atmosphere envelop us; to experience weight, suffocation, and the need for air; to take flight in kinetic exhilaration and freedom even as we are relatively bound to our theater seats; to be knocked backward by a sound; to sometimes even smell and taste the world we see on the screen [2004: 65].

Cinema speaks to the capacity to touch, to smell and to taste through vision and hearing, the two privileged senses in contemporary moving image culture. Therefore, the film viewer is best regarded as a "cinesthetic subject" making meaning through multiple senses. As much as, following a constructivist approach to the narrative film, the spectator comes to the movies ready to focus his energies toward the construction of the story and to fill the narrative gaps, his body is tuned to explore the sensual potentiality of the film and to "flesh out" the sensual gaps (what Sobchack calls a *sensual catachresis*). There is a kind of rebound effect in this latter process. The spectator not being able to literally touch, smell or taste what and who is on the screen soliciting his feelings or sensual desires, "[his] body's intentional trajectory, seeking a sensible object to fulfill this sensual solicitation, will *reverse its direction* to locate its partially frustrated sensual grasp on something more literally accessible. That more accessible sensual object is [*his*] *own subjective felt lived body*" (2004: 76, italics in original). Yet again, the horror genre fuels those two filling processes. Since it is "when we are afraid that we are telling ourselves the greatest short scary stories" (Perron, 2005b), our mind starts to imagine what could happen to us or others, in this way "fleshing out" our corporeal reactions.

At the beginning of "What My Fingers Knew," Sobchack refers to a small number of previous works which dealt with the carnal sensibility and density of the film experience. Two of those six "exceptions" are relevant here. The first one is the mostly Deleuze-Guattarian thoughts proposed by Steven Shaviro. For the author of *The Cinematic Body*, "[f]ilm is a vivid medium, and it is important to talk about how it arouses corporeal reactions of desire and fear, pleasure and disgust, fascination and shame" (1993: viii). What's more, "[c]inema invites me, or forces me, to stay within the orbit of the senses" (1993: 31). If psychoanalytic film theory kept the image at a distance, it is impossible, from Shaviro's perspective, to be detached from it. In accordance with Benjamin's idea of tactile film viewing, images might be seen as immaterial, "but their *effect* is all the more physical and corporeal" (1993: 51, italics in original). Accordingly, the psychoanalysis notion of identification also needs to be questioned. In a process of sympathetic participation, the subject is not stable or rigid, but made more fluid. "Mimesis and contagion tend to efface fixed identities and to blur boundaries between inside and outside. The viewer is transfixed and transmogrified in consequence of the infectious visceral contact of images" (1993: 53). Two genres best characterize the compelling and distressing experience of the viewer, an experience that goes beyond sight to show more than can be seen.

> This is why pornography and horror are so crucial to any account of cinematic experience. In the realm of visual fascination, sex and violence have much more intense and disturbing an impact than they do in literature or any other medium [non-interactive medium should we say to prepare the ground for the study of the horror video game]; they affect the viewer in a shockingly direct way. Violent and pornographic films literally anchor desire and perception in the agitated and fragmented body [1993: 55].

The analysis of George Romero's "living dead" trilogy (*Night of the Living Dead* in 1968, *Dawn of the Dead* in 1978, and *Day of the Dead* in 1985) provides Shaviro with the opportunity to specify his comments.

> More precisely, they [horror and porn] short-circuit the mechanism of fantasy altogether: they are not content to leave me with vague, disembodied imaginings, but excitedly seek to incise those imaginings in my very flesh. They focus obsessively upon the physical reactions of bodies on screen, the better to assault and agitate the bodies of the audience [1993: 101].

Horror films— and horror games— like zombie ones do not need to be believable, they need to be thrilling, and thrilling through bodies.

The "tactile convergences" are also at the center of Linda Williams' renowned study of pornographic and horror films. In "Film Bodies: Gender, Genre, and Excess," along with melodrama, Williams called these two genres "body genres" because they possess common features of bodily and ecstatic excess. Visually they both share a quality, which when applied to horror, provokes uncontrollable convulsions or spasms in the viewer's body "beside itself" in the grips of fear and terror. Aurally, the excess is marked by inarticulate screams of fear ([1991] 1995: 143). With low cultural status, melodrama, pornography and horror films are different from other genres because of "an apparent lack of proper aesthetic distance, a sense of overinvolvement in sensation and emotion" (1995 [1991]: 144). Moreover, "what may especially mark these genres as low is the perception that the body of the spectator is caught up in an involuntary mimicry of the emotion or sensation of the body on the screen, along with the fact that the body displayed is female [as the woman's body is indeed the primary embodiment of pleasure, fear, and pain]" ([1991] 1995: 143). Williams notes that the success of a horror film is "measured by the degree to which the audience sensation mimics what is seen in the screen," that is "in terms of screams, fainting, and heart attacks in the audience" ([1991] 1995: 144). Although the faints and heart attacks have to be taken in their figurative sense, Williams rightly emphasizes the importance of bodily responses.

As the reader might have already guessed, the above piecemeal account of the embodied experience of film, and particularly of the horror film, applies to the video game which leads to the main argument of my essay. Indeed, apart from any feminist aim, the survival horror can be defined as an "extended body genre." Because the body of the gamer is not only "caught up in an involuntary mimicry of the emotion or sensation of the body on the screen"—be it female or male, it is also urged to act and feel through its presence, agency and embodiment in the fictional world. If, as one game reviewer has stated (Thompson, 2007), video games can produce better horror than Hollywood, it is because of the gameplay. Consequently, I wish to study the bodily responses in relation to the three different bodies engaged in the videoludic horror experience: the body of the monster, the body of the player character and the body of the gamer.

The Monstrous Bodies

In the movie *The Blair Witch Project* (Daniel Myrick and Eduardo Sánchez, 1999), the eerie and terrifying events experienced by the three film students, who are attempting to document the legendary Blair Witch in the woods near Burkittsville, Maryland, do not lead to actual danger, but instead the (potentially) supernatural evil stays invisible and envisioned by both the protagonists and the spectators. This is not the case for the video game trilogy based on the myth of the aforementioned sorceress: *Blair Witch Volume 1: Rustin Parr* (Terminal Reality, 2000), *Blair Witch Volume 2: The Legend of Coffin Rock* (Human Head Studios, 2000) and *Blair Witch Volume 3: The Elly*

Kedward Tale (Ritual Entertainment, 2000). Right from the start of the first game, set in 1941, the player character's government special investigator Elspeth "Doc" Holliday faces various types of zombies, monsters and demons in her training mission. After a briefing with her boss and several short encounters with "Stranger"— the main character of *Nocturne* (Terminal Reality, 1999) which is a sort of prequel game also dealing with supernatural and malefic creatures, "Doc" is sent to Burkittsville to inspect the supernatural nature of the child murders committed by the hermit Rustin Parr. On the first night, she has a terrible nightmare in which she is attacked by the townspeople. On the second day, after getting a map, she ventures into the "surrounding forest for possible supernatural activity" (from the "things to do" list in her journal). But unlike the student filmmakers in the original film, "Doc" encounters— along with a wise Indian — actual evil foes, that is demon dogs, ghostly creatures and a giant spectral scorpion. Then, as Doc faces huge stick figures coming to life to attack her, one realizes to what extent the survival horror genre relies on an embodied threat (figure 2). What's more, compared to many horror movies, one does not wait until the end to finally face the monster (except for the final boss).

I have stated elsewhere: "the figure of the monster is at the core of the videoludic experience of fright" (Perron, 2005b and 2006b). Obviously, video games are not a departure from the norm.

> Central to the horror genre's identity is the configuration of the "monster," which has been redefined with each development in social and cultural history. The monstrous element in the horror text is usually an interrogation of the amorphous nature of evil, or an address to the limits of the human condition; physically, emotionally and psychologically [Wells (2000) 2002: 8].

The monstrous element is indeed what distinguishes horror from other genres. We might be scared to die in a war or a gangster video game. However, fear of dying is much deeper when death is personified by someone or something that is abnormally large and powerful, and when the end is expected to come through great pain and suffering, and/or is being portrayed in gruesome ways. For instance, while I'm writing this essay, one of *Gamespot.com*'s updates (Torres, 2008) highlights a new boss and the new kinds of pain experienced in the much anticipated *Resident Evil 5* (Capcom, 2009). Insofar as fear has an action-orienting quality and that the video game is intrinsically action-based, the confrontation with the monster(s) becomes inevitable in survival horror. The forces of evil don't stay unseen in the video game. The monstrous is always embodied. With the event schema "getting to the next place" (which underlines the adventure aspect of survival horror), "the gameplay experience of the survival horror genre revolve[s] around a main event schema: 'facing up to the monster.' This is not as much a narrative schema [knowing what can happen] as a gameplay schema [knowing how to deal with it in order to survive: flight or fight]" (Perron, 2006b: 67).

When talking about the videoludic monster, one should not forget to talk about its body, because the entire physical structure of this entity, its actions and reactions are what primarily assault and agitate the body of the gamer. It is the monsters—pre-

Figure 2: An embodied threat in *Blair Witch Volume 1: Rustin Parr* (Terminal Reality, 1999).

ferably in the plural since one never comes alone — that inhabit the fictional nightmarish world and move, pushing the gamer around in his "affective space." As soon as 3D engines gave them volume, they attacked quite rapidly across pre-rendered 2D backgrounds. It doesn't take more than a few minutes for a long-fanged monster to burst through the attic window of the haunted mansion called Derceto and for a zombie to emerge from a trap door in the floor to attack Edward Carnby or Emily Hartwood, the player characters in *Alone in the Dark* (Infogrames, 1992) — recognized as the origin of the survival horror genre. In *Resident Evil* (Capcom, 1996), the first living human the player character (Jill Valentine or Chris Redfield) encounters at the beginning of their search of the Spencer Mansion is a rotten one, eating a member of the missing Bravo Team. The hideous face of the zombie is shown through a cut-in pre-rendered 3D close-up, ensuring that the gamer immediately grasps and feels the horror that he is about to meet head-on.

> The zombies are impelled by a kind of desire, but they are largely devoid of energy and will. Their restless agitation is merely reactive. They totter clumsily about, in a strange state of stupefied and empty fascination, passively drawn to still-living humans.... They drift slowly away from identity and meaning, emptying these out in the very process of replicating them. The zombies are in a sense all body: they have brains but not minds [Shaviro, 1993: 86].

Zombies are a great (bio)hazard. Through contamination and proliferation, the group itself forms a threatening body — a body which evolved and grew in number in the *Resident Evil* series to become the Spanish (Los Ganados) and African infected people of, respectively, *Resident Evil 4* and *Resident Evil 5*. Zombies stand in the way of the gamer. They can be encountered in every corridor, come across in every corner, hidden behind any door. They respond to the sole presence of the player character, which is an effective way to call for inter(re)activity. It is no wonder why the living dead migrated from the silver screen to the video game and became the first important monster of the survival horror genre. Be it in a novel, a film or a video game, the figure of the zombie is abject and reminds the still-living of the inescapable decrepitude of their own material parts, to the point of repulsion.

The survival horror genre shares the obsession of the contemporary horror film with the invasion of the body by infectious agents and with the mutilation and destruction of bodies. Symptomatic of great social fears and of our schizoid relationship with our body, we witness on both screens frightful mutations. Like David J. Skal underlines in *The Monster Show: A Cultural History of Horror*:

> Many of the horror and science fiction films of the seventies and eighties began showing signs of imaginative kinship to the earlier visions of Francis Bacon and Salvador Dalí. John Carpenter's remake of *The Thing* (1982), with special effects by Robb Bottin, subjected the body to the most surrealistic stress and strain ever seen outside a gallery canvas. At least one of Bottin's grotesqueries, in fact, closely resembles a panel from Bacon's seminal triptych *Three Studies for Figures at the Base of a Crucifixion*. In a sense, the entire twentieth-century history of increasingly abstracted human forms in fine art was recapitulated in the pop medium of horror, science-fiction, and fantasy films [(1993) 2001: 313].

The video game has adapted this trend to its artistic possibilities. Because designers are creating computer-generated monsters and do not have to work with actual material like foam latex to provide a realistic look, their work remains closer to that of a painter. For instance, it is not surprising to learn that the favorite artist of Masahiro Ito, who has designed and modeled the creatures for the first three *Silent Hill* games (Konami, 1999, 2001 and 2003), is Francis Bacon and that Jérôme Bosch has been a great inspiration (see Beuglet, 2001 and 2003). Especially in 3D, monsters like the Patient Demons in their flesh straightjacket and the headless mannequins with their two pairs of legs from *Silent Hill 2*, or the huge, fat and decayed insane cancers and the numb bodies with no arms from *Silent Hill 3*, all seem to come alive straight from the works of the Irish and Dutch artists. Apart from the necessity of taking physics into account (monsters, if not immaterial and floating ghosts, have to be able to move in the game-world), computer graphics free the imagination and allow for the most disturbing abominations. What they lose in realism (something the increasingly realistic graphics rendered in the next generation games is coming to invalidate), they regain in expression. This is the case of the deformed Gum Heads, Bottoms, and the legless Siamese Victims in *Silent Hill 4: The Room* (Konami, 2004), and of the half-man half-woman Two Backs and dog-like Carrions in *Silent Hill: Origins* (Climax Studios, 2007). In the digital universe of survival horror, scientific experiments gone awry and submicroscopic infective agents cause horrendous mutations. The most famous are the Progenitor, Tyrant- (known as T-Virus) and Gene-Virus (G-Virus) of the *Resident Evil* series. Those have fathered not only zombies, but various frightening Bio-Organic Weapons such as the Lickers, the Hunters, the Tyrants, the Chimeras, the Drain Deimos, the Bandersnatches, the William Birkin/G, the Nemesis, etc. The Umbrella Corporation's research projects have also resulted in the increased size and aggressive behavior of ants, bees, spiders, snakes, sharks, worms, dogs, etc. Alien organisms infecting human bodies also lead to dreadful changes in the form or quality of the body. Such is the case in two games set in the Antarctic: the videoludic sequel of *The Thing* (Computer Artworks, 2002) and *Extermination* (Deep Space, 2001). The Russian oil rig in the middle of a stormy ocean of *Cold Fear* (Ubisoft, 2005) and the massive mining ship of *Dead Space* (EA Redwood Shores, 2008) are two other theatres of alien bodily invasions.

The most common survival horror monsters perfectly meet the requirement set by Noël Carroll in his definition of supernatural and alien art-horror in *The Philosophy of Horror or Paradoxes of the Heart*: they do not exist according to contemporary science. Although we can relate to their anthropomorphism, we are otherwise repelled by their impurity. They remain interstitial as they transgress distinctions such as inside/outside, living/dead, insect/human, flesh/machine and animate/inanimate. They are meant to be disgusting and disturbing, both through their look and sounds as they scream and growl, uttering cries of rage, fury and pain, making noisy and creepy movements, etc. They produce a "physiological state of felt agitation" (Carroll, 1990: 24). Even the unconventional opponent Maid Daniella in *Haunting Ground* (Capcom, 2005) seems to be a blend of machine, ghost and human. But the monsters are also, and above all, threatening. It is quite easy to conceive that those of the survival horror are dangerous: they are meant to put the player character to death. As previously stated, this is what constitutes the game, at least the action part which is an increasingly common and important element of the genre. The monsters possess all the strength necessary to maim and kill the player character. Hypertrophied massive arms like those of the Closers in *Silent Hill 3* and of the Siams in *Silent Hill: Homecoming* (Double Helix, 2008) are destructive. The huge claws of the Hunter in *Resident Evil* and *Dead Space* serve as great weapons. Combined with claws, the Humans and Troopers of *Extermination* spit infectious fluid. Slaughtering is so inherent to the nature of some foes that they literally have, as body parts, scythes (the Needlers in *Silent Hill: Homecoming*), swords (the Slayers in *The Suffering*, Surreal Software, 2004), blades (constituting the splitting head of the Schisms in *Silent Hill: Homecoming*) and guns (the Marksmen of

The Suffering). Smaller threats like cockroaches or spiders come in groups; and zombies bite and maul bodies.

The deadly behaviors of monsters, without a doubt, stress adaptive responses from the gamer. To stay alive in survival horror games chiefly means to escape and/or endure hostile face-to-face encounters. In fact, the player character exists only by and for the monsters: "Inverted figure, the monster is the hidden face of the hero and its founding virtues. It symbolizes the negative and destructive elements that the hero must fight to attain his full humanity" (Vandevyver, 2004: 74, freely translated). In the face of the monster's savagery, the player character has no choice but to reply with a similar and animal brutality. "Horror monsters exist, in large measure, to be destroyed" (Vorobej, 1997: 238). The boss battles are indeed unavoidable to progress. No one gets out of a nightmarish adventure without having defeated the final, most horrible and most threatening creatures: the Nemesis (*Resident Evil 3: Nemesis*, Capcom, 1999), the Rope Shrine Maiden Kirie (*Fatal Frame*, Tecmo, 2001), the bed-caged Mary (*Silent Hill 2*), etc. This is why the player character does not stick to a wooden plank, a survival knife, a handgun or even his own fists, but continuously collects better and more powerful weapons along the way. As much as the evil enemies make every effort to scare and to tear the player character to pieces, they are mutilated equally in return. "Lumps of flesh" and indistinct identities, zombies do not call for restraint. Rather, they inspire dirty deeds. The gamer can slow them down by shooting them in the legs, but inevitably, they must be shot in the head to kill them once and for all. A last kick is necessary to silence and terminate the abominable creatures met in the town of Silent Hill. Isaac Clarke does the same in *Dead Space* with more gruesome results. What's more, in order to kill the Necromorphs, he has to take them apart limb by limb. Decapitation is also the way "Doc" slaughters Burkittsville's townspeople in her nightmare at the beginning of *Blair Witch Volume 1: Rustin Parr*. It is in those moments of self-defense, but of great violence, that the survival horror becomes remarkable because it obliges the gamer to realize that "it is the man that makes the monster" (Vandevyver, 2004: 75, freely translated) and it reminds him that a monstrous Other is hidden inside each of us. *The Suffering* has exploited this facet perfectly. The game has an insanity meter. Every time the player-character Torque kills creatures, the meter fills. When it is full and pulsates, Torque can transform himself into a powerful creature, becoming as vicious and bloody as the Slayers or Mainliners attacking him (figure 3). The Black One, the final boss, whom Torque is fighting before leaving Carnate Island, is indeed the demon lurking within him. As Vorobej has so pertinently written: "the true object of fascination in horror is *ourselves,* and the human condition in general. Battling monsters is a highly veiled odyssey of self-exploration" (1997: 239).

The Specular Body of the Player Character

The odyssey of self-exploration is veiled in an interesting way in the survival horror genre because the gamer embarks on an adventure through some-BODY else, namely the main character he is required to play. If *to play* means to pretend to be someone else in the framework of a playful activity and to behave accordingly, it implies that the gamer forms one body — but not one mind as we'll see — with his player character: a head with a body in the game-world. Since the exploration of that world is not under the total control of an obliging assistant wheeling and flowing the gamer around through the time and space of the fictional world as in film but depends upon the movements of the player character, the narrative architecture of video games needs to be gone through — what the expression "walkthrough" refers to. The audio-vision of the gamer is transformed into a walk, a run, a flight.

Thinking about slapstick star Buster Keaton, I have underlined the fact that the player characters of the survival horror maintained a "stone face" during play (but not in cut-scenes) whatever the situation they were facing (Perron, 2004). It is not them who are meant to be scared but the gamer. With his helmet completely hiding his face, the player character of *Dead Space*, Isaac Clarke, has pushed this unemotional expression to the limit. Consequently, although they make themselves heard during their fights, Clarke and his fellow characters of the genre are generally defending themselves, and launching attacks on the monsters in a detached way. However, in examining horror, I had not evaluated all the implications of my reference to slapstick. Indeed, for Jean Louis Schefer: "The slapstick body is movable, malleable, transfusable as the real environment of all the adventures of the film. And in scenarios of very little interest, the body is the first place and the first object of the action — this is why this action is not dramatic" (1980:

Figure 3: A monstrous Other hidden inside Torque in *The Suffering* (Surreal Software, 2004).

60–61, freely translated). Schefer repeats that slapstick doesn't resort very often to the effects of close-ups since it is not necessary to detail the character outside a narrative. This responds to Steven Poole's comment about the relation between horror games and horror films: "the horror genre can easily do away with character and plot; it is the detail of the monsters, the rhythm of the tension and shocks that matter. Plot and characters are things videogames find very difficult to deal with" (2000: 79). During the interactive sequences, it is not the characters' reactions presented in close-up that calls upon those of the gamer — the action is always shown from a certain distance. It is the game's real-time representation synchronized with the gamer's actions that determine the effect. Even without the style or excessive way of the slapstick, the player characters of the survival horror remain the matter of/for the action. When they respond well or when they do not, even to the point of being rooted in place as Alyssa in *Clock Tower 3* (Capcom, 2003) and Fiona Belli in *Haunting Ground* panicking in front of the deformed and troubled castle's gardener and handyman, the body is experienced.

Following the "key" features distinguished by Jay McRoy in his study of the genre, survival horror games "are 'viewed' primarily from a third-person perspective framed in high-angle long shots intended to intensify the sensation of vulnerability, isolation, and, in certain 'key' moments, shock" (2006). Daniel S. Yu has said this in regard to *Alone in the Dark*: "Beyond the usual annoying aspects (like views changing during fights), the third[-]person perspective added to the dramatic tension by allowing the player to see things that would otherwise be lost in a first[-]person perspective, such as monsters chasing the player character and the player character running for his/her life at the same time" (2002). Even if first-person games like *System Shock 2* (Irrational Games/Looking Glass Studios, 1999), *Condemned: Criminal Origins* (Monolith, 2005) and *Condemned 2: Bloodshot* (Monolith, 2008) offer a great scary experience, which is often associated with the genre, we can argue — without wanting to be contentious — that the survival horror is in essence played in the third-person perspective. In this perspective, the gamer has to think according to the player character and to the position in which he or she is located: is he close or far in the frame?; is his movement leading to a new camera angle?; is he in an open or a closed space?; can he escape or will he be caught?; can he act?; etc. Above all, the third-person perspective intensifies the corporealized sensations. In games where death is calculated in multiple game over screens and consequently in many restarts, the survival horror's character does not, compared to the slapstick's "stone faces," always get out unharmed no matter what dangers or physical abuses one endures.

The gamer can be startled, scared, and overcome by panic in both first- and third-person perspectives. Yet, he is most certainly more effectively overcome by horror when he is actually seeing his player character being (b)eaten to death or slaughtered. This difference is made obvious in *The Suffering,* a game that can be played in first- or in third-person, or both by switching between the two points of view. In the first-person mode, every time a Slayer hits with its swords below the frame (i.e., Torque's point of view), there is a red flash on the screen to translate the hit. In the third-person mode, while the screen also turns red quickly upon a hit, the gamer also sees the violence. The swords run through Torque's body and the blood splatters. The more Torque is wounded, the more he will be covered with blood. In the vein of *Resident Evil* and following games such as *Cold Fear* and *ObsCure* (Hydravision Entertainment, 2005) where the player characters hold their stomach, Torque holds his left shoulder to convey his bodily pain and his health (a status only acknowledged by the meter in first-person). At last, the Slayer can cut off his head. Given that such an end is gruesome, it will — and Torque's other deaths also— always be shown in third-person, automatically switching to this perspective if the gamer is in the first-person mode. In *Fatal Frame* (and in the other games of the series), although without bloodshed insofar as it deals with visible disembodied souls of dead people, whether the attacking ghost is seen through the lens of the camera obscura or not, there is also and always a rapid cut to a short negative shot — images with tones reversed — showing the frail Miku being grabbed by the ghost.

Nevertheless, be it with a few spurts/pixels of blood when the head of the babysitter is chopped off by the maniac in the Atari 2600 *Halloween* (Wizard, 1983) or in a much gorier manner like the example of *Resident Evil 4* given in the introduction of the essay and the graphic dismemberment of Isaac Clarke by the Hunter in *Dead Space,* the blood does not stop spurting in the survival horror games. The various player characters and — they can't be forgotten — non-player characters (NPC) will have undergone all sorts of physical abuses: projected in all directions, beaten to death, stifled, struck down, stabbed, cut into pieces, eaten alive, etc. It is not surprising that some first-person shooters (FPS) shift their perspective as in the example of *The Suffering* to take advantage of the horrible images. As bad and boring as *Land of the Dead: Road to Fiddler's Green* (Brainbox Games, 2005) can be, it changes to a third-person perspective to show the player character being eaten by the zombies when he has lost all of his health. *Left 4 Dead* (Valve Corporation, 2009) is a grand deluge of visual and sonic information with its hundreds of zombies popping up in front of the gamers' eyes. But since you or your teammates (human- or computer-controlled) are never really seen mutilated during a furious attack by the flesh-eaters, the game misses (for a non–FPS gamer and horror aficionado like me) a dimension so important to the body genre.

The representation of the body on the videoludic horror screen is significant. As Chris Pruett has underlined, character design has a great influence in horror games (2005). It has an effect on the way we empathize with the characters, on the expression of vulnerability and danger, and on the game mechanics. For example, to create tension with characters like the members of the Special Tactics and Rescue Service, *Resident Evil* asks for more powerful enemies and a tighter rationing of save points and ammunition ("tension was created by making every shot count"). Frail young women such as *Fatal Frame*'s Miku, *Clock Tower 3*'s Alyssa or *Rule of Rose*'s (Punchline, 2006) Jennifer lead to situations playing on their inherent vulnerability (which "enables designers to achieve scares with less effort" writes Pruett). However, the ecstatic excess of survival horror games is not primarily based on uncontrollable convulsions or spasms of the body "beside itself" in the grips of terror on screen and the numerous inarticulate screams of fear as Williams underlined for films. In accordance with James Newman, we have to recognize that "the pleasures of videogame *play* are not principally visual, but rather are kinaesthetic" (2002).

> It [is] because the sense of being-in-the-gameworld derives from an interface-level connection rather than being a product of viewpoint that games such as *Super Mario World* that present their gameworld in a third-person viewpoint can be just as engaging as (pseudo-) first-person viewpoint games like *Quake* or even second (or dynamically shifting-) person games like *Super Mario 64*. During On-Line play, videogames are experienced by the primary-player first hand regardless of the mode of their presentation or content mediation. In recollection of their play, players talk not of playing or controlling but of "being" [2002].

Although it is not necessary, or even possible, to totally disregard the representational traits of the player character, it is essential to see "the constitution of character as sets of capabilities, potentials and techniques offered to the player" (Newman, 2002). As I suggested previously, it is by forming one body with his player character, to move through the game-world, that the gamer will survive the nightmarish adventure. One can highlight the fact that *Silent Hill: Homecoming*'s Alex Shepherd "is gifted with a martial prowess and combat training that the other Silent Hill protagonists lacked" (Anderson, 2008), but those fictional skills have to be synchronized with the game controls and the gamer's skills, and survival horror controls are notoriously clumsy. Personally, I did not feel I was given any more fighting capabilities with this soldier who was returning to his hometown than I had in the previous games of the *Silent Hill* series, on the contrary. However, I did take as much kinesthetic pleasure in moving Alex around town, encountering the monsters and defeating them. In my experience, one of the great levels in *Silent Hill: Homecoming* remains "Hell Descent," the one in Doc Fitch's office when Alex wakes up in a hellish and industrial environment where he finds Scarlet's doll. Without a map of the area, I made Alex drop down, climb down ladders, fight the few monsters, run without stopping and turn around in the various dead ends until I finally ended up, after the puzzle with the huge fans, in the room where Alex encounters Doc Fitch once again and meets with Scarlet. The breathtaking sequence I went through in this level was far more my experience than it was Alex's. In "As We Become Machines: Corporealized Pleasure in Video Games," Martti Lahti explains how this was intensified by my own empathetic bodily movements.

> [The] identification and immersive experience during the game play remains compelling, even addictive, because our surrogate body on the screen mirrors our desires and bodily experiences; it represents us. It is directly controlled and affected by us, and our (real bodies') actions, even involuntary ones (like blinking!) carry dire consequences for the game world. In this sense, our pleasure is based on blurring the distinction between the player and character: we jump, fly, shoot, kick, and race when we are actually clicking the mouse or tapping the controller [2003: 163].

As blurry as it may be, the distinction between the gamer and the player character still exists. For Carroll, we do not identify per se with the character in fiction. We assimilate his or her situation. Because the consumer of horror fiction and the protagonist share the same culture and the same knowledge about what might be horrifying, it is easy to understand the way the latter assesses a situation.

> To do this, we do not need to replicate the mental state of the protagonist, but only know reliably how she assesses it. And we can know how she feels without duplicating her feeling in ourselves. We can assimilate her internal evaluation of the situation without becoming, so to speak, possessed by her (Carroll, 1999: 95).

What's more, for Carroll, there is an asymmetry in the relation that we have with the protagonist. Because we see the situation both from her point of view and from outside, we can experience different emotions. For instance, as the protagonist will be frightened by a monster, we will be scared (empathy), but we'll also be concerned by the fact she is in anguish (sympathy). These observations are truly relevant for the third-person perspective of the survival horror genre. On the one hand, if the player character can keep a "stone-face" whatever situation she is facing, it is in part because the gamer can easily have a sense of the protagonists' assessment of the frightening situation without the classical facial reactions seen in films. On the other hand, if I can say that it is not the player character that is really meant to be scared, it is because of the asymmetrical relation describing the emotional responses of the gamer. Being subjected to artifact, fictional and gameplay emotions (see Perron, 2005a), his emotional journey is different and richer than the protagonist's.

The Gamer's Bodily Experience

Playing a survival horror game remains an "experience of the self": "The solitary experience of the character doubles the player's one whose body and mind are engaged by the manipulation of the controller, from which come moreover vibrations linked to the context of the game (heart poundings, physical pain)" (Chauvin, 2002: 39, freely translated). As for film, and to use Sobchack's terms, the "own subjective felt live body" of the gamer is still at the center of the video game's sensual address. However, the aforementioned link to the game context shows how the rebound effect brought forward earlier is now going through a new channel and how, ultimately, it is bouncing back at the screen in return. The video game activates in a more explicit manner multiple sensory systems.

With the family resemblance it shares with virtual reality (VR), the video game perfectly incarnates the digital technology in what becomes an extension of the body. It is difficult not to think about the "metaflesh game pod" of David Cronenberg's movie *eXistenZ* (1999). Once connected directly into the nervous system of the gamer, this controller literally turns into a new bodily part, a new erogenous zone. The gamer's consciousness is then made to believe that he or she is in another reality all together. Although current video games do not yet abolish the borders between the real and the virtual worlds (the gamer still has a framed image in front of him, i.e. a framework for clearly delimited play — what pervasive games are perverting), it nonetheless forces the gamer — referring now to Shaviro's expression — "to stay within the orbit of the senses"; for instance, through the force feedback or "vibration" function, the tactile sense adds to those of vision and hearing. This goes from the DualShock controller of the Sony PlayStation and the Microsoft Side-Winder Force Feedback joystick to the Ultimate Game Chair with different vibration sensation levels. Despite the fact that I was sitting on a normal sofa, I recall very well the little fright I got in *Silent Hill 2* when the player character James put his hand in a hole in the wall of Wood Side Apartment number 202; the DualShock 2 controller suddenly vibrated, making me feel what it is like to go and look for something unseen in a hole. The feedback really added to the creepiness of the cut-scene. I also remembered the odd sensation I had when the controller started to slightly pulsate for the first time to signify James' health status was low. I thought for a moment that it was my hands that were throbbing. The PlayStation games have made the most of this function. For example, on top of the red flickering screen and the monsters' strikes, the controller vibrates when Torque is hit in *The Suffering*; similar force feedbacks are used in *Dead Space*. The Wii remote has a vibration function as well, which provides, among others effects, more impact to the famous death of Leon from the chainsaw attack in *Resident Evil 4*— but I'll return to the Nintendo Wii a bit later.

While these tactile and haptic dimensions enhance the playing, the bodily experience of the games is not limited to these — quite the opposite. The frenzy of the videoludic audio-vision invites the body to immerse itself in a new sensitivity. Indeed, according to the semio-pragmatic approach of French film theoretician Roger Odin, the images and sounds of the video game induce an energetic reading, a reading aiming to immerse the gamer in the movement and to work on direct contact (2000: 167). The gamer becomes *attuned* (Odin's concept of *mise en phase*, 2000: 37–46) with the game; on the same wavelength as the game, he resonates to the rhythm of the events as they happen — a state close to the well-known notion of psychological flow. This might be clear for a movie spectator (I say "movie spectator" to draw the line between films and games, although contemporary cinema has remediated a great deal of video game aesthetics); the camera might move around too fast in the horrific game-world, the movements might be excessively jerky and the representation might become very confusing. Such responses may even take a concrete form for a non-gamer or a very casual one, who could end up not only being frightened, but feeling dizzy and having headaches or bouts of nausea during a game session. The vicarious kinesthesia of a video game stems from the connection between the gamer and his player character, not between a spectator and a gamer. Without a doubt, the spectator can transform himself into an assistant and help the gamer survive the horror by warning him about a forthcoming threat, directing him towards a clue and being startled with him upon the sudden appearance of a monster. The spectator has the option of being able to cover his eyes if it becomes too scary or too horrific: "It is a reflexive, protective action that attests to the literal body's reciprocal and reversible relation to the figures on the screen, to its sense of actual investment in a dense, albeit also diffuse, experience that is carnally as well as consciously meaningful" (Sobchack, 2004: 79). For his part, the gamer doesn't have this opportunity. It is in the interactive or ergodic dimensions that are situated in the ins and outs of this videoludic relation. The gamer has to do something.

Three notions remain essential to explain the experiential nature of the video game. The first one is the multidimensional concept of presence. Ron Tamborini and Paul Skalski (2006) survey this impression of "being" in the game-world and note that the spatial presence relies on the feelings of involvement and immersion. Survival horror worlds are scary and eerie, meaningful and rich sensorial environments capable of focusing the gamer's attention and isolating him from other stimuli. They are inhabited by copresent monstrous "others" showing an awareness of the player character, i.e. always going after him or her. What's more, additional inputs to haptic and orienting systems enhance "the ability of game technology to match expected *proprioception*, the anticipated sense of body orientation and movement" (2006: 228, italics in original). Survival horror games also enhance the presence by meeting the horizons of expectations about objects and events. As their narratives borrow from the many patterns and conventions of the overall horror genre, and use similar game mechanics over and over again, they generate a continuous flow more easily.

Agency is the second unavoidable concept at stake. Janet Murray has influentially defined it as "the satisfying power to take meaningful action and see the result of our decisions and choices" (1997:126). In addition to assimilating the situation in which the protagonist finds himself, the gamer can perform effective protective actions to keep the protagonist alive. To quickly summarize the comparative studies of films and games I have conducted elsewhere (Perron, 2004, 2005a and 2005b), the gamer is not only a witness in video games, but an active participant. The survival of the player character depends on his coping potentials at specific moments in a game and is based on the sets of capabilities, potentials and techniques highlighted by Newman (2002). Fear being a clear object- and goal-oriented emotion, it has a strong action tendency. The frightened gamer will be likely to try one of the three F's related to the emotion: freeze, flight or fight. The choice he makes will have a consequence in the game-world.

The blurred distinction between the gamer and the player character involves presence, agency, and a third notion to be fully grasped. As one will have deduced, it is the issue of embodiment I had overlooked until now. Andreas Gregersen and Torben Grodal emphasize perfectly the importance of our videoludic embodied experience. For them,

> interacting with video games may lead to a sense of extended embodiment and sense of agency that lies somewhere between the two poles of [body] schema and [body] image — it is *an embodied awareness in the moment of action,* a kind of *body image in action*— where one experiences both agency and ownership of virtual entities. This process is a fusion of player's intentions, perceptions, and actions [2008: 67, italics in original].

Video game interfaces map actions, that is, translate natural actions into virtual ones, in order to involve the gamer in the game-world. To carry out a wide variety of game actions, the gamer performs an actual body movement in relation to control interfaces, a movement which Gregersen and Grodal call primitive action (P-action). Contrasting the standard game controllers to the Wii remote, the authors observe how the former controller schemes couple minimal P-actions as pushing buttons and manipulating thumbsticks with maximal audiovisual effects— undeniably, the gamer only has to press R2 in *Dead Space* to squash a monster on the floor and splatter blood everywhere. Since the P-actions are mapped to the representation of the player character, the embodied effects rely strongly on the consequences of the actions of this body on screen. As long as his intentions, perceptions, and actions are fused, the gamer does not have to be possessed by the player character to "be" in the game-world.

The action mapping of survival horror games is meant to suit the obstacles, events and encounters the gamer will face. On a controller like the PlayStation's DualShock (and I'm looking at different instruction manuals here), the gamer will move the player character by moving the left thumbstick (accordingly or inversely depending on the controls setting). He will look around or control his aiming with the right thumbstick. He will use the directional buttons to navigate the inventory or change weapons. He will press (alone or in combination) various buttons to take actions: to search, to run, to jump, to turn around, to attack, to guard against attacks, to aim his weapon, to throw, to change targets, to reload, to recover his health, to display/hide a map or status, to change viewing mode (as in *Fatal Frame* and *The Suffering*), to change characters (as in *ObsCure*), etc. But as arbitrary and minimal as those P-actions can be, there comes a time where their use becomes intuitive. To bring into play Sobchack's expression, we could say that "our fingers know" how to make our way through the game-world. As the actions feel natural, the gamer has a sense of being-in-the-gameworld. He is taking meaningful actions that make him feel *as if* he was in the situation of the protagonist, *as if* he was in danger although his own body is not in danger. He is scared because he is in the moment of agency and ownership of actions, navigating a specular body. The physiological responses (changes in heart rate, respiration, skin temperature, hand moistness, muscular tension, etc.) agitating his body arise out of his own appraisal and coping. Controlling his thumbsticks, he has to successfully flee from dangerous situations. He has to press the right buttons at the right time to fight impure and threatening monsters. He has to find the more effective strategy to defeat the bosses. He has to search dark and creepy places to discover valuable and usable items. He is startled because he triggers a sudden apparition. He is very tense because ammo and health are low. Etc.

With the current multi-platform release of games, the survival horror genre did not escape the shift taken by the Nintendo Wii and its promise of a new kinesthetic experience. With its interface capturing the gamer's movements in front of the screen, the home video game console now not only asks for minimal P-actions, but also for more gestural ones. The "Nunchuk Style Play" (expression borrowed from the instruction manual of *Escape from Bug Island*, Secret Stash Games, 2006) mixes the P-actions performed on a standard game controller with the new P-gestures offered by the nunchuk and the Wii remote. Consequently, the gamer still moves his player character with the thumbstick of the nunchuk and presses various buttons. The combinations can also be arbitrary, as shown in the necessity in *ObsCure: The Aftermath* (Hydravision, 2007, Wii) to hold the Z button of the nunchuk to enter in an attack mode, to aim at an enemy with the pointer of the remote, to hold B to lock on it and press A to fire the weapon. In a similar vein of the light-gun arcade-style games such as *The House of the Dead* (Sega, 1998–2009, for home systems— of which are for the Wii) and the Gun Survivor series of games developed by Capcom at the beginning of 2000, the Wii remote (with or without a Wii Zapper or an Ergonomic Gun Grip to enliven the gameplay experience) can be used for a much more precise and faster aim anywhere on the screen. It is easier to move and fully control the whole arm than to direct a thumbstick. This functionality has been rightly praised for the Wii edition of *Resident Evil 4* (2007); all the differences in gameplay are located in those arm gestures. While pressing buttons, the gamer needs to wave the nunchuk and the remote up and down or left and right in order to perform different actions: to draw and to reload a weapon, to jump in the air, to execute a roll-ing dodge, to turn wheels, to shake things off, etc. In any case, the closest natural mapping is related to melee weapons. It might be a wooden stick in *Escape from Bug Island*, a baseball bat in *ObsCure: The Aftermath* or a piece of furniture in *Alone in the Dark* (Hydravision, 2008, Wii), and even if the player character holds it with two hands and a true force feedback is miss-ing, it feels intuitive to swing around the Wii remote to defend ourselves. The gestures are also matching the ones the player character is doing. This notion of similarity is important.

Gregersen and Grodal refer to "the well-known fact that observing other agents who perform bodily actions tends to activate parts of one's own motor system — and if the observing person also performs a motor action herself, the movements may be congruent or incongruent" (2008: 68). They also note how this activation and inference

> are due to specific mirror neurons (especially in the prefrontal motor cortex) that fire both when the subject observes an action and when she performs one herself; that is, they fire when a person plans and performs an act of grasping, but also when that person watches other people grasp. Such "shared circuits"-approaches argue that we are fundamentally intersubjectively attuned to the movements of other bodies [2008: 69].

Insofar as mirror responses have also been reported in both emotional pro-cessing and empathy (see Agnew, Bhakoo and Puri, 2007), we come to shed new light on Williams' comment about how the audience sensation of hor-ror mimics what is seen on the screen. While the observation of pain causes various degrees of the same reaction as experiencing it, the gamer is made to feel the bodily suffering of the player character. That may explain why extreme decapitations similar to the ones in *Resident Evil 4* and *Dead Space* leave the gamer aghast and send shivers down his spine. The account of the neural activation directs us toward another significant mechanism related to fear. For Joseph LeDoux, the fear system in the brain is "a system that detects dan-ger and produces responses that maximize the probability of surviving a dan-gerous situation in the most beneficial way" (1996: 128). The defensive nature of fear is prompted by two types of sign stimuli, called natural and learned triggers by LeDoux. On the one hand, the sight of a predator, its looks and sounds, is always automatically detected as a source of threat. On the other hand, the place the predator was seen and the sound it made when it was charging become knowledge, a knowledge appraised as dangerous and gaining control over tried-and-true ways of responding to those stimuli. It is easy to understand how the survival horror genre makes the most of the fear system. Monsters are clearly designed to be predators. The games play with a number of learned stimuli, for instance, conditioning the gamer about deadly encounters every time he enters a new space, about the lurking menace of dark corners, about the forewarnings of threats (it is difficult not to think about the white noise transmitted by the pocket radio in *Silent Hill*), about the increasing power of the foes further on, etc. When those natural and learned triggers are used well, they will always elicit strong bodily responses.

A Very Last Shudder

A head with a body. Although I have referred to many games and addressed many issues related to the carnal, corporeal, and physical dimension of the survival horror genre, this is what I hope the reader still is when arriving at this essay's end of the ride. Ultimately, the goal was to show how the video game intensifies the emotional experience of the horror genre and how all those monstrous bodies and the player character's body in the horrific game-worlds are needed to capture the imagination of the gamer's mind and to affect his own body. People playing survival horror games remain thrill-seekers. The survival horror is indisputably an extended body genre.

Works Cited

Agnew, Zarinah K., Kishore K. Bhakoo, and Basant K. Puri (2007), "The Human Mirror System: A Motor Resonance Theory of Mind-Reading," *Brain Research Reviews*, Vol. 54 No. 2, June, pp. 286–293.

Anderson, Lark (2008), "Silent Hill: Homecoming," *Gamespot.com*, October 21, available online at <http://www.gamespot.com/xbox360/adventure/silenthill5/review.html?om _act=convert&om_clk=gssummary&tag=summary;read-review>.

Beuglet, Nicolas (2001), *Silent Hill 2. The Making of. Alchemists of Emotion*, Fun TV, 33 minutes.

_____ (2003), *Silent Hill 3. Naissance d'une Renaissance*, WE Production/Konami, 26 minutes.

Carroll, Noël (1990), *The Philosophy of Horror or Paradoxes of the Heart*, New York: Routledge.

Chauvin, Jean Sèbastien (2002), "Du Singulier an pluriel," *Cahiers du cinéma*, Special Issue on Video Games, September, pp. 38–40.

Gibbs, Raymond W. (2007), *Embodiment and Cognitive Science* (2005), Cambridge: Cambridge University Press.

Gregersen, Andreas, and Torben Grodal (2008), "Embodiment and Interface," in Bernard Perron and Mark J.P. Wolf (eds.), *The Video Game Theory Reader 2*, New York: Routledge, pp. 65–83.

Lahti, Martti (2003), "As We Become Machines: Corporealized Pleasure in Video Games," in Mark J.P. Wolf and Bernard Perron (eds.), *The Video Game Theory Reader*, New York: Routledge, pp. 157–170.

LeDoux, Jospeh (1996), *The Emotional Brain. The Mysterious Underpinnings of Emotional Life*, New York: Simon & Schuster.

McRoy, Jay (2006), "The Horror Is Alive. Immersion, Spectatorship, and the Cinematics of Fear in the Survival Horror Genre," *Reconstruction*, Vol. 6, No. 1, available online at <http://reconstruction.eserver.org/061/mcroy.shtml>.

Murray, Janet H. (1997), *Hamlet on the Holodeck: The Future of Narrative in Cyberspace*, New York: The Free Press.

Newman, James (2002), "The Myth of the Ergodic Videogame. Some Thoughts on Player-Character Relationships in Videogames," *Gamestudies.org*, Vol. 1, No. 2, July, available online at <http://www.gamestudies.org/0102/newman/>.

Odin, Roger (2000), *De la fiction*, Bruxelles: Éditions De Boeck Université.

Perron, Bernard (2005a), "A Cognitive Psychological Approach to Gameplay Emotions," *Changing Views: Worlds in Play. Proceedings of DiGRA 2005 Conference*, Vancouver, available online at <http://www.digra.org/dl/db/06276.58345.pdf>.

_____ (2005b), "Coming to Play at Frightening Yourself: Welcome to the World of Horror Games," *Aesthetics of Play. A Conference on Computer Game Aesthetics*, University of Bergen, available online at <http://www.aestheticsofplay.org/perron.php>.

_____ (2006b), "The Heuristic Circle of Gameplay: the Case of Survival Horror," in M. Santorineos (ed.), *Gaming Realities: A Challenge of Digital Culture*, Fournos: Athens, pp. 62–69, available online at <http://www.ludicine.ca/sites/ludicine.ca/files/Perron — Heuristic Circle of Gameplay — Mediaterra 2006.pdf>.

_____ (2004), "Sign of a Threat: The Effects of Warning Systems in Survival Horror Games," *COSIGN 2004 Proceedings*, Art Academy, University of Split, pp. 132–141, available online at <http://www.ludicine.ca/sites/ludicine.ca/files/Perron_Cosign_2004.pdf>.

_____ (2006a), *Silent Hill: Il motore del terrore*, Milan: Costa & Nolan.

Poole, Steven (2000), *Trigger Happy: The Inner Life of Video Games*, London: Fourth Estate.

Pruett, Christopher (2005), "Designing Characters to be Scared For," *dreamdawn.com*, available online at <http://www.dreamdawn.com/sh/features/character_design.php>.

Schefer, Jean Louis (1980), *L'homme ordinaire du cinéma*, Paris: Cahiers du cinéma/Gallimard.

Shaviro, Steve (1993), *The Cinematic Body*, Minneapolis and London: University of Minnesota Press.

Skal David J. (2001), *The Monster Show: A Cultural History of Horror* (1993), New York: Faber and Faber.

Sobchack, Vivian (2004), "What My Fingers Knew: The Cinesthetic Subject, or Vision in the Flesh," *Carnal Thoughts. Embodiment and Moving Image Culture*, Berkeley: University of California Press, pp. 53–84; a first version was published in 2000 in *Sense of cinema*, No 5, April, available online at <http://archive.sensesofcinema.com/contents/00/5/fingers.html>.

Tamborini, Ron, and Paul Skalski (2006), "The Role of Presence in the Experience of Electronic Games," in Peter Vorderer and Jennings Bryant (eds.), *Playing Video Games. Motives, Responses, and Consequence*, Mahwah, New Jersey: Lawrence Erlbaum Associates, pp. 223–240.

Tan, Ed S. (1996), *Emotion and the Structure of Narrative Film. Film as an Emotion Machine*, Mahwah, NJ: Lawrence Erlbaum Associates.

Thompson, Clive (2007), "Gore Is Less: Videogames Make Better Horror Than Hollywood," *Wired*, August 28, available online at <http://www.wired.com/gaming/gamingreviews/

commentary/games/2007/08/gamesfrontiers_0827>.

Torres, Ricrado (2008), "Resident Evil 5 Update: New Boss, New Area, New Kinds of Pain," *Gamespot.com*, Decembre 18, available online at <http://www.gamespot.com/ps3/adventure/residentevil5/news.html?sid=6202542&tag=nl.e576>.

Vandevyver, Stéphanie (2004), "Humanité contre animalité," *Écran fantastique*, Special Issue, No. 6, Spring, pp. 74–77.

Vorobej, Mark (1997), "Monsters and the Paradox of Horror," *Dialogue*, No. 24, pp. 219–249.

Wells, Paul (2002), *The Horror Genre: From Beelzebub to Blair Witch* (2000), London: Wallflower Press.

Williams, Linda (1995), "Film Bodies: Gender, Genre, and Excess," in Barry Keith Grant (ed.), *Film Genre Reader II*, Austin: University of Texas Press, pp. 140–158; appeared originally in a slight different form in 1991 in *Film Quarterly*, Vol. 44, No 4, Summer, pp. 2–13.

Yu, Daniel S. (aka dsyu) (2002), "Exploring the Survival Horror Genre," *Joystick101.org*, March 18, offline.

Plunged Alone into Darkness: Evolution in the Staging of Fear in the *Alone in the Dark* Series

Guillaume Roux-Girard

Preconceptions of Fear: Between the Reception and Legibility of the Games

> It isn't what you see, but what you can't see. It's the suggestion; the subtle teasing of the subconscious; the lonely creaking of the floorboard resonating throughout an empty hallway; the slow advance around the corner; the swelling sense of dread as the ever-present evil that looms near refuses to reveal itself. Fear is not the adrenaline rush. It's that helpless feeling of being alone in the dark [Fahs, 2008].

This introduction to Travis Fahs' "Alone in the Dark Retrospective," available on the popular Internet website IGN, clearly illustrates the direction I want to take while exploring Infogrames' series. Moreover, it contributes from the outset to forge the reader's preconception of what this particular series is all about: giving a good chill to gamers who are reckless enough to engage themselves into its empty hallways. Official reviews and online fan evaluations of the *Alone in the Dark* series, which up to now is composed of five installments: *Alone in the Dark* (Infogrames, 1992), *Alone in the Dark 2* (Infogrames, 1993), *Alone in the Dark 3* (Infogrames, 1995), *Alone in the Dark: The New Nightmare* (DarkWorks, 2001) and *Alone in the Dark* (Eden Games S.A.S, 2008), contribute to highlight many elements constituting the videoludic staging of fear in survival horror games. Reviews participate in constructing the very "horizon of expectations" of what a scary game is, as people — myself included — usually refer to those texts when they need to find traces of the experience other gamers had while playing them. To take these horizons of expectations into consideration is essential to truly comprehend how contemporary gamers "have viewed and understood the work" (Jauss, 1982: 28). These expectations need to be objectified in order to prevent false readings originating from misconceptions about the games. As Hans Robert Jauss puts it:

> The analysis of the literary experience of the reader [or the videoludic experience of the gamer] avoids the threatening pitfalls of psychology if it describes the reception and the influence of a work within the objectifiable system of expectations that arise for each work in the historical moment of its appearance, from a pre-understanding of the genre, from the form and themes of already familiar works, and from the opposition between poetics and practical language [1982: 22].

However, because reviewers sometimes fail to state the limits—or properly "reconstruct," this horizon of expectations, consensus on what defines what is scary in a game is hardly reached. Criticism surrounding a title like *Alone in the Dark* does not always privilege the same approach, and the use of different analytic frameworks consequently multiplies the presumptions and perceptions gamers have of the games. Elements which according to some critics and gamers enhance the general quality of the series are considered very problematic by others. More interestingly, those debates often concern the elements defining the games as horrific. Since reviews often concentrate on the narrative structure or gameplay mechanics of games, they frequently neglect their formal treatment which predominantly supplies their staging of fear. Reviewers do point out to the sound and camera effects, but regularly fail to explain how their use induces fear. Likewise, those appraisals are sometimes biased by an affective bond experienced critics or gamers have for specific genres or game developers. Speaking of cinema, Christian Metz explained that we might become "groupies" of a director. Therefore, a movie might not be perceived exactly as what it is (the real object), but idealized and often confused with the imaginary object, what Metz called "the movie as it pleased us" (Metz, 1984: 19, freely translated). The interpretations some critics make of the games are occasionally filled with judgmental errors. For instance, fans of survival horror who consider that "[a]ll the games in the *Alone in the Dark* series are inspired by the work of H.P. Lovecraft" (Jong, 1997b) are wrong. Such misleading remarks distort the global image of the series and gamers who expected to find Lovecraft's influence throughout the series are bound to be disappointed as none of the following titles make direct references to his mythology.

While reviews modify the perception gamers have of the qualities and flaws held by the *Alone in the Dark* series in its attempt to stage fear, they also constitute a testimony of its evolution. Nevertheless, to truly understand how the *Alone in the Dark* games properly—or not—stage fear, a return to the original "objects" seams preferable. Following a statement Gilles Thérien made while attempting to theorize the breach between the reception of movies and their legibility, every game must first be read and experienced "as a singular and complex object which cannot be reduced to its abstract, but has to be considered in regards of the particular functioning of its imagery" (Thérien, 1992: 107, freely translated). Consequently, as for video games, one has to play them and study their formal structure and their gameplay.

Through an analysis of the *Alone in the Dark* series, this essay aims to take a closer look at how the games of the series constructed and responded to the horizon of expectations of gamers. By grounding itself in a formalist approach, this analysis aspires to bridge the gap between the general reception and the legibility of the games within the series. Extrapolating mostly from the eclectic interpretations of the critics and fans of the games, this essay will address the role of the series, in terms of game space, *mise en scène*, aesthetics and gameplay, to the evolution of the staging of fear in the survival horror genre. From crude polygonal shapes to high-definition graphics, and from the first use of off-screen monster sounds to a complex dynamic audio scripting, this essay looks at how the series has continuously evolved — positively or not — to intensify the gamer's emotional dread while playing alone, plunged into darkness.

"Fear needs to be staged": Creating a New Game Space

As Win Sical and Remi Delekta suggest in an article of the only issue of the *Horror Games Magazine*: "Survival Horror [can] not exist without a minimum of technical capacities: sounds, graphics, processing speed. Fear, to exist, needs to be staged, and this *mise en scène* needs means" (2003: 13, freely translated). Like Atari's *Haunted House* (1981) or remediated *slasher* movies titles such as *Halloween* (Video Software Specialist, 1983) or *Friday the 13th* (Pack-In-Video, 1987), a plurality of games developed in the eighties had attempted to integrate horrific elements into their narrative and gameplay structures. However, due to their abstract graphics— the spill of a few pixels hardly manages to stand for a gory moments, their potential to scare the gamer was quite limited compared to today's standards. For anyone going back to those games, it is indeed very hard to be scared or even think gamers were frightened by them. In fact, at that time, the horror was more lurking in the paratextual material than in the games themselves. As Mark J. P. Wolf explains:

> The boxes and advertising were eager to help players imagine that there was more to the games than there actually was, and actively worked to counter and deny the degree of abstraction that was still present in the games. Inside the box, game instruction manuals also attempted to add exciting narrative contexts to the games, no matter how far-fetched they were" [2003: 59 —for a longer historical account, see Perron, 2006: 19–42].

But, in 1992, one game somehow bypassed and even took advantage of some of those technical limitations to revolutionize action-adventure video gaming while bringing a fearful experience to gamers craving a horrific experience. Designed by Frédérick Raynal, *Alone in the Dark 1* (I'm adding the number to distinguish this first title from the whole series) shook up the entire videoludic scene by incorporating polygonal characters, monsters and objects in two-dimensional pre-rendered backgrounds. More than just creating new possibilities in gameplay, this simulated tri-dimensionality opened a new "game space" allowing "the game to depict a better, immersive horror world, [and] above all, a remediated cinematic one since the action will always be depicted from different fixed camera angles" (Perron, 2006: 31; translated by the author). In *Alone in the Dark 1*, threats could now materialize from every corner of a room; spiders could fall from the ceiling, and monstrous zombies could emerge from trap doors in the floor. This game space thus opened doors for a multitude of new strategies to improve the quality of the *mise en scène* of horror in video games. At the same time, the spatial representation was not constraining too much the gamer's interactions within the game, as opposed to point-and-click adventure games such as *Phantasmagoria* (Sierra On-line, 1996). As Brett Todd, from *Gamespot.com,* highlights in his "modern history of horror games": "*Alone in the Dark* and its two sequels were actually the only games during this period that allowed complete freedom of movement" (2001). For this reason, the original *Alone in the Dark* is often regarded by critics and the general gaming community as being the "Godfather of Survival Horror" (Fahs, 2008). This first title thus began to shape the identity of what would become the popular genre of survival horror and spontaneously forge a new horizon of expectations regarding this specific genre.

In *Alone in the Dark 1*'s narrative premises, Jeremy Hartwood, a recluse artist nourishing a passion for old occult manuscripts, has hanged himself in the attic of his huge Louisiana mansion: Derceto. Rumors say the manor is haunted and somehow rendered the owner insane, leading to his demise. Through the intervention of his avatar, the gamer must now enter the estate. Trapped inside, he must confront a plurality of nightmarish creatures while trying to get out alive. Immediately after choosing to start a new game, the gamer is prompted to make a choice between two player characters (PC): Edward Carnby, a private detective full of debts who is hired by an antiquary to recover a piano from Derceto's attic, or Emily Hartwood, a niece of the deceased, who wishes to further investigate the circumstances surrounding her uncle's death. The introductory text of the journal of either character, which in the 1996 CD-ROM version is also accompanied by a voice over, already contributes to depict the mansion as an old haunted house. For example, excerpts from Emily Hartwood's diary define it as a "creaking old mansion, with its unusual tales, its secret library door, the ancient upstairs clock, all those occult books." She also writes about her apprehensions concerning her return there: "I tremble at the thought of those dark corridors, those brooding portraits." Therefore, even though the gamer has not yet set foot in Derceto, he is already picturing the old Louisiana manor as a potential hostile territory. All these subtle indications about Derceto's space — a space which for the moment is still based on the gamer's spatial preconceptions of what an old mansion can look like — allow the gamer to somewhat anticipate its very experience.

The opening animated sequence brilliantly unfolds this game space before the gamer's eyes. From the luminescent outdoors of the Louisiana countryside to the dark pathway leading to the mansion, the camera follows the protagonist in a purely cinematic fashion. It even attempts a quick startle effect by switching rapidly from a long shot to a brief close-up (accompanied by a sounding croak) of the face of a toad trying to cross the road. From a long high-angle shot of the manor, the cinematic peak of this animation is reached when the camera switches to a cross high-angle subjective point of view from Derceto's window revealing the menacing long-nailed hands of the hellish creature stalking the protagonist's arrival. This presence, revealing itself only to the gamer since the avatar does not seem to notice it, confirms the lurking threat that might be encountered when entering the mansion. As the gamer enters Derceto, the camera follows his avatar up to the attic, establishing the third-person perspective as the gamer's vantage point. Once on the last floor, control of the avatar is given to the gamer.

In an interview, Frederick Raynal states that George A. Romero's and Dario Argento's zombie movies were his original influences for the game. This statement is opposed to the common belief that the author of the Cthulhu Mythos served as the main inspiration: "Lovecraft is something that was grafted over *Alone in the Dark* ... for the ambiance, to give roots to the mystery and to add a few creatures to the bestiary" (in Provezza, 2006: 54, freely translated). Still, "[s]harp observers [can] find references to the peculiar mythology crafted by Lovecraft and associates like Robert Bloch in nearly every room of Derceto" (Todd, 2001), investing the old mansion with a truly frightening aura. The narrative framework of *Alone in the Dark 1* is principally supported by the many books and parchments the gamer can find throughout the mansion's rooms. As Laurent Roucairol notes, everything is written in a style very similar to H.P Lovecraft's novel *The Case of Charles Dexter Ward* in which "horror does not count as much as the afterward description of the slow lurching into insanity of those who dared to walk alongside it" (2006: 50, freely translated). Therefore, *Alone in the Dark 1*'s treatment of horror is as much psychological and literary than physical and graphical. In this survival horror game, there is not much blood flowing and

Derceto's few monsters are simply the representation of a more powerful metaphysical threat eventually revealed as Pregzt, a demonic being enclosed in a dead tree located in the cavern laying underneath Derceto. As a result, even though *Alone in the Dark 1*'s horror mechanics generally rely on surprise effects—the long-fanged monster bursting through a window being the most prominent example, its plot succeeds in adding a certain dose of suspense (figure 1).

This first installment of the series developed most of the gameplay mechanics that contributed to the effectiveness of the *survival horror* genre. From clumsy control to limited inventory and scarce resources, everything is there to complicate the gamer's task to get out of the mansion alive. Carefulness is highly recommended and alternatives to fighting must be found. Luckily, the books also serve gameplay functions as they often contain clues to solve puzzles and avoid confrontation. For example, a parchment entitled "The Dagger of Sacrifice" explains how to get rid of a ghost that roams in the library. Without this book, a serious amount of trial and error would have proven necessary in order to find which dagger must be used to eliminate the dangerous threat. On the other hand, the books sometimes represent themselves a threat. For instance, the occult books of the library need to be read over a pentagram symbol carved in the library's floor. Doing otherwise revives "uncontrollable occult forces" killing the protagonist automatically.

As many reviews acknowledge, the main feature of the game remains its astonishing use of game space to implement dynamic camera framing "which for the first time," as Laurent Roucairol recalls, "participate as much in the

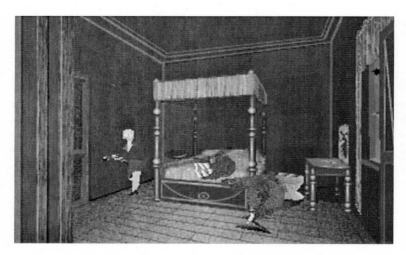

Figure 1: A long-fanged monster jumping through a window in *Alone in the Dark* (Infogrames, 1992).

visual impact of the 3D videogame, as in its ergonomic properties. We can talk of *mise en scène,* though the process never seems artificial nor to be done at the expense of ludic comfort" (2006: 50, freely translated). Indeed, the virtual cameras predominantly exploit fixed high-angle shots and bring a whole new dimension to Derceto's rooms. Not only does this framing strategy refer directly to horror film conventions, it also brings depth to the experience. Such camera work allows for spatial segmentation in an already confined space. Consequently, as viewed space is reduced to the borders of the frame, limits of the room no longer represent the boundaries from where menacing creatures might emerge. What seemed to be a perfectly safe space moments ago can now be filled with lurking threats ready to make the gamer shake in his boots. On the second floor, a long-fanged monster surprises the gamer right after he picks up old Jeremy's diary, leading to a violent enclosed fight. In the spirit of horror films, the use of the third-person perspective serves the horrific staging. It "[adds] to the dramatic tension by allowing the [gamer] to see things that would otherwise be lost in a first-person perspective, such as monsters chasing the player character" (Yu in Perron, 2006: 32, translated by Perron). This has the effect of re-establishing the gamer in a spectatorship position and is "intended to intensify the sensation of vulnerability, isolation, and in certain 'key' moments, shock" (McCoy, 2006).

Even more interesting is how the fixed camera angles of *Alone in the Dark 1* modify the relation existing between the player character (PC) and the game world. In her essay "Toward a Spatial Practice in Video Games," Laurie N. Taylor notes that the "fourth wall fixed perspective," used to define platform games such as *Super Mario Brothers* (Nintendo, 1985) and *Metroid* (Intelligent Systems, 1987), always centers the player character within the game world and therefore "comforts the player by letting [him] know where the PC is spatially and how the PC fits into that space" (2005). According to Taylor, survival horror games do exactly the opposite since they rather make the game world the focus of the game and the avatar merely "an aspect operating within the bleak landscape of the game world and one who is trapped and heavily weighted within the game world" (Taylor, 2005). Interestingly, Taylor attributes this transformation to the technical limitations modeling the design of *Alone in the Dark 1.* She clarifies: "The original survival horror game, *Alone in the Dark,* first used the bleak landscapes and fixed views to lessen the processing load so that its game world could be larger and more detailed when details warranted too much of the greatly needed processing power" (2005). Frederick Raynal confirms this observation as he explains that the cinematic treatment of the game is just a consequence of the technical limitations of the game rather than a deliberate choice of *mise en scène*: "Camera positioning ensued from ludic constraints which of course served fear, but without thinking about cinema. Imperatives were mostly regarded in terms of surface of play" (in Provezza, 2006: 54, freely translated). Accordingly, *Alone in the Dark 1*'s technical constraints did not only offer the possibility of a larger game world but also fashioned the formal treatment applied to the *survival horror* genre. Capcom's *Resident Evil* series (1996–2009) later followed this formula for many of its titles. Likewise, many horror video games used fixed camera angles and bleak spaces to preserve "the mood and the original feel of [those] game[s]" (Taylor, 2005), even though they were not required to do so for technical reasons anymore (examples of this can be found inside the series as it is the case with *Alone in the Dark: The New Nightmare*). From this point of view, the relationship between technological limitations and aesthetic choices largely contributed towards survival horror's evolution in the staging of fear.

While this new game space allowed for strategic uses of the visual dimension of survival horror games, it also created a brand new "playground" for imaginative sound designers. While *Alone in the Dark 1*'s sound design remains quite primitive, it nevertheless employs many of the sonic strategies games with less technical constraints currently used. Even though they are scarce, sound effects do adopt adequate typo-morphological criteria to induce fear. According to Pierre Schaeffer, typo-morphology "regroups as complementary the operations of typology and morphology constituting a stage of exploring, listing and describing sounds ... which, in principle refuses ... direct reference to their cause, origin or what they evoke" (Chion, 1983: 113, freely translated). For instance, the abrupt attack of the high pitched sound produced by the basement rats is sure to produce a strong emotional response of discomfort. This feeling of uneasiness is produced directly by the morphological nature of the sound itself, and not only because its source is a virtual rat. The same is true for the creaky sounds emitted by the avatar's footsteps or by the handling of opening and closing the mansion's doors. Of course, it is above all the spatial disposition of sounds that is innovative. The acousmatic sounds— defined as a "sound one hears without seeing its originating cause" (Chion, 1983: 19, freely translated)— populating the off-screen, induce fear because they create anticipation. In the attic, if the gamer has properly blocked both the trap door and window by pushing furniture over and in front of them, he will hear the sound of shattering glass and then a grainy low pitched growl he cannot yet associate to its source. Later identified as belonging to one of the long-fanged brown monsters, these growls originally create doubt as to what could have produced such a threatening noise. Therefore, the gamer might think twice before engaging himself in the stairs leading to the second floor. If heard again later in the game, these sounds will create further anticipation regarding the eminent arrival of one of those creatures inside the frame. Unfortunately, *Alone in the Dark 1* does not make much use of those off-screen sounds since most sounds are linked to a source directly present on the screen. At least, the possibility of a more cinematic sound was introduced and paved the way for a better use of sound effects and ambient tracks. The orchestral musical score also plays a large part in the building of the general mood of the game "with some genuinely unnerving discords struck" (Golding, 2004b). Music further contributes to some startling effects as string chords often punctuate the entrance of a monster in the screen. *Alone in the Dark 1* also uses silence to build up suspense. Zach Whalen mentions:

> As is the case with horror films, the silence ... puts the player on edge rather than reassuring him that there is no danger in the immediate environment, increasing the expectation that danger will soon appear. The appearance of the danger is, therefore, heightened in intensity by way of its sudden intrusion into silence [2004].

All of those sound strategies, combined with the visual, narrative, and gameplay stratagems, contributed without a doubt to making *Alone in the Dark 1* quite a scary game. Even though the game has aged considerably, it remains one of the genre's masterpieces as its revolutionary use of game space and cinematographic treatment has influenced numerous horror games.

Meet One Eye Jack: The Day Horror Died

Setting a proper space and implementing cinematic conventions is not nearly enough to induce fear. After all, for properly staged fear, one first needs something scary to put on stage. Consequently, although *Alone in the Dark 1*'s two sequels utilize the same graphics engine, fixed camera angles and confined spaces, they do not quite pull off the frightful experience which contributed to the success of the original title. *Alone in the Dark 2* (The PlayStation and Sega Saturn ports are entitled *Alone in the Dark 2: One Eyed-Jack's Revenge*) is undeniably the most problematic.

As noted by Marc Golding, the drastic change of ambience between *Alone in the Dark* and its sequel is mainly imputable to the fact that "Lovecraft did not make the trip to part two" (2004a). This unfortunate departure was itself the result of a conflict of interests at Infogrames. As Laurent Roucairol explains: "Frederick Raynal and Bruno Bonnel [the producer] did not agree in terms of game design. Bonnel wanted a very rhythmic episode with plenty of action sequences and various locales, while Raynal wanted to stick with the intimate approach of the first opus" (2006: 50, freely translated). Unhappy with the tangent the project was taking, Raynal left Infogrames, depriving the following *Alone in the Dark* titles from his vision. However, since Bruno Bonnel released the action-oriented blockbuster game he hoped to produce, it can be acknowledged that *Alone in the Dark 2* was not even supposed to be conceived as a frightening game. Since the game is still habitually labeled as *survival horror*, as it was publicized as "[picking] up where the first game left off" (EGM, 1995: 86) and because some critics seem to believe "we find in this sequel the same macabre ambiance we could find in the first title" (Mathieu, 2003: 20, freely translated), a look at *Alone in the Dark*'s follow-up remains mandatory.

Alone in the Dark 2's narrative premises differ a lot from its predecessor. After receiving a distress telegram from his good friend Ted Striker, another private detective investigating the kidnapping of a young girl named Grace Saunders, Edward Carnby embarks on a quest for justice leading him to California, more precisely to Hell's Kitchen, an old mansion serving as a hideout for the infamous One Eye Jack and his minions. As the gamer goes through the game, he learns the enemies he is facing are in fact eighteenth century pirates who were given immortality by signing a pact, thereby drawing its magic in the powers of the Voodoo witch Elizabeth Jarret. Considering that Voodoo is at the core of the Zombie mythology, one could have hopped for the presence of blood thirsty monsters. With the exceptions of Jarret and a single ghost, the game displays no horrific figures. Needless to say, to replace menacing zombies and horrendous monsters by immortal pirates posing as modern gangsters already disrupt a gamer's hope for horrific immersion.

In fact, the whole videoludic treatment breaks from the original game's staging of horror. Even though the spatial construction and camera work still allow for enemies to pop up from every corner of the screen, *Alone in the Dark 2* completely avoids using this possibility. Quoting Robert Baird's analysis in "The Startle Effect. Implication for Spectator Cognition and Media Theory," Bernard Perron mentions that three elements are necessary to create such an impact: "(1) a character presence, (2) an implied off-screen threat and (3) a disturbing intrusion [often accentuated by a sound burst] into the character's immediate space" (Baird in Perron, 2004:133). *Alone in the Dark* 2 fails to create startling effects because the game neglects the second and/or third element by either including the threat directly inside the frame, or emitting forewarning audio cues (varying between "Hi guy!," "Morning Sir!" and "Hey you!"), which, rather than building up suspense, gives the gamer just enough time to prepare for an ambush on the off-screen nuisance that is about to enter the frame. In addition, bad encounters have been multiplied exponentially and the gamer can expect a fight in almost every room of Hell's Kitchen, all detours of the gardens or in nearly each cabin of the Flying Dutchman ship. As a result, the gamer stays alert at all times, limiting the possibilities of being surprised as he is caught off guard.

Drastically outnumbering the protagonist could have proven a good strategy to provoke a certain level of uneasiness since survival horror games like *Resident Evil* (Capcom, 1996) do feature a large amount of enemies. To do so, the avatar's ability to defend himself has to be restrained so that the gamer will be encouraged to adopt a more conservative and prudent approach. Conversely, *Alone in the Dark 2* provides very effective weapons. Ammunition and healing flasks are also quite easy to come by and even when the game makes the gamer loses his inventory, it is not long before he is able to regain a decent arsenal. Moreover, in *Alone in the Dark 2*, the gamer's avatar does not play the role of a prey that is unwillingly trapped inside what becomes a hostile environment. For example, Edward Carnby blows up the gate to Hell's Kitchen with dynamite in order to penetrate a location he already knows to be unfriendly. Sometimes, the game, instead of building a pressuring atmosphere, even gives the gamer an advantage by letting Carnby eradicates sleeping henchmen by making a barrel of gun powder explode using the ship's cannon. With such gameplay possibilities, there is not much place left for victimization.

Yet, there is actually one part of the game where the gamer is not allowed to use firearms or melee weapons. After Carnby has been captured by the pirates, the gamer is given control of a new avatar: the young Grace Saunders. As Grace, he is allowed to carry only small objects and his main goal is to avoid getting caught while attempting to rescue Carnby. Put back into a *survival horror* context, this could have been a scary moment. Unfortunately, the gameplay is actually closer to a game like *Metal Gear Solid* (Konami, 1998) than to *Fatal Frame* (Tecmo, 2001). With most enemies already in sight, all the gamer has to do is to carefully navigate from room to room and sometimes use unorthodox techniques to get rid of unwelcome followers. In this segment, and throughout the game, the music's upbeat tempo also becomes an issue. Combined with Grace's bouncy way of walking and the clapping sound of her feet, she almost seems to perform a folkloric dance rather than flee from an incoming menace. For that reason, the game's music produces more comical effects than it induces fear. Since *Alone in the Dark 2*'s narrative framework and gameplay also include moonwalking gangsters, dancing immortal pirates and fights disguised as Santa Claus, slapstick plays a greater part in the game than horror (figure 2). Consequently, the game also fails to create any form of suspense.

Apart from the judgmental mistakes previously cited, the reception of *Alone in the Dark 2* seems ambivalent on the general quality of the game. This can be partly explained by a disparity between the horizon of expectations of the gamer and the game itself. As Jauss explains:

> If one characterizes as aesthetic distance the disparity between the given horizon of expectation and the appearance of a new work, whose reception can result in a "change of horizons" through negation of familiar experiences or through raising newly articulated experiences to the level of consciousness, then this aesthetic distance can be objectified historically along the spectrum of the

audience's reaction and criticism's judgement (spontaneous success, rejection or shock, scattered approval, gradual or belated understanding [1982: 25].

Therefore, while such disparity "create[d] much frustration in gamers who yearn[ed] for the intelligent gameplay [and eeriness] found in its predecessor" (Jong, 1997a) and in the eyes of those who were expecting a survival hor-

ror title, this does not mean the game is fundamentally bad. The game still holds all the ingredients found in a fun action-adventure game and thus must be analyzed in a consequent context, with different "constraints of genre" in mind. To fully appreciate his videoludic experience, a gamer must modify his expectations, and if he does not, he faces high risks of being disappointed. This analysis of *Alone in the Dark 2* did not aim to depict the game as a bad one, but to demonstrate why it cannot be considered a survival horror game and why it upset the community of gamers that was expecting one.

Figure 2, top: Carnby fighting T-Bone, the cook, in a Santa Claus costume in *Alone in the Dark 2* (Infogrames, 1993). *Bottom:* Carnby running away from a zombie outlaw in *Alone in the Dark 3* (Infogrames, 1995).

Going Back to the Basics: From Lovecraft to a Ghost Town

In 1995, *Alone in the Dark 3* tried to recover some of the elements that elevated the first installment to horror gaming cult, and almost achieved success in its attempt to stage fear. In this episode, Edward Carnby's adventure takes place in Slaughter Gulch, a ghost town where Emily Hartwood, who apparently abandoned her career as an antiquary to work with a film crew, mysteriously disappeared with all her colleagues. The introductory animated sequence is surprisingly promising. When the gamer's avatar crosses the bridge leaving the town, a desperado in black robes blows it up, cutting him off from his only way out. As Carnby regains his senses, the bandit vanishes through the ground like a ghost, announcing the mythological means of a horror themed game. A short film in the adjacent saloon confirms this hypothesis as a ghostly shadow attacks and kills a comedian during the filming of the said sequence. Sadly, the music fails to establish the mood, as the gripping orchestral score of the first opus is replaced by a bouncy guitar and mouth bow loop. On the other hand, most of the sound design, which includes other musical tracks, is pretty effective. For example, punctuated by a spooky spectral drone and strings music, every entrance by an assailant is quite enough to make a few hairs stand on end. Also, when an undead outlaw is killed, a shadow adopting the form of a devilish red-eyed cat often jumps out of his body emitting an upsetting shriek. The only downside to this revamped sound design is the insufficient use of off-screen possibilities to build up suspense.

Drawing from its predecessor's legacy, *Alone in the Dark 3* makes good use of its game space. Once again, locales are invested with a gloomy ambiance. There are dark colors and spider webs. Essentially, a fine camera decoupage "provides a truly movie like oppressive atmosphere where every corner may yet hide another danger" (Jong, 1997b). Consequently, some enclosed rooms are also full of surprises. Almost any gamer would jump out of their seat when, as they open a fireplace door, a massive zombie outlaw drops on them (figure 2). This episode also marks the return of the horror iconography as pentagrams, skulls and occult books can be found in some rooms. Following the tradition, documents dispersed throughout Slaughter Gulch carry the narrative background as well as giving precious clues on how to solve specific puzzles or avoid dangerous situations. The game also widens its horrifying strategies. In the "blood cavern," where Carnby has to jump from pillar to pillar, skeletons are entrenched in bloody rocky-organic matter. This is the first time that an *Alone in the Dark* title opts for a gory effect to induce disgust. *Alone in the Dark 3* also tries a rather bold narrative twist as it stages Edward Carnby's death, reincarnating him into a cougar who must now recover a golden eagle to regain his human form. This gameplay sequence, a predominantly stressful one as the gamer's health continuously decreases, is crowned by a beautiful animated sequence where Carnby rises from his grave, his hand bursting through the ground — a beautiful tribute to many horror films.

Once again, the main problem of the game is that it is too action-oriented. For the first two thirds of the game, resources are over-abundant, allowing Carnby to display too much firepower. In some way, this appears to foreshadow a tangent that horror games will take almost ten years later with *Resident Evil 4* (Capcom, 2004). Yet, the last portion of *Alone in the Dark 3* manages to salvage some of the *survival horror* spirit. Following the cougar sequence, right after regaining his human form, the gamer may become frustrated to realize that he has lost his entire inventory. From this point, as opposed to *Alone in the Dark 2*, weapons and healing flasks are rare. Therefore, even though this installment of the game is not embedded in horror mythology as much as the original title, it does hold certain qualities in its attempt to stage fear and does meet most of its gamers' expectations.

The Shadows Are Alive: Entering the New Nightmare

It took six more years for Infogrames to fully bring their franchise back on the horror track. Developed by Dark Works, the fourth title of the series, *Alone in the Dark: the New Nightmare* (herein referred to as *AITD: The New Nightmare*) was released in September 2001, and was "destined to give back to Infogrames its status as survival horror maestro" (Roucairol, 2006: 51, freely translated). With a new graphic engine, polished audiovisual aesthetics, and varied gameplay mechanics, the game was up for the challenge. Although *AITD: The New Nightmare* uses narrative premises resembling those found in the earlier titles of the series, the scenario benefits from some freshening up by moving the action from the twenties to the twenty-first century.

After learning that his friend Charles Fisk has been killed while attempting to recover three ancient Abkanis tablets on a mysterious isle called Shadow Island, Edward Carnby is recruited by Frederick Johnson to pursue his deceased friend's quest. Carnby, who accepted the mission mostly to avenge Fisk's death, will team up with an ethnology professor named Aline Cedrac, who was also enlisted by Johnson to retrieve the tablets. Like Carnby, Cedrac has her own reasons for going to the island since she was told by Johnson that Obed Morton, the archaeologist in charge of the Shadow Island project, is her father. While on its way, the plane carrying the two protagonists is attacked by an unknown creature who forces Aline and Carnby to parachute jump before impact. The drop separates the protagonists as they fall respectively in the forest and atop a mansion. From here, their adventure takes them to various frightful locales where they will discover dark secrets.

To appropriately stage fear, *AITD: The New Nightmare* recycles many of the techniques its predecessors established as survival horror games' conventions. It relies once more on a simulated tri-dimensional environment which perfectly supports the integration of fixed virtual cameras, and the borders of the frame are properly used to cause startling effects through a refined technique. This time around, the game repeatedly waits for the gamer to move his avatar near a specific border of the frame before sending in a creature, so available reaction time is considerably reduced improving the element of surprise. To achieve similar effects, the game also makes good use of linear perspective. For example, in Carnby's part of the game, a beautiful startle effect is staged by the combination of field of depth and ingenious camera positioning. A few seconds after the player character enters one of the long narrow corridors of the Morton's manor, a creature passes in front of the camera blocking the gamer's view, primarily diverting his attention from the progression of his avatar. The creature then passively pursues its way in an adjacent corridor. But, at the second the gamer's focus goes back to the actions of his avatar, another Creature of Darkness jumps into the frame right next to him. Coupled with the creature's attack growl, this intrusion is guaranteed to send the gamer's heart racing, even if, as Bernard Perron explains, "To trigger sudden events is undoubtedly one of the basic techniques used to scare someone. However, because the effect is considered easy to achieve, it is often labelled as a cheap approach and compared with another more valued one: suspense" (2004).

Sound also plays a bigger part in the staging of horror. *AITD: The New Nightmare* makes great use of off-screen possibilities. Sometimes used to give prior knowledge of incoming threats, these off-screen sounds contribute towards building quite a deal of apprehension. Occasionally, the sound designer will even "cheat" the mixing to accentuate the effects of forewarning and prolong the tension. As Aline rushes back from the observatory to the fort, hissing sounds, which can be attributed to the "plant monsters," are heard as soon as she sets foot on the ramparts. Since this kind of monster is undeniably one of the most dangerous of all the Creatures of Darkness, caution is advised. In this particular gameplay sequence, the gamer has limited time to reach the inner zone of the fort. As a result, he must continue his descent into the citadel anticipating the apparition of the said monsters each time the camera angle changes but, as the gamer finally notices, the "plant monsters" are located completely at the bottom of the courtyard. Misleading sonic intensity is therefore utilized to fake the proximity of the threat, thus building up suspense. *AITD: The New Nightmare*'s distorted music plays a similar role as it is occasionally used as forewarning, but mostly to punctuate gameplay action sequences.

"The core gameplay of *The New Nightmare* is something that anyone who has played a survival-horror game will instantly be familiar with: limited ammunition and health packs, vague puzzles and clues..." (Tracy, 2001). What's more, the game often takes from *Resident Evil* what had been left out by previous *Alone in the Dark* titles. For example, the game limits the gamer's opportunity of saving. Ink ribbons are replaced by "saving charms," but the beneficial result is the same: "having to go from one save point to another, or coming back to an early one by safety, create[s] a real and relevant dramatic tension since the whole game is precisely about being afraid to die" (Perron, 2006: 36). Those borrowings from the Capcom franchise, however, had a negative impact on the reception of *AITD: The New Nightmare*. The radical critics say the game "has degraded to a *Resident Evil* clone that's harder to save, not as fun to look at, and a generally worse time all around" (Golding, 2004c), while reviewer who are more moderate in their comments admit "it will never be recognised as a great game because it sticks too much with ludic mechanics of the *Resident Evil* series" (Roucairol, 2006:51, freely translated). However, not only does this installment differ from the *Resident Evil* series because — as in most of the *Alone in the Dark* tradition — it does not rely much on gory effects to stage horror, but *AITD: The New Nightmare* improves and innovates on a few concepts.

One of the game's main features is a two-poled narrative structure that allows the gamer to not only experience the game from different narrative points of view, but to experiment diverse gameplay styles. Since specific gaming structures favor one type of *mise en scène* over another, this option alters the means used to stage horrific elements. Choosing Edward Carnby offers a much more action-oriented experience, while picking Aline Cedrac mostly allows the gamer to demonstrate his puzzle-solving skills. Carnby's campaign takes place predominantly in the closed quarters of the mansion, the underground laboratory and in the narrow corridors of the World of Darkness. In those locations, confrontation is often inevitable and the gamer has to blast his way from room to room. In contrast, Aline Cedrac's route is more exploratory and challenging. It takes the gamer from the mansion to the graveyard, then to the fort, the observatory and finally to the underground Abkanis temple. Since Aline begins the game armed with only a flashlight, gameplay takes a notably different approach from Carnby's, encouraging the gamer to run rather than shoot. Although she eventually gets ample weaponry, the game still promotes evasion over action as a way to either save ammunition or save some time. The best way to highlight the differences between both characters' gameplay style can be achieved by analyzing the game's boss battles. With the exception of her first encounter with the mutated Howard Morton (Obed and Alan Morton's father), Aline's battles never actually require the use of firearms. Combat can even be shunned in her final encounter with the mutated Obed Morton, as a quick shift to the left while crossing the fallen cavern pillar leads Aline to safety. In contrast, Carnby's boss battles always require the gamer to blast the monstrous beasts into oblivion (figure 3). As a consequence, while both walkthroughs take advantage of the third-person perspective, the staging of fear in Carnby's gameplay relies mainly on startle effects provoked by a fast influx of monsters through a tight and dynamic visual decoupage, whereas Aline's gameplay draws principally from cinematic advantages to create panic effects.

The second main feature of *AITD: The New Nightmare* lies in its tremendous use of lighting effects. As opposed to previous *Alone in the Dark* titles, this installment represents an incredible exercise of light and shadows. "Oddly enough, ten years and a fourth installment were necessary for the series to respect its basic concept, which was to make good use of obscurity" (Roucairol, 2006: 51, freely translated). In *AITD: The New Nightmare*, the dichotomy between darkness and light is literally at the heart of every possible videoludic level. The narrative framework of the game is completely impregnated by this dichotomy because the main stake of this epic adventure is to prevent creatures from the World of Darkness to invade our world and "drink the blood from the creatures of light." From a gameplay point of view, light serves many purposes. It can sometimes be used as a weapon since some of the Creatures of Darkness are vulnerable to it. From time to time, light replaces guns as a weapon used to exterminate hideous monsters. The flashlight can also be used to find clues that lie in the shadows or to solve specific puzzles. However, the main use for those lighting effects is to create a dreadful atmosphere in which each bit of space can

Figure 3, top: Carnby unloading his shotgun at a flying boss monster in *AITD: The New Nightmare* (DarkWorks, 2001). *Bottom:* Carnby being attacked by Humanz in *Alone in the Dark: Inferno* (Eden Games S.A.S, 2008).

contain an unpleasant encounter. The on-screen space of *AITD: The New Nightmare* is no longer confined to the border of the virtual camera's frame, but reduced to the inside of the slender beam of a flashlight. To add a little spice to the mixture, the lights shut off occasionally when Creatures of Darkness materialize inside a room. Consequently, the game "forces the gamer to constantly search for new sources of light to be able to distinguish his enemies" (Mathieu, 2003: 23 freely translated).

If *AITD: The New Nightmare* is repeatedly discredited by critics for grasping too much of its strategies of *mise en scène* and gameplay mechanics from the *Resident Evil* series, it nevertheless sets new marks as it elaborately uses its narrative structure, gameplay mechanics and astounding aesthetics to deliver an effective scary experience.

Hell on Earth: The Return of Edward Carnby

The most recent game of the *Alone in the Dark* series tried to perfect some of the already established survival horror narrative and gameplay conventions. Regrettably, as a study of its reception will show, it also failed to meet the expectations of most gamers. As opposed to *Alone in the Dark 2*, this result is imputable to a poor execution rather than a disparity between the horrific treatment of the game and the said expectations. With tri-dimensional high-definition graphics and the possibilities of surround sound, *Alone in the Dark* (2008) should have provided the best support for a horror game. Unfortunately, potential technical capacity is not the only criteria necessary to properly stage fear. As many gamers complained, the Xbox 360 version — the first to be released — was "hobbled by its pervasive technical shortcomings" (Watters, 2008b). Even if the PlayStation 3 version — released a few months later under the title *Alone in the Dark: Inferno* (Eden Games S.A.S, 2008) — did overcome some of those flaws, it nevertheless fell short of the true potential that the game held. While the visual aspect of the game is respectable and contributes to the general ambiance with a great use of light and shadows, the sound design is as mediocre as it is inconsistent. Ambiances are poorly designed and sound effects are at times mixed so low it is impossible to hear them. Compared to the complex audio scripting of a contemporary game like *Dead Space* (EA Redwood Shores, 2008), *Alone in the Dark 5*'s sound design does not bring much to the sense of horror throughout the game.

To avoid too much rhetorical turnovers — as most critics themselves have never "been so conflicted about reviewing a game" (Lachel, 2008), it seems necessary at this point to moderate the previous statements. As Chris Matel underlines: "Eden Games has done some interesting things for not only the horror genre, but games in general with *Alone in the Dark*," but most of those characteristics are crippled in some way. As Tristan Kalogeropoulos specifies: "It holds in one hand a seriously interesting and innovative set of features and content and in the other an unpolished, unfinished feel, seeming as if it could have used a little more development time." (2008). As the goal of this essay is to understand how *Alone in the Dark 5* (while the official title does not include the number five, I have added the number in order to differentiate between versions within this essay) manages to scare its gamers, it seems constructive to evaluate some of the designers' ideas which, if they had been correctly executed, could have contributed to construct a frightful — or at least more frightful — experience. Therefore, the objective of this analysis is not to put *Alone in the Dark 5* on trial, but rather to emphasize the impact which the disparity between the good ideas and their poor execution has on the game's staging of fear.

Taking place in a modern-day New York City, the plot of this installment once again stages Edward Carnby as the main protagonist. Amnesiac by the exorcism of a demonic force that inhabited him, Carnby (who is the same Edward Carnby that defeated Pregzt in Derceto in 1924) is compelled to fight hellish monsters plaguing the Central Park area and prevent the imminent return of Lucifer on Earth.

Alone in the Dark 5 is divided into eight episodes which can be navigated through a DVD-like menu accessible on the main screen or when the game is paused. This option proposes a counterpoint to traditional survival horror games as most of them "aim to recreate the cinematic experience, but Eden Studio's *Alone in the Dark* aims for something different, aspiring for the high drama of an HBO series" (McGarvey, 2008). Whether this feature is seen as "an option to skip big chunks of the game" (Lachel, 2008) or simply to "skip the difficult bits without missing anything important" (Bramwell, 2008), the best use for this menu is that it allows the gamer to replay — or simply find — the noteworthy scary segments of the game without relying on a plurality of saved games.

As noted by Tristan Kalogeropoulos: "There are some decently creepy sections within *Alone in the Dark*, such as a severely claustrophobic museum storeroom, with well scripted events including, incredible use of lightning, poltergeists, and voices from beyond the grave" (2008). The Humanz — that is how the possessed humans are referred to in the game — look menacing and the black gooey floor that can swallow the avatar in a flash of a second contribute to the created anticipation (figure 3). But as most critics agree, the videoludic treatment and the narrative framework hold too few of these elements to really scare the gamer. In fact, most reviewers are quite ambivalent about the main attributes of the game.

According to Chris Watters in his online review of the game: "One of the most intriguing and well-executed elements of this adventure is the inventory and item system" (2008a). The original idea behind the inventory is to access it in real time. This means that monsters roaming in the area can still attack the avatar while the gamer is attempting to select a weapon or to combine some of his items into another. This characteristic forces the gamer to carefully plan his attacks. Moreover, this feature often constrains him to run from Lucifer's minions as time is often insufficient to counter attack. Since the inventory is directly located inside the avatar's coat, this strategy also aims to eradicate the frequent opening of non-diegetic menus or visual interfaces, leading towards a sense of videoludic immersion. Following Chris Matel's line of thought: "By implementing various in-game mechanics for real time action, it's possible to find [the gamer] feeling a bit more anxious than [he] would with loads of menus to navigate" (2008). As Matel remarks about the limited spaces for inventory storing, "survival games have always limited [gamers] to what they can carry" (2008). This signifies that *Alone in the Dark 5* is "[s]ticking with the tradition" (2008). But for most reviewers and fans, this inventory system is "the worst feature of the game" (Mills, 2008). Such an assertion is attributable to the fact that "the way to mix items to create others ... was badly done" (Mills, 2008) In the Xbox 360 version of the game, objects must be combined in a precise order. To assemble a Molotov cocktail, the gamer has to pick the tissue first and then combine it with the bottle. Doing the opposite does not work. Those gameplay quirks almost make it impossible to construct weapons without being attacked. Alas, due to many of the fan complaints, the real-time feature, instead of being polished, was removed from the PlayStation 3 version, meaning that the game actually pauses itself while the avatar reaches in his coat or heals himself. This modification relieves the game from huge frustrations but, in the event that this feature would have been properly implemented — mostly considering the item combining issue was fixed in the *Inferno* version, it also deprives the gamer from a dose of game generated anxiety.

Another good idea in its essence was the weapon system. The infernal creatures of the game are only vulnerable to fire, implying that melee weapons and regular bullets can only slow them down. Though Molotov cocktails and fire bullets prove to be quite effective, the lack of inventory space drastically limits their use and confrontation regularly needs to be avoided in order to preserve enough firepower for when fights are obligatory. Therefore, the gamer always needs to find new ways to expose the creatures to flames, such as igniting pieces of wood to bash the monsters right back to hell. Unfortunately, while those techniques are impressive, they weakens the gameplay in some segments of the game. It is particularly the case in the eighth episode where Carnby is asked to get rid of demonic roots spread around Central Park. The roots can only be destroyed with fire. In order to remain within the survival horror concept, the game does not give enough combustibles to destroy the roots efficiently. The time necessary to accomplish this redundant quest, as the gamer must stride in the park over and over again to find means to burn the roots, becomes almost ridiculous. As a result, once again the game generates much more irritation than fun for many gamers.

The Xbox 360 controls and camera work, for their part, are deeply broken — and once again needed fixing for the PlayStation 3 version. Such negative comments about the bulky controls and fixed camera of survival horror games had already been seen in reviews of previous *Alone in the Dark* games. But for the first time, the negative opinions are not only generated because the constraints of the genre are misunderstood. Tristan Kalogeropoulos explains:

> Survival horror titles often use their control as a means of creating a more oppressive world for the [gamer]. Their on-screen avatar's tank movements cause enemies that could deftly be manoeuvred around in an action game to become more imposing than they would be should the controller allow for completely free locomotion, thus creating a greater sense of foreboding [2008].

Apart from Kalogeropoulos, what most critics fail to highlight is that the first mistake of the game is that it tried to mix too many different genres. Part survival horror, part action-adventure game, part platformer, *Alone in the Dark 5* includes them all. The game even borrows from open-ended world action RPGs as, similarly to role playing games' experience points, Carnby must acquire a certain "spectral vision" level by burning demonic roots in order to gain access to the end of the game. While cinematic camera angles and "tank controls" are great when it comes to the staging of fear, they are not adapted for "*Prince of Persia* style traversing environments" (Kalogeropoulos, 2008) or *The Elders Scrolls III: Morrowind* (Bethesda Softworks, 2002) type of gameplay mechanics. In the end, even though *Alone in the Dark 5*'s ambitious ideas tried to improve certain elements that survival horror games had not yet fully exploited, it did not add much to the overall genre.

Conclusion

The *Alone in the Dark* series did not only invent the genre of *survival horror*, it also played an important part in its development. Although the staging of fear in some of the *Alone in the Dark* titles did not hold up to the quality of the first installment, each chapter brought something new, and added some valuable strategies to be used in the survival horror genre. As the reception of the games is mostly conditioned by the horizon of expectations gamers have in regard of the genre, games which fail to meet those expectations are bound to either modify the said horizon of expectations—

like in the case of the original *Alone in the Dark*—or provoke a negative response. However, even though reviews represent a good testimony of the genre evolution, they sometimes fail to clearly objectify the gamers' horizon of expectations, occasionally leading to false interpretations. Therefore, in order to fully understand why the *Alone in the Dark* games received such distinct acclaims, it was necessary to return to the games.

Works Cited

Bramwell, Tom (2008), "Alone in the Dark Review," *Eurogamer.net*, June 8, available online at <http://www.eurogamer.net/articles/alone-in-the-dark-review>.

Chion, Michel (1995), *Le Guide des objets sonores: Pierre Schaeffer et la recherche musicale* (1983), Paris: Buchet/Chastel.

Editorial Member (1995), "Alone in the Dark 2," *Electronic Gaming Monthly*, Vol. 1, No. 69, April, p. 86.

Fahs, Travis (2008), "Alone in the Dark Retrospective," *IGN.com*, June 23, available online at <http://retro.ign.com/articles/883/883558p1.html>.

Golding, Marc (2004a), "If You Can't Take the Heat, Stay Out of Hell's Kitchen," *Honest Gamers.com*, January 14, available online at <http://www.honestgamers.com/systems/content.php?review_id=1826&platform=PC&abr=PC&gametitle=Alone+in+the+Dark+2>.

_____ (2004b), "The Superb Lovecraft Love-In," *HonnestGamers.com*, January 14, available online at <http://www.honestgamers.com/systems/content.php?review_id=1825&platform=PC&abr=PC&gametitle=Alone+in+the+Dark>.

_____ (2004c), "When the Stars Are Right," *HonnestGamers.com*, January 14, available online at <http://www.honestgamers.com/systems/content.php?review_id=1802&platform=PlayStation&abr=PSX&gametitle=Alone+in+the+Dark%3A+The+New+Nightmare>.

Jauss, Hans Robert (1982), *Towards an Aesthetic of Reception*, Minneapolis: University of Minnesota Press.

Jong, Philip (1997a), "Alone in the Dark 2," *AdventureClassicGaming.com*, November 5, available online at <http://www.adventureclassicgaming.com/index.php/site/reviews/36/>.

_____ (1997b), "Alone in the Dark 3," *AdventureClassicGaming.com*, November 2, available online at <http://www.adventureclassicgaming.com/index.php/site/reviews/34/>.

Kalogeropoulos, Tristan (2008), "Alone in the Dark Review: Burning brightly, or left in the dark," *Palgn.com*, July 25, available online at <http://palgn.com.au/article.php?id=12186>.

Lachel, Cyril (2008), "Alone in the Dark Review," *GamingNexus.com*, August 19, available online at <http://www.gamingnexus.com/Article/Alone-in-the-Dark/Item1930.aspx>.

Matel, Chris (2008), "Alone in the Dark Review," *Gamershell.com*, August 13, available online at <http://www.gamershell.com/xbox360/alone_in_the_dark/review.html>.

Mathieu, Bruno (2003), "Alone in the Dark: mieux vaut ne pas rester trop seul dans l'obscurité," *Horror Games Magazine*, No. 1, July-August, pp. 18–23.

McCoy, Jay (2006), "The Horror Is Alive. Immersion, Spectatorship, and the Cinematics of Fear in the Survival Horror Genre," *Reconstruction*, Vol. 6, No. 1, available online at <http://reconstruction.eserver.org/061/mcroy.shtml>.

McGarvey, Sterling (2008), "Alone in the Dark (X360)," *Gamespy.com*, June 25, available online at <http://xbox360.gamespy.com/xbox-360/alone-in-the-dark-360/884413p1.html>.

Metz, Christian (1984), "L'imaginaire et le 'bon objet' dans le cinéma et sa théorie," *Le signifiant imaginaire*, Paris : Christian Bourgeois, pp. 9–26.

Mills, Steven (2008), "Alone in the Dark," *Worthplaying.com*, December 7, available online at <http://www.worthplaying.com/article.php?sid=58086>.

Perron, Bernard (2004), "Sign of a Threat: The Effects of Warning Systems in Survival Horror Games," *COSIGN 2004 Proceedings*, Art Academy, University of Split, pp. 132–141, available online at <http://www.ludicine.ca/sites/ludicine.ca/files/Perron_Cosign_2004.pdf>.

_____ (2006), *Silent Hill: il motore del terrore*, Milan: Costa & Nolan.

Provezza, Bruno (2006), "Interview Frederick Raynal," *Mad Movies*, Special Edition, April, pp. 52–57.

Roucairol, Laurent (2006), "Tenebrae," *Mad Movies*, Special Edition, April, pp. 49–51.

Taylor, Laurie N. (2005), "Towards a Spatial Practice in Video Games," *Gamology*, June 21, available online at <http://www.gameology.org/node/809>.

Thérien, Gilles (1992), "La lisibilité au cinéma," *Cinémas*, Cinéma et Réception, Vol. 2, No. 2–3, Spring, pp. 107–122.

Todd, Brett (2001), "A Modern History of Horror Games Part I," *Gamespot.com*, available online at <http://www.gamespot.com/gamespot/features/pc/history_horror_pt1/index.html>.

Tracy, Tim (2001), "Alone in the Dark: The New Nightmare Review," *Gamespot.com*, June 26, available online at <http://www.gamespot.com/ps/adventure/aloneinthedarkthenn/review.html>.

Watters, Chris (2008b), "Alone in the Dark: Inferno Review," *Gamespot.com*, December 5, available online at <http://www.gamespot.com/ps3/action/aloneinthedark/review.html>.

_____ (2008a), "Alone in the Dark Review," *Gamespot.com*, June 26, available online at <http://www.gamespot.com/xbox360/action/aloneinthedark/review.html>.

Whalen, Zach (2004), "Play Along — An Approach to Videogame Music," *Game Studies*, Vol. 4, No. 1, available online at <http://gamestudies.org/0401/whalen/>.

Wolf, Mark J. P. (2003), "Abstraction in the Videogame," in Bernard Perron and Mark J.P. Wolf (eds.), *The Video Game Theory Reader*, New York: Routledge, pp. 47–65.

Patterns of Obscurity:
Gothic Setting and Light in
Resident Evil 4 and *Silent Hill 2*
Simon Niedenthal

Obeying an urgent summons contained in a mysterious letter, the narrator approaches his destination on a "dull, dark, and soundless day in the autumn of the year, when the clouds hung oppressively low in the heavens" (Poe, 2003: 90). Although this opening is taken from Poe's *Fall of the House of Usher*, it also applies in an almost literal way to the first cut scenes and misty environments of the survival horror digital game *Silent Hill 2* (Konami, 2001).

Echoes of the themes, settings, and ambience of Gothic literature are so frequent in games from the *Silent Hill* (Konami, 1999–2008) and *Resident Evil* (Capcom, 1996–2009) series that it is possible to argue that survival horror games constitute a new form of the Gothic, one in which player activity drives the unfolding of the action. The emotions resulting from enforced player vulnerability — a hallmark of the survival horror genre — as experienced within the narrative themes, player tasks, and virtual architecture of the game worlds, offer a new venue for exploring the depths of fear, terror, and the sublime that were first plumbed by writers such as Anne Radcliffe, Edgar Allen Poe, Matthew Lewis, and H.P. Lovecraft.

Supplementing historical texts with contemporary eyetracking technologies and emotion research demonstrates that these games depend as much upon architectural setting and ambience as they do upon traditional narrative concerns or game balance for the unique power of the emotions they elicit. Patterns of obscurity set the groundwork for the player's ability to appraise and act upon challenges in their environment, as they move through the castles, caverns, and labyrinths of this gruesomely satisfying gothic new media genre.

Survival Horror Games and Gothic Fiction

Broad correspondances between Gothic fiction and survival horror games immediately become apparent when one compares literary definitions of Gothic fiction and emerging attitudes towards the survival horror game genre:

> Gothic novel: "The locale was often a gloomy castle furnished with dungeons, subterranean passages, and sliding panels ... and made bountiful use of ghosts, mysterious disappearances, and other sensational and supernatural occurrences.... The principal aim of such novels was to evoke chilling terror by exploiting mystery and a variety of horrors" [Abrams, 1999: 111].
>
> Survival horror: "Survival horror is a prominent video game genre in which the player has to survive an onslaught of opponents, often undead or otherwise supernatural, typically in claustrophobic environments in a third-person perspective" [www.Wikipedia.org, accessed 13 Dec. 2006].

These entries suggest an intersection of shared concerns around supernatural themes, haunted and claustrophobic settings, and specific effects upon the reader or player. Deeper resemblances can also be traced, and I will argue that an understanding of the Gothic genre, and more particularly the sense qualities of Gothic settings, such as illumination and atmosphere, can enrich our understanding of the experience of survival horror video games. But first, we need to look more closely at the ways in which our experiences of fiction and other non-interactive media, such as film, differ from those of interactive media.

The psychological effect upon the reader or player — whether described as fear, terror, or horror — is central to both the gothic and survival horror genres. Both genres are vehicles for exploring emotional extremes. To return our definition of Gothic fiction:

> The term "Gothic" has also been extended to a type of fiction which lacks the exotic setting of the earlier romances, but develops a brooding atmosphere of gloom and terror, represents events that are uncanny or macabre or melodramatically violent, and often deals with aberrant psychological states [Abrams, 1999: 111].

But it must be noted that the emotional experience of reading fiction and playing a game are very different. Perron (2005a) has drawn upon the film psychology work of Tan, and emotion research of Frijda, to sketch a framework for understanding the emotional impact of interactive media. Frijda argues that emotions are not just passive experiences, but orient us towards action. Initial appraisals of situations are conducted to determine the relevance to one's interests and well-being, and are followed by an evaluation of what can be done, actions that can be taken. Perron further quotes Grodal (2003: 150) as an example of how this process can work in the case of video games:

> It is the player's evaluation of his own coping potential that determines whether (a) confrontation with a monster will be experienced as fear (if the evaluation of his coping potential is moderate), despair (if he feels that he has no coping potentials), or triumphant aggression (if he feels that he is amply equipped for the challenge). This entails that the emotional experience will vary over time, due to the learning processes leading to a change in coping potentials [Grodal, 2003: 150].

It is thus the capacity to act that differentiates interactive media, such as games, from fiction and film, and the emotional experience of interactive media emerges from the intertwined processes of evaluation and action.

One key way in which survival horror games create their emotional effect is by maintaining a state of player vulnerability. The Wikipedia entry emphasizes the way in which this is achieved through game balance and resources: in comparison to shooter games, for example, "the player is made to feel underpowered, generally fighting alone for the bulk of the game, with limited supplies" ("Survival Horror," *Wikipedia: The Free Encyclopedia*). This is of course inherent in the paired terms in "survival horror": the first — survival — indicates a player goal, while the second — horror — refers to an emotional state as well as an existing film and literary genre. The word "survival" indicates that we are in a world of diminished expectation; it isn't called victory horror. One primary activity is self-defense. The player is never free enough to go on the offensive, as in a strategy game, but is maintained in a reactive posture. We begin with simple weapons like blunt sticks. We play alone, but are also often responsible for characters who cannot fully defend themselves (such as Ashley in *Resident Evil 4* or Maria in *Silent Hill 2*), and we face tough bosses such as Pyramid Head in *Silent Hill 2*, who cannot be defeated, only survived. These features of survival horror games underscore the limited powers of the player, and the fact that our tendency must be to evaluate our resources as limited.

Defensive struggle is not the only hallmark activity of survival horror games; drawing from earlier adventure games, there is a fair component of puzzle solving. The player is also suspended in a state of incomplete knowledge. This establishes a varied pace in which moments of feverish activity are leavened with moments of cognitive challenge. It should be noted that puzzle-solving is an important theme in Gothic literature as well, whether explicit, as in the cryptographic challenges of Poe's *The Gold Bug* (1843), or implicit, as in *The Pit and the Pendulum* (1842), in which the narrator has to solve the problem of how to escape a torture device that threatens to vivisect him.

It is not only game resources and cognitive challenges that contribute to the psychological effect of survival horror games. A sense of vulnerability is also produced through the perceptual conditions of the game worlds. I have replayed *Silent Hill 2* and chapters 3 and 4 of *Resident Evil 4* (Capcom, 2005) with knowledge of how to solve the puzzles, as well as armories of weapons bolstered by previous trips through the games. My in-game resources and cognitive preparation were tiptop, yet the games still produced goosebumps. As in my first time through the games, I was compelled forward to the conclusion, almost against my will. And even in the first time through, I wasn't particularly compelled by the narrative framework for either game. In *Silent Hill 2*, we are introduced to James Sunderland and his quest to understand a mysterious letter from his dead wife, while narrative drive is supplied in *Residen Evil 4* by the kidnapping of Ashley, the president's daughter, and subsequent search for her by the intrepid Leon Kennedy. Understanding goosebumps, our physical and psychological response to these compelling games, directs us to look beyond game resources and narrative, to a deeper consideration of the conditions which lead to the emotions of fear, terror, and awe.

Gothic and the Sublime

Much has been written on the distinctions between fear, terror, and horror; these distinctions are relevant to our understanding of the survival horror experience. Perron notes that horror is an emotion that is overwhelming and annihilating in character, and that our experience of games such as *Silent Hill* has little to do with it. Fear is the relevant emotion; in survival horror games, as well as non-interactive media, we seek a "bounded experience of fear" (Perron, 2005b). Writers of gothic fiction were also very interested in the nuances of this particular emotional range. In her essay *On the Supernatural in Poetry*, the Gothic novelist Anne Radcliffe distinguished between terror and horror, arguing the literary value of the former, as well as outlining a poetics of how terror emerges from imagery:

> Terror and horror are so far opposite, that the first expands the soul, and awakens the faculties to a higher degree of life; the other contracts, freezes and nearly annihilates them ... and where lies the great difference between horror and terror, but in ... uncertainty and obscurity [Radcliffe, 1826: 6].

Obscurity in this sense enhances a sense of vulnerability (uncertainty) and is thrilling because it is makes the object of terror indistinct. It should be noted that the opposite of obscurity is not light, but clarity; thus obscurity can be produced by anything that thwarts clear perception: darkness, atmospheric phenomena, or occlusion. Radcliffe compares the experience of reading to that of real life, anticipating the greater range of action possible in survival horror games: "Now, if obscurity has so much affect on fiction, what must it have in real life, when to ascertain the object of our terror, is frequently to acquire the means of escaping it?" (p. 6)

Radcliffe's discussion of obscurity owes a debt to the discourse on the nature of the sublime, which established many of the emotional and aesthetic terms underpinning the Gothic. "Sublime" is a term which has continued relevance in the discussion of how one designs the psychological effect of fictional worlds in which terror is the desired end. Edmund Burke's *A Philosophical Enquiry into the Origin of Our Ideas of the Sublime and Beautiful* (1757) contributed the most to the association of obscurity with terror. In this book, Burke attempts to describe the emotion that corresponds to the sublime, which he defines "the strongest emotion which the mind is capable of feeling" (Burke, 1998 [1757]: 86), and explores the aesthetic means and perceptual conditions by which it can be encouraged. Burke's discussion of the sublime object or setting focuses upon issues of scale and qualities of description; vastness is the favored scale, and obscurity is the favored mode of representation: "To make anything very terrible, obscurity seems in general to be necessary. When we know the full extent of any danger, when we can accustom our eyes to it, a great deal of the apprehension vanishes" (p. 102). Burke goes on to look at the ways in which light, color, and other visual phenomena contribute to these particular effects, with attention to the way in which contrasts can be created:

> I think then, that all edifices calculated to produce an idea of the sublime, ought rather to be dark and gloomy, and this for two reasons; the first is, that darkness itself on other occasions is known by experience to have a greater effect on the passions than light. The second is, that to make an object very striking, we should make it as different as possible from the objects with which we have been immediately conversant [p. 122].

The relationship between indistinctness of representation and that particular emotional response associated with the sublime, first explored by Burke, has been further elaborated in current game studies literature. Grodal (2003) points to a class of video games in which "associative processing of perceptual input is just as important as the motor output." These games are experienced as a "mismatch between grandiose input and blocked output" that was, as Grodal notes, called "'sublime feelings' by the preromantic and romantic poets" (2003: 151).

Burke's emphasis upon scale, vastness and grandeur, coupled with indistinctness of representation, is echoed in contemporary research on an emotion associated with the sublime: the experience of awe. In "Approaching Awe, a Moral, Spiritual, and Aesthetic Emotion," Keltner and Haidt outline a prototypical description of the emotion, with reference to two key features: vastness and accommodation.

> Vastness refers to anything that is experienced as being much larger than the subject, or the subject's ordinary level of experience or frame of reference.... Accommodation refers to the Piagetian process of adjusting mental structures that cannot assimilate a new experience.... The concept of accommodation brings together many insights about awe, including that it involves confusion

(St. Paul) and obscurity (Burke), and that it is heightened in times of crisis, when extant traditions and knowledge structures do not suffice (Weber). We propose that prototypical awe involves a challenge to or negation of mental structures when they fail to make sense of an experience of something vast.... We stress that awe involves a *need* for accommodation, which may or may not be successfully accomplished. The success of one's attempts at accommodation may partially explain why awe can be both terrifying (when one fails to understand) and enlightening (when one succeeds) [Keltner and Haidt, 2003: 306, authors' emphasis].

There are a number of features of survival horror games that also challenge existing mental structures. The theme of the supernatural, for instance (receiving a letter from one's dead wife, or being confronted by zombie monks), requires a thematic accommodation by the player, while the visual qualities of survival horror game worlds require a perceptual accommodation, as we seek to penetrate fog and darkness and make our way in the world. The dual nature of awe — which can lend itself to both terror and enlightenment — helps us better understand the peculiar power of the survival horror genre. Keltner and Haidt also note that the physical marker of awe is piloerection, or goose bumps. Awe and terror are, as Burke originally noted, two sides of the same emotional coin.

At their best, survival horror games create a compelling play experience because they suspend the player in a state of awe and terror. To return to Frijda's terms, obscurity is one means by which the appraisal period is extended, and the player is frozen in a state of uncertainty, in which action is considered but not yet possible (this is one difference between survival horror and first-person shooter games, which are much more about reflex action). Often this is accomplished through strategies of visual obscurity related to darkness, atmosphere, and spatial occlusion.

Positioned in the Labyrinth: Spatial Occlusion and Obscurity

The player begins Chapter 3-1 of *Resident Evil 4* in the empty entrance courtyard of a castle, silent except for the chirp of crickets and the sound of wind. Night and stillness predominate; the gray stone walls are washed with a silvery blue moonlight. Going through a doorway (and waiting for a new scene to load), he works around a curved terrace to the left, and then triggers a cutscene that functions almost like a helicopter shot: moving straight up and panning to the side, revealing an enormous castle complex, in which the evening blue is punctuated by warm flickering torchlight. The overall tone is strikingly similar to Emily's first view of of Radcliffe's castle of Udolpho:

... the gothic greatness of its features, and its mouldering walls of dark grey stone, rendered it a gloomy and sublime object. As she gazed, the light died away on its walls, leaving a melancholy purple tint, which spread deeper and deeper, as the thin vapour crept up the mountain, while the battlements above were still tipped with splendour.... Silent, lonely, and sublime, it seemed to stand the sovereign of the scene, and to frown defiance on all, who dared to invade its solitary reign. As the twilight deepened, its features became more awful in obscurity ... [Radcliffe, 1794].

The effect of the cut-scene is complex. It occurs as the player moves into a new segment of the game, after leaving the muted daylight of a village and its surrounding countryside. As an introduction to a new game environment, the cut-scene grants the player a foretaste of the qualities of the space to come, but at the same time avoids giving away any information about the adversaries that will be immediately encountered upon moving forward. As the player moves forward after the cut-scene, one hears a low, unintelligible chanting sound without a visible source. Moving around a corner, she spies sentry monks patrolling on a parapet, circulating perpendicularly to the player. A few sniper shots, or a carefully lobbed grenade, and then it is up the stairs, to where the fiery catapults await.

Resident Evil 4 could be described as a game of positioning. It is not possible to both run and shoot at the same time, depriving the player of the strafing capabilities of a first-person shooter. Like Kevin VanOrd has noted in his review of the Nintendo Wii version of the game: "Once you've drawn your weapon, you can't walk, but you can aim. It all feels very deliberate, but it's perfectly countered by the measured speed at which your enemies approach you" (VanOrd, 2007). The player moves, assesses the environment and its threats, takes a position, and acts. Flight and fight are both good options, but he can't do both, one must make a decision. The importance of the avatar's relationship to the virtual space (and attendant sense of player vulnerability) is compounded by the slow speed with which one is able to rotate one's perspective. The fact that the game is one of positioning means that one must master the environment as much as one must master opponents. The deliberate nature of the game as noted by VanOrd means that the player is forced to engage in a more conscious decision-making process with reference to navigation and threat assessment, and suspends the player in a particular mode of action and reaction. It is here that we can perhaps most clearly understand what Grodal means by a "mismatch between grandiose input and blocked output." The relationship between game environments and the deliberate nature of player activity constitutes one of the sources of the power of *Resident Evil 4*.

As Burke mentions, our experiences are often shaped through contrast; we feel things more strongly when opposites are juxtaposed. The modulation of contrasting perceptual states contributes to the pace and rhythm of playing through *Resident Evil 4*. Spatial perception and visual occlusion in the castle section of *Resident Evil 4*, for example, is shaped by navigation through environments in which regularity and axial symmetry is contrasted with meandering features. This contrast is often felt when we move from the ceremonial and regular spaces of the castle (Hall of Rites, Hall of Water, for example), to the winding tunnels and passages beneath the ground level, such as the Mine and Processing plant. Purposeful navigation and visual perception on the horizontal plane is often stymied in *Resident Evil 4* and *Silent Hill 2* by labyrinthine spaces. These spaces correspond closely to the Gothic prototype. With reference to the stories of Poe, David Leatherbarrow contends that:

> The labyrinth is the form of most of Poe's interior passages. Spatial movement in Poe's fiction is typically an ongoing negotiation with unexpected obstacles and unforeseen changes in direction.... In such a place one was always without external reference and fixed orientation. Any sequence is alternately redirected by intermediate walls and panels as well as vertically by steps in ascent or descent [Leatherbarrow, 1986: 13].

Labyrinths in survival horror games come in several varieties. There are spaces that are explicit labyrinths, such as the nighttime hedge maze inhabited by wolf-like Colmillos in Chapter 3-2 of *Resident Evil 4*. In this setting, tight quarters, frequent turnings, and slow avatar rotation, combined with the speed of the opponents, add to the sense of vulnerability. There are also spaces that are implicitly labyrinthine. Perhaps most fiendish, and effective, is the labyrinthine section of *Silent Hill 2* in which navigation through a banal interior space is rendered much more difficult when the map function, upon which the player has relied, becomes unreliable. Normally, the player locates a map for a new environment upon entering it, and progress (such as doors that have been opened, or tried and found to be locked) is updated continually. In the labyrinth section, no overview is granted. The map is only updated to show player progress, sketching hallways as they are traversed. It cannot be used for wayfinding or to plan one's movement. Frequent backtracking is necessary, which is complicated by the fact that Pyramidhead prowls in a random fashion through the suterannean sections of the labyrinth.

Navigation on the vertical axis is also an important contrast in both games. In *Silent Hill 2*, vertical movement often takes the form of jumping into darkness, where one cannot see the bottom of the pit. Confronting this primal fear within the safe confines of the game is the only way to move forward. It has been argued that there is an aesthetic of the vertical in video games (Johansson, 2003); in virtual spaces devoid of gravity, one is freer to play on this dimension. And indeed, one experiences a kind of extension of the vertical dimension in the middle section (Silent Hill Historical Society and Toluca Prison) of *Silent Hill 2*, in which one jumps and descends repeatedly, seemingly travelling great vertical distances to go a very little way in the actual space of the game world, moving from the level of the town down to the shore of Toluca Lake through the prison section. Upward vertical movement is also important in the castle sequence of *Resident Evil 4*, in which the climactic boss fight is preceded by a lengthy ascent to the top of a tower, the ascent to which is foreshadowed by a cut-scene at the beginning of Chapter 4-3. Once again, these spaces correspond to the archetypal spaces of gothic fiction. Hennelly argues that the figure of the cathedral unites the varying archetectonic forces of the gothic, playing vertical aspirations against underlying caverns, natural forms against artificial symmetry: "The artifice in Gothic cathedrals mocks the natural models of forest trees, stressing especially the vertical tension between spiritual spires and charnel/carnal catacombs, what The Monk terms 'vaults above and caverns below'" (2001).

Darkness and Obscurity

Dark environments are a cliché within the horror genre. Therefore, it is important to reiterate that darkness is only one means of creating the obscurity that lends itself to the sublime terror of the survival horror genre. That said, it is possible to note that the patterns of darkness that one experiences in *Resident Evil 4* result from several different dynamics. First, *Resident Evil 4* exhibits a single day/night cycle over the game as a whole, beginning in the daytime, followed by dusk and night, and the final cut-scene image is a sunrise (this pattern is very similar to *Silent Hill 2*). The bulk of the action in the game takes place at night, or under moonlight, though much occurs in interior spaces where we are less aware of changes in the time of day. The differences between day and night illumination are, according to the design team in the "Making of" *Resident Evil 4* video (Capcom, 2008), deliberately dramatic, and are intended to support variations in the way in which enemies are perceived. Other patterns of darkness emerge not from the structure of value in the overall form of the game, but arise rather as a function of player navigation through simulated 3D spaces. Light and dark in the games often correspond to the implied source of simulated illumination in the scene, whether coming from torches, incandescent lighting, or flashlights. Movement from exterior to interior environments also creates changes in overall illuminance levels.

Besides supporting an overall sense of spatial and temporal progression through the game, the distribution of light and dark illumination in *Resident Evil 4* environments also displays a logic that enhances a sense of player vulnerability through obscurity. The darkest environments in the game occur in the middle of the castle sequence, in the almost completely black Storeroom (Chapter 3-4). One plays through this sequence as Ashley, the character with the most limited health and defensive resources, and hence the greatest vulnerability. This segment is notable for being the only one in the game in which the source of illumination is a flashlight shining from the perspective of the player's avatar. The scene, in which the dusty Armaduras, first revealed in Ashley's flashlight's beam, subsequently come to clanking, dangerous life, is a striking moment, a passage of intense creepiness, and one that invites comparison to other survival horror games, such as *Silent Hill 2*, in which the flashlight is frequently the main source of illumination.

Another important strategy of obscurity through darkness in survival horror has to do with exploiting the darkness edge in individual environments. A good example of this is the behavior of the split-head hounds in *Silent Hill 3* (Konami, 2003). In the Silent Hill amusement park and subway sections, they often lope along just outside pools of illumination, just barely perceived in the darkness, before making forays towards the player's avatar. The edge of darkness functions in these cases as a focus of attention (and worry) in itself.

Tracking the Edges: Atmospherics and Obscurity

The opening sequence of *Silent Hill 2* must be considered a masterpiece of game exposition. First the letter, a bathroom, a winding trail, a smear of blood on the asphalt, a blunt piece of wood, and, finally, we experience the terror of the writhing, unrecognizable human form (reminiscent of the "floundering, squealing white thing on which Sir John Clave's horse had trod one night in a lonely field" in H.P. Lovecraft's *Rats in the Walls* (1923)). Told through cut-scene, voiceover and music, experienced through player navigation and exploration, the opening sequence introduces us to a character and his motivation, and we learn on our own how to move forward into Silent Hill. Most of all it is the mist that serves as the binding substance of the exposition; fog in *Silent Hill 2* is a fluid, permeable medium that is endlessly fascinating, as it both hides and reveals.

Strategies of obscurity involving atmospherics are exploited fully in *Silent Hill 2*. In contrast to the prototypical gothic environments of *Resident Evil 4*, the settings of *Silent Hill 2* owe more to the North American small town gothic of David Lynch. No castles here; rather, the haunted house becomes the haunted community. Vastness is exchanged for the familiar and quotidian, and dramatic lighting is replaced with fog and grainy indistinctness. The environments of *Silent Hill 2* contain fewer of the traditional settings of the gothic sublime, but rather participate in the "uncanny," the *unheimlich*. As

Vidler writes, "for Freud, 'unhomeliness' was more than a simple sense of not belonging; it was the fundamental propensity of the familiar to turn on its owners, suddenly to become defamiliarized, derealized, as if in a dream" (1992: 45). In many parts of the game, when one is on the streets of the town, large portions of the frame are simply rendered as darkness or atmospheric fog. Against a background of anticipatory sound, punctuated by growls and radio static, obscurity enhances the sense of vulnerability and suspense.

The degree to which the fog of the opening scenes of *Silent Hill 2* dominates our attention is revealed in eyetracker studies. Gustaf Berg, Niklas Norin, Staffan Persson & Johan Ögren — students at Gotland University in Sweden — conducted eyetracker studies of the first exterior environments of the game, as well as segments inside the Woodside apartments (2006). Running tests with subjects of differing degrees of survival horror experience and skill, they analyzed the data by plotting eye fixations (where the players looked, and how long) at one-second intervals. The players spent an average of 31.5 percent of their playing time scanning the fog edge, which is defined as the transparent area just on the border of visibility. This data supports just how important the strategy of obscurity through fog is in the opening sequence of *Silent Hill 2*. This is especially true if we are new to the game, and are not yet sure of what we will encounter. The students also compared the fog edge with the darkness edge that results from flashlight usage within the Woodside apartment complex interior sequences, which are mostly played out in small rooms and tight hallways. Here they found that the darkness edge was much less emphatic, drawing the attention of the players only about 5 percent of the time. One interpretation is that this attention is a function of felt vulnerability. In expansive, outdoor environments, sources of danger can approach from almost any direction, while in claustrophobic spaces there are much more limited angles of access. The darkness edge in the Woodside apartments often overlaps with interior architecture and walls. As Perron has noted, this dynamic is different in survival horror games such as those from the *Fatal Frame* series (Tecmo, 2001–2008), in which ghosts can approach through walls.

Conclusion

Whether our journey takes us through labyrinths, darkness, or mist, in the end, survival is its own reward. Our journey through the caverns, castles, and haunted houses of survival horror games is a compelling experience in which we can taste the emotion of fear most fully, because we can (eventually) act in the face of our fears. It is the process of perception and action — scanning, anticipating, feeling, and doing — that is exercised by these games.

The magnificent gothic spaces of *Resident Evil 4* and the uncanny, fogbound and surreal ambiance of *Silent Hill 2* offer two quite different explorations of gothic themes in interactive media. They provide a new media playground for an established genre.

Acknowledgments

Thanks to Charlotte Sennerstein and Craig Lindley for sharing the eye-tracking work of their students from Gotland University. Thanks also to Gustaf Berg, Niklas Norin, Staffan Persson & Johan Ögren of Gotland University for their hard work and useful insights. An earlier version of this article was presented at the Gothic and Horror in Literature, Film and Computer Games Conference, Lund University, Sweden, in December of 2006. The conference was organized by Claes-Göran Holmberg.

Works Cited

Abrams, M. H. (1999), *A Glossary of Literary Terms, Seventh edition*, New York: Harcourt Brace.

Berg, Gustaf, Niklas Norin, Staffan Persson, and Johan Ögren (2006), Looking for the Invisible: Eyetracking within Limited Visual Spaces, unpublished student paper, Charlotte Sennersten, supervisor, Gotland University, Sweden.

Burke, Edmund (1998), *A Philosophical Enquiry into the Origin of Our Ideas of the Sublime and Beautiful* (1757), London: Penguin Books.

Grodal, Torben (2003), "Stories for Eye, Ear and Muscles: Video Games, Media and Embodied Experiences," in Wolf, Mark J. P. & B. Perron (eds.), *The Video Game Theory Reader*, New York: Routledge, pp. 129–155.

Hennelly, Mark (2001), "Framing the Gothic: From Pillar to Post-structuralism," *College Literature*, Fall, available online at <http://findarticles.com/p/articles/mi_qa3709/is_200110/ai_n8985157/pg_14>.

Johansson, Troels Degn (2003), "Vertigo and Verticality in Super Monkey Ball" in M. Copier & J. Raessens (eds.), *Level Up*: Digital Games Research Conference, Utrecht University, Utrecht, Netherlands, pp. 374–381.

Keltner, Dacher, and Jonathan Haidt (2003), "Approaching Awe, a Moral, Spiritual and Aesthetic Emotion," *Cognition and Emotion*, Vol. 17, No 2, pp. 297–314.

Leatherbarrow, David (1986), "The Poetics of the Architectural Setting: A Study of the Writings of Edgar Allan Poe," in M. Martin (ed.), *VIA 8*, New York: Rizzoli, pp. 7–15.

Lovecraft, Howard Phillips (1923), *The Rats in the Walls*. Available online at <http://www.dagonbytes.com/thelibrary/lovecraft/theratsinthewalls.htm18/4/2008>.

Perron, Bernard (2005a), "A Cognitive Psychological Approach to Gameplay Emotions," *Changing Views: Worlds in Play. Proceedings of DiGRA 2005 Conference*, Vancouver, available online at <http://www.digra.org/dl/db/06276.58345.pdf>.

_____ (2005b), "Coming to Play at Frightening Yourself: Welcome to the World of Horror Video Games," *Online Proceedings, Aesthetics of Play Conference* University of Bergen, Bergen, Norway, available online at <http://www.aestheticsofplay.org/perron.php>.

Poe, Edgar Allan (2003), *The Fall of the House of Usher and Other Writings*, London: Penguin Books.

Radcliffe, Ann (1794), *The Mysteries of Udolpho*, available online at <http://www.gutenberg.org/browse/authors/r#a114718/4/2008>.
_____ (1826), *On the Supernatural in Poetry*, available online at <http://www.litgothic.com/Authors/authors.html>.
VanOrd, Kevin (2007), "Review of Resident Evil 4 (Wii)," Gamespot.com, June 19, available online at <http://www.gamespot.com/wii/action/residentevil4/review.html?om_act=convert&om_clk=gssummary&tag=summary;review>.
Vidler, Anthony (1992), *The Architectural Uncanny: Essays in the Modern Unhomely*, Cambridge, Massachusetts: MIT Press.

Hair-Raising Entertainment: Emotions, Sound, and Structure in *Silent Hill 2* and *Fatal Frame*

Inger Ekman and Petri Lankoski

Introduction

Playing video games is an emotional experience. This should come as no surprise to anyone who has touched a gamepad, keyboard or joystick. But precisely what is it in horror games that makes people react emotionally and how does game design influence what emotions the player is likely to experience? In this essay we will attempt to answer both of these questions, focusing on a particular element of game design and its application in horror games: *the use of sound.*

The horror genre is interesting to analyze for several reasons. In terms of affective impact, horror games work with an exceptionally broad selection of emotions — ranging from visceral feelings of disgust to ecstasy, loathing to sympathy, suspense and fear to relief. Particularly, the survival horror genre is fascinating in its extensive use of negative affect; and the experience of playing such a game is a thrilling series of shocking, frightful and disgusting events. Horror also relies to a great deal on sound for creating and supporting those emotions. Regarding the early horror film, Whittington mentions how sound became one of the main tools for maintaining narrative cohesion in films that otherwise would have lacked tension and suspense (Whittington, 2007: 131). The emphasis on sound has remained important even as the genre has matured. We suggest a reason for this resides in sound's ability to tap into emotional responses in a way that is extremely powerful, yet subtle enough to escape our conscious attention.

The typical emotional effects of horror can be categorized as suspense and usually relate to worry and fear. Carroll (1990) further suggests that horror relies heavily on monsters, invoking a unique combination of the emotions fear and disgust. In this essay we will introduce a framework for

181

understanding emotional sound in games. We will use this framework to analyze how sound has been applied in practice, and compare the use of emotional sound design techniques in two different horror games: *Silent Hill 2*
(Konami, 2003) and *Fatal Frame*, aka *Project Zero* in Europe (Tecmo, 2001).
We will examine how these games employ both traditional audiovisual tools,
as well as techniques unique to games, in order to create and manipulate
player emotions. This analysis will allow us to look at concepts central to the
horror genre, and in particular at how sound contributes to the horror-
specific emotions of fear and disgust.

The essay is structured as follows: next, we will introduce the central concept of this essay, emotion, and present a framework for analyzing emotional
game sound. We will then proceed into the details of the framework, looking at the various influencing factors involved in the process of creating emotion, and apply them to the analysis of sound in *Silent Hill 2* and *Fatal Frame*.
We will consider in particular how the identified features contribute to two
emotions typical to horror: fear and disgust. The investigation will be limited to a very specific set of games, as the two games under investigation have
been selectively chosen both by theme (horror), but also by genre (action
adventure). We conclude with a discussion about the generality of our
findings, and the particular aspects that the horror genre introduces in terms
of sound design.

Understanding Emotion in Games and Game Sound

A central concept throughout this essay is emotion. For most people,
the word *emotion* would seem intuitive. Let us nevertheless consider briefly
what having an emotion implies. Oatley and Jenkins describe emotions as
evaluations of a specific (visceral and urgent) type, which signal events of
critical importance and relevance to the perceiver (1996: 96). An emotion is
experienced as a distinctive type of mental state, sometimes accompanied or
followed by bodily changes, expressions, and actions. Emotions provide the
perceiver with an evaluation of the event, (typically) producing either a positive or negative sensation referred to as *valence*. Emotions also create a sense
of urgency. The activation part of emotions is called *arousal*.

The above description of emotion only considers what an emotion is. It
does not take into account how or what causes emotions, other than saying
that emotion emerges as the result of evaluation. Looking at the function
emotions serve can help us understand why emotions arise.

The emotional system is optimized for, but by no means restricted to
survival-related evaluations. Emotions are a fundamental part of all decision-making, and they influence so called "rational" decisions, also such deci-

sions that experientially would appear non-emotional. Moreover, even if the word *evaluation* is suggestive of conscious, deliberate reasoning, only a small part of the evaluations that underlie emotional reactions are made consciously. Much emotional processing takes place unconsciously, and some emotional reactions precede cognition (Damasio, 2005: 125–164; Zajonc, 1980). The body employs emotions much like an alarm system, signaling evaluations that pertain to our survival. In terms of experience, an important function of the emotional system is to ensure that whenever something of significance happens, we pay attention. Emotions involve mental and bodily changes that are all geared towards the purpose of survival, ensuring we take appropriate action when it is needed (Damasio, 2005: 165–180).

In the following sections we shall consider how games engage the emotional system. We will pay special attention to the functions of sound in creating and contributing to emotions. The analysis combines various theories explaining emotional reactions to interactive audiovisual media.

Ekman (2008) underlines three aspects that contribute to the emotionality of game sound. Part of the emotions during play arise as a result of cognitive evaluations, either related to (1) narrative comprehension or (2) goal-related evaluations. Sound influences interpretations through its functional role of providing or withholding information necessary for making such evaluations. Additionally, sounds trigger (3) low-level emotional responses and are involved in automatic processes. These low-level responses modify perception and tint the experience with emotion, while the processes by which they function remains outside conscious attention.

It is necessary to remember that the presence of game structures or representational qualities that are capable of causing emotion by no means guarantee that the player will have a certain experience. Especially with consciously made evaluations (but as we will see, less so with automatic responses), the process is guided, one might well say determined, by personal characteristics of the player: skills, knowledge, musical preferences, and personal history.

Ekman's framework will serve as a starting point for our analysis. We will first look at the evaluative systems at work in gameplay and introduce the underlying emotional theory, identifying the game elements that have a central role in conscious emotional evaluations. We will then proceed to look at low-level emotional responses and other automatic processes and the emotional possibilities this introduces for game sound.

Evaluations, Emotions and Sound Design

Games utilize many of the same representational techniques as traditional audiovisual media, such as film and television. Many games incorporate momentarily movie-like elements, so called "cinematics." They include everything from pre-scripted animation to cut-scenes and can be used to create emotion in games much in the same way that they are used in any linear production.

The addition of player activity extends the available techniques for eliciting emotion beyond audiovisual tools. Therefore, thinking about game emotions only as an extension or development of film is not satisfactory. In terms of activity, playing is characterized on the one hand by challenge, and on the other by the player successfully overcoming those challenges and thus gaining access to continued playing. Players are making choices and forming strategies, executing plans, and facing both mental and motor challenges, which open up for new tools of emotional design through interaction design and game structure.

According to Ekman (2008), when it comes to eliciting emotions, narrative comprehension and goal-oriented evaluations are two approaches linked in a contradictory manner in terms of the sounds they utilize. However, Lankoski (2007) suggests that the player character provides a common ground for making both narrative and goal-related evaluations. For this analysis, we will extend Ekman's framework to accommodate the sonic representations of player character as an attempt to find points of contact between the two evaluative systems.

SOUND, PLAUSIBILITY, AND NARRATIVE COMPREHENSION

The primary way of creating emotion with cinematics and film-like techniques in games is through empathy: as viewers, we typically attend to the fates of characters. The characters of a story allow us both a way to reflect on the emotional impacts of events, and reasoning about the intentions of characters provides a strategy for understanding the story (Smith, 1995; Currie, 1995). Whenever we empathetically relate to certain characters (usually the protagonist), we also come to have a vested interest in how the story progresses. Our empathetic relation allows us to associate emotional content to *narrative comprehension*, and also explains why we can have such strong feelings about fictive events (Tan, 1995; Tan and Frijda, 1999; Smith 1995).

Tan (1995) suggests that a sense of *apparent realism* is a prerequisite for experiencing empathetic emotions in film. In terms of supporting narrative comprehension, the key role of sound is to make both the characters and the events that happen around them appear plausible (enough), so that the viewer can relate empathetically to them. For example, event sounds such as the crash of impacts add a sense of physical body to images depicted on the screen. An important point to note is that apparent realism is heightened not by realistic sound, but by sounds with high *narrative fit*—sounds that seem realistic in the context of the story, style, and culture (Ekman, 2008). This is why we hear explosions in space films even if in reality, there would be no sound in a vacuum.

Sounds can also facilitate narrative comprehension in ways other than making events appear real. They aid story comprehension by selectively attracting attention to events which are important for understanding the story; in the constructed reality of film, nonsignificant events may simply be left without sound. Sounds also bring forth particular aspects of objects and characters, for example, highlighting the clumsiness of a person by emphasizing their movement sounds. The way sound is portrayed can signal shifts between subjective and objective view. For example, accompanying a shot of a conversation with a muffled dialogue creates a sense that the scene is being viewed (by someone) excluded from the conversation, for instance a secret observer. Sound is also essential in representing the passage of time, and it structures the larger narrative by influencing perception of pace and direction. When sound develops smoothly over cuts, it provides continuation (to the point of masking cuts altogether), making scenes feel like they link together.

FUNCTIONAL SOUND AND GOAL-RELATED EVALUATION

Several scholars explain the emotionality of gameplay. Perron (2005) extends Tan's framework with a category for gameplay emotions that relate to the evaluations the player makes while playing. Lankoski (2007) and Ravaja et al. (2006) make similar suggestions, again, linking emotion to the structural content of games. The common evaluative context for game emotions in these accounts is the relation between player and the goal set. In general, *goal-driven evaluations* link actions with emotional effect (Oatley, 1996; Power and Dalgleish, 1997). Furthermore, in playing, no single event is evaluated in isolation. Just like films evolve as they go along, sequences of actions in games allow deeper emotional development. Every minute of playing is an investment, and every advance in the game brings the player closer to a goal (and also contributes to the construction of a story). Within this system, sequential actions combine to build up more complex emotions—for example, care, commitment or loss (Bura, 2008).

The function of game sound in goal-related evaluations is tied to action. Sound provides necessary information for decision-making, thus serves a functional role in achieving goals. Ekman (2005) and Joergensen (2007) both note that most often games are not even trying to portray the game world's sounds very realistically. Instead, sounds are overly simplified, and they tend to match game actions categorically. Further, the manner in which sounds portray events in the game appears purposefully unrealistic. These apparent inconsistencies, however, appear logical when considered in terms of function. The sound design favors simplicity and clarity in order to be helpful to the player — to allow distinguishing important events, detecting changes in game state and planning and executing actions. Game sound is free to challenge narrative fit since it is primarily serving a function other than maintaining narrative plausibility: its role is to facilitate gameplay and help the player make meaningful choices (Joergensen, 2007).

The functional role of sound opens up a new possibility for emotional effect. The *functional fit* refers to the ease by which sound provides information for performing actions (Ekman, 2008). Challenging or enhancing the functional fit of sound changes how readily a player can access the information they need to make gameplay-related evaluations. Through this function, sound influences goal-related evaluations.

The contradictory relation between sound with high *functional fit* and sound with high *narrative fit* necessitates selectivity in the design process. However, this does not exclude the possibility of using both narrative and gameplay-related effects within the same game. The contradictory relation between the two sound strategies suggests only that one and the same sound is unlikely to have high narrative and functional fit at the same time. Thus, in any game, there will be some sounds that are more plausible in a narrative sense, while others emphasize functionality. Nevertheless, players' interpretation of sounds will always be influenced jointly by both aspects. In fact, the contradictory relation between the two approaches can be used for emotional purposes as well. Purposefully creating sounds that evoke maximally contradictory evaluations can invoke a heightened sense of uncertainty and confusion by providing mixed signals. For example, one could choose sounds that are totally out of narrative context to support gameplay, instead of simplified realistic sounds.

THE MEETING OF STORY AND GAMEPLAY: THE PLAYER CHARACTER

To reiterate, the two evaluative frameworks based on *narrative comprehension* and *goal-related evaluations* are basically contradictory. The typical story, with linear structure, leaves little room for player choice. Similarly, an interactive structure defies linear storytelling. Yet, alongside gameplay emotions, many games invite the player to form empathetic relations to characters. Particularly, the *player character* can bridge the empathetic (narrative comprehension) viewpoint with gameplay (Lankoski, 2007). The evaluative process of story and gameplay combine whenever the player character's narrated goals meet with the game goals. In its most simple form, this is expressed by emphasizing that the survival of the player character is prerequisite to continued play.

Further possibilities are introduced if making goal-related decisions requires understanding the player character, such as reasoning about the characters' skills, thoughts or feelings (Lankoski, 2007). Likewise, the design of character sounds and expressions can fulfill both a narrative and a functional role at the same time. For example, expressions and vocalizations of the player character evoke empathy, and also signal to the player how an event is to be interpreted in terms of success or failure.

Low-level Emotional Responses and Automatic Processes

Empathetic emotions require attending to the story, while goal-related emotions require taking an interest in the game. However, part of the emotions we have while watching films have nothing to do with *consciously evaluating or even attending to the events* in terms of story (Tan 1995). The same applies to games. Much of the emotional impact of both film and games rely on these unconscious evaluations. It has been suggested that this is how music influences the perception of events when viewing film (Cohen, 2001; Marshall and Cohen, 1988) and the concept has also been applied to sound effects in games (Ekman, 2008).

Unconscious Emotion

When viewing a film or playing a game, part of our emotions are essentially just reactions. They nevertheless pertain to a wide variety of emotional experiences, and emotional reactions can completely change the evaluations we make at higher levels of processing. In fact, extreme emotions can override all reasoning. People with phobias know this well. Even when rational thought tells them that a picture of a spider could not possibly harm them, they cannot help but be frightened or disgusted by it (LeDoux, 1996; Power and Dalgleish, 1997: 174–184).

In general, every perceived element of a game arouses emotion. As players, we are constantly moved emotionally, if ever so slightly, as we consciously or unconsciously evaluate the events we encounter. However, most of the time, we will be too busy focusing on a very small subset of events to notice the vast number of other events that influence how we feel at a given moment. In terms of representations, visual primacy (both as a perceptual phenomenon and cultural convention) usually insures that sound receives less conscious attention than the picture. Moreover, whereas visual information in games is limited to the screen, sounds (changes in air pressure) extend into space, even interacting with it. Sounds create continuity and presence, and as a result, confuse the borders of fiction. This is partly what makes sound such an effective shortcut to emotions.

ESTABLISHING AGENCY

A special case of unconscious emotion is related to the player's feeling of *agency*. Agency, here, refers to a perceived causality between one's actions and the events in the game. By introducing action, games necessarily provide the players some access to the fictive world portrayed by the game. Sound is essential in shaping this relation. In film, the coupling of action and representation relies on synchrony, both the action and the sound are representational (visual and sound) (Chion 1994). In games, instead of merely observing events as they take place, players discover the game world by active exploration; they don't just watch objects collide, but instead make them collide. Because the sounds of the game world are linked to action, sound can take on functions similar to real-world interaction. Not only does game sound tell us something about objects on screen, it also tells us about the relation between players own actions and the sounding object within the game (Ekman, 2005).

In games, the simultaneity of action and response allows the player to perceive actions performed at the physical interface as actions performed within the game. The quality of such action sounds serves as a confirmation of the action-control relation between player and character. Chion (1998) writes about "ergo audition," referring to the experience of hearing one's own actions in the world. He emphasizes the importance, even pleasure, of this feedback, and the subjective experience of having access to and impact on the world. In games, the player character sounds—walking, jumping, and hitting—serve as ergo audition. They establish and also symbolize the player's access to the world, presence within it, and control of actions. The feeling of being in control (or not) is a typical unconscious emotion. It precedes cognitive evaluation of goal structure or story progression—it shapes these processes. Interfering with the sonic feedback of actions decouples action from effect, removing the sensation of control within the game and replacing it instead with an experience of fiddling with the controller.

AFFECTIVE MIMICRY

Humans have a tendency to automatically mimic emotional expressions. This phenomenon, termed *affective mimicry*, is an unconscious emotional process in which a person will automatically mirror emotions of others. According to this theory, a smile (or any other emotional expression) is contagious: simply seeing someone smile will make us smile as well. Experimental research investigating affective mimicry suggests that this mimicking is completely involuntary and fully autonomous and it can range from small (invisible to the eyes) muscle movements to perceivable expressions (Dimberg, Thunberg and Elmehed, 2000). Affective mimicry appears to underlie the social behavior of humans and to provide a neurological foundation for empathy (Jackson and Decety, 2004). Indeed, the similarity of brain responses between performing and perceiving actions has prompted researchers to suggest that mimicry more generally forms the basis of understanding others (Jackson and Decety, 2004; Niedenthal et al., 2005).

In games with recognizable characters, it is likely that affective mimicry plays a role in the process of invoking empathetic emotions. Affective mimicry differs from narrative comprehension in that the reaction is hardwired. Mimicry precedes understanding of story. It arises automatically, mirroring the feelings of the person we are watching, or hearing. This means we can empathize with characters we do not sympathize with, which would not be the case if all empathetic emotions were evaluated through vested interest in the character's survival.

Tricks and Treats of the Survival Horror Genre: A Comparison Between Silent Hill 2 and Fatal Frame

In the preceding section of this essay, we have covered how emotions arise as a result of evaluative processes during gaming. These evaluations can be the result of cognitive processes. Emotions are also caused in a reactive manner, through the various low-level responses we have with our environment. Emotional responses to story elements rely on representation enhancing narrative comprehension, while gameplay emotion benefits from focusing design efforts on functionality and facilitating performance. The player character provides an exception, as it is capable of communicating goals simultaneously through representation and function. However, in all other representations, the contradiction between the two frameworks prompts either choosing one strategy over the other, or using the contradictions intentionally for added tension. This understanding has guided our investigation towards particular elements of interest in terms of emotional design. In terms of representation, key videoludic elements are game *characters* on the one hand (both the player character and non-player characters), and the *environment* on the other. There are two conceptual elements that are central in terms of goal-related evaluations: *threat* and *goal*. We will now look at how these elements and effects are used in *Silent Hill 2* and *Fatal Frame*.

Introducing *Silent Hill 2* and *Fatal Frame*

Silent Hill 2 revolves around a character named James Sunderland. Mary, James' wife, has died three years ago due to a serious illness. In the game, James has received a letter signed with her name, so he travels to Silent Hill to investigate the source of the letter. During his search, he encounters the strange and unnatural creatures that occupy Silent Hill. The game guides its player through the town, and in particular places that James is said to have visited with his late wife. The gameplay consists of solving puzzles, while sneaking past or fighting monsters.

The main character in *Fatal Frame* is a young girl, named Miku Hinasaki. She is looking for her brother, Mafuya Hinasaki, who has disappeared after going into a cursed mansion, where he was seeking his mentor. The game posits Miku and the player against the ghosts inhabiting the mansion. The game begins with a playable flashback in which the player controls Mafuya — this section of the game also acts as a tutorial. After the introduction ends, the game fades in to Miku saying that it has been two weeks since she last heard from her brother. The gameplay of *Fatal Frame* consists of searching for clues, solving puzzles, and unraveling the past of a haunted mansion, fighting spirits with a mystical camera.

Monsters and Threat

The emotional impact of playing the two games revolves largely around suspense, relating to worry and fear. Power and Dalgleish suggest that *fear* relates to situations in which a person perceives that their personal survival, or their objectives are in danger. A threat can be physical or psychological. A particular psychological threat is related to social roles, and a person can fear conflicts, loss of status or isolation from the rest of the community (1997: 199–156). On top of that, the specific feature of horror, as suggested by Carroll (1990) is invoked through disgust, particularly through use of monsters. Indeed, monsters and disgust are important in both games.

Monsters in *Silent Hill 2* and *Fatal Frame* threaten players' goals and thus are likely to prompt fear. Monsters in *Silent Hill 2* constitute a straightforward threat; they are always unambiguously malevolent and the emotional reactions they provoke are likely to be clearly negative. However, the monsters in *Fatal Frame* are not only threatening, but they are also shown to suffer. Such is the case with a ghost of a blinded female, who keeps crying in pain "oh, my eyes." The player is forced to witness the pain and suffering that the persons experienced before turning into ghosts (e.g., being blinded or strangled in a ritual). The game associates several different kinds of emotional triggers to ghosts; players will fear ghosts, but they are also invited to sympathize with the tormented ghosts and pity their lost souls.

The two games also portray two very different kinds of *monsters*: in *Fatal Frame* they are spirits of dead people, and in *Silent Hill 2* they are various kinds of non-human and unnatural creatures. This brings us to consider how the two games invoke emotional responses of *disgust*. Disgust relates to situations in which one perceives something as physically or psychologically contaminating (Power and Dalgleish, 1997: 345–276). In terms of survival value, the disgust reaction serves to ensure that risky substances (such as spoiled food or infectious agents) are avoided. Feelings of disgust are not bound to factual contamination; instead, underlying the feeling of disgust is precisely a desire to avoid contact. Disgust is also strongly associative: the idea of eating a soft, warm, brown heap that looks exactly like dog droppings is likely to be revolting even if it is revealed that the heap is in fact made of chocolate.

Further, disgust reactions need not be linked to physical impurity—for example morally unacceptable deeds and thoughts can be perceived as contaminating. Power and Dalgleish (1997) use a particularly illuminating example, citing a study in which among a range of objects, the object that was assessed as the most disgusting was Hitler's shirt. The morally disgusting factor (Hitler's deeds of terror) is in no way transmissible by a shirt, nevertheless there is a notion of something rubbing off that underlies the reaction towards it.

Carroll (1990) suggests the monsters of horror are built to create a disgust reaction. Clearly, there is no real risk of contamination involved in contact with video game monsters. Nevertheless, fictive monsters can activate notions of contamination or trigger disgust reactions by associating monsters to substances and concepts that somehow pose a threat to the purity of the player. At the same time, monsters also typically pose a real threat towards the player's objectives. The player is thus invited to feel both fear and disgust in relation to monsters. Indeed, on the level of player experience, the two emotions are likely to interact and may be hard to distinguish from each other.

In terms of invoking disgust, *Silent Hill 2* seems to be focusing on physical contamination and gustatory based disgust reactions. Some of the monsters in *Silent Hill 2* are depicted as rotting or covered in blood. The disgust reactions to these are based on the repulsiveness of physically contaminating substances, such as spoiled food and (other people's) body fluids (Power and Dalgleish, 1997). The sounds speak of excess, with elaborate and intimate sounds contributing to the vivid and visceral experience of disgust created by the game. Sounds and graphics partly fill in for the olfactory and tactile sense that is lacking from the medium. Monsters in *Silent Hill 2* make burp-like or hissing gaseous sounds and when they are successfully hit, the impact sounds wet and mushy. Sounds are also important in drawing attention to significant visual details that might otherwise go unnoticed, or disgust signals that would otherwise be visually ambiguous (e.g., due to low resolution), such as slimy or sticky surfaces.

Monsters in *Silent Hill 2* systematically break the categories of human and non-human: for example, the "pyramid head" is a humanlike creature with a block-like triangular formation instead of a head. Other monsters pertain to insect-related disgust reactions, either by movement reminiscent of scurrying insets or by visual appearance. Synchronicity between sounds and visuals is used to create further contrast between human-like movement and sounds that go against the human; some of the monsters sound almost mechanical. At times, creatures change suddenly from bipedal walking to insectal scurrying. These abnormalities introduce a threat of contamination because they are blurring the categorical borders between what is considered human versus non-human. This is enough to trigger both disgust and fear.

Fatal Frame also uses the breach of humanness, this time in terms of living and dead. The monsters here are the hostile dead spirits of the mansion. These spirits are visually connotative of corpses, which can trigger disgust reactions. Many spirits are also portrayed in unnatural and painful positions, activating body mimicry and invoking images of pain, or deformation. In general, however, *Fatal Frame* is utilizing disgust not in a gustatory aspect, but rather the notion of mental contamination, fear of insanity and spiritual decay. The monsters mainly use human vocalizations: they sigh, moan or lament. The sounds are often overly simplified and repetitive, which can be interpreted as another sign of mental incapacity. Spirits in *Fatal Frame* are hostile dead agents, but the main threat is not death, but a death without spiritual release. Again, the ambivalent nature of the spirit-monsters opens the way for multiple emotions: the player is invited to feel fear for and pity with the trapped souls, followed by joy as the spirits are relieved of their torment.

Establishing the World and Communicating Action Possibilities

Considerations of a possible or probable (yet unrealized) threat cause emotional anxiety. According to Power and Dalgleish, *worry* is an example of a complex emotion that combines basic emotions or adds cognitive appraisal. In worry, fear reactions are triggered not by observing the threat itself, but by expecting it (Power and Dalgleish, 1997). To invoke worry, both games keep players constantly alert. In *Silent Hill 2*, the environment visually suggests imminent threat. Rooms can have blood trails that imply that someone has been killed on the spot. Blood trails also serve the purpose of triggering disgust (blood is a typical source of disgust). However, the strongest factor in establishing threat is through the function of game elements. In

Fatal Frame, spirits appear at different spots and follow the player through walls, effectively signaling that the player is not safe anywhere. Both games use typical structural tools for establishing a sense of dread: limited choice and limited resources (ammunition). The environment is portrayed as hostile, and a failure to keep the player character alive will terminate the game.

In both game worlds, worry is provoked further by using two themes typical of horror: loneliness and anthropomorphism. The loneliness of the player character, at least with respect to human allies, is evident in both games. In *Fatal Frame* the mansion is empty except for the ghosts. *Silent Hill 2* has a few human inhabitants (Maria, Angela Orosco, Eddie Dombrowski and a child named Laura), but their behavior suggests that they may be unreliable, and some of them are outright threatening. For example, little Laura will trick the player into dangerous situations and Eddie will try to kill James. This confirms the fact that the player character will have to manage alone, with no other characters to rely on.

Establishing loneliness is also effective in increasing a general tendency to perceive anthropomorphism, which attributes human characteristics and motivations to nonhuman agents. This tendency is inherent in humans, and it is strengthened whenever people are in absence of social connection to other humans, or have a high need to interact effectively with their environment (Epley, Waytz and Cacioppo, 2007). Furthermore, anthropomorphism is encouraged by a desire to understand and act (or witness action) based upon the situation and to unwind the story that is being told. Games massively exploit the tendency to see life in inanimate objects and anthropomorphism forms the basis of perceiving characters as persons.

In terms of general mood, the games further create anxiety by playing noisy and unpredictable environment ambient sounds. Both games feature an abundance of event sounds with no evident cause, sounds not plausibly attributed to an inanimate environment — scraping, chiming, rustling, and shuffling. Signaling that the game world is alive also gives it the potential to be (intentionally) malicious. In both *Silent Hill 2* and *Fatal Frame,* the whole game world breathes with life, suggesting that somehow the environment itself is alive, sentient, and capable of taking action against the player. Both games use sighing and groaning winds in a manner typical of horror movies. *Fatal Frame* uses human vocal expression — partly melding together the animacy of the mansion and the legacy of ghosts haunting it.

A living environment is indicated by the way in which the environment responds to player action. For example, after the player has passed through, the doors in *Fatal Frame* close as if by an inner will. Also, some sounds that otherwise would have a clear source seem to be unlocalized, and come from everywhere, or change position randomly, which creates a feeling of omnipotent power at work in the mansion. *Silent Hill 2* will sometimes introduce a second sound of footsteps alongside the walking sounds of the player character. These sounds respond in a way that suggests that someone is following the player character: if the player stops, the sounds instantly go silent. Typically, the shuffling sound will reappear sometime after walking resumes. Together, the pattern by which the sound responds to player action and the sound of footsteps create a strong sense of being observed.

Both games use sound as a primary signal of threat: *Silent Hill 2* provides a radio for this purpose and *Fatal Frame* introduces a metallic ringing and throbbing sound. The way sound represents threat is illustrative of the type of threat proposed in the game. *Fatal Frame* relies on the disgust factor of mental contamination and utilizes sound for emotionally enunciating the character's experience of that threat. When Miku is in the presence of ghosts, the soundscape is transformed to reflect a subjectively changed point of audition. *Silent Hill 2*, on the other hand, outsources the warning signal to a radio which produces static noise when it is near monsters.

The utility of sounds for informational purposes ensures that the player will be constantly listening for clues. Utilizing sound as a source of information is further motivated by limited visual clues: *Silent Hill 2* uses thick fog and darkness to limit what can be seen and *Fatal Frame* sports more or less invisible ghosts in a dark mansion. Nevertheless, the typical background of these games is an environment that makes it hard to listen for information. Furthermore, even when a threatening sound is heard, the sound is poorly localized (which in itself can increase the fear associated with scary sounds, according to Ekman and Kajastila, 2009). These features work against the utility of sounds, and challenge the *functional fit* of sound in a way that creates a general sense of unease (Ekman 2008; Joergensen, 2007). Daniel Kromand (2008) points out that horror games also tend to use "false alarms." Thus, when the usefulness of a certain sound has been established, it is sometimes used in vain, just to make the player more alert. This uncertainty of the functionality and role of sounds contributes to the deeply disturbing effect of sounds. In *Fatal Frame*, a similar effect is created visually by making some objects move by themselves. This is important, since the mansion is otherwise empty except for ghosts. Objects that move by themselves make observing movement ambiguous and reacting to changes in the environment more complicated, because not all movement in the environment is a sign of threat.

Generally, unpredictable and arrhythmic environment sounds will resist listener adaptation. The soundscapes of the games (even when there are no clues) will require constant attention and listening, which is taxing to the player. This is one type of low level affective "trick" that can be used to create an emotional effect. Both games also use sudden loud sounds. *Fatal Frame* especially exploits abrupt sound cuts and bursts of noise together with fragmentary cut-scenes. Similar fragmented soundscapes accompany the sudden visual effects of encounters with ghosts. *Silent Hill 2* draws as well on culturally imprinted danger symbols. For example, it mixes the archetypal rising and sinking tone of sirens with the environmental ambiance to create strong associations to danger, panic, and imminent threat. Here again, unconscious emotion is recruited to add to the scariness of the environment.

In a tense situation, the player character's well-being is further endangered by the forced use of playing mechanisms that, on the one hand, advance playing but on the other pose a threat to survival. The player is thus forced to put the character in danger in order to perform game tasks. This is the case with the flashlight and radio in *Silent Hill 2*. In the dark, monsters don't see James and if the radio is also off he can go completely unnoticed. However, the radio provides an essential clue to the player. The flashlight is also unavoidable: there is no way to search the rooms without light. The decision to turn these devices on and risk being spotted by monsters is likely to cause worry. *Fatal Frame* does not function in the same explicit manner, but the game nevertheless uses similar associations to increase the tension during gameplay. Moving around in the mansion is extremely noisy: floorboards creak audibly at each step and opening doors make loud impact sounds. The exaggerated movement sounds are prone to worry the player because the game is suggestive of stealth; a natural player assumption is that monsters (especially within this genre) are able to hear the player character and that loud sounds will attract monsters. Here, emotion arises at the mismatch between the two functions of sound: the action of walking is represented as loud, but the goal against which walking sounds are evaluated is to remain silent.

THE PLAYER TO CHARACTER RELATION

Both games start by establishing a relation to the player character that is unambiguously sympathetic. The games also make it clear that in order to succeed, the player must keep the player character in good health. This establishes a double basis for care. In addition to the functional role, the sympathetic relation enhances the chances that the player feels allied with the player character and the successes and failures of the character are more likely to have emotional impact (Lankoski and Björk, 2008). Positive evaluation is typical when a character is beautiful, expresses affection or fear, or when the character is evaluated as morally good (in relation to standards set by the game).

Silent Hill 2 spends a lot of time building a positive image of the player character, only to turn these evaluations upside down in the final cut-scenes of the game. Throughout the game, James is presented as a loving and caring character. In the end, these positive evaluations are heavily contrasted by revealing that James has killed his own wife. The information is likely to modulate the whole pleasure of reaching the goal as a re-evaluation of events. Indeed, after the turn of events, players may even associate disgust with James. The success of the effect, however, necessitates that James is first perceived as sympathetic and likable.

Miku of *Fatal Frame*, on the other hand, remains cute and approachable throughout the entire game. *Fatal Frame* also exaggerates her weakness. Whenever Miku is attacked by spirits, there are relatively long animations during which the player is removed of control and can only listen to and watch the whimpering girl as she is being attacked. Miku is also rather slow to move. The value of keeping her not only alive but unharmed is enhanced by the fact that if she is not in good condition, some spirits can kill her with a single attack. In addition to functional aspects, the generally fidgety behavior of Miku will invite the player to feel empathetic fear.

In general, both *Fatal Frame* and *Silent Hill 2* offer multiple chances to relate to the emotions of the player character through affective mimicry: when attacked, the characters make scared rather than aggressive sounds and cut scenes are highly evocative emotionally, including close up pictures of facial expressions and emotionally expressive voice acting. By default, both *Fatal Frame* and *Silent Hill 2* use third-person mode, which allows monitoring both the player and his or her immediate environment. Nevertheless, the games sometimes limit vision by using fixed camera angles so that at some locations the player is able to see only very little of what is ahead. In *Fatal Frame*, the player can at any point choose to activate the first-person view of the camera finder, but that limits the player's possibilities to monitor the back of the player character. The search view of *Silent Hill 2*, that normally enables the guiding of the camera, is disabled or limited part of the time. This camera usage is likely to prompt worry.

In an unpredictable and threatening environment, staying in control becomes an emotional issue. In terms of vested interest, the level of control also reflects the level of protection a player can provide to the player character (this, of course, also depends on the player's skill). Cut-scenes and cinematics temporarily remove control. In situations where the player would like to act or is prepared to do so, cut scenes can be used to generate a sense of helplessness, heightening anxiety. *Fatal Frame* uses the loss of control during cut-scenes to increase the intensity of worry when the player is anticipating a fight. Whenever a ghost attacks, a very short cut-scene is displayed. This is in some sense beneficial, since it leaves players some time to orient to the ghost. At the same time, however, players are also stripped of control, since they cannot react to the ghost at the precise moment when the cut-scene is playing. The temporary loss of control intensifies the threat.

Simple action sounds are crucial in signaling the level of activity available to the player. During cinematics and cut-scenes, simple player-responsive action sounds are removed, and often substituted by other foreground sounds, such as dialogue. *Silent Hill 2* uses the special relation players have to footsteps in a particularly interesting way to create a sense of worry. The game posits the camera at varying distances in relation to the character and ties point of audition to the camera, so that the volume of the footstep sounds varies as the character walks closer to, or away from, the camera. In some cases, the player character will walk so far away that one cannot really hear the footsteps any longer. Depriving the player of the usual response of walking sounds creates an eerie feeling of loosing control. Footsteps, as instantly responsive to controls, first make apparent, then continue to communicate the agency of the player.

Conclusion

The typical emotional effect of horror can be categorized as suspense and relates to worry or fear and disgust. We have introduced a framework for understanding emotions, and have identified emotional techniques that pertain to horror games. We have analyzed how these emotions are elicited in two different horror games: *Silent Hill 2* and *Fatal Frame*.

The horror genre must somehow combine audiovisual and game-related emotions, as horror requires very specific representational aspects in order to realize. Survival horror games use both traditional audiovisual means, as well as action-specific techniques, to prompt fear and worry. We fear for the character, because we empathize with the character, but also because we need to keep the character in good health in order to pursue game goals. In the two survival horror games that were analyzed, the necessity of the player character as a tool combined with emphasis on threat is particularly strongly used to create fear and worry. Structurally, both *Silent Hill 2* and *Fatal Frame* use limited resources and imminent danger to constantly keep the player in a state of worry. The environment is portrayed as hostile and a failure to keep the player character alive will end the game. In order to succeed, the player must keep the character in good health, which establishes a basis for care. Care is further supported by emphasizing the weakness of the character.

Our analysis suggests that sounds are essential in shaping fear through goal-related evaluations. This functional aspect introduces a unique way of creating fear with game sound. In both of the analyzed games sound is used as a warning element, establishing sound as necessary for gameplay. Sounds are also central in communicating a feeling of control that underlies all game action. A particular sense of unease is created with sounds that cause contradictory evaluations: loud sounds accompany actions that would best be silent, or unpleasant noises provide vital clues. These contradictions are made possible by the fact that sounds are simultaneously subjected to multiple evaluative strategies, both on the conscious, and on the unconscious level.

In terms of establishing threat, the single most important structural element in both games is the monsters. Monsters in *Silent Hill 2* and *Fatal Frame* threaten players' goals and thus they are likely to prompt fear. However, the visual and auditory presentation of monsters implies they are not only frightening, but contaminating. It is the unique element of disgust and a notion of contamination that makes the two games precisely *horror*. Our example games show two approaches to the representation of monsters. *Silent Hill 2* focuses primarily on physical contamination and gustatory based disgust reactions. Here, sound compensates for the limited sensory capabilities of the medium, particularly for the lack of tactile information. *Fatal Frame*, on the other hand, uses a notion of insanity, and uses sound to enunciate the subjective viewpoint of the player character. In both cases, games use narrative techniques in order to invoke disgust. Sound is employed to stretch the limits of the medium and to act as a surrogate for missing senses. The choice of sound also helps establish the non-human nature of monsters on the one hand, and contributes to create an animate the environment, on the other. By considering only gameplay and the structural properties of these games, one could not explain the unique playing experience they offer. In its reliance on disgust, horror has a necessity-based relation to specific representational content.

Works Cited

Bura, Stéphane (2008), "Emotion Engineering: A Scientific Approach for Understanding Game Appeal," *Gamasutra*, available online at <http://www.gamasutra.com/view/fea tur/3738/emotion_engineering_a_scientific_.php>.

Carroll, Noël (1987), "The Nature of Horror," *The Journal of Aesthetics and Art Criticism*, Vol. 46, No. 1, pp. 51–59.

_____ (1990), *The Philosophy of Horror; or, Paradoxes of the Heart*, New York: Routledge.

Chion, Michel (1994), *Audio-Vision: Sound on Screen*, New York: Columbia University Press.

_____ (1998), *Le Son*, Paris: Nathan.

Cohen, Annabel (2001), "Music as the Source of Emotion in Film," in Patrik Juslin and John Sloboda (eds.), *Music and Emotion*, Oxford: Oxford University Press, pp. 249–272.

Currie, Gregory (1995), *Image and Mind: Film, Philosophy, and Cognitive Science*, Cambridge: Cambridge University Press.

Damasio, Antonio (2005), *Descartes' Error: Emotion, Reason, and the Human Brain*, New York: Penguin Books.

Dimberg, Ulf, Monika Thunberg, and Kurt Elmehed (2000), "Unconscious facial reactions to emotional facial expressions," *Psychological Science*, Vol. 11, No. 1, pp. 86–89.

Ekman, Inger (2008), "Psychologically Motivated Techniques for Emotional Sound in Computer Games," *Proceedings of AudioMostly*, Piteå, Sweden, pp. 20–26.

_____ (2005), "Understanding Sound Effects in Computer Games," *Proceedings of Digital Arts and Cultures 2005*, Copenhagen, CD-ROM.

_____, and Raine Kajastila (2009), "Spatialization Cues Affect Emotional Judgments— Results from a User Study on Scary Sound," *Proceedings of AES 35th Conference on Game Audio*, Feb. 2009, London, CD-Rom, available online at <http://meaningfulnoise.blogsome. com/p23>.

Epley, Nicholas, Adam Waytz, and John T. Cacioppo (2007), "On Seeing Human: A Three-Factor Theory of Anthropomorphism," *Psychological Review*, Vol. 114, No. 4, pp. 864–886.

Jackson, Philip L., and Jean Decety (2004), "Motor Cognition: A New Paradigm to Study Self— Other Interactions," *Current Opinion in Neurobiology*, Vol. 14, No. 2, pp. 259–263.

Joergensen, Kristine (2007), *"What Are Those Grunts and Growls Over There?" Computer Game Audio and Player Action*, Ph.D. dissertation, Copenhagen University.

Kromand, Daniel (2008), "Sound and the Diegesis In Survival-Horror Games," *Proceedings of AudioMostly 2008*, Piteå, Sweden, pp. 16–19.

Lankoski, Petri (2007), "Goals, Affects, and Empathy in Computer Games," *Proceedings of Philosophy of Computer Games*, Reggio Emilia, available online at <http://game.uni more.it/Papers/Lankoski_Paper.pdf>.

_____, and Staffan Björk (2008), "Character-Driven Game Design: Characters, Conflict, and Gameplay," *Proceedings of GDTW08*, Liverpool, pp. 59–66.

LeDoux, Joseph (1996), *The Emotional Brain*, New York: Simon and Schuster.

Marshall, Sandra, and Annabel Cohen (1988), "Effects of Musical Soundtracks on Attitudes toward Animated Geometric Figures," *Music Perception*, Vol. 6, No 1, pp. 95–112.

Niedenthal, Paula M., Lawrence W. Barsalou, Piotr Winkielman, Silvia Krauth-Gruber, and François Ric (2005), "Embodiment in attitudes, social perception, and emotion," *Personality and Social Psychology Review*, Vol. 9, No. 3, pp. 184–211.

Oatley, Keith, and Jennifer M. Jenkins (1996), *Understanding Emotions*, Blackwell Publishing: Cambridge.

Perron, Bernard (2005), "A Cognitive Psychological Approach to Gameplay Emotions," *Changing Views: Worlds in Play. Proceedings of DiGRA 2005 Conference*, Vancouver, available online at <http://www.digra.org/dl/db/06276.58345.pdf>.

Power, Mick, and Tim Dalgleish (1997), *Cognition and Emotion: From Order to Disorder*, Hove: Psychology Press Ltd.

Ravaja, Niklas, Timo Saari, Mikko Salminen, Jari Laarni, and Kari Kallinen (2006), "Phasic Emotional Reactions to Video Game Events: A Psychophysiological Investigation," *Media Psychology*, Vol. 8, No. 1, pp. 343–367.

Smith, Murray (1995), *Engaging Characters: Fiction, Emotion, and the Cinema*, New York: Oxford University Press.

Tan, Ed S. (1994), "Film-induced Affect as a Witness Emotion," *Poetics*, Vol. 23, No. 2. pp. 7–32.

_____, and Nico H. Frijda (1999), "Sentiment in Film Viewing," in Carl Plantinga, and Greg M. Smith (eds.), *Passionate Views. Film, Cognition, and Emotion*, Baltimore: Johns Hopkins University Press, pp. 48–64.

Whittington, William (2007), *Sound Design & Science Fiction*, Austin: University of Texas Press.

Zajonc, Robert B. (1980), "Feeling and Thinking: Preferences Need No Inferences," *American Psychologist*, Vol. 35, No. 2, pp. 151–175.

Complete Horror in *Fatal Frame*
Michael Nitsche

Introduction

The following pages will look at the *Fatal Frame* video game series and will investigate some aspects of photography and embodiment to outline how this specific survival horror game series instigates terror. So far, the *Fatal Frame* series (originally published as *Zero* in Japan) has seen four install-ments: *Fatal Frame* (2001) (in the following called *Fatal Frame I* to distin-guish it from the overall series), *Fatal Frame II: Crimson Butterfly* (2003), *Fatal Frame III: The Tormented* (2005), and *Fatal Frame IV: The Mask of the Lunar Eclipse* (2008). All of them were produced by Keisuke Kikuchi and directed by Makoto Shibata. The exception is the latest installment *Fatal Frame IV: Mask of the Lunar Eclipse* which was co-designed by Goichi Suda (*aka* Suda 51) but Shibata and Kikuchi remained connected to the title. The first two titles were initially published for the PlayStation 2 and later, with some changes, for the Xbox (2002 and 2003 respectively). *Fatal Frame III: The Tormented* is a PlayStation 2 exclusive, and at the time of writing, *Fatal Frame IV* has only been released in Japan for the Wii. All titles were developed by Tecmo except *Fatal Frame IV*, which was a co-production with Grasshopper Manufacture. Furthermore, the *Fatal Frame* franchise has been adapted to other media including the amusement park 3D cinematic ride *Zero4D* (2004) and the cell phone game *Real: Another Edition* (2004), as well as numerous other formats from fan made card games to comics and short films. Despite this range of titles, this essay will treat the four main titles and the franchise as one consistent game world. It will not concentrate on the close reading of one individual title or on a comparative approach between them. Instead it aims to investigate some aspects of one element that is prominent in all four original games, namely photography in a virtual world. It is possible to dis-cuss *Fatal Frame* as one coherent franchise instead of four (or six) separate titles because the core design of the overall series remains clear and consis-tent throughout. This stands in contrast to, for example, the development of the *Resident Evil* (Capcom, 1996–2009) or *Alone in the Dark* (Infograms, Dark-work SA, and Eden Games S.A.S., 1992–2008) franchises which have both seen fundamental changes in their gameplay, such as the inclusion of Quick Timer Events, significant changes of pace, and representation. None of this applies to the *Fatal Frame* games. Whenever there are alterations of the core formula, as seen in the Xbox versions, they still deal with the main mechanics and copy them in a slightly different way. This overall consistency gave the series the chance to mature within a given framework.

The core design in the *Fatal Frame* series is a simple concept: the player controls a virtual character who has to survive a haunted environment where some kind of past ritual has gone terribly wrong and some sacrifice is needed to correct it. During the exploration of these haunted worlds, ghosts can attack the virtual hero at any time from anywhere. There is only one kind of weapon available in all of these titles: a magic camera that has exorcist powers and can destroy the otherwise immaterial ghost spirits through the act of photographing them. This basic mechanism is re-used in all titles without much change.

While this core principle remains, the games' various storylines are very complex and interwoven. For example, although there is usually one main heroine in each game, you always have control over at least two characters over the time of the gameplay. This offers different perspectives to the same events and the more recent titles increasingly play with that shift. The main heroine of *Fatal Frame I*, Miku Hinasaki, is searching for her brother, who disappeared during his investigation of a secluded mansion. Miku soon discovers that the mansion is haunted because an ancient ritual of self-sacrifice was not completed. *Fatal Frame II* features two twin sisters, Mio and Mayu Amakura, who are lured into a haunted village where they are supposed to perform a ritual sacrifice of one of the sisters to appease a hellish force that lurks in a bottomless abyss. The female protagonist of *Fatal Frame III* is Rei Kurosawa, who follows an apparition of her dead fiancé and becomes infected with a curse that manifests in the form of a growing tattoo. Originally the tattoo was a sign for a ritualistic self-sacrifice of a priestess for the sake of the community. But once again, the ritual failed and the curse turned the Manor of Sleep, where the infected experience their dreams, into a haunted environment like the mansion and the village before. *Fatal Frame IV* has not been released in the West at the time of writing and will receive the least attention in this essay. However, it still provides the same kind of haunted setting, this time on an island. The island was host to a terrible crime that seemed solved. But ten years later, with Ruka Minazuki as the main heroine, the surviving young women have to re-visit the island to bring the horror to an end. Once more, the disaster was caused by failed rituals.

Different games refer to each other and main characters re-appear as supporting ones or are alluded to in other titles. For example, a number of characters or relatives of characters from the first games reappear in *Fatal Frame III* including Miku Hanasaki from the first installment as a playable character in the third. The games, thus, create an interconnected framework of cross-references between characters, items at work, and parts of the back-story. Another consistent element of the series is that these back-stories remain rooted in Japanese tradition and culture. All playable heroes are Japanese and all events are staged in Japanese locations. Some of the games try to connect their virtual locations more specifically to factual Japanese regions. The first *Fatal Frame* was even marketed with the tag line "Based on a true story"—a marketing strategy that tried to connect it to local Japanese folklore and urban legends. The games continue this cultural reference, often using traditional Japanese attire, architecture, and symbols. Shinto traditions, for example, are alluded to not only in the back-story but also in the roles of the ghosts and their position within the specific game setting. This cultural grounding is in contrast to basically all other main Japanese survival horror franchises from *Resident Evil* to *Silent Hill*. The *Siren* franchise is based more closely on Japanese tradition but even *Siren* (Sony Computer Entertainment Japan, 2004–2008) sidesteps these references by introducing American heroes visiting the haunted Japanese grounds, thereby changing the perspective into one of the visitor looking into the Japanese horror. In comparison, the *Fatal Frame* series remains within the chosen cultural frame and provides a clearly Japanese perspective. It concentrates its horror on a more psychological subsection of what has been termed J-Horror from where parallels to the *kaidan/ avenging spirit* film can be drawn. McRoy exemplifies some specific motifs of these films as dealing with ghosts and haunted houses, often citing Japanese folklore, and mentions visual themes like the dangerous stare and the long black hair of the women (McRoy, 2005: 3)—all of which are present in the *Fatal Frame* series. That does not mean that no changes to the game were applied for the localization of *Fatal Frame* titles. Miku, the heroine of the original game, for example, was adjusted in age and in appearance to appeal to Western audiences (Di Marco, 2007). However, the fundamental design, look, and functionality of the franchise remain intact, not only between different platforms and across different markets, but also between the various installments of the game series. For these reasons, *Fatal Frame* offers itself for an analysis that interconnects the different games and highlights the consistent features at work in basically all of them.

As previously stated, this essay investigates these mechanics and treats the *Fatal Frame* games as one body of work. Specific references to individual and title-specific points will be traced back to the respective game. First, the essay investigates the use of photography in the game and how the specific qualities of the photographic image are part of the horror in *Fatal Frame*. The main argument is that *Fatal Frame* utilizes the ambiguity of the photographic image as both a document and a manipulation to evoke terror. The two main points in this discussion are the use of the camera itself and the concept of spirit photography in the game. Secondly, the essay looks at the function of the avatar as a connecting medium to better transmit the horror to the player. Almost as a mirror to the mediating effect of the photograph, the avatar will be interpreted as a kind of medium itself: one that uses the axis of agency and interaction with the game world to transcend the horror from the virtual out to the real world. It ultimately situates the player in a horrific situation not only in the game space, but also in the real world. The key points here address the interaction design that leads to a specific positioning of the player and the role of the avatar and her body in the game world.

The Photograph

The use of photography in *Fatal Frame* hinges on its core gameplay element: the use of a magic camera, called "camera obscura," which is the single most important object in the game space. One can roughly divide the gameplay in *Fatal Frame* into two main parts: exploration and fighting. The default visualization during the player's exploration of the haunted world in *Fatal Frame I-III* is a third-person view. The game has a number of pre-defined viewpoints that are activated depending on where the player steers the main heroine. The player, thus, looks at the avatar as she explores the game universe with no direct control over this viewpoint. Whenever the player activates the camera obscura, the game switches into a first-person point of view through the finder of the camera (figure 1). In this state, the player can — and has to— directly control the viewpoint. The camera obscura can be used as an explorative device, as it allows the player to investigate the virtual surroundings. Mostly, though, it is used as a weapon. During her journey through the haunted grounds the heroine is attacked again and again by translucent ghosts that try to grab and kill her. The camera obscura is the only way to fight back against these attacking ghosts, as its photographs have exorcist powers. During the fight, the player has to keep the attacking ghost in the central ring of the viewfinder as this allows the camera to gradually charge its exorcist powers. The longer the player waits and manages to charge the camera, the more powerful the shot will be. The most effective moment is the "fatal frame," which usually occurs a split second just before the ghost reaches the player's avatar. It is the most dangerous, but also the most rewarding moment to take the shot, as it causes the most damage to the ghost. Over time, the camera can be improved and equipped with better lenses, films, and extras, but the core interaction stays the same. All *Fatal Frame* games follow this same principle.

THE CAMERA

The motif of the camera as weapon has clear parallels to seminal horror films like *Peeping Tom* (Michael Powell, 1960). In both cases a camera is the killing device albeit in different ways. The *Fatal Frame* camera kills spirits through the exorcist power of its images, while the *Peeping Tom* camera kills humans through a knife hidden in its tripod. In both cases, the looking at a victim and the distance to this victim are crucial for the operator. The camera operator experiences the kill through the viewfinder and both cameras support their murderous use in the way their viewfinders are shaped. Mark Lewis' murder weapon in *Peeping Tom*, a Bolex 16mm handheld film camera, cuts the picture into a cross hair like shape. This cross hair shape is a divergence from the original finder and serves as a visual marker for the camera and its use to document and conduct the murders. The camera obscura devices in *Fatal Frame* are fictitious but clearly mirror this function with various forms of visual aides for aiming and powering up effects in the finder. They work to assist in the timing of the shot and are generally markers for the camera's supernatural capabilities. Like in *Peeping Tom*, the player sees the ghost exorcism through the viewfinder. One is always killer and witness at the same time. Like Mark Lewis' snuff films, the *Fatal Frame* cameras also document the events for later re-viewing. All pictures can be stored in a virtual photo album to keep track of ghosts and spooks. To complicate the fights, the ghosts often move erratically, teleport, or disappear altogether — making it difficult to keep them in the viewfinder. This puts even more emphasis on the timing of the photograph in the game itself.

Notably, timing is not an issue of the original camera obscura set up. The original apparatus of the historical camera obscura has neither a shutter, nor a finder, unlike the camera in *Fatal Frame*. The principle of the camera obscura, Latin for "dark chamber," is based on

Figure 1: **An approaching ghost is seen through the viewfinder of the camera obscura in *Fatal Frame III: The Tormented* (Tecmo, 2005).**

the way light beams pass through a small opening to create the projection of an inverted image of the original objects in a secluded room. The timing of the projection is the same as that of the depicted objects. Its value is precisely the fact that it is an ongoing and accurate image; although, it does not necessarily have to be a realistic projection. The effect has been used to create entertaining visual effects by Arnold Villeneuve (Arnoldus de Villa Nova) as early as the 13th century and later by Giovanni Battista della Porta. Della Porta describes the possible set up of a camera obscura in his best selling *Magica Naturalis* of 1589:

> In a tempestuous night the image of anything may be represented hanging in the middle of a chamber, that will terrify the beholders. Fit the image before the hole, that you desire to make to seem hanging in the air in another chamber, that it is dark; let there be many torches lighted around about. In the middle of the dark chamber place a white sheet, or some solid thing, that may receive the image sent in; for the spectators that see not the sheet, will see the image hanging in the middle of the air, very clear, not without fear and terror, especially if the artificer be ingenious [quoted in Hammond, 1981: 19].

The visual effect and its frightening impact fit the way that the half-transparent ghosts materialize in *Fatal Frame*: hanging in the middle of the air, without body, like projections from another world. They even tend to float into the scene through some wall, coming from some outside and otherwise invisible space. However entertaining the early visual effects might have been, they do not reflect the original value of the camera obscura as a scientific tool. Its precise reproduction of an image made the original camera obscura useful as an instrument for various technical and scientific observations, from the observation of eclipses of the sun to the training of soldiers for World War I (Hammond, 1981: 103). Its principle of the visual reproduction and projection is both precise visual instrument and visual effects tool. At times, the borderlines between the two blur, as seen in the works of alchemists like Villeneuve, who also used the camera obscura. His work did not always distinguish between hard science, folkloristic alchemy, and sheer magic. On the one hand, Villeneuve discovered new factual elements; on the other, he was on the hunt for the mythic Philosopher's Stone to achieve eternal life. His controversial work forced him into exile and saw his writings burned in Paris (Thompson, 2002: 82).

With the camera as the central device, the *Fatal Frame* series copies these references to alchemy and alchemists. *Fatal Frame* positions the character of Kunihiko Aso, the fictional inventor of the camera obscura devices, in this mix of hard scientific achievement and dubious alchemist endeavors. Like Villeneuve, Aso practices the occult in addition to the accepted sciences. The results of this work are the cameras as well as other media devices, such as radios, and projectors, that connect the world of the living with that of the dead. The camera obscura in *Fatal Frame* inherits these alchemistic traits and the interconnections they draw between the real and the unreal world. It is both scientific device and obscure occult object; a threshold item and interface into the ghastly otherworld. As such, its task is to bring the unreal haunted virtual world closer to the player — make it more "real." In this role of the threshold media object, the camera also fulfills the task of an early warning system into the "real." It senses the presence of virtual spirits and indicates the danger visually through a glowing warning signal that appears onscreen and — more importantly — through a vibration of the physical controller. Whenever a ghost is near, the PlayStation controller vibrates to alarm the player. This stretches the anticipation of the onslaught and thereby increases the impact of the horror (Perron, 2004). It also emphasizes the connection between the camera device itself and the controller. If the camera is the alchemistic device that senses the otherworld, then it originates the real world vibrations of the controller. The physically shaking controller connects the player closer to the virtual camera interface and the fictional world of the game.

The game continues with this subtle but direct mapping of the camera onto the game controller and enhances its function as a threshold object. Both the controller and the camera are usually held with both hands and the player uses the right index finger to take a picture. The PlayStation games map the same functionality onto the game controller and reference the handling of a real camera in a tactile way. While the effect is subtle and obvious changes apply — the controller is held horizontally and the camera vertically — this mapping is continuous. Unlike the guns, knives, rocket launchers, and other weaponry used in *Resident Evil, Silent Hill,* or *Siren,* the player in *Fatal Frame I–III* only has this single weapon and the interface remains the same throughout, giving this tactile reference the necessary time to establish itself. *Fatal Frame IV* deviates from that and offers an additional flashlight with exorcist powers, as well as the entirely different control scheme of the Wii.

The camera interfaces in *Fatal Frame I–III* combine multiple traits: operational weapon, familiar every-day device, and occult instrument. The camera works and feels like a household item but functions at the same time as an occult weapon. The camera as a tool for horror in *Fatal Frame* builds on this combination of familiarity and unfamiliarity. The apparatus both locates and simultaneously blurs the threshold from the virtual to the real. Like the true camera obscura — that demanded its users step into the darkened chamber to perceive the image projection, the viewfinder could be read as the pinhole into the virtual game world. The player's chamber is the living room, into which the seemingly real haunted ghost world is projected.

SPIRIT PHOTOGRAPHY

Bazin stated about photography that "[f]or the first time, between the originating object and its reproduction there intervenes only the instrumentality of a nonliving agent. For the first time an image of the world is formed automatically, without the creative intervention of man" (Bazin, 1967: 13). Much has been written on the level of creativity in photography, and spirit photography is a good example of a constant expression of creativity in the generation of images, while still alluding to their value as "instrumental" documents of reality. In spirit photography, the camera apparatus functions like a spiritual medium that somehow detects the presence or aura of an otherwise invisible spirit world. The result is usually an image that merges the real physical world with a spiritual presence. The image often combines the clear picture of the real person with that of a faded apparition of another being, such as a dead relative or a historic figure. These images seem to provide some proof of a parallel world existing around the real. Seemingly documenting this world, the photography draws on the element of the mechanical unaltered reproduction of what is in front of the camera's lens. This reproduction is focusing on the material image itself. In fact, some spirit photographers claimed to be the spiritual medium and to develop the images they only needed to hold a sensitive plate in their hands (Gunning, 1995: 52–53). Gunning expands the discussion of spirit photography and includes documentation of real-world effects such as materialization of ghosts or ectoplasmic manifestations. In both cases, Gunning continues:

> The Spiritualist encounter with photography reveals the uncanny aspect of this technological process, as one is confronted with doubles that can be endlessly scrutinized for their recognizable features, but whose origins remain obscure. Although mere images, photographs remain endlessly reproducible, able to survive the physical death of their originals. While serving, on the one hand, as evidence of a supernatural metaphysical existence, spirit photographs also present a uniquely modern conception of the spirit world as caught up in the endless play of image making and reproduction and the creation of simulacra [Gunning, 1995: 67].

The "play of image making" in *Fatal Frame* uses multiple references to spirit photography.

First, there is an exploratory element in the way the player uses the camera obscura in the game. At times, the player has to take a picture of a location or of an object that radiates spiritual energy but does not present any ordinary visible spirit materialization. Only once the photo is taken, will the player notice that the original picture gradually morphs into a different image that indicates the solution to a puzzle or provides some other hint. This mechanism remediates the idea of the original spirit photography as a chemical/mechanical visualization of an otherwise invisible ghostly presence. The material image serves as proof of the ghost world. The better and more reliable this proof is, the more "real" the horror of the ghost world can become. Needless to say that in the diegetic game world of *Fatal Frame* each hint is relevant and valuable for the player's progress through the game. There are no wrong hints or false prophecies in these images, instead they are always "true" and operate like help functions in the game.

Second, the camera play can turn into a visual ghost hunt. Not all of the ghosts one encounters in *Fatal Frame* are enemies. On many occasions, ghosts materialize in the game world and disappear again after seconds without attacking the player character. These ghosts can indicate certain spots of interest or provide yet another surprising spirit encounter to de-stabilize the player. Instead of following the usual reaction, which would be to run away and search for a good location for the photo-fight, the player has to race toward the ghost and try to get the best snapshot possible. Notably, these photos lack any exorcist powers and leave the captured ghosts unchanged. Although they are taken with the same camera, they are of a different kind than the shots taken during the fighting sequences. These photographs are parts of a reward system. If the player manages to shoot a photo of these elusive materializations, additional bonus points can be gained and these can be used to upgrade the camera obscura. The player turns into a ghost hunter who gains profits from his glimpses of the unreal. If the first form of spirit photography is exploratory, then this second form is the paparazzi shot. The successful ghost hunter collects ever more pictures in his virtual photo album, all proof for the existence of the ghost world, and is rewarded for it in the form of ever better camera equipment to deliver yet more evidence.

The third, and most dominant, reference to spirit photography is the use of the camera as a weapon against attacking ghosts throughout all games. The fact that the ghosts in *Fatal Frame* are visible without the help of any camera, initially works against the original idea of spirit photography. Not all characters in the *Fatal Frame* universe can see the ghosts but all playable virtual heroes can; usually because they have encountered the ghost world before or have a natural sixth sense. They do not need another medium to visualize the spiritual. However, *Fatal Frame* puts its emphasis on photography as a means to document the reality of the ghosts. Proving the ghosts' existence is directly connected to their exorcism. The camera continuously proves the presence of the ghosts and at the same time fights them through its exorcist powers. Photography is the proof as well as the means to destruction and the player constantly engages in a form of destructive documentation. This might be the most radical form of spirit photography, as it not only presents but also exorcizes the spirit through pictorial representation. A soul is literally captured on film and once the ghost is defeated, these pictures are its last remains.

The combination of the three outlined forms of spirit photography in *Fatal Frame* presents a broad range of references to spiritualist photographic practice. The two functions of spirit photography, as creative, as well as documentary practice, are both present and used to enhance the terror. However, unlike the traditional forms of spirit photography that look at the images after their production, *Fatal Frame* puts the player into the active role of the photographer at the time and location of the shot. It is most important to find the best split second timing for the snapshot in order to defeat and document a ghostly presence. This adds a heightened relevance and immediacy to the production of the image. To take the best possible picture, the player has to put herself in the greatest danger, facing the attacking ghastly creature and waiting as long a possible to allow the camera's exorcist power to build up. Traditional spirit photography was mainly aimed at audiences visiting the selected photographer for a sitting. The player of *Fatal Frame* becomes both the manipulative spirit photographer and the contact to the spirit world. He is the producer of the trick. But who is fooled by it? Instead of manipulating somebody else (a client or some visiting audience), this arrangement is set up to help the player to support her own suspension of disbelief. The pictures are staged as continuous evidence for the reality of the terrifying apparitions; because the player took the photograph herself and with much effort, the photographic image is even more believable. The player creates more and more convincing proof to support her own horror experience. As Makoto Shibata, the series' director stated himself:

> In the *Fatal Frame* series, I pursue the fear which is generated by the player himself, and condensed as the essence of Japanese horror to generate the kind of fear which I personally believe is the most horrible [Shibata, 2005].

Through this creative documentation, the image plane in *Fatal Frame* becomes the continuous threshold and an interface into the world of the ghosts. It exceeds classic spirit photography by emphasizing and dramatizing the act of photography itself. To support this central position of the photograph, the visualization of the game has a materiality to the image that is not common in most other survival horror series. Through the remediation of the photographic image, *Fatal Frame* uses photography as a documentary tool and a trick effect. Through the positioning of the player as the producer of these images, it involves them in the trickery.

The Player

Gunning's discussion of spirit photography includes references to Freud's principle of the uncanny. He identifies the uncanny in the (re)productive qualities of photography — and as the discussion above indicates, these (re)productive powers also apply to *Fatal Frame*. However, in addition to the qualities of the photograph, *Fatal Frame* creates a connection between the avatar figure and the photographic medium to ultimately evoke fear in the player. The body of the virtual hero avatar is used as the link between the player and the fictional game world. For example, the motif of the uncanny is not limited to the reproductive qualities of the photographic image but appears also in the doubling of hero bodies in the game. Hoeger and Huber discuss this specifically for *Fatal Frame II*, which features two identical twin sisters as the playable heroines, and wherein the story culminates in a ritual that demands one twin to strangle the other (Hoeger and Huber 2007). The player encounters fragmented bits of information that often point toward a doubling/twin world throughout this title, such as traces of earlier twins who conducted the ritual and ghosts, as well as survivors of former rituals. Although Hoeger and Huber's argument manifests most clearly in *Fatal Frame II*, traces of this doubling can also be found in other titles of the series. The complicated storylines of the games often link different bodies and souls, present the same character but at different ages, or apply possession of ghosts and bodies, so that one character might be connected to others. Even when soul mates part they might stay connected, as seen in one ending of *Fatal Frame III*, when the main heroine Rei meets her (dead) fiancé Yuu again, only to loose him to the world of the dead as he announces: "When you die then I will be gone forever. As long as you go on living, a part of me will continue to live on." In various ways the souls and spirits of characters, their death, life, and salvation seem to be connected and dependent on the bodies of others.

The *Fatal Frame* series deals with spirituality and a division between the physical and the immaterial, which can be used to create these uncanny doublings and interconnections. The antagonists, in competing franchises such as *Resident Evil* or *Alone in the Dark*, are usually physical creatures whose physicality is often emphasized through the use of blood, gore, and graphic details. *Fatal Frame*'s terror, in contrast, evolves around the basic distinction between body and soul. Much of the series' horror is not necessarily physical but spiritual and its presentation is accordingly less tangible. It also avoids a clear differentiation between good and evil in the ghosts. The antagonistic ghosts are often victims of a bigger calamity, usually condemned to suffer some horrible situation or event, often tortured and possessed themselves. They are trapped in a horrible state and only the player avatar can release them as her virtual body moves gradually closer to the final source of the evil in order to heal the world and release the spirits from their curse. This division between body and spirit is constantly crossed and there are multiple signs for this crossover in the games: tattoos on the "real" hero's body are signs of her spirit's curse in *Fatal Frame III*; the "real" hero twins of *Fatal*

Frame II are mistaken for another pair of twins, long dead, that fulfilled the ritual; the "healed" antagonist ghost in *Fatal Frame I* has to use her body to seal the gate to the demon world once her spirit has been cleared; one hero in *Fatal Frame IV* seems to be a supporting character but is ultimately revealed to be a ghost himself. *Fatal Frame* games are not only opening up the body-spirit division, they are actively developing it over the course of the gameplay and through their background storylines.

Because it is not a mere detail of the back-story but a fundamental part of the gameplay, the dualism of body and soul can be translated to the player-avatar situation in a reversed way. As Hoeger and Huber already argue for *Fatal Frame II*, the "oscillation between same and other that occurs between twins is mirrored in the player/avatar situation" (Hoeger and Huber, 2007: 154). This can be extended to the whole series. The avatar herself becomes a form of medium, trapped in the very same situation as the ghosts and intimately connected to it, a wanderer between the worlds. This function of the hero is directly alluded to in the games themselves. Once touched by the ghost world, all heroes have the ability to "see things" or have visions that can be triggered either by merely looking at or touching objects. Since these abilities play out in the interactive gameplay, the player can be seen as the spirit to the virtual medium-body. Therefore, the player is equally trapped in the horror, through the connection to, and control of, the virtual hero's avatar body. In this way, *Fatal Frame* is ultimately the story of a haunting: that of the player.

Because this haunting is evoked through the body of the main heroine as medium it seems necessary to investigate what kind of terror they mediate. Most playable characters in *Fatal Frame* are young women, which raises the question as to how the series uses these characters, their bodies, and presentation in its horror scenario.

DAMSELS IN DISTRESS?

Although this essay has pointed to a paparazzi-like use of the camera obscura and although it drew parallels to Powell's voyeuristic *Peeping Tom*, the photo camera in *Fatal Frame* notably lacks the widely spread notion of intrusive and obviously sexual voyeurism. There are numerous examples portraying the use of the camera in a voyeuristic stance in games, starting from the earliest CDi pieces like *Voyeur* (Entertainment Software Partners, 1995), where the player observes the murderous and erotic events in a fictional mansion in a *Rear Window* (Alfred Hitchcock, 1954) style. However, the photographic first-person view in *Fatal Frame*, as discussed so far, does not share this specific trait. The player does not use the camera to invade the ghosts' space or intimacy — it is the virtual body of the heroine that enters the haunted world. Instead of an outside camera peering into a living room or bedroom (as in *Voyeur*), the player steers the virtual heroine through those deserted bed chambers, play rooms, living rooms, kitchens and other interior spaces. It is the hero avatar who looks through peepholes, broken windows and into closets. The view of the photo camera, which has been a central element of the argument so far, does not have the "phallic gaze" that Clover attributes to a wide range of horror films using an "assaultive gaze" (Clover, 1992: 182). It does not follow traditional gender roles either: ghosts are both male and female and the virtual photographer during the fight sequences is predominantly female. The first-person perspective through the viewfinder of the virtual camera is instead a visual sign of empowerment and a sign for the heroine fighting back. However, this first-person perspective is not the only camera work implemented in *Fatal Frame*.

Next to the fighting sequences, the second main gameplay mode consists of exploratory sequences in which the player steers the main character through the haunted environments (figure 2).

The visualization during these sections in *Fatal Frame I-III* is not the first-person perspective used during the photographic battles, but instead a third-person perspective of cameras seemingly spread throughout the virtual game world. The main heroine is shown from pre-defined camera perspectives set in the game world that are activated depending on her spatial position. Whenever the player steers the avatar into a new environment or crosses into new sections of the game world, the camera cuts to a new perspective

and shows the relevant portion of the world with the heroine in it. Over the course of the game, the camera therefore concentrates exclusively on the young girl-woman from countless perspectives. Notably, *Fatal Frame IV* diverges from this strategy and uses a kind of following camera that is more directly tied to the player's actions. This shifts the experience of the

Figure 2: The virtual heroine is exploring the haunted game world of *Fatal Frame II: Crimson Butterfly* (Tecmo, 2003).

game, as critics have stated: "We've trodden these creaky paths before, but with a Resident Evil 4-styled shift from fixed camera to over-the-shoulder character trailing, the ornate mansions and hospital corridors are near unrecognisable" (EDGE, 2008). In comparison to such a following camera, the original third-person point of view in *Fatal Frame I–III* contributes to a more voyeuristic perspective, because it uses cameras as separate entities looking at the avatar as object from every possible angle — not unlike a stalker or secret observer. In contrast, the following camera is directly controlled by the avatar's movements and shows her almost exclusively from behind. In itself the third-person view does not necessarily constitute Clover's "assaultive gaze." But the appearance of the main hero, and especially the unlockable costumes, support this evolving voyeuristic gaze. Finishing a *Fatal Frame* game in one of the various play modes unlocks new costumes for the characters. In the case of the predominantly young female heroines, this varies between the platforms and installments, but includes traditional kimono styles in varying lengths, as well as gothic Lolita outfits, schoolgirl uniforms, and bikinis. As an in-game reference, the Xbox version of *Fatal Frame II* includes the extra outfits of two characters from the *Dead or Alive* (Tecmo, 1996–2006) fighting game series, which gained some notoriety for the presentation of its female fighters. Thus, the reward for solving the game includes the option for a more sexualized appearance.

Fatal Frame III puts even more emphasis on the avatar's body as it uses a magic tattoo that represents the curse as it gradually spreads over the main heroine's skin. This combination of terror and sexuality was envisioned by the game's director Makoto Shibata:

> The magical and mysterious meanings of the tattoo, the fear that you cannot get rid of the tattoo once you have it in your skin, the erotic image when the tattoo invades the woman's skin.... I wanted those concepts in my game and I chose the special tattoo as a key visual image of the game [Shibata, 2005].

The heroine is clearly eroticized in staging and visual representation. Shibata furthermore hints at masochistic elements in this use of the tattoo:

> We designed the heroine to be the type of person [who] would look good with a tattoo. She endures the pain, sometimes accepts it or even wishes the pain upon herself. I think that the situation itself is very erotic [Shibata, 2005].

Another sign of such a sexualized theme are the spin offs made by parts of the fan community. It is not atypical that fan fiction picks up (or projects) sexual tension into a game setting. However, *Fatal Frame II* did inspire a commercial erotic movie, *Lusty Brown Butterfly* (n.n., Japan 2004) that was produced and marketed based on the *Fatal Frame II* setting. Although there is the element of a sexualized presentation of the women in *Fatal Frame* and a semi-masochistic eroticism in the horror and pain they have to endure, this does not mean that they are helpless victims. Even if they might be looked at as eroticized objects of interest, these women remain strong in their role as the active heroines in control. In fact, women also feature as important antagonists, as each title includes a female final opponent. *Fatal Frame* pits these women, who might have fallen under horrible spells that turned them into scary and destructive ghosts, against the player-controlled avatars who have to defeat them to cure the curse. Women are both the danger as well as the savior of the community. This responds to what Martinez outlined for the depiction of Japanese women in popular culture at large: "It then becomes possible to depict Japanese women as both symbolically dangerous ... as well as the very source of all that is Japanese ... and thus able to mediate between the two poles..." (Martinez, 1998: 7).

Strong women also feature in the predecessors to the series. In part, the *Fatal Frame* series points back to Tecmo's older *Deception* franchise: *Tecmo's Deception* released (1996), *Kagero: Deception II* (1998), *Deception III: Dark Delusion* (2000), leading up to the 2005 release of *Trapt*. Kikuchi and Shibata were both involved in this series, where the player controls a woman on a revenge mission. *Deception*'s game design allows players to set up elaborate traps and lure enemies into these often highly inventive killing mechanisms. The female body functions as bait — in *Tecmo's Deception* the body appears in the same first-person point of view as seen in *Fatal Frame*, just replacing the camera with external traps — that attracts the usually male invaders. However, even as a targeted victim, the female character remains dangerous. The connection to the series is manifested in *Fatal Frame* in the dual role of the women as victims of some curse as well as decisive heroines. It is also directly alluded to in another costume-based cross-reference: players of the Xbox *Fatal Frame* version can unlock the costumes of the *Deception II* and *Deception III* heroines as extras.

No matter how sexualized the appearance of these video game heroines might be, no matter how they are staged as targets and victims, they manage to stay in control and refuse to succumb to a victim-role. In *Fatal Frame*, their control visually manifests in the use of the magic camera, the cut to the first-person point of view, and the new options that this perspective opens up for the character. The gaze onto the female body ends abruptly and becomes the view of the woman herself looking outwards through the viewfinder. This cut emphasizes the role of the virtual female hero as a powerful character in *Fatal Frame* and — at the same time — it strengthens the player's engagement. The player-triggered cut to a first-person perspective "is the reinforcement of the player positioning in the game space through the interactive cut. (...) Interactive access and player positioning are applied and reinforced" (Nitsche, 2005: 33). The player's reinforcement of control goes hand in hand with the hero's. These women are not helpless damsels in distress;

on the contrary, they actively deal with the fate that threatens the fictional game world. They might be staged as— at times eroticized — victims but they are strong enough to overcome this role through the gameplay and through the participation of the player. Maybe this is one reason why the *Fatal Frame* games attract a seemingly large female audience. Judging from the online forums such as *Beyond the Camera's Lens* (http://www.cameraslens.com/) or YouTube channels focusing on the *Fatal Frame* series, there seems to be a solid female fan base for the franchise.

ACTION RESTRICTION

The *Deception* series provides an accurate reference to describe the power of the woman that fights back, at the same time it highlights fundamental differences between the two game series. *Deception* games are basically about revenge. *Fatal Frame* has far more complex background stories. Heroines in *Fatal Frame* do not set out to destroy their enemies but usually look for other people (brother, sister, lover, or friend) and they are drawn into the cursed world because they want to help. They are not luring others into dangerous situations but are themselves drawn into the world of ghosts. This reversed perspective also manifests itself in the use of the environment in both game series. In *Deception*, the heroine controls the environment to fight off intruders. In *Fatal Frame*, the haunted world and its ghastly inhabitants try to fight off the intruding heroine. Likewise, the range of interactive options available to the player is more reactive and restricted in *Fatal Frame*. Heroes in *Fatal Frame* never consciously attack with their camera, not even indirectly as seen in *Deception*'s trap system. Instead, all fighting in *Fatal Frame* is counter attacking. Players have no idea from where the next ghost might appear and can only respond to the event. Even experienced players, who might have played the situation before and know the particular ghost and its behavior, have no chance to use this knowledge for a surprise attack. The way the camera operates prevents the player from any kind of preemptive strike. One can only react to a ghosts attack.

Such a reactive stance draws connections to Kryzwinska's suggestion that survival horror games often feature moments of restriction of interactive access. She continues: "these moments actively work to produce the crucial sense of *being out of control* that is inherent to the experience of horror" (Kryzwinska, 2002: 216–217, italics in original). During *Fatal Frame*, the effect of "*being out of control*" is called upon on numerous occasions, often in the form of shocking and well-staged cut-scenes that introduce new ghosts and scary situations. The motif of control is also at work in multiple other aspects of the *Fatal Frame* universe, often alluding to gruesome rituals, unchangeable fate and destiny. Like in many other horror scenarios, *Fatal Frame* is in large parts a battle against one's virtually declared fate.

Yet dealing with fate in *Fatal Frame* is more complicated than in the *Resident Evil* series or *Clive Barker's Undying* (Dreamwork Games, 2001)—which are the main reference points for Kryzwinska. Even if the heroines in *Fatal Frame* manage to succeed and the particular game story's curse might be lifted at the conclusion of the title, the divide between body and spirit continues. The "good" endings of each title show spirits leaving the haunted world and traveling to their final destination. The haunting comes—at least for now—to an end. At the same time, many of these endings include motifs of self-sacrifice that question the flawlessness of the victory. In *Fatal Frame I*, the released antagonist becomes the savior and closes the demon gate by chaining her body in front of it, trapped in that torturous position for eternity; the entire setting of *Fatal Frame II* revolves around the concept of the twin sisters sacrifice, and even in what might be seen as the most positive ending, wherein both sisters survive, one looses her eyesight as she saves her twin; the hero in *Fatal Frame III* might survive but has to let her love go forever. In other words, there is no easy way out of the *Fatal Frame* universe. As Hoeger and Huber argue for *Fatal Frame II*:

> Upon completion of the game, the player is left with no increased understanding or reward; it is unclear whether survival or a "happy ending" was achieved. The avatar could possibly be dead. Instead, finishing the game provides relief from responsibility and escape from its horrors [Hoeger and Huber, 2007: 156].

Resident Evil 4 (Capcom, 2005) finishes its horror off with a final rocket hitting the last beastly monster to send it to its spectacular death. It distinguishes between good and evil and although the antagonistic Umbrella Corporation is soon to re-emerge for the sequel, the ending demonstrates clearly that good prevails if the player performs well enough. In *Fatal Frame*, the solution is never so easy. The problem remains open because the presence of the ghost world itself is not resolved. Instead of ending the evil through the destruction of its last manifestation, the player, at the end of *Fatal Frame*, has assembled the largest collection of proof of the presence of spirits. The curse has been defeated but the player keeps the unsettling proof of the spirit world's existence as the final reward: a virtual photo album full of ghost photos. In that way, the image continues to destabilize the "safe" real world. The curse might be gone but its underlying reason is not.

The same technique is found in horror films such as *Ringu* (Hideo Nakata, 1998) or *The Grudge 2* (Takashi Shimizu, 2006). In a most memorable scene of *Ringu*, the ghost invades the cursed victim's living room through the television screen. At that moment of the film, the curse remains active and deadly even though the corpse of the murdered child who turned into the ghost was found and taken care of. Although the body is taken care of, the ghost still continues to kill through the imagery. *The Grudge 2* opens with a scene in a darkroom, where a photographer develops photographs that show a ghost's shadow figure. This figure starts to move on one image, its black shadow taints liquid in the developing tray and finally the ghost literally appears from the development tray and launches into the darkroom. Where *The Grudge 2* and *Fatal Frame* reference photography, *Ringu* uses video: the video cassette, its copying and the way it is watched. All three pieces set out to cross their media thresholds to ultimately push the fear beyond the image and into the real space. Just like *Ringu* invades the living room through the evil video spirit, *Fatal Frame* attacks the player's home through the consistency of the still images produced by the camera obscura. The horror extends from the virtual game world into the player's play space. Like *Ringu*, the *Fatal Frame* series manages to leave the player with a final question instead of an answer. The dilemma goes on and even at the end, these pieces destabilize through the use of the imagery. Although the path of the heroines is largely pre-set in *Fatal Frame*, it, thus, fails to deliver a simple solution to the player.

Screams in Disneyland

This essay set out to describe some basic features of the production of terror in the *Fatal Frame* series. With the image as an active medium for the connection into the virtual, we arrive at a point that has been discussed manifold in new media: the question of simulations and simulacra. *Fatal Frame* can be seen as gradually trying to create a horror "hyperreality," where the horror attempts to escape the game world to enter the player's real space. Technically, this is best illustrated in the cell phone game spin off *Real: Another Edition* (Tecmo, 2004). In *Real*, players use their cell phone cameras to snap pictures that combine a virtual ghost apparition with real world backdrops. In this installation of the *Fatal Frame* franchise, the ghosts have left the game world for good and spread into the real. At the same time, this concept reveals the surrounding world to be a horror playground. The theme park attraction *Zero4D* and its 3D cinematic imagery is a second form of this spilling over of the franchise into real physical space. Baudrillard argues that Disneyland

> is presented as imaginary in order to make us believe that the rest is real, whereas all of Los Angeles and the America that surrounds it are no longer real, but belong to the hyperreal order and to the order of simulation. It is no longer a question of a false representation of reality (ideology) but of concealing the fact that the real is no longer real, and thus of saving the reality principle [Baudrillard, 1994: 12].

This essay does not necessarily follow Baudrillard's final conclusion for our society at large — namely that "the real is no longer real" — but agrees that mechanisms of this principle can be traced in *Fatal Frame* as it certainly attempts to achieve that hyperreal effect. The game is no longer a mere representation of something real — no matter how much the marketing tries to create this connection. The game is no longer hiding the real or masking it — it confines itself no longer to an illusionary world contained in the TV set. Instead, it tries to reveal the reality of the surrounding "real" world through itself — namely that we are surrounded by ghosts. This belief is, as so many other influences in *Fatal Frame*, part of Asian traditions where spirits of ancestors are often seen as coexisting in our physical world and influencing it. Playing off this principle, *Fatal Frame* questions the "reality principle" through visual techniques that transport the virtual ghosts into the physical play space. *Ringu* refers to "a new cultural logic, a logic of the simulacrum according to which copies of copies vary continually from an always already lost original" (White, 2005: 41). *Fatal Frame* tries to copy the ghosts from the virtual into the real through the medium at hand: an interactive video game and its gameplay based on photography.

As discussed in the first half of this essay, *Fatal Frame* diverges from Baudrillard. *Fatal Frame* remediates media by focusing on their materiality. This remediation includes the camera, the photograph and the heroine's virtual body as forms of display to connect the player to the ghost world. As Bolter and Grusin argue against Baudrillard: "all mediations are themselves real. They are real as artifacts (but not as autonomous agents) in our mediated culture" (Bolter and Grusin, 1999: 55). Using the "reality" of its virtual media, *Fatal Frame* falls in-between these two perspectives. Its game simulation uses remediation techniques in order to question, not only the depicted fantasy environment, but also, the world we live in. *Fatal Frame* does not settle for the scares inside the game world — it aims to put the terror into your everyday life. Certainly ambitious, and when it succeeds it is also very scary.

Works Cited

Baudrillard, Jean (1994), *Simulacra and Simulation*, transl. by Sheila Glasner, Ann Arbor: University of Michigan Press; "Precession of Simulacra" available online at <http://www.egs.edu/faculty/baudrillard/baudrillard-simulacra-and-simulation-01-the-precession-of-simulacra.html>.

Bazin, André (1967), *What Is Cinema?* Berkeley: University of California Press.

Bolter, Jay, and Richard Grusin (1999), *Remediation: Understanding New Media*, Cambridge, MA: MIT Press.

Chien, Irene (2007), "Playing Undead," *Film Quarterly*, Vol. 61, No. 2, pp. 64–65.

Clover, Carol (1992), *Men, Women and Chainsaws: Gender in the Modern Horror Film*, Princeton: Princeton University Press.

Di Marco, Francesca (2007), "Cultural Localization: Orientation and Disorientation in Japanese Video Games," *Revista Tradumàtica — Traducció i Tecnologies de la Informació i la Comunicació: Localització de videojocs*, No. 5, November, available online at <http://www.fti.uab.es/tradumatica/revista/num5/articles/06/06central.htm>.

EDGE (2008), "Review: Fatal Frame 4," *EDGE-online*, October 15, available online at <http://www.edge-online.com/magazine/review-fatal-frame-4>.

Hammond, John H. (1981), *The Camera Obscura. A Chronicle*, Oxford, UK: Taylor & Francis.

Hoeger, Laura, and William Huber (2007), "Ghastly multiplication: *Fatal Frame II* and the Videogame Uncanny," in Akira Baba (ed.), *Situated Play: Proceedings of the Third International Conference of the Digital Games Research Association DiGRA '07*, Tokyo: University of Tokyo, pp. 152–156, available online at <http://www.digra.org/dl/db/07313.12302.pdf>.

Gunning, Tom (1995), "Phantom Images and Modern Manifestations: Spirit Photography, Magic Theater, Trick Films, and Photography's Uncanny," in Patrice Petro (ed.), *Fugitive Images: From Photography to Video*, Bloomington and Indianapolis: Indiana University Press, pp. 42–72.

Kryzwinska, Tanya (2002), "Hands-On Horror," in Geoff King and Tanya Kryzwinska (eds.), *Screenplay. Cinema/Videogames/ Interfaces*, London: Wallflower Press, pp. 206–225.

Martinez, Dolores (1998), "Gender Shifting Boundaries and Global Cultures," in Dolores Martinez (ed.), *The Worlds of Japanese Popular Culture: Gender, Shifting Boundaries and Global Cultures*, Cambridge, UK: Cambridge University Press, pp. 1–19.

McRoy, Jay (2005), "Introduction," in Jay McRoy (ed.), *Japanese Horror Cinema*, Honolulu: University of Hawaii Press, pp. 1–11.

Nitsche, Michael (2005), "Games, Montage, and the First Person Point of View," in Suzanne de Castell and Jennifer Jenson (eds.), *Changing Views: Worlds in Play. Selected Papers*, New York: Peter Lang, pp. 29–35, available online at <http://www.digra.org/dl/db/06276.11074.pdf>.

Perron, Bernard (2004), "Sign of a Threat: The Effects of Warning Systems in Survival Horror Games," *COSIGN 2004 Proceedings*, Art Academy, University of Split, pp. 132–141, available online at <http://www.ludicine.ca/sites/ludicine.ca/files/Perron_Cosign_2004.pdf>.

Shibata, Makoto (2005), "Fatal Frame III Developer's Diary #3," GameSpy.com, October 28, available online at <http://ps2.gamespy.com/playstation-2/fatal-frame-3/662607p1.html>.

_____ (2005), "Fatal Frame III Developer's Diary #4," GameSpy.com, November 4, available online at <http://ps2.gamespy.com/playstation-2/fatal-frame-3/664167p1.html>

Thompson, C.J.S. (2002), *Alchemy and Alchemists*, Mineola, NY: Courier Dover Publications.

White, Eric (2005), "Case Study: Nakata Hideo's Ringu and Ringu 2," in Jay McRoy (ed.), *Japanese Horror Cinema*, Edinburgh: University of Edinburgh Press, pp. 38–47.

Gaming's Hauntology:
Dead Media in *Dead Rising, Siren*
and *Michigan: Report from Hell*
Christian McCrea

Game horror's ability to overwhelm us, its tangible and tactile power, is measured by our quickened heartbeat, the sweat on our skin, and our silent shout. Yet alongside horror's hot breath on our necks, there is also that subtle intellectual tickle — a play with genre, form, or media history. Disbelief is not so much "suspended" as "bound up tightly"; the navigation of both physical and intellectual registers has to dovetail, one folding over the other, in order to affect us fully. We want to feel fear in its absolute, and yet possess everything we need to conquer it. Agency and control well up from the player's history of mastering games, while powerlessness and the monstrous apparitions of horror look to chip away at their confidence. This dialectic is not limited to any one media or text; the scope of horror's generic elements spills far over its borders, and leaves persistent stains on genres such as the first-person shooter and the role-playing game. Yet even as game horror feeds other genres, an increasingly rich textuality is becoming part of its tradition that makes the intellectual pleasure of agency and control very different. Games have taken up their place in the hall of media mirrors, looking for ways to make sense of themselves through known media forms. That layered media history is increasingly becoming a literal part of the arsenal players equip against the wicked foulness lurking in the bleak surrounds of their castles, mansions, and abandoned towns.

Photography, video, non-linear databases, and other forms of media now feature heavily in helping characters and players through their nightmare. The game image increasingly splits into photographs, videos, tapes, notes, databases, interruptions, and cut-scenes. When Jay David Bolter and Richard Grusin engaged with "remediation," it was the immediacy/hypermediation dialectic that drove their analysis of media appearing in other media.

(Bolter and Grusin, 2000: 29). Part of horror gaming's pleasure is that the media being remediated the most is gaming itself. The formal structures of games are laid all the more bare when film, video, and other media come in to interrupt.

One primary fascination will drive the following exploration of specific horror games. That is, how precisely the player sees gaming's formal properties and how these gain visibility through the shifting and changing layers of other media — this conceit will be explored under the rubric of "hauntology." In the process of following these traces between media, more and more questions are asked of the figures we face in horror games, interpreting them as central embodiments of both our player experience, and the experience of the machines we play with. These gaming (un)dead require their own specific form of address to distinguish them from the immaterial, virtual horrors of other media, a mapping of their deviation which in this essay is termed "teratology."

The location of our senses in this continual paradox is the focus of much horror game scholarship. Bernard Perron, for example, wrote in 2004 on the processes by which survival horror games produce mechanics of forewarning. Expanding on Noël Carroll's concept of audience-victim synchronicity, he examined the relationship between gamer and victim, noting that in survival horror, while "emotional responses run parallel to those of the characters, their way of feeling fear is different" (Perron, 2004). Even as this "way of feeling fear" changes as game horror matures, there remains a central binding problem that fascinates gamer and researcher alike — "the ability of the player and the inability of protagonists cross over and manifest at the worst (and best) possible moments." Perron writes again in 2005 (expanding upon the work of Isabel Cristina Pinedo) that "the horror film is as much an exercise in terror as 'an exercise in mastery, in which controlled loss substitutes for loss of control'" (Perron, 2005). The continual disturbing of the control paradox underpins the entire textual fabric, as cut-scenes form part of the player's episteme in a genre driven by direct experience. Tanya Krzywinska writes about the rhythm of playable sequences and cut-scenes, arguing that it "takes on a generically apposite resonance within the context of horror because it ties into and consolidates formally a theme often found in horror, in which supernatural forces act on, and regularly threaten, the sphere of human agency" (Krzywinska, 2002: 206). This keenly focuses on the visibility of moral forces and the role of agency in providing horror's elemental power — a zone in which the breadth of consequences are teased out. Supernatural forces act to set things in motion, while the character struggles to effectively react — a deeply different formulation than most action scenarios, where the player's supernatural ability forces the entire game-world to react in turn.

In an article titled *"Resident Evil's* Typewriter: Survival Horror and Its Remediations," Ewan Kirkland directly addresses the role of the analog media apparatus in several survival horror titles, including *Siren* (SCE Japan Studio, 2004 — aka *Forbidden Siren* in Europe and Australia). Kirkland specifically links the process and history of remediation to the splintering of concerns about temporarily and the encroaching anxiety of history: "Horror video games' emulation of white noise, photographic blurring, and celluloid imperfections, produces the uncanny impression of an older, ghostly or undead analog media seeping into, contaminating and enveloping the digital" (Kirkland, 2009). Kirkland identifies the functional role of these apparatuses as a means of deploying verisimilitude — the Keeper's diary entries, in *Resident Evil* (Capcom, 1996), ends ominously with "Itchy. Tasty.," which instantly transforms the Keeper into a zombie in the player's expectations, and turns a simple note into an indicator of a threat to come. This verisimilitude is not limited to supporting the game's narrative, but often operates ludically, for example with the use of photography in games which "underlines the image's reliability in revealing truth, contrasting with the phantasmagorical virtual digital game world of wandering spirits and magically imbued objects" (Kirkland, 2009). It is precisely the image's reliability which makes the game, in an important sense, ultimately unreliable — something becomes more effective in play terms when it can be filmed in game, or photographed, or somehow turned into another media form. Paradoxically, perhaps, it is the other media forms that make the player's movements through the game spaces and the progression possible.

What Remains to Be Seen

It is the dead themselves who are often the apparatus of memory:

> Once memories and dreams, the dead and ghosts become technically reproducible, readers and writers are no longer in need of the powers of hallucination. Our realm of the dead has withdrawn from books, in which it resided for so long. As Diodor of Sicily once wrote, "it is no longer only through writing that the dead remain in the memory of the living" [Kittler, 1999: 34].

There is no concept of the dead without one of the trappings of memory; Friedrich Kittler's influential 1999 monograph *Gramophone, Film, Typewriter*, on the development of the media apparatus, begins, tellingly, with the ghost story of modernity. At each turn and development in media technology — the telegraph, the camera, or the animated image — a new fascination with contacting and representing the dead erupts. The dead are, after all, disconnected by time and distance, two great barriers brought down by the wire, the broadcast, and the filmstrip. But more than that, each new technology captures and represents the dead, fakes the dead, and fools the incredulous. The more the machine makes sensible what we already know to be real, the more that the opposite — the doubtful but ever-present threat of the arisen corpse or spirit — becomes provable. Kittler proposes that the more we advance into modernity's apparatuses of capture and display, the more fascinated we are with the dead and their imprints.

This is what Jacques Derrida cheerily described as "hauntology," in reference to Karl Marx's persistently present but persistently dead hope of Communist revolution in Europe (Derrida, 1994: 5). A postulation more than a neologism, hauntology encapsulated "the paradoxical state of the specter, which is neither being nor non-being" (Derrida, 1994: 4). The term has slowly percolated through to music criticism and elsewhere, where it naturally found itself pronounced dead on arrival. If Derrida's hauntology is useful as a concept or as a way of seeing, it is through making forms and beings that are "out of joint" with their times and place (Derrida, 1994: 34); the rule rather than the exception. This means that hauntology accepts that changes in a form sometimes occur in one-off echoes and nuances, mutant evolutions and most importantly, anachronistic reflections. It is one way to come to grips with the muddying of traditions, the ability for figures to permeate across fictive boundaries, and the impact of the audio-visual archive on the ability to remember and forget. Derrida goes on to say that "haunting is historical, to be sure ... but it is not *dated*, it is never docilely given a date in the chain of presents, day after day, according to the instituted order of the calendar" (Derrida, 1994: 4).

Gaming's own hauntology is keenly felt in games where technologies of representation find themselves arrayed to combat the dead, or to navigate around them. Hauntology is not limited to the undead, but the appearance of the past "out of joint" more generally, media's own ghosts. So, that the gaming hauntological is most visible along genre borders speaks to the centrality of horror to game culture and design, rather than to a literal connection between the specters of media and the specters of the dead. This natural, deep media historicity and the multiple ways in which it seeks to represent the dead are, above all, traces.

The idea of the trace, so emphatically underlined by Gayatri Chakravorty Spivak in her translator's introduction to Derrida's *Of Grammatology*, is "in part the mark of the absence of a presence, an always already absent present, of the lack at the origin that is the condition of thought and experience" (Spivak in Derrida, 1974: 10). That is to say, if they are traces, both the apparition of the apparatus and the gaming dead are doubly haunted — they are resolutely about what they are not, or are no longer. They are stains and bookmarks hinting at other things, always missing an origin.

It becomes useful to think through games this way when considering game history as part of media history. For example, the continually dysfunctional familial relationship between game studies and cinema studies has produced some of the best new criticism of both fields, precisely because media forms haunt each other, and jostle for the right to genre, to archetype, to memorialization. What Jay David Bolter and Richard Grusin in part term "remediation" is also a broader autopsy of contemporary media (Bolter and Grusin, 2000: 29). Espen Aarseth, perceiving a "land grab," wrote in 2004 of the fear that it "will be a long time before film critics studying computer games will understand the difference (between the game gaze and cinema gaze)," in doing so asserting that visual pleasure came somehow after 'kinaesthetic, functional and cognitive' pleasures" (Aarseth, 2004: 313).

If this was true for game studies, from the perspective of contemporary cinema studies, it seemed a non-sequitur — after all, the cinematic gaze is not resolutely visual in the same way that cinema itself is not merely about light and color. For example, Jonathan Crary's 1979 monograph *Techniques of the Observer* described visuality as becoming mechanized and torn from the other senses, imperfectly and incompletely (Crary, 1979). Since then, as varied as the streams of cinema criticism are, there has been a concerted turn to constructing an adequate language to discuss the affective, embodied, phenomenological experience of the moving image. In the face of that turn, it would be intellectual anathema to suggest cinema and its theory was not broadly "kinaesthetic, functional and cognitive." Guiliana Bruno's *Atlas of Emotion* proposed a "geographic notion of the haptic" using media to speak to the history of media (Bruno, 2004: 120). In a similar vein, Vivian Carol Sobchack wrote in 2004 of the hope that:

> ... image-conscious and visible culture might re-engage materialism at its most radical and come to recognize as precious both the grounded gravity and transcendent possibilities, not only of our technologies and texts, but also of our flesh [Sobchack, 2004: 9].

Technologies. Texts. Flesh. This triad is gaming's birthright, and it is in tracing the relationship between the three that game studies scholars have spoken with the most lucidity and impact. Following the trace from gaming technology, game texts, and game flesh, and back again allows us to illuminate the haunt, the revenant, the corpse of other media. Gaming's hauntology — reading very different to Derrida's intent — is a way to see what remains to be seen.

In the second section of the essay, we will seek out how game mechanics, dynamics, and aesthetics make sense of technologies, texts, and fleshes in three close examples. In each, an analog media technology appears in the play mechanics, which affect the ecology of dynamics (primarily through chronology manipulation), and in turn feed into the central aesthetic of agency/helplessness that game horror is attuned to.

Haunting the Apparatus

In the wake of the success of the *Silent Hill* series (Konami, 1999–2008), the director of the first game (Keiichirō Toyama) and other members of "Team Silent" moved to work on an original title for Sony Computer Entertainment Japan Studio. *Siren* would emerge in late 2003 as a dark revisitation of the *Silent Hill* formula, which had by then begun to delve deeper into mystery-solving and demonology. *Siren* reimbursed the investment of *Silent Hill* fans with familiar tropes: a remote country town (Hanuda, characterized as both geographically and culturally isolated), a nightmarish resurrection/eschatology cult, and torchlight as a gameplay mechanic. The undead are *shibito*, "corpse people," who are all the more monstrous because they seem willing participants in their undeath — the story reveals that the townspeople were called into the blood-red lake that sits near the town by the siren Datatsushi, where they were transformed.

Unusually, *Siren*'s character models exist as plain surface models with photo-mapped faces, the resultant characters appearing rigid and still. Rather than synchronized lip movement, the faces fade from one image to another — from open mouth to closed or closed mouth to stern, furrowed brow. Perhaps as a result, many of the cut-scenes simply do not contain many medium shots or close-ups. The deeply uncanny sensation of watching *Siren* characters speak has an immediate impact on the game's experience — if *Silent Hill*'s horrors are more architectural, some of *Siren*'s horrific elements are facial and bodily, visible on the creeping, stuttering skin of the characters. They are, even in a genre of outlandish design, truly different.

The world they inhabit is dark, unforgiving, and systematic. To open a door in the game's very first mission controlling Kyoya Suda, the player has to first press the action button at the door, and then immediately confirm the action in a yes/no sub-menu. Finding keys on a table and then getting into a car throws up similarly disquieting breaks in the flow of action. It becomes apparent very early on that these are design choices, intermeshing with a cold and starkly designed interface which contains a massive database of information, as well as a timeline and character profiles that vibrate with bureaucratic malice. At every stage, *Siren* breaks itself down — the brutal, continuous interface interruptions on one hand, and the characters' mannequin-like appearance on the other, form a different kind of suspension of disbelief — "I can't believe this is happening *like this*." Progressing through the game is a baroque interconnecting web of ten survivors, as the playable character shifts from level to level and to different parts of the chronology, shown in a sub-menu after each event or cut-scene. As you progress, you begin to see the chronology fill, and the fates of the survivors unfold, segment by segment. The massive database begins to take on a life of its own, as missing elements of the puzzle niggle at the players' instinct for a revisit of the area to search again.

The mechanic for which *Siren* is most well known — "sightjacking" — is described by Kirkland as "[resembling] the experience of searching through static for television channels to tune into" (Kirkland, 2009). In a sense, the experience is not only about resemblance, but also mimicry and palpability. The left analog stick on the DualShock 2 (or other) controller was the tuning mechanism; in a mimic of older television sets' use of analog rotary tuners, players gingerly rotate the stick through VHF-style static to find an image. The image is, in fact, the viewpoint of one of the *shibito*. Players can then use knowledge of what the *shibito* is looking at, or what their routine is, to triangulate safe passage through the game.

Each level is played with an equal ratio of escaping from the *shibito*, database checking, and sight-jacking. Because the changes occur so often, taking the player from the minds of the *shibito* (complete with within-head-muffled groans and sobs), to third-person, to behind the eerie central characters, the end result is a continually disjointed experience that adds to the horror, rather than providing a break from it. This continual disjointing is distinct from the multitude of titles with similarly multiple layers because the tone of *Siren*, and the horror it deploys, are cumulative. For example, while entering the menu system may remove the immediate stress of a threat, the ever-present bureaucratic horror of the information system adds to the sense of menace. Similarly, while "sightjacking" performs a tactical role and acts as the player's main instrument for evading the *shibito*, it concentrates the affective horror nonetheless. This occurs because the faux–VHF signal is so stark and planar, where the game world is deeply shaded and dimensional, and because the static hiss of "sightjacking" is set to be louder than the sound of normal play.

Where *Fatal Frame* (Tecmo, 2001) would achieve its horror by making the player see ghosts everywhere in Himuro mansion and therefore remain continuously expectant of threats, or where *Silent Hill* would crescendo with a monster's approach, *Siren* snaps in and out of modes of vision, from static to *shibito* perspective to character perspective, so often that interruption becomes part of the horrific core of the game. The monsters of *Siren* are not just the three-dimensional *shibito* in the foothills surrounding the lake, they are the broader sensory palpability of the *shibito* — the monsters are in the signal band of the right analog stick.

Horror writer China Miéville's essay "*M.R. James and the Quantum Vampire: Weird; Hauntological; Versus and/or and and/or or?*" contains a potent phrase that foregrounds his interest in a hauntology: "Teratological specificity demands attention" (Miéville, 2008: 223). Or, more bluntly, "this monster is different." Being the study of the abnormal body, either medical or monstrous, "teratology" offers an opportunity for a productive confusion between exceptional forms that nevertheless assert uniqueness. The context of this quote is a defense of Miéville's interest against what he sees as Terry Eagleton's "cavalier hand-waving" when he in turn dismisses the "rash of books about vampires, werewolves, zombies and assorted mutants, as though a whole culture had fallen in love with the undead" (2006: 45). We might say that most cultures have always been in love with both the dead and the undead. More importantly, though, is the opportunity for the horror student's careful parsing: two of the four monsters Eagleton lists are not undead at all — mutants and werewolves are shifts in the state of life, viral and vectoral anomalies. What does bind the four categories, however, is their virtuality. Only in their proximity and to the actual do we make sense of the vampiric, lychanthropic, zombified and mutagenic. Even the mutagenic, which crosses categories by assembling both real (birth defects) and unreal (super-powered mutants) figures, is a deeply complex and productive way to think through our bodies.

So if "teratological specificity demands attention," each of the categories of the "undead" (for Eagleton) forms a limit case for internalized categories of being: hunger, violence, automation and irruption. This concept of a limit case, or extended exceptionality, is one of the great articulations that game horror has brought to bear on the wider genre. A game monster can be an expression of a particular limit case merely by being monstrous, but if the game and control mechanics cohere to that monstrosity, by making us participate or react to them in a palpable way, that monstrosity is effectively expanded. So, the *shibito* are the fulcrum by which a teratology (study of monstrous difference) and hauntology (study of ghostly traces) of *Siren* becomes possible. These monsters are different. They are broadcast horrors.

If we read the central horror apparatus of *Siren* to be a series of sensory feedback loops between the sightjacking (using VHF aesthetic), the database, and event timeline (using a bureaucratic aesthetic) and the unusual character forms (using what could be termed a *maquillage* aesthetic), then we appreciate the location of horror in *Siren* to be not merely in tensions, but in aesthetic breaks (figure 1).

This is all the more appreciable in the face of the changes made in the sequels. *Siren 2* (SCE Japan, 2006) changed the control system to dispense with confirmation prompts and the archive system to make it more interactive and less imposing. It also introduced a simplification of the sightjacking system that greatly reduced the amount of static on the "dial," in favor of filling the "spectrum" with the *shibito* signals. The PlayStation 3 title *Siren: Blood Curse* (SCE Japan, 2008, aka *Siren: New Translation* in Japan) retells the events of the first game with changes aimed at a broader audience; more combat-oriented levels and a mixed American/Japanese cast. Most importantly, the game exchanged the sightjacking's VHF tuning aesthetic for a heavily distorted split-screen option more readily coherent with high-definition imagery. Both *Siren: Blood Curse* and *Siren 2* diverge from the original game's sightjacking sensibility, and the massive, static database by which players navigated. As the games evolved and became more accessible, the *shibito* did too, becoming more driven to fight the players' characters than their thirst for blunt and quick murder witnessed in the first game.

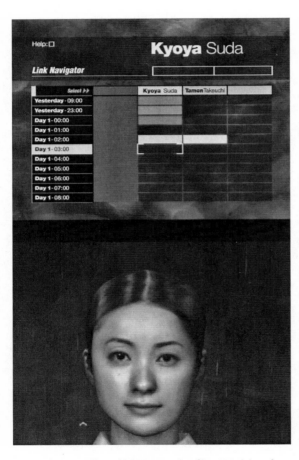

Figure 1: Siren (SCE Japan Studio, 2004) involves the parsing of multiple layers of media. Above, the database begins to grow as the player experiences levels and watches cut-scenes. Below, an eerie photograph replaces the usual 3D facial model of contemporary games.

Haunting Space

In every sense, Keiji Inafune's *Dead Rising* (Capcom, 2006) is a black comedy. Players are presented with Frank West, a fast-talking photographer-journalist molded in the vein of Bruce Campbell's character Smitty in the Coen Brothers' *The Hudsucker Proxy* (Joel and Ethan Coen, 1995). While the world of *Dead Rising* is a carnival of clichés from films and games, the clear framing intent is to parodically embrace the mall horror scenarios of *Dawn of the Dead* (George A. Romero, 1978; Zack Snyder, 2004), though an unsuccessful series of lawsuits rose and fell in the wake of their similarities.

The central game mechanics of *Dead Rising* are combat (often articulated through slapstick; shopping carts, hot frying pans, CD cases) and photography. West's camera is the main method for players progression; photographs of zombies taken around the mall are automatically sorted into categories of "erotica," "horror," "outtakes," "drama," or "brutality." These photos in turn generate "Prestige Points" which give Frank access to higher levels of health, fighting abilities—which unusually, can accrue, despite the player dying and restarting.

The apparatus-horror of the *Dead Rising* camera is an odd system; it does not change or upgrade in the same sense as *Fatal Frame*, yet through it, combat skills are developed. Just as *Siren*'s sequels moved away from that game's central dynamic, *Dead Rising: Chop Till You Drop* (Capcom, 2008) for the Nintendo Wii, removes the camera entirely to allow for more action-driven play. If *Siren* managed experience in small bureaucratic sizes, *Dead Rising* creates a laissez-faire economy of action; missions arrive now and then with greater or lesser urgency, and the player is free to take them up or ignore them. As a result, a hauntological trace is possible through the camera mechanic; observing ratios of the different categories is not clearly defined as a reward structure or goal, but as the game opens into an initiative-led experience, the player returns to photography as the mainstay of experimentation. Even this is somewhat of a euphemism; the game plainly circulates around mass slaughter and the subsequent photography thereof. *Dead Rising*'s pleasures are not merely sensory because they are concerned with bodily extremes—playing with corpses, running them over with a lawnmower, etc.—but because the combat is often connected to the camera.

Just as the left analog stick in *Siren* provided the broadcast dial in a moment of palpability, a trigger button on the top of the controller in *Dead Rising* mimics any camera's exposure button. It is worth considering these sensorial mimicries and connections as a type of expanded realism. Talking about the horror film, Brigitte Peucker offers a working model:

> Supplementing the activity of the eye with that of touch, taste and sometimes even smell, the horror film engages its spectator in a multisensory, yet nevertheless aesthetic experience that promotes a certain type of illusion. Horror, like the picturesque, overlaps with realism in its expanded sense, with realism anchored in the response of a spectatorial body whose sensations and affects promote the effect that the image is real [Peucker, 2007, 24].

In apprehending the location of the horrific, an establishment of its considerable wealth of elements is necessary. For example, we cannot establish with any strength that all images of the dead are horrific per se. Peucker's promotion-of-the-real is a dynamic, specifically textual way to think around the problem of realism. Coming across a corpse in a specific textual space (say, a specific game and a specific play experience) forces the unanimated body to stand in for a number of other vectored forces. The presence of a still body, or better yet a manipulable body, does not assert realism. Rather, it is the body's proximity to the real — how real it seems, how manipulable it is, what we can see when we linger over it — which is coded as a pleasure act. Rather than gaming *realism* or a functioning sense of the *realistic*, we are interpolated into gaining pleasure from bodily exhibition, not dissimilar to a wax-work museum. It is fun — a fun idiosyncratic to gaming — to linger over a virtual body and marvel in its realistic construction. This pleasure is neither based in gaming nor narrative logic, but from the pleasure of spectacle itself. In a 2004 article on *DOOM 3* (id Software, 2004b), Angela Ndalianis expands on this idea:

> In the sensorial assault that continues, the player is invited to believe that the illusion they perceive is perceptually real ... imitation and representation evoke alternative "realities" that reflect the ability of the effects to trigger emotional responses and almost instinctive reactions from the player [Ndalianis, 2004b: 109].

While this doubling of reality or promotion of the real literally makes sense, the role of the fallen or falling body in this situation is increasingly central. The body, animated and otherwise, is the zenith concentration point of game materiality, where the senses are interfacing most often, and of course, where most of the production system is oriented. Animation, facial mapping, high quality texturing, all concentrate on the bodies and forms we face. So it is that the virtual body becomes the invitation card to this doubled reality.

What is traded, either explicitly or otherwise, is the promotion of a realistic effect; the game body, because it ceases to provide ludic affordances, signifies the literal luxury of the game space, an ornament and trophy. The opportunity to play with the body — corpse-play — is the conduit through which horror rushes into game texts which otherwise bear no generic relation. *Dead Rising* is a comedic experience, but one which gathers horror elements through sensorial connections, like the camera and the corpse-play. Like Peucker's sense of the picturesque, the horror highlighted here is in an expanded sense. The exhibition of the corpse produces a literally sensible point of reference, a portal through which sensibility of the game space can be understood. In cases where these bodies disappear soon after death, an evaporation of visible labor occurs.

In *Siren*, the gaming body of the *shibito* has a mnemonic twin; the apparatus of the aerial and the database. The zombie hordes of *Dead Rising* have theirs; the hands-off mission structure which can be forgotten, and a (hitherto unmentioned) save system which perverts years of conventional game design. Where most modern games give total memory control to the player, *Dead Rising* only allows one save game at a time, and offers a circular question upon the player dying — where "save status and quit" means to save the state of the character but begin the game anew, and "load game" results in the player losing their progress. The result is that players are encouraged to experience the first sections of the game multiple times. As Jay McRoy explains: "This experience of an elliptical, yet forward progression may at first seem like a considerable, or perhaps even a radical, departure from traditional reading or viewing practices" (McRoy, 2006). The game is thus designed to be played through, but also to be failed. When players save their progress, they are saving Prestige Points and a growing health bar, even though Frank West dies and dies again.

It is for these reasons that *Dead Rising* begins to take on an expansive, ornamental style when the player has smashed dozens or hundreds of zombies in absurd ways, their bodies persisting longer than most horror games due to the affordances of the platform and the game's cultural role as an early high-definition exhibition piece. The swarming masses of *Dead Rising* are distinct from the *Dawn of the Dead* zombies by virtue of their relationship to the mall; zombies are largely indigenous to the mall and each new area to explore has a new set of largely stationary, but slowly encroaching zombies. It does not take long to sense that if Romero's zombies were shopping to remind us of the futility and inhumanity of consumer routine, we would shop for Inafune's zombies ourselves— they are functional ornaments. In doing so, they fulfill many of the requirements of Angela Ndalianis's "neo-baroque," that other time-out-of-joint that "combines the visual, the auditory, and the textual in ways that parallel the dynamism of seventeenth-century baroque form" (Ndalianis, 2004: 5) which is characterized by excess and waste. Excess in the cultural sense, as Ndalianis had discussed elsewhere, "does not just imply more ... excess involves a process that causes the mind of the spectator to rebel because expectations have been shattered" (Ndalianis, 2002: 511).

If we began by accepting Sobchack's articulated hope that we might re-engage a materialist approach to culture through technology, text, and flesh, we find ourselves with some resolute and stark early impressions— where flesh and technology coincide, memory and chronology twist in response. In *Siren*, a galaxy of segmented experiences wheels and turns in the bureaucratic database, so the more we play and experience in-flesh, the more the text expands. Like many games in which the saves on the memory card are doubled by the revealing of notes and artifacts, *Siren* requires us to refer to the database with increasing frequency. In *Dead Rising*, a shopping mall is a measuring cup for the creeping flesh we are encouraged to play with, experiment with, and turn into photographic ornament. The element of apparatus capture in Inafune's mall horror is less concerned with building up a history, than with a spectacular collection of extreme images. The natural site of enquiry for both is the apparatus that makes the memory — the vectoral dynamic that turns one type of experience into another.

Haunting Lack

A lesser known example in the short history of survival horror is the B-grade cult title *Michigan: Report from Hell* (Grasshopper Manufacture, 2004). As part of the long-tail economy of highly successful consoles, publishers such as 505 Gamestreet have appeared in European (including Australasian territories) markets, thanks to very cheap license agreements with equally down-market Japanese publishers. The business of B and Z-grade game publication, while chronically under-researched, is easily mappable to the economies of scale in game labor; as a particular popular platform becomes easier and easier to develop for, the bar for effective game production is continually lowered. *Michigan: Report from Hell* emerges not out of B-grade production per se, but was published in Europe only due to the success of far less complex games featuring nameless low-polygon models of generically designed characters. *Michigan: Report from Hell* attains cult status through *Suda 51* (Goichi Suda), who would go on to direct and plan *killer7* (Grasshopper Manufacture, 2005) and *No More Heroes* (Grasshopper Manufacture, 2007). Both of the latter games are stylistically brave, featuring a depth-modeled cel-shaded style and highly unusual mission-based gameplay and mission design. In each of those games, elements of apparatus horror create unique gameplay dynamics—despite neither being strictly horror experiences. *Michigan: Report from Hell* was afforded none of the stylistic flourishes, suffering a wide range of otherwise fatal bugs and design flaws.

Michigan: Report from Hell is played from the perspective of a nameless cameraman for ZaKa TV, who is seeking to investigate a mysterious mist that has enveloped the city. He embarks on this endeavor with a sound operator called Brisco and a series of reporters who— surprisingly, for the first time player —form the functional memory for the player. The player's view of the game-world is styled on the viewfinder of a digital video camera. Gameplay dynamics are limited to filming strange events, combat, conversations and investigation. Like *Dead Rising*, the game uses categories: "Suspense," "Erotic" and "Immoral." By interacting with the environment with a simple "tag" command, the player can set the circumstances for the different categories of filmable action. After "tagging" an object, the reporter accompanies the cameraman to the market and performs the action, as the player-cameraman "films" the results. This routine of call-and-response is the primary means of moving through the game, as the witness-mechanics of the ZaKa TV cameraman rarely call for any form of direct combat or action. However, it is not powerlessness or the lack of agency which provides the horror mechanics. Despite what we have seen with other examples, and how apparatus horror can often translate to a deep use of memory architecture, it is *Michigan: Report from Hell*'s utter lack of functional memory that provides the horror element. Through error or inaction, the reporters can die — and rather than give the player a punishment, it simply moves them to the next level. This way, the game can be rapidly completed through ineptitude. The central reason for not completing the game rapidly is to experience several moments of "Immoral" gameplay; complex play sequences which culminate in the player letting a support character die in order to film it. However, the reward is shallow. Seeing one of your star reporters buckles unconvincingly after a spider lurches at her legs ultimately fails to fulfill any category, "immoral" or otherwise.

Michigan: Report from Hell can hardly be seen as a template for Suda 51's later games *killer7* and *No More Heroes;* where both games share stylistic concerns, and segmented level structure with lesser or greater degrees of freedom, the earlier game offers only the barest conceit of traditional game design. Progress and success are, for the most part, completely disconnected. In this almost comically barren game, one of the most intriguing uses of memory to foreground horror is hidden — by design, or more likely by accident. The sensory link that ties the apparatus to history is almost untraceable; in its place, we have an explicit relationship between memory and play. When we fail to protect the reporters, we never see their bodies— we see a flash of VHF static and just move on.

Many of *Michigan: Report from Hell*'s dynamics circulate through the dispersal of memory itself. The central plot, unraveling the cause of the mist which has descended over the town, is doubled by the mist itself, a convenience to close the draw distance between the player viewpoint and horizon. The haze turns the people of the town into fleshy proto–*Silent Hill* horrors, but also hides the relatively low-budget game engine. During repeated playthroughs, a player will find fewer and fewer clues about the origin of the mist (a rogue bioweapon) since ludic success is not concomitantly rewarded. Rather, with voice-acting at the barest quality, repeated play in the game environment leads to a more and more experimental play-style. Finding "immoral" and "erotic" value scenes and objects becomes the skein of reward, and the main ludic activity (figure 2).

With a game as glitchy and sparsely produced as *Michigan: Report from Hell*, the core horror elements then migrate out of plot, out of sensory display, and into the player's memorial capacity. Logic breaks down in ways which sometimes causes the game software to crash, as opposed to the playful ontology breaks in the *Metal Gear Solid* series (Konami, 2001–2008) and *Eternal Darkness: Sanity's Requiem* (Silicon Knights, 2002). Fatal and nonfatal glitches that behave like this— reminding us of the material circumstances of games— are by nature, frustrating. They can also allow other pleasures to grow alongside normal correct play and change the experience out of the bounds of narrative, or of ludic experience. The mist that sits at the centre of play has to be thought of as part-glitch itself, since it binds the proscenium of play in a shroud of doubt. The repetitions of scenes and inexplicable jumps in the plot do not accumulate to resolve amnesia, but to enforce it. In Don Delilio's novel, *White Noise* (1985), the quintessential "Airbourne Toxic Event" produces a sense of *déjà vu* in those it comes into contact with, where the reliability of memory is the final signal of death's power spreading into life — the media apparatus being the means by which our memory becomes erratic, suffuse, and cloudy. Delilio's novel uses the Airbourne Toxic Event as a kind of purposeful miasma; the memory-devouring presence by which the panic of everyday life resolves. In *Michigan: Report from Hell*, it is not a sense of *déjà vu* but amnesia that the mist comes to represent; the possibilities of play are only those within the draw distance. Unlike *Silent Hill*'s grim fog, which shrouds the town in white, the grey-black mist of *Michigan: Report from Hell* acts as a far harder limit. In many buildings throughout the game, the opposite end of a room diminishes into the bleakness.

Conclusion: Haunting Memory

Marc Augé's 2004 book *Oblivion* concerns the problem of memory as one of cultivation, in which forgetting allows remembrance, and feeds the processes of grief, of memorialization, and so on.

Remembering or forgetting is doing gardener's work, selecting, pruning. Memories are like plants: there are those that need to be quickly eliminated in order to help the others burgeon, transform, flower. Those plants that have in some way achieved their destiny, those flourishing plants have in some way forgotten themselves in order to transform: between the seeds or the cutting from which they were born and what they have become there is hardly any apparent relationship anymore. In that sense, the flower is the seed's oblivion [Augé, 2004: 66].

Figure 2: Michigan: Report from Hell (Grasshopper Manufacture, 2004), by Goichi Suda, gives the player the role of a cameraman in a kind of undead apocalypse. Here, the non-player characters puzzle over an unexplainable, but filmable, situation.

As removed aesthetically as this is from a computer game of say, dragons and zombies, trolls and monsters, the sense of cultivated *space* is immediately recognizable as the prior form of game movement. We leave the inanimate behind to go and find things to do with the animate, annihilating them. Remembering our concern with *Dead Rising's* neo-baroque, we can begin to use this trace of oblivion itself to weed out the aesthetic core.

Bodies left by the player are not always our murder victims, but can act as our symbolic architecture of passage, leaving place where space once stood. In each game text, if we are to speak of specificity, a different context of memorialization through the corpse's lack of animation is true in each game, and in each gameplay. In many of these contexts, inanimate bodies are the crumbs leading out of the forest. Playing through a game which involves violence situates the player as a figure that cultivates other figures, knocking animation cycles away and returning them to the oblivion of computer memory. When we avoid other figures, such as in *Michigan: Report from Hell,* and *Siren,* we are austere, and the construction of memory matters more than ever. What makes this reading of the milieu relatively compelling is that we as players assume an almost digestive role, turning gaming bodies and their constituent labor — remembering that characters are the site of most game production work — inside out as we move through or as we linger. A body in the next hallway is digested, we move through, the remains linger until the next memory purge.

Augé's formulation of remembrance is open to both rapid, violent passage, and lingering over the body we've found, made, or mutilated. His concept of the cultivated garden is a neat poetic metaphor for how computers handle memory and data. If we adapt his formulation in this way, we can read certain games as memory-recuperation activities— our violence acting much like Marc Augé's proverbial pruning shears. Zombies fall to the ground, dissolve, and free up random-access memory (RAM).

If where we look makes the world, which is increasingly true with contemporary video and computer games, then it follows that when we look at the dead, we make the dead. To look away is to annihilate.

From here, how we articulate the gaming body's moment of death becomes vital.

> The definition of death as the horizon of every individual and distinct life, while obvious, nevertheless takes on another meaning, a more subtle and more everyday meaning, as soon as one perceives it as a definition of life itself— of life between two deaths. So it is with memory and oblivion. The definition of oblivion as loss of remembrance takes on another meaning as soon as one perceives it as a component of memory itself [Augé, 2004: 73].

This sense of death being a kind of life between two deaths in material and memorial terms is immediately readable to the gamer, and especially the horror gamer, who experiences memory and life in such specifically demarcated ways that the aesthetic confluence cannot help but be a consideration of the "life between two deaths."

These monsters are different. In each case, we see an atypical but strong relationship between apparatus, meaning and body — technology, text, and flesh. The gaming dead, however, are not in the same category as the zombies and ghosts of those worlds. They are indigenous only to absence itself; neither ghosts nor monsters, but somewhere in-between and resolutely constituent, persistent where a game needs to display its sense of the real, or totally absent where only the directive of the genre or narrative matters. It is their constituency in the memory of the apparatus, both literally and figuratively, that generates their pneumea. The hauntology that can chase down the relationships in each specific case, looking for those traces of dead media to find the next link, often finds itself face to face with something more horrible that it imagined.

Works Cited

Aarseth, Espen (2004), "Genre Trouble," in Noah Wardrip-Fruin and Pat. Harrigan (eds.), *First Person: New Media as Story, Performance, and Game*, Cambridge, MA: MIT Press, pp. 45–54.

Atkins, Barry, and Tanya Krzywinska (eds.) (2007), *Videogame, Player, Text*, Manchester, UK, and New York: Manchester University Press and Palgrave.

Augé, Marc (2004), *Oblivion*, Minneapolis: University of Minnesota Press.

Bolter, Jay David and Grusin, Richard (2000), *Remediation: Understanding New Media*, Cambridge, MA: MIT Press.

Bruno, Giuliana (2002), *Atlas of Emotion: Journeys in Art, Architecture, and Film*, London and New York: Verso.

Buse, Peter, and Andrew Stott (1999), *Ghosts: Deconstruction, Psychoanalysis, History*, New York: St. Martin's Press.

Crary, Jonathan (1990), *Techniques of the Observer: On Vision and Modernity in the Nineteenth Century*, Cambridge, MA: MIT Press.

DeLillo, Don. (1985), *White Noise*, New York: Viking.

Derrida, Jacques (1976), *Of Grammatology*, Baltimore: Johns Hopkins University Press.

_____ (1994), *Specters of Marx: The State of the Debt, the Work of Mourning, and the New International*, New York: Routledge.

Eagleton, Terry (2006), "Mark Neocleous: The Monstrous and the Dead: Burke, Marx, Fascism," *Radical Philosophy*, No. 137, May-June. pp. 45–47.

King, Geoff, and Tanya Krzywinska (eds.) (2002), *Screenplay: Cinema/Videogames/Interfaces*, London and New York: Wallflower Press.

_____, and _____ (eds.) (2006), *Tomb Raiders and Space Invaders: Videogame Forms and Contexts*, London: I. B. Tauris.

Kirkland, Ewan (2009), "*Resident Evil*'s Typewriter: Survival Horror and Its Remediations," *Games and Culture*, Vol. 4, No. 2, April.

Kittler, Friedrich A. (1999), *Gramophone, Film, Typewriter*, translated by Geoffrey Winthrop-Young and Michael Wutz, Writing Science Series, Stanford, CA: Stanford University Press.

Krzywinska, Tanya (2002), "Hands-On Horror," in Geoff King and Tania Krzywinska (eds.),

Screenplay: Cinema/Videogames/Interfaces, London and New York: Wallflower Press, pp. 206–23.

McIntosh, Shawn, and Marc Leverette (2008), *Zombie Culture: Autopsies of the Living Dead*, Lanham, MD: Scarecrow Press.

McRoy, Jay (2006), "The Horror Is Alive. Immersion, Spectatorship, and the Cinematics of Fear in the Survival Horror Genre," *Reconstruction*, Vol. 6, No. 1, available online at <http://reconstruction.eserver.org/061/mcroy.shtml>.

Miéville, China (2008), "M. R. James and the Quantum Vampire: Weird; Hauntological: Versus and/or and and/or or?," in Robin Mackay (ed.) *Concept-Horror*, Collapse IV, London: Urbanomic, pp. 105–128.

Ndalianis, Angela (2004b), "'Hail to the King!'—the Return of Doom," *Journal for Media History* (Tijdschrift voor Mediageschiedenis), No. 2, pp. 100–117.

_____ (2004a), *Neo-Baroque Aesthetics and Contemporary Entertainment*, Cambridge, MA: MIT Press.

_____ (2002), "The Rules of the Game: Evil Dead II ... Meet Thy Doom," in Henry Jenkins, Tara McPherson and Jane Shattuc (eds.), *Hop on Pop: the Politics and Pleasures of Popular Culture*, Durham, NC: Duke University Press, pp. 503–516.

Perron, Bernard (2005), "Coming to Play at Frightening Yourself: Welcome to the World of Horror Video Games," *Aesthetics of Play. A Conference on Computer Game Aesthetics*, University of Bergen, Norway, available online at <http://www.cosignconference.org/downloads/papers/perron_cosign_2004.pdf>.

_____ (2004), "Sign of a Threat: The Effects of Warning Systems in Survival Horror Games," *COSIGN 2004 Proceedings*, Art Academy, University of Split, pp. 132–141, available online at <http://www.aestheticsofplay.org/perron.php>.

Peucker, Brigitte (2007), *The Material Image: Art and the Real in Film*, Cultural Memory in the Present Series, Stanford, CA: Stanford University Press.

Sconce, Jeffrey (2000), *Haunted Media: Electronic Presence from Telegraphy to Television*, Durham, NC: Duke University Press.

Sobchack, Vivian (2004), *Carnal Thoughts: Embodiment and Moving Image Culture*, Berkeley: University of California Press.

Wardrip-Fruin, Noah, and Pat Harrigan (eds.) (2004), *First Person: New Media as Story, Performance, and Game*, Cambridge, MA: MIT Press.

Whalen, Zach, and Laurie N. Taylor (2008), *Playing the Past: History and Nostalgia in Video Games*, Nashville: Vanderbilt University Press.

The Rules of Horror:
Procedural Adaptation in
Clock Tower, Resident Evil,
and *Dead Rising*
Matthew Weise

Introduction

Procedural adaptation, the concept of taking a text from another medium and modeling it as a computer simulation, has hitherto been characterized as something theoretical, as a tool to imagine the future of computer-based art rather than describe its past or present. It is my view that quite a few procedural adaptations already exist in the commercial sphere of video games. Particularly in the case of horror games, which often have extremely clear, highly codified subgenre conventions to work from, procedural adaptation has a long and complex history. Horror games span a wide array of game genres—from action platformers, to graphic adventures, to text adventures, to first-person shooters—and use many different types of game conventions to model, embody, and express the logics of various horror subgenres. This essay will explore two specific case study examples of procedural adaptation in horror games: those modeled on the stalker film subgenre, which I will refer to as "stalker simulations," and those modeled on the zombie film subgenre, which I will refer to as "zombie simulations."

Procedural Adaptation

Procedural adaptation, as I use it in this essay, is a variation on procedural translation. Procedural translation is a concept developed by game scholar Ian Bogost, which he describes as "taking themes and figures from poetry, literature, film, and television [...] and asking how such themes are/could be represented in games" (2006). This is an extension of Bogost's theory of procedural rhetoric, which he defines as "the practice of authoring arguments through process" (2007: 29).

> [Procedural rhetoric's] arguments are made not through construction of words and images, but through the authorship of rules of behavior, the construction of dynamic models. In computation, those rules are authored in code, through the practice of programming [Bogost, 2007: 29].

Rather than authoring rules and systems dynamics in such a way that they make an argument, procedural translation is the practice of authoring rules and systems dynamics in such ways that they model the situational logics implied by texts from other media. Developing a game system that expressed Marxist ideology would be procedural rhetoric. Developing a game system that let the user experience what it would be like to be Laurie in *Halloween* (John Carpenter, 1979) would be procedural translation.

I prefer the term "adaptation" over "translation" for a few reasons. First of all I want to emphasize that the process of which I'm speaking is creative, not prescriptive. It is an authored process, by which conscious choices are made in how to change, manipulate, and re-arrange elements of an existing media text so that it conforms to an author's interpretation. Game scholar Jesper Juul calls this a process of abstraction, by which certain elements are chosen to be modeled in a game system while others are omitted (Juul, 2007). Adaptation is a term already associated with the arts, as in the case of novel-to-stage adaptations or stage-to-screen adaptations, and implies a similar process of abstraction to what Juul describes, a process of choosing which elements to focus on and which to ignore, which will vary significantly depending on one's creative vision. Translation, by comparison, is a term that has connotations of accuracy and correctness I would like to avoid. I do not believe there is such a thing as an "accurate" procedural translation of a film into a game just as I do not believe there is an "accurate" procedural translation of a novel into a film. While it is true that translation in some circumstances can be a creative process (as in the case of language translation when there is a word in one language with no analog in the other), adaptation is closer in spirit to the practice of artistic creation I wish to discuss.

Procedural adaptation is the term that I feel best encapsulates what video games do when they codify the conventions of horror texts.[1] Yet this does not mean that visual, audio, and story components are irrelevant. Media scholars Diane Carr and Diarmid Campbell and game writer Katie Ellwood describe the video game adaptation of John Carpenter's *The Thing* (1982) as a case where "ludic and representational features operate in tandem" (2006: 161). Although Carr, Campbell and Ellwood do not use the term procedural adaptation, their discussion of *The Thing* (Computer Artworks, 2002) falls easily under its rubric. *The Thing* is a horror game that attempts to simulate various aspects of Carpenter's film — such as trust, social stability, and an alien that can secretly take the form of any human comrade — in its rule system. This rule system does not exist in a vacuum however, as it is entirely derived from and reinforced by the fictive context — the setting, the characters, the visual and audio design — which give the rules purpose and coherence (Carr, Campbell and Ellwood, 2006: 161). I argue that this is what procedural adaptation is in the world of commercial game development: games that use both ludic and representational elements to adapt a text from another medium, yet do so in a way in which the removal of the ludic elements would cause a game's identity as an adaptation to evaporate.

The games I will discuss—*Clock Tower* (Human Entertainment, 1995), *Clock Tower 2* (Human Entertainment, 1997), *Resident Evil* (Capcom, 1996), *Resident Evil 2* (Capcom, 1998), and *Dead Rising* (Capcom, 2006)— all fit this model of procedural adaptation. These games are all adaptations of horror subgenres. As such they embody logics that one might find in several horror films of the same sub-category (like stalker films) as opposed to a single film (like *Halloween*). However, even among adaptations of horror subgenres, it is common for a game to single out a specific film as its model. This is most clearly the case with *Dead Rising*, which bears as much in common with the specific zombie film *Dawn of the Dead* (George Romero, 1978) as with zombie films in general. For the purposes of this essay I will be focusing on such examples for their generic qualities mainly, since my purpose is to illustrate how adaptations of genre logic evolve over several different games. I will illustrate this first in the case of *Clock Tower* and the stalker film, and then in the case of *Resident Evil* and the zombie film. For each game I will discuss the rule systems that make up the game world (i.e. the gameplay mechanics) and then explain how these systems are derived from their filmic sources. I will discuss how procedural adaptation differs in complexity from game to game, i.e. how game developers selectively choose to codify certain conventions of their subgenre but avoid others because of technical or aesthetic reasons. Finally, I will discuss how all these nuances strengthen or weaken a game as a procedural adaptation.

Simulation and Experience

In addition to procedural adaptation, there are other key terms I will use throughout this essay that bear defining. Simulation is a term I have already used to describe the games I will be speaking of. Game scholar Gonzalo Frasca claims "to simulate is to model a (source) system through a different system which maintains (for somebody) some of the behaviors of the original system" (2003: 223). When I refer to simulations, I will be referring to rule systems that are intended to replicate the behaviors one finds in — to use Frasca's terminology — the source system. In the case of procedural adaptation, the source is not a system explicitly but a certain set of genre conventions. These conventions imply systems through their apparent cause and effect logic. The genre conventions of stalker films and zombie films in particular imply certain logics based on the situational experience of their stock protagonists (that of a young girl versus an unstoppable serial killer or that of a survivor versus an army of flesh-eating undead). Although there are undoubtedly additional logics implied by stalker and zombie films, the logics bound up in the situation of the protagonist are the ones explicitly modeled by the games I will discuss.[2]

"I want *Resident Evil* to give the player the feeling that he's the main character in a horror movie," game creator Shinji Mikami states (1996a). This is the user experience both stalker simulations and zombie simulations generate. They replicate, within certain limits, the experience of a film's protagonist, allowing players to discover "what they would do" in the protagonist's situation. This maps neatly to film scholar Noël Carroll's claim that horror audiences do not identify mentally and emotionally with horror protagonists so much as "assimilate their situation."

> When I read a description of a protagonist in a certain set of circumstances, I do not duplicate the mind of the character (as given in the fiction) in myself. I assimilate her situation. Part of this involves having a sense of the character's internal understanding of the situation, that is, having a sense of how the character assesses the situation [Carroll, 1990: 95].

Carroll argues that the protagonist's mental state need only be comprehended, not shared, in order for audiences to engage with a horror text. This suggests a sympathetic connection between audience and text in traditional media, rather than an empathetic one. Procedural adaptations like stalker and zombie simulations offer users the opportunity to experiment with this gap between sympathy and empathy. Watching someone run from a serial killer and running from a serial killer oneself are not the same experience, for example, but stalker simulations give users the opportunity to experience the latter, albeit in a highly mediated form. In the process, the player might discover they are more like the horror film protagonist than they think they are, or less. It is this sense of discovery that procedural adaptations offer the player, of how ourselves personally — not someone else — might act when confronted by horrific circumstances.

Horror vs. Survival Horror

For accuracy's sake, I will refer to my examples as horror games. Survival horror, the term which in recent years has come to mean virtually all horror-themed video games, is problematic for a variety of reasons. It is specifically tied to the *Resident Evil* franchise, which originated in 1996 and was highly influential.[3] Survival horror did not exist as a phrase in popular video game terminology prior to that, yet games are often retroactively labeled as survival horror in spite of the fact that they predate *Resident Evil* by several years. This is a problem because the *survival* aspect of survival horror is strongly connected to the combat-oriented gameplay popularized by *Resident Evil* and does not necessarily apply to all horror games.[4] There are many horror games which predate *Resident Evil* that are not primarily based on combat — and hence not on survival — including *Dark Seed* (Cyberdreams, 1993), *Alone in the Dark* (Infogrames, 1992), *The Lurking Horror* (Infocom, 1987), and *Uninvited* (ICOM Simulations, 1986). The gameplay of these games is based primarily on puzzle-solving and exploration, and several of them have point-and-click interfaces which are not suited to action mechanics. The fact that *Clock Tower* predates *Resident Evil*, has a point-and-click interface, and features no combat is a good argument for a more inclusive term, of which "horror games" seems the most obvious choice. All survival horror games are horror games, but not all horror games are survival horror.

The Stalker Simulation

Stalker simulations are what I call the group of horror games that model themselves after the stalker film. Stalker simulations include *Clock Tower*, *Clock Tower 2*, *Clock Tower 3* (Capcom, 2004), and *Haunting Ground* (Capcom, 2005). Also known as slasher films, examples of the stalker film include *Halloween*, *The Texas Chain Saw Massacre* (Tobe Hooper, 1974), *Friday the 13th* (Sean S. Cunningham, 1980), *Nightmare on Elm Street* (Wes Craven, 1984), and *Slumber Party Massacre* (Amy Holden Jones, 1982). Film scholar Carol J. Clover describes the stalker film as:

> [T]he immensely generative story of a psychokiller who slashes to death a string of mostly female victims, one by one, until he is subdued or killed, usually by the one girl who has survived [1992: 21].

Clover breaks down the stalker film into several reoccurring components: the Killer, the Weapon(s), the Terrible Place, the Victims, and the Final Girl (1992: 24). The killer is the main antagonist of the story, who remains the same for the entire film, and has an iconic look, often involving a mask of some sort; he uses a signature weapon or weapons, which are always primitive. The Terrible Place, usually the killer's home, is where the final sections of the story happen, in which the killer's sick family past (which serves as an explanation for his psychosis) is revealed. The victims are the people — usually women — who are killed by the killer, always in sudden, spectacularly gruesome ways. The Final Girl is the main protagonist who survives the killer's onslaught and emerges triumphantly, either to be saved or to kill the killer herself.

The way Clover describes these components is not particularly systemic. She speaks of plot elements that each stalker film must hit, such as the eventual arrival at the Terrible Place. However, in addition to set plot elements, Clover speaks often of behaviors each character type — specifically the Final Girl — must exhibit in order to satisfy the genre. The Final Girl is one who:

> ... encounters the mutilated bodies of her friends and perceives the full extent of the preceding horror and of her own peril; who is chased, cornered, wounded; whom we see scream, stagger, fall, rise, and scream again. She is abject terror personified [Clover, 1992: 35].

Conversely, the Final Girl is also "resourceful and intelligent in a pinch" crafting weapons to defend herself, performing daring feats of escape, and outsmarting the killer through stealth (Clover, 1992: 39). Together these qualities form a map of the Final Girl's core behavior set. She is one who runs, hides, escapes, tricks, overcomes, and fights back. Her keys to survival are a combination of quick reflexes, even quicker wits, and sheer will power. Her goal is survival and escape, not direct physical confrontation. Her triumph is her own ability to rise above her abject terror, to manage it and ensure it does not jeopardize her judgment. In a sense, her goal is to survive her own fear, as well as the physical threat the killer represents, because failing to master the former means failure to master the latter.

The above paragraph is as accurate a description of the core game mechanics of *Clock Tower* as I can imagine.[5] In the game, the player assumes the role of Jennifer, a young orphan girl who is adopted, along with several other girls, by a mysterious woman and taken to live at her mansion. *Clock Tower* has a point-and-click style interface derived from graphic adventure games. The player as Jennifer explores the mansion — including its giant, spooky clock tower from which the game gets its title — looking for clues, and solving puzzles in her attempt to escape from the murderous Scissorman, a masked killer welding a giant pair of scissors who stalks and kills the orphan girls one by one.

Jennifer is a textbook Final Girl. As a video game character she embodies all the behaviors of the Final Girl and offers them to the player as her core affordances. To survive the player must run, hide, and outsmart Scissorman. Combat is not an option. If Scissorman should corner the player, in a bathroom or at the end of a hallway, Jennifer will begin to panic. She stops responding to player input as fear takes her over, causing her to shake uncontrollably. At this point the player's only option is to press the B button as quickly as possible to break Jennifer out of her panic. If successful, Jennifer will gain a sudden burst of will, pushing Scissorman off balance and quickly running away. If unsuccessful, Scissorman does to Jennifer exactly what is expected and the game is over.

Clock Tower is primarily a point-and-click adventure game, meaning the player directs Jennifer's attention around the screen with a cursor. The point-and-click interface is not commonly used for reflex-based action games, which is what *Clock Tower* becomes when Scissorman shows up, seemingly at random. He may pop out of a closet, through a window, or simply be waiting in a room when Jennifer enters. The player gets the feeling very strongly right from the beginning that Scissorman could be anywhere; it's just a matter of time before he appears. His appearances are not scripted or predictable, however. They are part of the game system. Scissorman is the never-ending enemy of *Clock Tower*, the player's cursed pursuer who cannot ever, under any circumstances, be permanently stopped. He can only be outwitted, delayed, or temporarily subdued.

Even when it seems as if Jennifer could just grab his scissors and kill him herself, like when she's just knocked him unconscious, the player is never given the opportunity to do this. Jennifer is too scared. She only has enough emotional stability to escape at the first opportunity, regardless of whatever strategic advantage the player may have created for her. The player's agency is entirely contained within Jennifer's psychological limits as a Final Girl.

> Angry displays of force may belong to the male [Killer], but crying, cowering, screaming, fainting, trembling, begging for mercy belong to the female [Final Girl] [Clover, 1992: 51].

Clock Tower puts the player in a world of these gendered actions.[6] It is interesting to observe that, in virtually all other horror games, player avatars never express fear during gameplay. The protagonists of *Resident Evil*, *Silent Hill*, and most other popular horror franchises are calm and collected when faced with fantastic terrors. Jennifer in *Clock Tower*, however, is a basket case. The player has to learn and respond to her emotional state; else they will never be able to maneuver her away from Scissorman. This focus on fear management and emotion is not just relegated to chase sequences: it permeates the entire game. In the moments between scrapes with Scissorman the player's goal is to search around the mansion and look for a way to escape. Following the conventions of point-and-click games, the player can inspect all sorts of objects to see if they are useful. However, many of these objects can scare Jennifer, further unhinging her and leaving her in a worsened state.

There is a picture of Jennifer's face on-screen at all times in *Clock Tower*. By default, the area surrounding it is blue and her expression is calm. However, if Jennifer should hear a weird noise or find something scary (like a blood-filled sink!), her expression will change and the color will move from blue to red. Like Scissorman, many of the environmental elements that scare

Jennifer are random. If the player looks at a mirror once nothing might happen. But looking at the same mirror again later may cause a ghostly hand to reach through it and grab Jennifer, causing her fear level to spike. The more scared Jennifer is when facing Scissorman, the more rapid button presses it takes to break her out of the depths of her terror if cornered. This makes the player judge every room, every moment of the game, as a potential psychological minefield. Things that might not scare a macho warrior will scare Jennifer, and this is something the player must deal with whether they like it or not. The player must learn to manage Jennifer's fear, to work within her mental faculties in order to survive. The extent to which the player is able to do this—the extent to which they are able to display the perceptiveness, wits, and determination of an effective Final Girl—determines whether or not they will survive to see the end of *Clock Tower*.

These rules are at the center of *Clock Tower*'s gameplay: its core mechanics. They are the reason *Clock Tower* qualifies as a procedural adaptation of the stalker film. *Clock Tower*'s design strategy for becoming a stalker simulation is to become a Final Girl simulation. The core transmedial pleasure lies in the player getting to step into the Final Girl's role and discover the emergent dynamics of her iconic peril for themselves. They get to finally discover what it's like to be the person they've mocked by shouting "Don't go in there!" at so many times. In the process they may discover that surviving an unstoppable, psychically superior killing machine with nothing but a cotton dress and their wits isn't as easy as it always looked from the safety of the darkened theater.

Of course, *Clock Tower* uses more than just mechanics to achieve its effect. The setting and story also fit the conventions of stalker films. Scissorman perfectly fits the profile of the Killer, complete with mask, signature weapon, and past drenched in family dysfunction. In exploring the mansion, the player inevitably uncovers the history of the Barrows family, the matriarch of which is the one who adopted Jennifer and her friends. Scissorman, it turns out, is one of the deformed Barrows children. Their father, the player discovers, is a feral madman kept in a cage out in the courtyard shed. Their mother, Mary Barrows, presides over her sick family and brings them victims to kill for pleasure. The player eventually discovers that Jennifer's father, a doctor, was murdered by Mrs. Barrows after delivering her horrid children.[7] The mansion itself, where all this family sickness festers and which the player gets to fully explore during the course of the game, is an interactive form of the Terrible Place. It is interesting how *Clock Tower* alters the plot structure of the stalker film to make it fit within with contours of a video game. Clover describes the Terrible Place as a location which usually appears in the third act of a story, yet in *Clock Tower* it is the single location in which the entire story takes place.[8] Further emphasizing this storytelling difference is the role Jennifer's friends play in *Clock Tower*, which are miniscule compared to traditional stalker films. The first two acts of the stalker film, which inevitably feature various characters meeting their fates one by one until only the Final Girl is left, is here compressed into a brief prologue. *Clock Tower* begins with Mrs. Barrows leaving all the children alone in the foyer, at which point the cursor appears and the player can walk around and talk to each of Jennifer's friends. This is when the player gets to know their names and faces. After a few minutes, the girls get worried that Mrs. Barrows hasn't come back and elect Jennifer to go look for her. The player has only gone down one hallway, however, when a scream makes Jennifer's fear level spike. Upon inspecting the foyer again, all the girls are gone.

This is when the game proper begins, which is the point a stalker film would not typically reach until near the end. The entire game of *Clock Tower*, not just the end, is comprised of a one-on-one struggle between the Final Girl and the Killer in the Terrible Place. Along the way the player discovers the horribly murdered bodies of Jennifer's friends (which have devastating effects on her fear level), much in the way a Final Girl would in the final sections of a stalker film. The key difference is, unlike in the voyeuristic world of cinema, the deaths of Jennifer's friends are not seen in *Clock Tower* ... unless, of course, they are seen by Jennifer.[9] The locking of the player in the Final Girl's perspective makes the three-act structure and multi-view point approach of the classic stalker film impossible. *Clock Tower* is not just a procedural adaptation of the stalker film. It is specifically a procedural adaptation of the *last act* of a stalker film, because these are when the elements of the stalker film most clearly align with the conventions of single-player exploration-based video games.

Subsequent stalker simulations have expanded on *Clock Tower*'s approach to adapting the stalker film. *Clock Tower 2* attempted a more complicated plot structure that more closely resembles traditional stalker films. In *Clock Tower 2* Jennifer is again the main character, although this time she is joined by a host of other characters, each of whom play a greater role within a clear three-act structure.

Clock Tower 2 begins some years after the events of the original game, with Jennifer receiving psychiatric treatment for the trauma she experienced. Her caretaker is a psych student named Helen at a local university, where both she and Jennifer live and study. Unlike the original game, *Clock Tower 2* has several locations: the student dormitory, the university library, and finally another mansion owned by the Barrows family.[10] This new Barrows mansion makes up the final third of the game. Once Jennifer and her friends arrive at the new Barrows mansion — the Terrible Place — *Clock Tower 2* becomes much like the original *Clock Tower*. All Jennifer's friends disappear, and the player discovers them slain one by one while simultaneously trying to avoid the ever lurking, ever stalking, ever pursuing Scissorman. Previous to this final section, however, *Clock Tower 2* has two other, similar sections of gameplay taking place at other locations which are not the Terrible Place. They are normal, everyday locations only made terrifying by the fact that Scissorman shows up in them to stalk and kill innocent people. The gameplay of these sections is identical to both the third act of *Clock Tower 2* and the original *Clock Tower*: the player must run around, looking for ways to escape, all the while being pursued by Scissorman. Thus *Clock Tower 2* features three sections of stalking/fleeing gameplay that correspond to its three acts (called "scenarios" in the game), the final of which takes place in the Terrible Place. This allows the game to follow the narrative sequence of the stalker film more closely. *Clock Tower 2*'s principal innovations are narrative, not procedural, owing to the fact that the behavioral formula of the stalker film was already established quite firmly in the original *Clock Tower*.

The biggest difference between *Clock Tower* and *Clock Tower 2* is that the player gets to know the cast of supporting characters before they are snipped into pieces by Scissorman. The opening dialogue sequence from *Clock Tower* (where the player could speak to Jennifer's friends) is expanded into long, expository dialogue sequences that take place before each act. In these sections — which always take place during the day — the player can navigate Jennifer around different campus locations and speak to people. In the main gameplay sequences — which always take place at night — the player must avoid Scissorman. This alternation between pure character interaction and stalking/fleeing puts *Clock Tower 2* more in the traditional narrative rhythm of a stalker film: exposition and character development is punctuated by moments of action, horror, and violence that eventually lead to a final, epic confrontation in the Terrible Place. In the final new Barrows mansion sequence, most of the characters Jennifer has befriended over the course of the first two acts end up mutilated.[11]

In addition to plot structure, *Clock Tower 2* does one more important thing that pushes it closer to a traditional stalker film formula. Jennifer is, in fact, not the only playable character. The player is given a choice near the beginning of the game of whether they wish to play as Jennifer or Helen. In other words, they are given the choice of who will be the Final Girl. This is significant because Helen fits the archetype of Clover's Final Girl more closely than Jennifer does:

> The Final Girl is boyish, in a word. Just as the killer is not fully masculine, she is not fully feminine — not, in any case, as feminine in the way of her friends. Her smartness, gravity, and competence in mechanical and other practical matters, and sexual reluctance set her apart from other girls [Clover, 1992: 40].

Jennifer is very feminine. As a young adolescent girl in the first game she had long, dark hair and wore a dress. In *Clock Tower 2*, as an older adolescent, she wears a tight skirt with knee-high boots. And though she still seems sexually inexperienced, she has a boyfriend. Helen, by contrast, is more androgynous than Jennifer. She wears a suit and trousers, has much shorter hair than Jennifer, and no boyfriend. Her interests, it seems, are entirely professional. The main relationship she has in the story is with a detective, who helps her but is in no way a romantic interest. She is thus a more prototypical Final Girl than Jennifer.

Figure 1, top: Jennifer flees from Scissorman in *Clock Tower* (Human Entertainment, 1995). ***Bottom:*** Helen blasts Scissorman with a fire extinguisher in *Clock Tower 2* (Human Entertainment, 1997).

It is arguably a factor of *Clock Tower 2*'s great emphasis on following narrative formula that it offers the player the choice between a sexy Final Girl and a more androgynous Final Girl. The core gameplay mechanics of exploration, fear management, and fleeing/outsmarting Scissorman are still present from *Clock Tower* and are the same for both Jennifer and Helen (figure 1).

This makes the choice between the two characters somewhat cosmetic, the only difference being that the un-chosen character is relegated to a supporting role in the story. Yet even this fact becomes interesting when viewed through the lens of procedural adaptation. In the stalker film the Final Girl is:

... the first character to sense something amiss and the only one to deduce from the accumulating evidence the pattern and extent of the threat; the only one, in other words, whose perspective approaches our own privileged understanding of the situation [Clover, 1992: 44].

The primary gameplay of both *Clock Tower* and *Clock Tower 2*, aside from escaping Scissorman, revolves around perception and investigation. This is a mainstay of the point-and-click tradition this series follows. The point-and-click interface shapes the user experience toward observing one's surroundings and then investigating potential points of interest, making it effective in games which feature detective themes, such as *Police Quest* (Sierra, 1987) and *Blade Runner* (Westwood Studios, 1997). In *Clock Tower* and *Clock Tower 2* the detective-like affordances of the point-and-click interface map directly to the role of the Final Girl. The player, unlike all the other characters, has the ability to explore, interact with, and perceive potential dangers in the environment. The implication of the player's lone agency in this manner is that all other characters don't perceive any of these dangers, hence they die. If only they had the perceptiveness of the player — of the Final Girl — they might have lived. If the player chooses Helen over Jennifer, Jennifer loses this agency, this perceptiveness, and ends up as dead as the other secondary characters. The same happens to Helen if Jennifer is chosen. Although Jennifer and Helen embody different aspects of the Final Girl, the final piece — the Final Girl's decision-making ability — can only be supplied by the player. This allows the player to decide what kind of Final Girl they want to be. Helen may be a more likely archetype for such resourceful intelligence, but if the player chooses Jennifer the fact that she, through the player, behaves resourcefully and intelligently makes her a believable Final Girl.

Although *Clock Tower* was a true procedural adaptation in the behavioral sense, *Clock Tower 2* built a more complicated edifice around its core mechanics to enhance the overall experience of being in a stalker film. The reliance of *Clock Tower* and *Clock Tower 2* on common, yet seldom combined, groups of gameplay conventions creates a picture of how procedural adaptation can exist within the constraints of existing gameplay genres. The model *Clock Tower* and *Clock Tower 2* adopted to approximate the tensions and drama of the stalker film could be called the "interrupted adventure game." In point-and-click adventures the user typically interacts with the gameworld via indirect manipulation (Fernández-Vara, 2008:221). The cursor is the only thing directly manipulated by the player, with the character performing actions only after a command has been given. Point-and-click adventure games have historically been filled with mental challenges (i.e. puzzles) rather than reflex-based challenges, which would require direct manipulation of the character. *Clock Tower*, however, toys with the player by forcing them to respond to reflex-based challenges using indirect manipulation. One moment the player is moving about slowly, trying to solve a puzzle, and the next they are forced to run for their life using controls not designed for action.[12] This sudden oscillation between two gameplay styles is at the heart of *Clock Tower*'s strategy for building tension. The player never knows when the gameplay mechanics will switch on them, forcing them to think in a different mode. For players familiar with point-and-click adventure games there is an additional dimension, since the sudden demand on reflexes seems transgressive — a betrayal of genre expectations. Jennifer is not *in* an action game, one might protest, so it is not fair that she is pitted against an unstoppable killer. But that's precisely the point. It's not fair. Jennifer is not a space marine. She is a teenage girl who can't fight, and has to rely completely on her wits. That is the challenge and the promise of the stalker simulation.

Clock Tower and *Clock Tower 2* effectively illustrate how procedural adaptation can function within the realm of commercial video games. They are prototypical examples of the stalker simulation, the way *Halloween* or *The Texas Chain Saw Massacre* are prototypical examples of the stalker film. It would be interesting to explore a complete history of the stalker simulation, discussing in detail how games like *Friday the 13th* (LJN Toys, 1989) made rudimentary attempts to model stalker film conventions, or how the stalker simulation has struggled to retain its identity post–*Resident Evil* in games like *Clock Tower 3* and *Haunting Ground*, which adopt certain conventions of survival horror. If one is merely looking to illustrate how procedural adaptation functions in relation to stalker films, as I am here, one needs look no further than *Clock Tower* and *Clock Tower 2*: the two most textbook examples of the stalker simulation.

Writing about the stalker film, and its subsequent adaptation into the stalker simulation, is in some ways very easy. Clover sets out a clear series of conventions to discuss, and those map neatly to the overarching design of several individual video games. In addition, the stalker film is a relatively recent, self-contained subgenre. It originated in film, as opposed to literature, and it is only about 30 years old. It is therefore much easier to define, contain, and map than other horror subgenres that have richer, more complicated transmedia histories. The zombie film, which will be my next example of procedural adaptation, is one such subgenre.

The Zombie Simulation

Zombie simulations are what I call the group of games modeled after the modern zombie film. Examples include *Dead Rising*, the *Resident Evil* series, and *Left 4 Dead* (Valve, 2008). The zombie films from which these games derive their conventions take some work to define. To begin with, zombies are not the domain of a single genre, subgenre, or medium. It is a figure, like the vampire, that appears first in legend and then in various forms of literature before arriving in film. I am not about to undertake a complete cultural history of the zombie, so I will limit my discussion of the zombie to variants that, arguably, have most directly inspired zombie-themed video games. Those variants, defined by their shared "rules" of how zombies function, can be traced back to the zombie films of George A. Romero.

The zombie films of Romero were, of course, not the first zombie films, being preceded by *I Walked with a Zombie* (Jacques Tourneur, 1943), *White Zombie* (Victor Halperin, 1932), and many others. These films were rooted in the folklore and mysticism of Haitian voodoo practices and featured "zombies" which were quite different from those of later horror films. The origins of the zombie figure are profoundly bound up in the colonial horrors of Europe's conquest of the Caribbean. A voodoo zombie is a corpse that has had its soul removed by a sorcerer and been reanimated to do his bidding: an eternal living-dead slave (Russell, 2005: 11–12).[13] They do not eat flesh or spread like a disease. The term "zombie" decisively shedding its voodoo connotations and becoming largely synonymous with flesh-eating, autonomous walking corpses correlates strongly with Romeo's *Night of the Living Dead* (1968), a film which rewrote the rules of zombies significantly. "From that moment onward cinematic zombies would almost always be flesh eaters," claims author Jamie Russell, explaining the film's definitive impact on the subgenre (2005: 68). The list of films that follow *Night of the Living Dead*'s template of zombie behavior is too long to mention. Some of the most famous ones are *Children Shouldn't Play with Dead Things* (Bob Clark, 1972), *Zombie* (Lucio Fulci, 1979), *Return of the Living Dead* (Dan O'Bannon, 1985), *Braindead* (Peter Jackson, 1992), and more recently *Shaun of the Dead* (Edgar Wright, 2004). One of the major recurring themes of these films is apocalypse. The sudden and inexplicable appearance of flesh-eating zombies in real world settings creates a situation where "the whole basis of civilization — and man's sense of mastery over his environment — is instantly altered" (Russell, 2005: 68). Mankind's failure to master this environment — where zombies are streaming endlessly into homes, businesses, police stations, hospitals, government buildings, military installations, and every other safe haven imaginable — is the narrative framing device for a significant number of zombie films, including Romero's own *Dawn of the Dead* (1978), *Day of the Dead* (1985) and *Land of the Dead* (2005). In these films the shrinking possibility of any safe haven from zombies is framed as the core problem characters must solve, forcing them to search for protection in increasingly desperate locations. The most iconic of these is the mall in *Dawn of the Dead*, where survivors attempt to wait out the apocalypse in a consumer playground.

It is this zombie film — the modern apocalyptic zombie film — that has had the largest impact on video games. Although zombies appeared in some video games in the '80s and early '90s, it is in *Resident Evil* that Romero's influence becomes explicit.[14] *Resident Evil* producer Shinji Mikami claims:

> I saw [*Dawn of the Dead*] as a junior high school student, and the image is still burnt into my brain. Of course, it was just a movie and I couldn't do anything to recreate it as a game, but it made me daydream about living in a realistic world in which zombies appeared. Like "what if it was me who was in that situation? Well I'd do this, and I'd do that...." I'd daydream like this since I was little and I thought "since [*Resident Evil*] is a videogame, wouldn't it's be possible to recreate that?" Of course no one wants to actually live in such a world, and get killed, but with a game it's possible to satisfy your imagination and feel like you're actually experiencing it [1996b].[15]

The above statement establishes two important things. First, that *Resident Evil* was inspired heavily by Romero and, second, that *Resident Evil* was deliberately selective in its efforts to simulate Romero's apocalyptic vision.[16] These two observations imply a trajectory in which it is possible to chart the evolution of the zombie simulation, from modest attempts at modeling basic zombie behavior to increasingly more complex attempts to model larger apocalyptic scenarios.

For the purposes of this essay, I will limit my view of zombie film conventions to two aspects: the behaviors of the zombie itself, and the dynamics of dwindling safety which are the common dilemma of zombie film protagonists. The first aspect is a fairly straightforward "rule set" which maps easily to games. The second is a bit more complicated, having a lot to do with how in-game space is designed and what affordances the player is given to alter that space to promote their own safety. It is in the combination of these two aspects that the apocalyptic sensibility of the zombie film most clearly finds procedural expression. The more complex zombie behaviors become, and the more complex the environments they inhabit become, the more complex the question of safety becomes for the player. As we shall see, the apocalyptic scope of a zombie simulation is greatly affected by these core elements.

The modern zombie is associated with a clear set of behaviors, which could just as easily be called "rules." According to these rules a zombie is a creature that: violently attacks any human in sight, eats human flesh, cannot move quickly, cannot use tools, possesses no reason or higher intelligence, and cannot be killed except by a blow or shot to the head. The final rule is that any human bitten by a zombie will eventually die and become one themselves.[17]

These rules are clearly laid out in *Night of the Living Dead*, partially by example and partially by dialogue.[18] These rules have very few exceptions, like when a zombie uses a rock to bash in a window in *Night of the Living Dead* or when a zombie uses a gun in *Day of the Dead*.[19] The apocalyptic aspects of the zombie film are not so much rules as they are the survival dynamics that arise from the intersection of the zombie figure with familiar settings. In *Night of the Living Dead* a group of survivors barricade themselves in a farmhouse to escape the growing horde of walking dead, using nails and furniture to block doors and windows. As barricades are overwhelmed, survivors fall back to individual rooms, relying more on weapons. This concept of the "shrinking fortress" is a mainstay of the subgenre, finding expression in virtually every zombie film, whether on a small scale as in *Shaun of the Dead* (a pub) or on an epic scale as in *Land of the Dead* (an entire city).

These zombie film conventions are rudimentally modeled in *Resident Evil*. In it the player assumes the role of either Chris Redfield or Jill Valentine, two members of an elite rescue team sent to a remote mansion in a deep forest. They are there to investigate the source of murders that have taken place in the surrounding woods. The gameplay begins when Chris and Jill enter the mansion and realize it is infested with flesh-eating zombies. The player's goal is to explore the mansion and discover the source of the zombie outbreak, being careful along the way to avoid a grisly, gory death.

Resident Evil's gameplay primarily revolves around zombie combat. The game takes place entirely in one location — the mansion — which is mostly made up of narrow corridors and small rooms. Each of these areas contains a number of zombies, which the player has to kill or avoid to get to the next room. The player has various firearms at their disposal — like pistols and shotguns — but there is never enough ammo available to kill every single zombie. As a backup the player has a knife, but this weapon is extremely inefficient, forcing the player to attack within biting distance. The result is that the player must strategize, making effective use of their resources to survive, and thoroughly observing the zombie rules to their best advantage. The zombie rules *Resident Evil* follows are based on Romero in several clear ways. Firstly, its zombies are slow. The player can easily outrun them. Secondly, they are stupid. They will not notice the player until he or she is close by, and even then they may simply walk into a wall. Thirdly, they will bite the player if not shaken off. This causes the player to lose health and, eventually, die as other zombies join in the feast. Fourthly, they can be instantly killed by a blow or bullet to the head.

There are a few important ways in which these rules differ from Romero. First and most obviously, being bitten by a zombie does not turn the player into a zombie. Chris or Jill can be bitten over and over again, but they will never become zombies. Second, although destroying the head is the quickest way to kill a zombie, it is not the *only* way. Zombies in *Resident Evil* can be killed simply by shooting them (or stabbing them) over and over in any part of their body. If they sustain enough damage, they will eventually not get up.

It is easy to see these alterations as concessions to existing game design practice. *Resident Evil* features a classic video game health system, in which the player can sustain a certain amount of damage before dying. This is where much of the challenge comes from, since health-refilling items are scarce and enemies are numerous. By adhering to such a conventional mechanic *Resident Evil* denies itself the possibility of modeling the zombie film more closely. In zombie films the fatalism of even the smallest zombie bite is absolute. The difference between life and death is not gradient but binary: a survivor is either uninjured or doomed. In *Resident Evil* the player can have their flesh chomped within an inch of their life and still fully recover. This makes the stakes and sense of risk associated with engaging zombies different than those of the zombie film. The player can afford to make mistakes in ways zombie film protagonists cannot.[20] Additionally, the fact that zombies can be killed by brute force alters the logic depicted in the films. *Resident Evil*'s interface does not include precision aiming, owing to the fact that it employs real-time 3D characters moving across pre-rendered 2D backgrounds. This strategy allowed early 3D games (which *Resident Evil* was) to have highly detailed backgrounds at the expense of camera-control. While this certainly made *Resident Evil* moody and atmospheric, it also excluded the ability to aim in a first-person view. *Resident Evil* only gives the player control over lateral gun movement, meaning they can choose which zombie to shoot, but not where to shoot them. The player does have some extremely limited control over height, in that they can aim either up at a 45-degree angle or down at a 45-degree angle, but this means the player is either aiming far above or far below a zombie's head. It is thus impossible to aim at a zombie's head in *Resident Evil*, ironically enough, as all shots hit either zombies across their mid-section or not at all. Yet even within these constraints *Resident Evil* takes pains to emphasize the head as the zombie's ultimate weak point. If successive hits down a zombie, the zombie will grab Chris or Jill's leg. If the player presses the X button at this moment, Chris or Jill will smash the zombie's head with their foot, resulting in instant victory. In addition, if the player is equipped with certain powerful firearms shots will instantly destroy the head. A magnum, for example, will invariably make a zombie's head explode. Even though the player has no control over aiming, the importance of the head as the zombie's weak point is still reinforced, albeit indirectly, through the unique affordances of such weapons. Ultimately the destruction of the head signals the player's triumph over the forces of the undead.[21] It is the most decisive outcome possible of any zombie encounter. The fact that it is dependent on certain weapons, as opposed to the player's aiming skills, is indicative of how *Resident Evil* attempts to get around the limitations of its chosen format to provide a recognizable zombie experience.

There are many ways in which the technology of *Resident Evil* stood in the way of it being a more complex zombie simulation. While some alterations were no doubt aesthetic — like not dying from bites, for example — others were arguably rooted in the game's combination 3D/2D format, which meant space was hopelessly fragmented. Because doors were part of static 2D backgrounds, they could not be shown opening or closing. Furthermore, each room had to be a separate space, with no possibility of zombies following the player from one to another. In *Resident Evil* the player goes through doors by walking up to them and pressing the X button. At this point the default third-person view fades out and a first-person view of the opening door appears. The screen fades back to first-person and the player is in the next room. This "door sequence" was designed to disguise the load time it took the original PlayStation hardware to load each room into memory. Consequently, the rooms in *Resident Evil* were entirely separate spaces that only the player character — and no one else — could pass between. This made the "shrinking fortress" concept so central to zombie films difficult to express in *Resident Evil*. The player always knew they were safe when they reached a door, since doors were inaccessible to zombies. Furthermore, the nature of how the load screens worked made doors magical safe zones. Even with a small horde of zombies blocking a doorway, the player could still escape at the touch of a button as long as they were able to touch the door. This made *Resident Evil*, essentially, a series of microcosmic instances of zombie dynamics, none of which were allowed to mix together into something larger. The game effectively recreated the experience of being in a zombie film on the level of a single room. But anything beyond that was out of the question.

Although *Resident Evil* was an extremely limited exploration of the zombie simulation, it did manage to simulate certain aspects of the zombie film for the first time. Its microcosmic recreations of zombie combat were, within their limitations, very faithful to Romero. The experience of having to deal with slow-moving zombies, even if it was just in a single hallway, was something anyone familiar with zombie films could instantly recognize. And even though the fragmentation of space made shrinking fortress dynamics impossible, *Resident Evil* managed to make the construction safe zones one of its prime player activities. It encouraged players to exterminate all zombies in certain key hallways, making them "safe" and thus useful as strategic fall back areas. Interestingly, the fragmented nature of space is what made such planning reliable, since the player knew there was zero chance of zombies wandering into an area they had previously cleared. Limited ammo forced the player to decide which zombies would be the most useful to exterminate, which reinforced both strategic thinking and the feeling of being in a zombie film, since planning which zombie to shoot and which zombie to run past is a common dilemma of the film protagonists.

While *Resident Evil* achieves a certain, contained feeling of being a zombie film protagonist, its apocalyptic aspects are minimal. *Resident Evil 2* attempts to introduce more apocalyptic elements, yet is still bound by many of the same aesthetic and technical limitations. *Resident Evil 2*, unlike its predecessor, takes place in a city. The city has been completely overrun by zombies, resulting in the exact sort of apocalyptic imagery found in *Day of the Dead*. Cars are overturned, buildings are abandoned, fires run rampant, and zombies litter the streets. The player begins the game as either Leon Kennedy or Claire Redfield (the sister of Chris) who must reach safety and figure out a way to escape the town.

The gameplay of *Resident Evil 2* is largely unchanged from its predecessor. Zombies behave more or less the same, and it is still impossible to aim for their heads.[22] The 3D/2D format — with all of its spatial limitations — is still present, which means the "city" setting is largely cosmetic. The 2D backgrounds display complex cityscapes, but the microcosmic isolation of each area still applies. Each environment basically amounts to rooms and corridors, only this time they have the visual appearance of being outdoors. This ruse isn't kept up for long, as the player is quickly shoehorned into a series of indoor locations including a police station, a sewer, and a factory. Given that *Resident Evil 2* has the same limitations as its predecessor, however, it does do some interesting things to evoke (though not actually simulate) zombie film conventions not present in *Resident Evil*. In certain areas of the police station zombies will punch through windows and reach for the player. In other areas they will come entirely through, sliding over the railing and onto the floor. There is even a puzzle which allows the player to close the shutters of these windows, permanently stopping zombies from coming through.

None of these things push *Resident Evil 2* towards becoming a more complex zombie simulation, since none of these things are actually rule-based. They are all static, one-time events with no dynamic possibility. Regardless, they do suggest that the makers of *Resident Evil 2* wanted to evoke the apocalyptic aspects of the zombie film more strongly than in the first game, while working more or less within its formula. Capcom is a developer famous for its conservative stance on innovation in regard to successful franchises, which may explain why its expansive apocalyptic scope occurs mostly in the form of back story and not gameplay.[23] The game's main location, the police station, is littered with evidence of a past shrinking fortress scenario. Windows are boarded up, doors are fortified, and hand-written notes tell of desperate last stands. None of this actually happens to the player, of course, meaning it does little to simulate the experience of being in a zombie film. If anything, it simulates the experience of arriving *late* to a zombie film, when all the fun is over.

Although there have been many games featuring zombies since *Resident Evil* and *Resident Evil 2*, it is difficult to find one that attempts to procedurally model a large scale zombie apocalypse scenario.[24] One that does represent such an attempt is *Dead Rising*. This game is a much more complex zombie simulation than the earlier *Resident Evil* games, laying a wide procedural foundation of complicated zombie behaviors and environmental interactions that mix together into to form a impressive range of emergent possibility. This has much to do with the fact that *Dead Rising* features huge, sprawling environments that are filled with literally thousands of zombies.

In *Dead Rising* the player assumes the role of Frank West, a photojournalist who's paid a freelance helicopter pilot to illegally fly him into the center of a city mysteriously under quarantine. The city, it turns out, is completely overrun with zombies. Smelling a story, Frank asks to be set down on

Figure 2, top: Jill is cornered by a flesh eating zombie in *Resident Evil* (Capcom, 1996). *Bottom:* Leon trudges through deserted city streets in *Resident Evil 2* (Capcom, 1998).

the roof of the local mall. In exactly 72 hours the pilot will return, and Frank has until then to penetrate the mystery. Aside from this simple set-up, *Dead Rising* does not shoehorn the player into any specific chain of events, giving them free reign over the entire zombie-infested mall. Aside from being an obvious reference to *Dawn of the Dead*, the mall is a vast network of large-scale environments. There are four separate wings, each with their own stores, as well as a massive courtyard and a complicated series of underground parking lots. There are cars, toys, food, sporting equipment, power tools, clothes, and countless other consumer goods one would conceivably find in a mall, all of which the player can interact with. *Dead Rising* presents this world — one much closer to the realistic world of Mikami's zombie movie daydreams — and allows players to simply react.[25]

The zombies in *Dead Rising*, like those in *Resident Evil*, faithfully follow Romero's model within certain limits.[26] They are slow, flesh-eating imbeciles who die by fatal headshots. Players in *Dead Rising*, however, are given a vast number of possible interactions with these creatures. First of all, the player is able to aim. Holding the R trigger causes Frank to draw his gun (should he have one) at a camera angle which shows his point of view, allowing the player to use whatever marksmanship skills they may have to take down the shambolic masses. As in Romero's films, a single bullet in the brain will do it every time. If the player is moderately skilled with a controller, performing headshots is relatively easy. This fact, combined with the subtle dynamics of *Dead Rising*, give us our first glimpse into its value as a procedural adaptation. One of the recurring mistakes of zombie film characters is to underestimate the threat of slow, stupid zombies. This is famously illustrated in *Dawn of the Dead* when Roger, the SWAT team member, becomes drunk with his own power at being able to kill zombies easily. He is so confident that he becomes careless, and before he knows it he is overwhelmed, bitten, and on his way to becoming an undead. *Dead Rising* — especially for players weaned on *Resident Evil* — creates the same deceptive feedback loop. Zombies are so slow, so easy to kill, that beating up on them is a deeply satisfying power trip. Downing one, two, three, even four zombies is much fun. It's so fun that the player may fail to notice that, in the time it has taken them to kill four zombies, seven more have appeared to their left, twelve have appeared to their right, and a good thirty or forty may have appeared behind them. The player may turn around, triumphant, only to be staring directly into a vast ocean of the undead. At this moment the player may realize, to their embarrassment, that the "stupid" character they used to make fun of in the zombie film is, in fact, them ... and that they are about to meet the same horrid fate.

As with *Clock Tower*, *Dead Rising* delivers players the opportunity to discover what they would do in a zombie film. Often, this discovery is unflattering to player's intelligence, but such is the value of simulation: one can always try again. In *Resident Evil*, trying again merely meant attempting the same pre-designed room or hallway over again. In *Dead Rising* it means something new every time, since zombies are never in the same place twice. They have a "life" of their own, so to speak, shambling in endless hordes that roam every last inch of the gameworld. In a sense, they don't just inhabit the environment; they are the environment. The zombies themselves are one massive obstacle course of shifting dangers. Players must look for gaps in the ocean of zombies or for garbage bins they can climb for a momentary breather before making the final break for it to an elevator, car, or door. *Dead Rising* reverses *Resident Evil*'s strategic thinking: firearms are deathtraps whereas melee weapons are lifesavers. Often the only way to survive is to simply hit zombies with whatever is closely at hand, whether it be a $4,000 LCD television or a custard pie, and make a run for it. In *Dead Rising* the consumer toys of our collapsing civilization become the player's tools of survival, the value of them shifting towards their usefulness in the present environment. Players soon discover that a lawnmower, a chainsaw, or even a rake is much more valuable than a diamond necklace, which can be thrown at zombies but has no other use. As the player's thinking becomes tailored to this value system, *Dead Rising* edges towards post-civilization survival logic worthy of Romero.

The strategic elements of navigation and tool usage find their highest expression in the challenge of leading survivors to safety. If the player should so choose they can spend much of their time in *Dead Rising* trying to save people. This is where the apocalyptic rears its terrible head most obviously in *Dead Rising*, which constructs the entire mall from the outset as a giant shrinking fortress. When Frank first arrives, the mall's in-

Figure 3, top: Frank stares down a tidal wave of zombies in *Dead Rising* (Capcom, 2006). *Bottom:* Frank leads a survivor to safety in *Dead Rising* (Capcom, 2006).

habitants have successfully barricaded the front doors. Things go wrong immediately, zombies swarm into the mall, and the classic shrinking fortress scenario has begun.[27] There is one safe zone left — the roof — which all the scattered inhabitants must reach in order to survive. Most of these people, however, are panic-stricken and need guidance to reach safety. Frank, it would seem, is the only one who can get them there.

Each survivor can be found in their own shrinking fortress of sorts, holed up under a shop counter, in a closet, or behind a bunch of boxes they've stacked in front of a door. The player can attempt to pull them out of their pathetic fortresses that will soon be overcome and lead them to the roof. These events are all part of *Dead Rising*'s game system. If the player waits too long on the 72 hour timer, zombies will overrun a survivor's barricade and kill them. At this moment giant text will appear on the screen proclaiming their death. If the player wishes to save these people, they have to reach them in time, fight off the zombies, and use all their knowledge of zombie behavior to create a safe path between their hapless companion and the elevator to the roof. Simply creating a better fortress where the survivor was found is out of the question. Players can try by moving large objects — such as benches, boxes, or even cars — in front of doors so zombies cannot get to the survivors, but this tends not to work so well, since zombies will always break through eventually. Just like in the films, the fortress never stops shrinking. The only hope is to get everyone to the roof so they can be rescued when the helicopter returns. This makes *Dead Rising* a game which almost literally models the last 30 minutes of *Dawn of the Dead*, when the zombies finally break through the mall's barricades and the survivors attempt to reach the roof together and escape in the last helicopter. *Dead Rising* gives players the opportunity to re-enact this scenario, to feel the guilt of leaving a screaming companion to be devoured by zombies, or the triumph of spearheading a daring and heroic group exodus.

Dead Rising is not the only game that has taken a deeply rule-based approach to zombie film conventions.[28] Yet it is one of the few that explicitly positions itself in the player's imagination as a simulation of the modern zombie film. The box cover for *Dead Rising* suspiciously reads, "This game was not approved, developed, or licensed by the owners or creators of George A. Romero's *Dawn of the Dead*." The reason it has to make such a guilt-ridden claim is because it is obviously a procedural adaptation of Romero's film. The plot and storyline of *Dead Rising* have nothing to do with the plot and storyline of *Dawn of the Dead*, but the situations of the film, and the complex logic they imply, is the naked blueprint for *Dead Rising*. One of the surest ways to recognize a procedural adaptation is to watch the film and ask oneself if a viewer would understand how to *play* the game simply by watching the movie. If the answer is "yes," there is arguably some amount of procedural adaptation going on, of systemic logic being-reverse engineered out of narrative and transformed into a simulation. In the case of *Dead Rising* there is a very iconic film in mind, which is both famous in its own right and famous for extending the groundwork of a subgenre. *Dead Rising* is riffing on both these aspects of *Dawn of the Dead*, and although much else could be said about this game in terms of how it adapts this particular film, the way it uses *Dawn* as a template for a prototypical zombie simulation is most significant to this discussion. Zombie film aficionados have known for almost four decades what the rules of zombie survival are. But getting to actually test those rules in practice — short of a real zombie apocalypse — has only recently been made possible by the medium of video games. The apocalyptic anxiety that the zombie film taps into, its ability to haunt our imaginations with questions of "what would I do," is at the heart of the subgenre's lasting appeal. Games like *Resident Evil* and *Dead Rising* also driven by this anxiety and produced by professionals who understand that the video game medium is probably the only medium in which this lurking, morbid curiosity can be satisfied.

Games like *Resident Evil*, *Resident Evil 2*, and *Dead Rising* help paint a picture of how the zombie simulation has evolved over time, adapting the zombie film at different levels of abstraction based on a variety of aesthetic, commercial, and technical factors. Although functional for my core argument, this is not a complete picture of the subgenre's development by any means. A comprehensive history of the zombie simulation would be a huge undertaking and would include many examples of games which fill the eight year gap between *Resident Evil 2* and *Dead Rising*. It would include additional games within the *Resident Evil* series like *Resident Evil: Outbreak*, one of the few zombie simulations to model infection as part of its game system. It would also include many games outside the *Resident Evil* series like *Time Splitters 2* (Free Radical Design, 2002), one of the few games in which a bullet to the head is literally the *only* way to kill a zombie, not just the best way. It finally would include recent zombie simulations like *Left 4 Dead*, which attempts to bring large-scale shrinking fortress dynamics into the realm of multiplayer cooperation while pitting players against the "fast zombies" popularized by *28 Days Later* and the *Dawn of the Dead* remake.

Conclusion

Procedural adaptation is not merely a theory or something relegated to the domain of "art games." It is a powerful tool for understanding experience design in existing commercial video games. Horror games in particular, because of their strong connection with the horror subgenres of film and

literature, offer rich examples of how procedural adaptation works. I have
tried to illustrate that richness throughout this essay, in the case of stalker
simulations and zombie simulations. There are many other examples that
could be discussed, though perhaps few that are based on as well known subgenres. There are a number of horror video games, for example, based on the
works of H. P. Lovecraft. Although Lovecraft does not qualify as a complete
subgenre, his work, like Romero's, is widely identifiable by certain core features, many of which have proved inspiring for game makers. The logics of
human perception, cognition, and emotion in Lovecraft are distinct enough
to have inspired systemic interpretations of concepts like "sanity" in various
horror games, both digital and non-digital.[29] Games like *Eternal Darkness:
Sanity's Requiem* (Silicon Knights, 2002) and *Call of Cthulhu: Dark Corners
of the Earth* (Headfirst Productions, 2005) attempt to model the experience
of being a Lovecraft protagonist by attempting to model the experience of
battling one's own madness. It would be possible to discuss in detail these
and other Lovecraft-inspired games the same way I've discussed stalker simulations and zombie simulations. Other interesting prospects include certain
games featuring vampires as protagonists, such as *Castlevania: Symphony of
the Night* (Konami, 1997) and *Blood Omen: Legacy of Kain* (Silicon Knights,
1996), which adapt the core vampire rule-set directly from Bram Stoker's
Dracula (1897). Although it would not be accurate to call either of these games
adaptations of Stoker's novel, the fact that their rule-based model for vampires can be traced explicitly back to this text is grounds, within certain
boundaries, for procedural adaptation-based analysis. Though the adherence
to particular sets of subgenre rules might not be as complete in these cases
as they are in games like *Clock Tower*, *Resident Evil*, and *Dead Rising*, the lens
of procedural adaptation could still yield illuminating observations about
how these games construct user experience.

The transformative ability of video games to give us the experience of
being horror film protagonists, as opposed to watching them or reading about
them, situates games differently in relation to horror experience than in other
media forms. Traditionally horror stories provoke us to imagine our own
behaviors and solutions were we faced with the same fantastic terrors as unfortunate protagonists. The fact that we remain separate from these protagonists, protected from their horrible situations by the fact that we are just
voyeurs or readers, allows us the luxury of never discovering what our fate
in such a situation would be. To use Noël Carroll's terminology, we assimilate the protagonist's situation. We comprehend it. We understand it. But we
do not experience it. Horror games adapted from other media forms tempt
us to cross this boundary, to risk the safety of our imaginations and discover
what hitherto was impossible to discover. In doing so they give us the opportunity not just to experience familiar horror situations for ourselves, but to

transform them beyond what is even seen in the static formulas of genre. As protagonists we have to face the same terrifying challenges we've watched film characters face — and be destroyed by — our whole lives. As players we make mistakes, try different solutions, and explore the limits of what's possible in ways film characters do not. The fact that it is possible, depending on player performance, to actually save some of Jennifer's friends in *Clock Tower 2*, or the fact that one can devote oneself to saving *everyone* in *Dead Rising*, gives players the cathartic experience of rewriting genre logic. There is no such thing as a stalker or zombie film in which no one dies, but this possibility can be explored in video games if the player is willing to endure a brutal learning process. The trial and error of mastering a game, in a certain sense, allows a player to earn one's status as a successful horror film protagonist. The performance of an unskilled player is likely to resemble the behavior of a doomed character in a horror film, while the performance of a skilled player is likely to resemble the cool-headed crisis management of a surviving character. First time players of *Clock Tower* will not behave like Final Girls, and will see Jennifer snipped into pieces countless times before they do. Procedural adaptations allow players to try and try again in such familiar fictional worlds, to face their iconic dangers via the safety of computer simulation.

Notes

1. The conventions of horror texts and the conventions of video games should not be confused. The former includes things like themes, images, stylistic devices (like lighting or editing), settings, character types, plot structures, and a host of other elements that traditionally combine to form a generic or textual identity. The latter includes things like rules, goals, mechanics, dynamics, and other procedural elements which define video games and video game genres. On the most basic level, this paper seeks to explain how a certain subset of these conventions— specifically themes, situations, character types, and plot structures— serve as the basis for rules, goals, mechanics, and dynamics in video games.

2. There are games which derive their rules from horror subgenres but do not use them to replicate the protagonist's experience. For example, *Stubb the Zombie* (Wideload Games, 2005) is a comedic game where the player takes the role of the zombie, not of the survivor.

3. The phrase was part of a *Resident Evil* load screen: "You have once again entered the world of survival horror. Good luck."

4. Media scholar Ewan Kirkland, in his discussion of *Resident Evil*'s influences on *Silent Hill* (Konami, 1999), describes "fighting off monsters with limited ammunition, energy and means of replenishing it" as a defining component of survival horror (2005: 172).

5. The *Clock Tower* I am referring to is the original version released on the Super Famicom, which never saw release outside Japan. This game should not be confused with the North American 1998 Playstation release bearing the same title. The North American PlayStation release is in reality *Clock Tower 2*, the sequel to the Super Famicom original. When I refer to *Clock Tower* and *Clock Tower 2*, I will be using the Japanese release numbering, not the North American release numbering.

6. Gender politics play a huge part in Carol J. Clover's interpretation of horror films

and horror film audiences. It is impossible to ignore her observations on gender since they are foundational to her theory of the stalker film. I will mention them when they are directly relevant to *Clock Tower*'s adaptation process. More complicated observations belong in a essay exclusively about the gender politics of stalker simulations.

7. Many of these plot elements are lifted directly from Dario Argento's *Phenomena* (1985), which featured 14-year-old actress Jennifer Connelly being menaced by a psychotic woman and her deformed son who kills people with scissors. While it would not be accurate to consider *Clock Tower* a procedural adaptation of *Phenomena* (owing to the fact that *Phenomena* deviates significantly from Clover's formula), it is clearly a major source of inspiration. *Clock Tower* is, in some sense, *Phenomena* re-imagined as a stalker film and then modeled as a stalker simulation.

8. While it is true that the Barrows mansion gets more and more terrible as the player explores it further—culminating in the discovery of an underground dungeon in which the other, exceedingly more horrific Barrows child is kept—the entire gameworld roughly fits Clover's description of the Terrible Place ... some parts of it are just more terrible than others.

9. The voyeuristic thrill of watching people die in ever more gruesome ways is not as absent from *Clock Tower* as one might assume. The frequency of the player's own death, and the subsequent feedback loop of trial and error that sustains it, arguably substitutes the visceral representation of multiple murders in the stalker film. Instead of watching supporting characters die in new and shocking ways, the player watches Jennifer die in new and shocking ways, over and over again. While the voyeuristic implications are not exactly the same as with stalker film Victims, the presence of multiple displays of gory death is a persistent aspect of *Clock Tower*.

10. There is a fourth location, a house, which is optional. This does not affect *Clock Tower 2*'s three act structure, however, since the house location simply replaces the library location depending on certain choices the player makes. It is impossible to play all four locations in one play-through.

11. Depending on the choices the player makes, some of Jennifer's friends can actually be saved. This is also true to a smaller degree in the original *Clock Tower*. It is an interesting way both *Clock Tower* games deviate from their source material, giving the Final Girl a level of agency beyond that typically found the stalker films. I will discuss this more in my conclusion.

12. The original *Clock Tower* (though not *Clock Tower 2*) does feature some limited direct manipulation of Jennifer. Pressing the left or right shoulder buttons will instantly force Jennifer to break into a run in case she needs to escape quickly. However, in every other respect *Clock Tower* functions like a traditional point-and-click adventure game. Any complex evasive action, like opening a window to escape from Scissorman, must be performed indirectly with the cursor.

13. The notion of being stripped of one's identity and forced into manual labor forever has obvious significance in a culture where slavery is the ultimate horror. "For most Haitians, the predominant fear was not of being attacked by zombies, but of *becoming* one" (Russell, 2005: 11).

14. Games like *Alone in the Dark*, *Vampire Killer* (Konami, 1986), and many others—both horror and non-horror—feature zombies as an enemy-type. The explicit notion of the 'zombie game'—in which zombies are the main enemy-type—was popularized by *Resident Evil*.

15. The interview this quote is from was sloppily translated from Japanese. The text refers to *Dawn of the Dead* as "Dome of the Dead," which I corrected.

16. The other film Mikami has mentioned as a major influence on *Resident Evil* is *Zombie* (also called *Zombie 2* or *Zombie Flesh Eaters*) which was an Italian-made semi-sequel to *Dawn of the Dead* made possible by the fact that *Dawn* was a joint Italian-American co-production (1996a).

17. The rule concerning the speed of zombies has come under dispute in recent years

in the wake of films like *28 Days Later* (Danny Boyle, 2002) and the *Dawn of the Dead* remake (Zach Snyder, 2004), both of which feature fast-moving zombies. Although in this essay I am focusing only on games that feature slow zombies, it should be known that the 'fast zombie' variant does crop up in some zombie simulations, most notably *Left 4 Dead*.

18. One of the most famous scenes in *Night of the Living Dead* involves a television interview with a local militiaman who outlines how to deal with zombies. He imparts "If you have a gun, shoot 'em in the head. That's a sure way to kill 'em" and other such wisdom.

19. Even these occurrences can be seen as an evolution, not a contradiction, of the core rule set. There is an increasing trend over the course of the films in which zombies, in the right circumstances, remember more and more of their past lives. This is why in *Dawn of the Dead* zombies congregate in a mall, why in *Day of the Dead* a zombie is taught to appreciate music, and why in *Land of the Dead* a highly intelligent zombie leads an organized zombie revolt on the last surviving humans.

20. This is no doubt a concession to the entertainment goals of a commercial video game. To reiterate Mikami, "no one wants to actually live in [a zombie infested] world, and get killed" (2006b).

21. This fact is driven home memorably in a scene from *Dawn of the Dead*. A helicopter pilot fires his weapon again and again at a zombie, repeatedly hitting it in the chest. As he stands confused, a professional SWAT team member smugly pushes him aside, like a parent instructing a child, and downs the zombie in one shot with his superior aim. This is what some might call a teachable moment.

22. Interestingly, *Resident Evil 2* did not incorporate a feature added to *Resident Evil: Director's Cut* (Capcom, 1997), a special re-release of *Resident Evil* with added features. One of those features was the probability of making a fatal head shot each time the player fired the handgun. This made it seem as if Chris or Jill were trying to aim for each zombie's head every time they fired, with occasional success.

23. Aside from *Resident Evil*, its two most famous franchises are *Street Fighter* (1988 — present) and *Mega Man* (1987 — present), both of which typify Capcom's strategy of adding only modest changes between installments once a commercially successful formula has been established.

24. Two might be *Resident Evil: Outbreak* (Capcom, 2004) and *Left 4 Dead*, both of which I will briefly mention later.

25. Ironically, Shinji Mikami was not involved in the production of *Dead Rising* in spite of its being developed at Capcom. *Dead Rising* instead represents the brainchild of producer Keiji Inafune, who worked previously with Mikami on *Resident Evil 2*.

26. Similar to *Resident Evil*, *Dead Rising* omits the rule of biting turning people into zombies. However, unlike *Resident Evil*, it contains an explanation for such alterations. There is an amusing conversation in *Dead Rising* which makes it clear that, contrary to what horror-films suggest, zombie infection is not spread by biting. This is in stark contrast to *Resident Evil 2* where, in the opening cinematic, a truck driver clearly turns into a zombie as the result of a bite, whereas in the actual game no amount of biting will infect Claire or Leon.

27. This is all shown in a brief cinematic near the game's beginning. The in-game action picks up the instant the zombies break through and begin ripping nearby survivors to shreds.

28. *Resident Evil 4* (Capcom, 2005) deserves special mention here. It draws inspiration from many other types of films, not just zombie films, but the bits it does take from zombie films are impressively dynamic. It manages to re-create the shrinking fortress mechanics of *Night of the Living Dead* with fantastic fidelity. It features many large-scale rural environments in which the player can run into farmhouses for safety and even push furniture in front of doors. These moments essentially amount to a procedural recreation of the last 30 minutes of *Night*, when the protagonists are besieged in a farmhouse. Unfortunately, *Resident Evil 4* does not adhere strongly to zombie film conventions in other ways, making it ultimately not as complete an example of procedural adaptation as *Dead Rising*.

29. Any discussion of procedural adaptation in relation to Lovecraft would have to mention non-digital games such as *Call of Cthulhu* (Choasium, 1981) and *Arkham Horror*

(Chaosium, 1987) which pioneered the concept of sanity mechanics before their introduction into digital games.

Works Cited

Bogost, Ian (2007), *Persuasive Games: The Expressive Power of Videogames*, MIT Press.

_____ (2006), "Special Topics in Game Design and Analysis," course syllabus, *School of Literature, Culture, and Communication, Georgia Tech*, available online at <http://www.bogost.com/teaching/videogame_adaptation_and_trans.shtml>.

Carr, Diane, Diarmid Campbell, and Katie Ellwood (2006), "Film, Adaptation and Computer Games," in Buckingham, David, Andrew Burn, Diane Carr and Gareth Schott (eds.), *Computer Games; Text, Narrative, and Play*, Cambridge: Polity Press, pp. 149–161.

Carroll, Noël (1990), *The Philosophy of Horror, or, Paradoxes of the Heart*, New York and Londres: Routledge.

Clover, Carol J. (1992), *Men, Women and Chainsaws: Gender in the Modern Horror Film*, Princeton, NJ: Princeton University Press.

Fernández-Vara, Clara (2008), "Shaping Player Experience in Adventure Games: History of the Adventure Game Interface," in Olli Leino, Hanna Wirman and Amyris Fernandez (eds.), *Extended Experiences: Structure, Analysis and Design of Computer Game Player Experience*, Rovaniemi: Lapland University Press, pp. 210–227.

Juul, Jesper (2007), "A Certain Level of Abstraction," *jesperjuul.net*, available online at <http://www.jesperjuul.net/text/acertainlevel/>.

Kirkland, Ewan (2005), "Restless Dreams in *Silent Hill*: Approaches to Video Game Analysis," *Journal of Media Practice*, Vol. 6, No 3, December, pp. 167–178.

Mikami, Shinji (1996a), "Shinji Mikami Interview," *GamePro Magazine*, No. 91, April, pp. 32–33, available online at <http://residentevil.planets.gamespy.com/sec/features/articles/00003.htm>.

_____ (1996b), "Shinji Mikami Interview," September, English translation available online at <http://www.bioflames.com/miscsection5.htm>.

Russell, Jamie (2005), *Book of the Dead: The Complete History of Zombie Cinema*, Godalming: FAB Press.

Reanimating Lovecraft: The Ludic Paradox of *Call of Cthulhu: Dark Corners of the Earth*

Tanya Krzywinska

Franchises that cut across media platforms have become common currency within contemporary culture and the allure of pre-branded product has grown more central to large-scale media companies' marketing strategy. Inevitably, somewhat dormant, and largely academic, debates around adaptation and translation have found new purchase in this age of convergence. While we might be cynical about the commercial conversativism of "recycling" cultural material, it is nonetheless essential to analyze the aesthetic and cultural ramifications of branded artifacts that spin out across diverse media platforms. This is particularly the case if we are to better understand the way that different media shape engagement, orchestrate experience, and offer pleasure in our digital age. While identification of divergence across media is certainly enlightening, and indeed might well aid in the process of identifying what is new and exciting about video game media, it is nonetheless important not to ignore characteristics that might be shared or similar across a given franchise.

Through an appraisal of *Call of Cthulhu: Dark Corners of the Earth* (Bethesda, 2005), I will show how the core characteristics of the "Cthulhu" brand are treated within the terms of video game media and through the design choices made by this particular incarnation's producers. It is then an essay about a direct adaptation, in this case the source for the game is several short stories written by H.P. Lovecraft, yet it is also an essay about the transformations made to the horror genre more generally by the cybernetic qualities of video game media. Our journey through the gamescape of adaptation will take us through some aspects of both video game history and the horror genre and eventually open up some testing questions about the nature of the video game industry, its markets, and what might be said to constitute good or bad design. I am concerned in this essay with aesthetic values, particularly those related to the Cthulhu brand and genre, bounded as they are by commercial imperatives, and their relation to the way games commonly offer an experience where orchestration is woven with the ludic and participatory.

Call of Cthulhu: Dark Corners of the Earth is a peculiar game, as befits its heritage. Like so much horror, it's the deformed offspring of the popular and the cultish. Yet more refined artistic sensibilities are conjured into focus against the flickering backdrop of the generic, as was also the case with Lovecraft's own approach to commercial fiction writing. To understand better to what particular drums *Call of Cthulhu: Dark Corners of the Earth* dances, the game demands to be seen in the broader context of horror and horror games.

Throughout the history of games made for the commercial market, a surprising number use elements that we might recognize as drawn from horror. There is no platform bar to their use. We find games like *Castlevania: Dawn of Sorrow* (Konami, 1986/2005) on the handheld Nintendo DS, through to a game such as *Dead Rising* (Capcom, 2005) designed to showcase the visual pleasures of high definition facilitated by developments in television technology and the Xbox 360. While we might speak of games within the terms of the horror genre, the picture is made more complex however because *ludic* features are what tend to define genre in the context of video games rather than story type or iconographic sets, as is the case of film or fiction. *Silent Hill 2* (Konami, 2001) could be described as a horror-based first-person shooter game, *Quake 4* (id Software/Raven, 2005) a horror-based First Person Shooter (in space no-one can hear you scream — horror-SF hybrid), or *Planescape Torment* (Black Isle, 1999) a horror-based Role-Playing game.

It is clear that multiple categories are in play in the definition and marketing of products, as is often the case in other media. Yet unlike other media, the specific characteristics of video game form plays a strong role in the constitution of genre definition. The picture is made even more complex because there are also differences in the type of "horror" on offer in games that need to be accounted for. Games range from those that use what might be termed "cute" horror (largely less sensationalist and designed for broader consumption) that lend themselves well to the smaller screens of hand-held devices exemplified by the more recent games in the *Castlevania* series, to games that might use elements of "serious" horror (often highly sensationalist, overtly transgressive, suspenseful, working with spectacles of pain and gore) that lend themselves to higher-end platforms and larger viewing devices, the *Silent Hill* series for example. A high proportion of video games generally employ techniques, tropes, iconography, character, or narrative types developed elsewhere within the broader generic context of horror. The entry of horror into the high-tech world of video games is testimony to the compelling draw of the genre's rhetoric as a creative, fictional framework into which can be placed a particular set of textual strategies, sensations and experiences. The evolution of horror in game media, however, is keyed into developments in hardware and software (graphics and audio technologies in particular) which have widened the scope, over the past decade or so, of the types of experiences games are able to offer, as we shall now see.

The Call of Cinema

Phantasmagoria (Sierra On-Line, 1995) is a third-person, 2D, point-and-click game. Its name and the box-cover art clearly marked it out to players as a "horror game." It ran on domestic PCs that were, at the time, relatively high spec. Yet despite the new, vastly improved capacity of CD media on which the game was distributed, resources had to be carefully managed. Constraint often acting as the mother of invention, the result was some innovative and interesting ways to produce what is essentially an interactive horror story, requiring certain actions of the player to progress that story (see Ndalianis, 2004: 109–114). The story itself is however very far from innovative: a woman has to investigate the grisly history of the remote house she has moved into, which eventually "possesses" her husband and drives him to try to kill her, restaging thereby similar events that had happened before with another couple. But to have delivery of the story, the player must investigate and collect objects to be used later in the game — if you've not found some object you risk several grisly types of death. The core game mechanic is much the same as is used in *The Secret of Monkey Island* (LucasArts, 1990) yet, while the former is highly playful, lightly absurd comedy, *Phantasmagoria* strives for serious, rather than cute or comedic horror, marrying realism and the grotesque. The game is composed of a number of adjacent interior and exterior locations represented by a series of static, computer modeled images (each room having two or three static framed views), through which the player directs the protagonist to walk. Like *The Secret of Monkey Island*, the game's construction of space might be compared to that found in a comic book: space constructed through adjacency, implication and correspondence, yet the use of static, overtly artificial backdrops to indicate location also resembles the conventions of creating space found traditionally in proscenium theatre, a feature that more generically echoes the game's Grand Guignol thematic. Unlike the backgrounds, the key human figures in the game are not drawn using a computer-based graphic program instead they are real people filmed doing a small variety of actions (walking, picking up objects, running, etc.), the loops of which are pressed into action when the player points the cursor showing on the screen and clicks to indicate a certain direction or action. Because of film's capacity to convey the nuances and extremes of human emotion through posture and facial expression, the presence of filmed characters (particularly the main character through whom we play the game and are asked to identify) lends realism to the affective situations, yet these are also made more strange by their juxtaposition with the overtly artificial backgrounds they inhabit.

For the purposes of this essay, *Phantasmagoria* illustrates two foundational points. First, the game demands specific actions from the player for progression to occur. This contractual condition between game and player is very different to other media and one that ultimately affects the way in which we expect horror to be delivered. Second, the game is haunted by the expressive characteristics and narrative format of cinema (figure 1).

There is a clear intention to provide for the player an experience equivalent to that produced by a horror film (testimony to Bolter and Grusin's notion that a new medium works with the tropes developed by established media [2000]) — even if the game fails *on those terms* to achieve this goal because of its agonizingly slow pace and repetitive cycles (outcomes of the ludic dimensions of the game). Presented in third-person perspective throughout, the game resembles in terms of framing that which we'd expect from a film. Once the player has decided what to do and clicked on the screen, they are then able to watch the character walk to where she's been directed. Similarly with use of objects — the player initiates an action through a couple of clicks and then sits back to watch the effects of that action. Emphasis is largely on uncovering the story through a fairly limited range of possible actions (far fewer in fact than are made available by the "verb" based action set of *Secret of Monkey Island*). Even though events are put into action by the player, story and plotline are pre-scripted, with little variation

Figure 1: Haunted by cinema: *Phantasmagoria* (Sierra On-Line, 1995) aimed to provide an experience close to that of cinematic horror.

in outcome — indeed the aim is to produce the "ideal" outcome; other outcomes are presented as failures, or perhaps, using movie-watching as the model, functioning as ill-formed guesses at what will happen. If you don't use the right objects or have the right objects at a key moment then death is the probable outcome — inducing reloads from previous saves, the path to progression is therefore set. It is story, character, audio, and visual effects of the type found in cinema that lend much of the interest, even though the player has to be more attentive to clues and put into order a set of actions. The game's more cinematic elements are privileged over player choice or intervention, even though it is clear to see that the particular characteristics of game media, even at this stage in their evolution, are disturbing and transforming the beat of the game's cinematic drum. In many respects this is a game based on observation, which is underpinned more by a debt to cinema than ludic activity and player agency. The latter however increased to a greater degree in horror games with the development of 3D graphics technology, where a play between orchestration and agency continues but with more freedom for designers to find ways of exploring this balance according to intention rather than at the dictates of available computing resources.

Despite the strong emphasis placed on the analysis of ludic dimensions by some academic commentators on games, it is nonetheless the case that cinema has acted, and continues to act, as a game industry benchmark — something to aspire to in terms of immersion, expressive "art" form, and commercial success. Often films within a franchise are marketed more strongly than tie-in games and act as the "authorative" text; it is still the case that large blockbuster movies bring in more money than games due to larger audiences (easier access and lower levels of time commitment seeming good explanations for such). Cinema can be regarded as providing a certain authority for a medium regarded by many as still in its primitive phase of evolution or designed to "simply" keep children and troublesome teenagers amused. I would contend that the pulply, ludic elegance of the first-person shooter makes exquisite use of video game medium, while I concur with the notion that the medium is far from fully explored, I am suspicious of the teleological, condescending and taste-based claim that games need to "grow up." But in line with its parental legacy, *Phantasmagoria*, now a pensioner in the video game time-line, orchestrated very closely the player's experience with the aim of producing suspense, tension, horror-style whimsy and a few visceral frights in the manner of cinema. Games in 3D changed this situation significantly, implicitly by opening up space for players to travel through. Rather than appearing to be "on rails" (with no scope for exploration or freedom of movement), as in platform games or vertical or horizontal scrolling games, far greater scope for player agency in terms of travel and the investigative gaze became available. As such players' movements became less predictable and with that came the loss of facility for managing and creating shock effects, suspense, and narrative tension, of the types found in cinema. This is then absolutely central to the way in which game media makes some substantial transformations to established rhetorics of horror. The opening up of space and time, which engenders a far more willful and unpredictable player, meant techniques different from those used in cinema had to come into play to generate the types of sensations and emotions associated with horror.

Adaptation at the Doorstep

It's important now to identify some edges and overlaps between games and films if we are to understand more closely the transformational developments in the use of the genre within games that offer various freedoms to players. Readers, players, and viewers of horror accumulate knowledge of the particular, and often evolving, patterns used in any given genre over time — some people set great store by such knowledge and seek to expand it, others wear their knowledge more lightly. At times, horror cinema has within certain sub-genres become heavily formulaic and as a result producers have tended to make self-conscious use of well-known conventions, which are often presented as a kind of diegetic "folklore" or urban myth. Such rhetoric makes for predictability and familiarity (perhaps required to ameliorate the evocation of the real of horror and the Other), yet providing a necessary basis to enable expectations to be played with. From the conventions that are used for, say, dispatching a vampire or werewolf, through to the apparent moral and gendered rule-set that determine who's killed in what way in a slasher film, horror has very frequently made explicit use of the viewer's genre knowledge to create affective twists and surprises. Classic horror narratives for example tend to pitch the forces of evil against those of good, a means that has worked well for getting all kinds of horror passed by regulators, and such films regularly conform to the well documented, classical Hollywood story arc of order, disorder, and containment. The values carried in these forms are ideologically driven, creating a safety net wherein the fantastic, the terrifying and the preposterous can be experienced without too great discomfort. Perhaps one of the reasons that zombies appear so frequently in games is that they are cheap cannon-fodder, insulating the player from any guilt produced by relentless, unreflective trigger-happy death-dealing (as I have argued elsewhere).

"Master of horror," Alfred Hitchcock, explained in interview (Gottleib, 2003 [1972]: 87) that editing provides a major rhetorical device for the creation of suspense, now often referred to as his "bomb theory." Imagine two people sitting discussing fairly trivial matters over lunch. If the viewer is not given sight of the bomb planted under the couple's table, then no tension is created. A cutaway shot to the bomb changes entirely the meaning of the scene for the audience, who know what the couple does not. The viewer is placed in a privileged position of knowledge, albeit knowledge they are unable to utilize — cinematic couples being deaf to the warnings of the audience, no matter how shrill. A state of suspense and considerable tension is generated for the expectant viewer, who may, as intended by the design of most classical films, by this time have considerable investment in the two characters and their relationship. In games the situation bears some similarities but is tellingly different. Many of the *Resident Evil* games for example employ cutaway shots of events that take place outside of the player-characters immediate vicinity. These are wedged disruptively into the otherwise anchored and seamless point of view of the player-character in an effort to create precisely a sense of tension and suspense for the player, as outlined by Hitchcock, by showing them what awaits around the corner. The effect of this disturbance to visual continuity is jarring and has quite different resonances in the largely unified point-of-view structure of a game than in a film, the fabric of which is a tapestry of different points of view by virtue of editing. While it is cogent to argue that this breaks the illusion that the player is in control of their own destiny (as I have argued elsewhere, Krzywinska, 2002) through this blatant reminder that the game can wrest control from the player at potentially any time, it also acts for the player as a signifier to be acted upon in the dimension of the ludic. It says "prepare yourself for the upcoming event," creating suspense in the manner of Hitchcock's rhetoric, but due to its ludic function it is also a transformed type of suspense. This dimension ameliorates, at least to some extent, the potential rupture in the player's qualified belief in the diegesis because, once it has happened a couple of times it is understood as part of the game's specific grammar (the patterns that make up a game and with which the player becomes familiar as they progress through the game).

A similar rupture to an otherwise seamless welding of point-of-view with player-character can be found in *Call of Cthulhu: Dark Corners of the Earth*. Here the player is often given a first-person point of view from another character entirely. This is thematically and narratively motivated in this case, rather than directly ludic however. The cutaway to the stalking monster's point-of-view, from places that humans would find extremely difficult to reach, reminds the player they are being hunted by something other than the freaky hybrid fish-human people, instead by something that is not in any way human. This alternate view is contextualized, at least ostensibly in the beginning, because of the split identity narrative that is signaled very clearly in the game's exposition (and of course if the player has read the stories the game is based upon). But borrowing techniques that depend upon cutting into the otherwise seamless continuity between point-of-view of character and player as means of creating suspense is not the only way to create the types of sensations associated with horror. There are some sensation-production devices that can only be created through the particular characteristics of game media.

Reanimator: The Alien of Video Game Media

In 3D games, space is not implied and constructed in the player/viewer's mind by a set of different camera angles and continuity editing. Instead, it is seamless and exists — at least in nascent digital form — whether or not a player enters it. Space is constructed and made available for the player to explore, even though the scope for exploration might vary from game to game, or indeed area to area, and exploration is very often integral to a game's ludic features. Many games provide environmental cues as to where the player should turn their attention — learning to read these clues is part of learning the particular syntactical pattern of a given game (much like learning the meaning of a cutaway). The "cookie-crumb trail" device, as I will call it, provides game designers with a means of controlling the order in which a player encounters events, the predictability of which can mean that that cinema-style shock tactics can be more easily employed. The trail is both hermeneutic and rhetorical and can be played with to create shocks, surprises, work up a strong sense of trepidation and in many cases function as a means of acting as both environmental story-telling and warning of terrors to come (the trails of discarnate flesh in the game version of *The Thing* (Computer Artworks, 2002) provide an indicative example). In the celebrated case of the use of fog in *Silent Hill* (Konami, 1999) we find a particularly strong model of the way that the game media transforms horror rhetoric in terms of space. As the player runs for the *first time* into the town Silent Hill, full of trepidation and likely unused to the game controls, they are enveloped in a thick mist that restricts vision and brings about the iconic claustrophobia and metaphoric live burial that Eve Sedgwick Kofosky regards as an integral aspect of the gothic (1980: 5). Unable to see more than a few feet in front of you when danger is imminent and potentially coming from any direction certainly ratchets up the tension; the suspense intensifies when the radio carried by the player-character begins to play the static crackle that indicates a monster is nearby. As the sound becomes louder the player flails around, turning 360 degrees to try to identify the direction of the incoming monster. Aiming blindly into the impenetrable murk, trying to set up an unfamiliar weapon, a monster suddenly appears in view a few feet above the player-character's head. Suspense is broken and panic sets in as the monster attacks; any sense of control is diminished to nothing, most likely leading to a ragged, failed attempt to shoot the clawing, flying monster. This type of horror experience is one that is produced precisely through the particularities of game media, where player participation and representation work alongside one another and from which a new dimension is given to the generic rhetorics of horror.

After, in all likelihood, a player-character makes a mess of their first encounter with the flying monster and they are returned to an earlier time in the game to allow them to go back and tackle the fight again, a new perceptual framework comes into play informed by hindsight that shifts suspense onto different ground (even if *literally* the same ground is covered). This example shows how time is constructed and experienced differently in games than in cinema. Repetition is core to the structure of many games, intrinsic to their learning curve and part of their hermeneutic construction. You encounter something, if you fail — you try again; this time attempting to take notice of what you learned from the last encounter. Thus suspense is relocated from the sphere of "what will happen?," to that of "will I get through this time?" This is because games tend to be predicated on a structure of repeated actions, which is integral to the way most games proffer to players a challenge, the mastery of which requires skills to be learned through repetition. The pleasures of novelty and surprise are replaced with a question about one's own ability to know and do what is required by the game. Suspense is therefore tied here to the ludic and, importantly, to player performance. Herein lies an essential difference between games and cinema: games work with what we might call, borrowing from Nietzsche, the will to power — something far from diminished or blunted by a ludic context and that can easily and sometimes necessarily dominate over what Bernard Suits calls the "lusory attitude" (1990: 35) (in other words a "playful" approach to as task). It would not be wrong to argue that cinema is far better able to solicit a wide range of emotions than games, but I would suggest that games are very powerful machines for soliciting certain types of emotions and in particular a dynamic between frustration and elation — emotions that often sit alongside edgy wariness making for a perfect preparation for inducing horror-related affect such as suspense, trepidation, and fear. To return to the *Silent Hill* example, alert wariness can be ramped up to nerve-jangling degrees when it is accompanied by a unearthly cacophony of dissonant sounds that creak, squawk, and rumble their way at the very edges of the bearable and through which the player has to pick out the unstructured sound of radio static (after all, diegetic non-being and stasis are the outcome of failing to respond adequately). When horror games work their dark magic most effectively, claustrophobia is manifest visually, aurally, thematically and, notably, in terms of the player's ability to act when hijacked by panic. While the sound or other cues in cinema prompt the spectator to imagine they have to act, in games it is incumbent on the player to act on what they hear and see.

In cinema, the viewer is unable to do anything to effect what happens on screen (even taking into account slippage in signifying conventions, closing eyes, going to the toilet or personal reading). In games, whatever you do whether bungled or brilliant, affects the state of things on screen. In this sense games are far more intently focused on performance than spectatorship. Here looking, reading, and interpreting the rhetorics and syntax of a game become core to player performance — looking for clues, patterns and, more than this, tying that information into the physical skills required to play a game. To make sense of these processes and to give greater meaning to the activity of learning a game, many horror games (and indeed other games) seek to provide suitably strong motivation through rhetorics of death and survival to learn such skills. They triangulate death and survival with action — games such as these very often make "being" in the game world/space conditional on "doing" and very often in survival horror this means shooting monsters, as can be seen in a range of examples. *The House of the Dead* (Sega, 1998–2009, for home systems) arcade-style games requires players to move through game-space automatically, as if on rails and to shoot down as many zombies that come their way without paying much heed to anything else. *Typing of the Dead* (Smilebit, 2000) has a similar approach, even though here key presses translate into deadly words rather than bullets that dispatch the zombie threat. *Dead Rising* (Capcom, 2006), although fully 3D, combines shooting with guns and cameras the hordes of zombies populating a small town Mall (and outlying area). *Clive Barker's Undying* (Dreamworks, 2001) has a slightly more rounded and gothic story and the player can "see" into the family's secrets yet the primary game mechanic nonetheless remains "shoot-shoot-shoot to survive." *American McGee's Alice* (Rogue, 2000) has eccentric characters, a wonderfully quirky storyline and graphics, yet the player-character still has an armory with which to "shoot" threatening monsters. There are many, many games built on this premise. Beginning with *DOOM* (id Software, 1993), shoot-and-survive rhetoric has achieved the status of archetype within the world of games.

So why has horror proved such a popular mode for games? Why have certain horror based rhetorics made it into games while others haven't? Certainly within the media industry horror is perceived to be a predictable, tried, and tested market and that market dovetails with a traditional younger male market (added to which is the general and strangely suitable ageless appeal of the gothic to a broader audience). The genre also has the advantage of dealing in strong emotions through narratives that deploy archetypal situations — survival, death, fear, sex, transgression; themes that are often appealing to exploratory, sensation-seeking teens. Game designers can borrow from a set of established conventions and familiar brands, re-molding and exploring the new media, and in so doing retaining some familiarity for potential players to identify the product in the marketplace. Horror permits the impossible and the supernatural, something easily achieved when creating digital content. Good versus evil narratives are simple and strong, easily understood, providing clear motives for violence that also insulate against censorship. The pursuit of mastery rhetoric used in games, suits action-based horror extraordinarily well. Now, some of these dimensions fit quite well the task of translating Lovecraft's rhetorics and ethos into popular video game form, but other very crucial elements do not.

"...in the black seas of infinity..."

Howard Phillips Lovecraft (1890–1937) wrote short stories, the latter group of which fall neatly under the sub-generic label of "cosmic horror" (although "weird fiction" is also a commonly used descriptor). These were published during the late 1920s and 30s, mainly in the popular magazine *Weird Tales*. A certain ethos and world/cosmos, as used in a fantasy genre sense, grow out of these tales. Lovecraft was himself keen for others to write stories that made use of the mythos he had conjured into being, as has indeed been the case. For purposes of this essay I'll briefly outline the main characteristics of what I'll call "Cthulhean rhetoric." The stories are very different to the type of approach found in other work published in those magazines—Lovecraft did not write the muscular action fiction found in his friend Robert E Howard's Conan stories. Instead the stories are marked by inaction and characters are frozen in terror; rather than act on their situation in an effort to master it, they are more likely to be consumed by dread, wits thrown asunder as certainties and reason fall to ash and slide down into the dark waters of oblivion. The pessimistic rhetoric of the mythos is neatly, bleakly, summed up by the first line of "The Call of Cthulhu": "The most merciful thing in the world, I think, is the inability of the human mind to correlate all its contents. We live on a placid island of ignorance in the midst of black seas of infinity; and it was not meant that we should voyage far" (Lovecraft, 1999 [1926]: 139). To give a further example, Lovecraft helpfully sets out his pitch in a letter:

> Now all my tales are based on the fundamental premise that common human laws and interests and emotions have no validity or significance in the vast cosmos-at-large. To me there is nothing but puerility in a tale in which the human form — and the local human passions and conditions and standards— are depicted as native to other worlds or universes. To achieve the essence of real externality, whether of time or space or dimensions, one must forget that such things as organic life, good and evil, love and hate, and all such local attributes of a negligible and temporary race called mankind, have any existence at all. Only human scenes and characters must have human qualities. *These* must be

handled with unsparing *realism*, (not catch-penny *romanticism*) but when we cross the line to the boundless and hideous unknown — the shadow haunted *Outside*— we must remember to leave our humanity and terrestrialism at the threshold [cited in Joshi, 2004: 77 (italics in original)].

The invocation of cosmic terror found in Lovecraft's tales corresponds with uncanny neatness to an aspect of the Lacanian conception of the "Real" (one of the spheres that he uses to describe psychological function, the other two are Symbolic and Imaginary; the Real is that which exceeds or is remaindered by these latter two). In particular that awe-inspiring, belittling aspect of the Real; the sublime Real that Slavoj Zizek is drawn-in by and elaborates in his work on cinema (Zizek, 1991), a dimension of the Real that is radical, crashing into our bubble of speech and imagination and literally stops us in our tracks, rather than its more mundane counterpart (the Real father for example, as opposed to the imaginary or symbolic father). In other words, and indeed paradoxically, the Real is that which resists symbolization, breaching thereby the outer contours of human understanding and rationality, where the imagination can easily locate monstrous terrors; this in turn corresponds with romantic notions of the sublime, derived from Edmund Burke, who claimed during the mid 18th century, back when Gothic fiction was in its infancy, that

> ... terror is in all cases whatsoever either more openly or latently the ruling principle of the sublime [Burke, 2008: 58].
>
> The passion caused by the great and sublime in nature ... is Astonishment; and astonishment is that state of the soul, in which all its motions are suspended, with some degree of horror. In this case the mind is so entirely filled with its object, that it cannot entertain any other [Burke, 2008: 57].

In the yawning maw of the Cthulhean, all certainties and comforting correspondences become merely the blown dust of illusion. There is no redemption or salvation, and the Other that diminishes human-scale to nothing can never be contained or mastered. Nor is there "good" or "evil" in the classical sense. Instead there is simply no occulted moral order, no power that guarantees or safeguards human existence. Religion and other human-centric institutions are revealed as rhetoric dreamed up by the social order to give structure and meaning to everyday selves and lives. All the protective whimsy present in earlier tales, through the influence of Lord Dunsany's tales, is denied in these later ones; even the language that was inclined, Poe-like, to be encrusted with adjectives and complex rhythms and sentence structures has become more simplified, powerful and, by virtue of that, less of a distracting consolation. All these factors seem far from recommendations for the translation of the Cthulhean rhetoric into the shoot-and-survive, morally polar world dimensions of video games with their placatory visual glitter and auditory profusion. However, the broader game format has proved a fertile spawning ground for Cthulhean remediation.

First amongst these are Chaosium's tabletop role playing games sold under the title of "Call of Cthulhu" (see www.chaosium.com), developed by Sandy Peterson, who also worked on the tabletop RPG *Runequest* (Chaosium, 1978) and the video game *DOOM*. The franchise has wide acclaim among tabletop role-play gamers, while this support is not of blockbuster commercial proportions it has attracted sufficient commercial interest to sustain it over the past 25 years (the 25th Anniversary edition came out in 2006). Players become detectives of the Cthulhean conspiracy, placed in a wide range of eras and locations with each edition, using various skills, yet running the fairly high risk of dying horribly or going insane. A common criticism of the games is that they tend to stray from the Cthulhean ethos into the domain of action-based adventure with storylines pitching the group in the task of saving the world. Like video games, table-top role-play games do tend, perhaps because of their core market, to focus on action, often fighting in amongst exploration and character development. In line with the traditional form of table top systems, role-players expect to be active agents in the game. To be able to initiate action and prevail over adversity is, in this format and also in video games, geared as the mark of player presence and participation. Fighting and winning is something that does not tally with the Cthulhean; here we see how the dominant "act-and-prevail" rhetorics of popular participatory entertainment flounder on the bleak, pessimistic, shores of Lovecraft's ethos. This is an aspect that we need to consider in relation to video game rhetorics generally and the *Call of Cthulhu: Dark Corners of the Earth* video game particularly.

To provide a better understanding of the game as both adaptation and artifact I'll outline some of its core features. The game makes use of names and locations drawn from mainly two tales: "The Shadow over Innsmouth" (Lovecraft, 1999 [1931]) and "The Call of Cthulhu" (Lovecraft, 1999[1926]). Its setting is contemporary to the time these stories were written, allowing the game some latitude to justify various aspects of the tale as well as, one suspects, excusing some racism carried by Lovecraft's conception of Cthulthean terrors. The player is Jack Walters, a detective (figure 2).

We learn very early on in the game's preface that he has lost six years of his life to an alternative personality after an encounter (seen in cut-scene) with some very ET-ish looking "Old Ones."

The game is played in first-person, yet it can hardly be described as a first-person shooter. In fact, much of the early part of the game is spent without any form of weapon. It is, as suits the shade of this collection of essays, a dark game that can only barely be played during daylight. The color palette is tonally very dark, with only small variations on grey, blue, black, and brown; it's not sepia, but it's not far off (a common means of indicating the past by using color associated with contemporary photography). Innsmouth, and its interiors, is exceedingly dingy and run-down, the overall effect of the decaying-chewed-toffee colors is to give the player a sense of claustrophobia, underpinned by the presence of many boundaries that restrict the player's explorations. In addition to the cloying darkness of the game, the player is at the start instructed to play the game at night — suggesting the game's designers recognize that horror and its concomitant suspension of disbelief is very sensitive to context. The music is melancholy and low-key, resonantly opposed thereby to the heavy-metal groove of adrenalinized shoot-em-ups. Having established how the player-character lost his mind and spent time in an asylum, skipping forward to the future, Jack is reluctantly engaged to find a missing person in the town of Innsmouth — local myth has it that few ever go there now and even fewer return. Jack is then engaged in a series of tasks of the type expected of an adventure game. The objective missing person is a shop-boy, but even at this early stage the player is likely to understand that the journey might also subjectively be about searching for that which would restore self-continuity. The player-character searches the town for clues, learns much from various non-player characters' conversations, begins to understand the grammar of the game in spatial terms (including the location of save points), dodges the attention of fish-men and avoids looking too closely at horrific spectacles. While a weapon is available further on, much of the game is spent running from those who will kill Jack, and getting to know and using the environment to evade enemies. We also hear Jack's thoughts, as if we are at least at times one with his thoughts. He has no useful side-kick to talk to, a factor that isolates him, working thereby in a dif-

ferent way to many solo-play RPGs that give players an AI controlled group to play in. Jack's thoughts (prerecorded audio loops) are often played back-to-back, perhaps inadvertently helping make him seem even more unstable. Some of what he thinks aloud is practical and banally objective ("This is a key."), yet directly helpful to the player, while at other times he makes far

Figure 2: Jack Walters, a detective teetering on the edge of sanity after being caught up in the Cult of Cthulhu.

more subjective statements that build for the player a sense that he is not what he seems.

In acknowledgement of the written source of the game, and indeed of the way that Lovecaft's stories themselves are often woven out of an assortment of written sources, drawn from and pertaining to various places and times (letters, newspaper articles, etc.), the game makes frequent use of writing that must be read by the player. A diary is provided which logs what the player-character has done and seen, scraps of ancient grimoires encountered provide back-story and indeed help create a sense of the mythos, inter-titles of the type found in contemporary pre-talkie movies are common — often quoting lines directly from the stories or from Lovecraft's letters and articles. This is one way that the game retains something of the particularities of his writing and its peculiar rhythms and idiosyncrasies. In addition the game collects player statistics, a nod not to the primary source but instead to the system that lies behind the table-top games. This further emphasizes player performance, and acts as recognition of the time and effort a player puts in to complete the game within certain timescales. When the player complete the game within a set time, secrets are unlocked and players are given the opportunity to play the "mythos specialist" (these features encourage players to play the game over again).

One of the features of the game that pleased some reviewers (see Simmer, 2005) was the way the game took the shooter format with its normally "thin" story line and gave it instead, through the mythos, a thick story (as those coming to the game with a knowledge of Lovecraft would perhaps have expected this). Working with a range of themes common to horror — otherness, transformation, alienation allied to a twist on the central tenets of detective fiction, the game has a narrative depth but this is certainly by virtue of the source texts. A core thematic of the game's story is "denial"; a theme often present in Lovecraft's stories (and horror stories generally — a convention often used in popular horror is where the protagonist has to come to believe in the supernatural and irrational, neatly exemplified by the film *Night of the Demon* [Jacques Tourneur, 1957, UK]). This theme is keyed into the game not just in terms of story — what the player-character has forgotten (lost years and an occulted heritage), but also, importantly, in terms of the core game mechanics. Here is where the medium comes into its own and the adaptation extends beyond the source into a new dimension. This is also apparent in another aspect of the game.

Bruce Kawin (1984) has argued that the horror film tends to punish the transgressive gaze. This notion is supported by a number of examples where those that look at the forbidden are paid back for their action. It is perhaps most strongly emblemized in the infamous bullet-in-the-eye scene in Dario Argento's *Opera* (1987) where the trope is over-determined and *in extremis*, yet the punishment of the eye is a common feature in horror films. This frequently used rhetorical device can be seen as part of the way in which horror films seek to involve their audience, in this case punishing the audience by proxy for their interest in the "forbidden." A film like Michael Powell's *Peeping Tom* (1960) works reflexively with this convention. Here he aligns the audience with the look of the killer's victim rather than the look of the photographer/killer; the victim sees their face in a mirror attached to the camera as they die, after being stabbed with the camera's sharpened tripod by the photographer. This image of the screaming victim in the mirror is shown in first person, as if it were the face of the viewer. Like cinema, games place importance on looking, even, as I argued above, taking the hermeneutic visual code a step further because they demand of the player an acute investigative gaze if a game's challenges are to be negotiated with skill. In this sense the gaze is less likely to be punished, because it is not simply allied to visual pleasure, as it is in films. Careful and informed looking, that leads to specific actions, is part of the player's contract with the game (figure 3).

One of the core selling features of the *Call of Cthulhu: Dark Corners of the Earth* is its "Insanity Effects." In centralizing these as a core gameplay mechanic, the game acknowledges most deeply the Cthulhean approach to horror. These effects have a host of implications. They provide a very direct way of linking the character's psychological state to the perceptual and action field of the player, providing in some way an equivalent of literature's unreliable narrator. *Eternal Darkness: Sanity's Requiem* (Silicon Knights, 2002),

a video game that is indebted to Lovecraft but is not a direct adaptation of one of his stories, also makes use of the hallmark insanity of the Cthulhean ethos. Here it is imposed on the player in different ways, and in so doing breaks the fourth wall (a tradition found in horror genre from Grand Guignol theatre to the "ghost-train" auditorium

Figure 3: The debilitating spectacle of death in *Call of Cthulhu: Dark Corners of the Earth* (Bethesda, 2006).

antics of director William Castle in the 1950s). During play, the game image occasionally dissolves into TV static making it look to the player as if the console has failed; other times colors change and sounds start to echo and distort. Suggesting to the player that something has gone wrong with the console or software, such devices affect directly play with the boundary between the imaginary and diegetic sphere and that of the real; breaking in that sense the frame of representation and even fundamentally the game grammar we are used to. *Call of Cthulhu* does not go in for these "breaking the frame of representation" type devices. Instead the player does in fact have some control over how "insane" they become. Importantly, and to return to the issue of punishment for "looking," the player will induce hallucinations and impair their ability to act in the game world if they gaze too intently at the spectacles of horror that are littered throughout the game (using morphine to "heal" oneself also has this effect but with a different resonance). And, if you do this too often your already fairly minimal skills are deeply diminished and the player-character can barely function, at least temporarily. This is not *just* insanity. The deployment of this device, where you are asked "not to look" and it is reinforced by the game mechanics, undermines one of the fundamental rhetorics of games and in some respects looks back to the punishment of the gaze rhetorics used within cinema. This device represents therefore, one of the major paradoxes of the game. It is one that also ties very neatly to the theme of denial which is structural to the game's narrative. It is realized in such a way that the player gets a more direct sense of it because the normal actions they would expect to carry out in a game are given this defamiliarizing twist. In some regards the insanity effects work necessarily against the rhetorics of mastery that are intrinsic to popular culture artifacts and games particularly, with their "doing" dimension. But still, the game itself is designed for the player to progress, and master, however under-powered, the challenges that arise. Players of the game rarely prevail in the type of categorical manner made available in more "muscular" games, instead it is more of a case of scraping through, a feature that provides a very diluted version of Roger Caillois' *agon* (competition). The controller itself in the Xbox version seems at times to work against the player; the affects of fear making it pulsate, becoming more present and not in a helpful manner. The increasing intensity of the sound of the heartbeat works with primal responses. Occasionally the camera jumps into close-ups, again showing Jack's terror at the spectacles of horror he regularly encounters (mainly rotting bodies). It is often Caillois' other term *ilinx* (vertigo) that pertains more directly to the experience solicited by the game; not the literal vertigo of *Mirror's Edge* (EA/ DICE, 2008), but the vertigo produced by terror.

What I have to admit is that fairly early in the game I became completely stuck; I found this "aporia" (Aarseth, 1997: 125) rather interesting as an academic, although supremely frustrating as a gamer, and it leads into some conclusions about game design practice and the very specific characteristics of video game form. Jack is asleep, awoken by fishmen at his hotel room door, clearly come to bludgeon him to death established in the preceding cut-scene. This sequence is told in Lovecraft's original story retrospectively, presented as a recalled event rather than, as in the game, in the present tense. It is clear in the story that he's escaped, by contrast in the game we have to escape, creating perhaps a stronger sense of suspense and anxiety. However, in the game we do know that the fishmen have come to kill the character, whereas in the story their intentions are far less clear; the character is himself in a state of suspense because he could only barely hear what those outside his room are saying or what they are doing. In the game, escape can only be made by dexterous and precise actions on the part of the player. Wardrobes must be moved, doors locked and unlocked, under timed conditions, with only fractions of seconds to spare, even when done with exactitude. This involves the player in moving their point-of-view to frame the objects precisely, as well as requiring other actions: you must move across the room in an optimum way, look up, throw a bolt, look down, open the door, go through the door, look up, throw the bolt, push a wardrobe to cover a further door — an object that moves extremely slowly. They're coming, you can see them in your peripheral vision, their breath is loud, they hit you, you're dead, back in the bed where you started out, and they are at the door once more. After 15 tries and still quite calm, I am thinking this is all very Cthulhean because of the repetition, inability to act, and the very tangible sense that powers far greater than me affect my sphere of action (aka the fiendish game designers). After 30 tries, my thoughts affected very deeply by my growing frustration, I conclude that this is terrible game design!! My suspension of disbelief broken, and what *was* a world, a mythos, becomes all too apparently a set of mechanical actions demanded by a game machine, and a broken one at that. Panic and frustration now subsided; it occurs to me that this is an extraordinary game. I am used to games with very new-user friendly learning curves, game that are afraid that the player will reject the game if they encounter any stiff challenge. With markets for games widening the trend is for the simple. *World of Warcraft* (Blizzard, 2004–2009) is lauded for the ease with which it introduced new users to the MMORPG format. Wii games are designed on the whole to appeal to families, with games that tend to be more intuited than learned. Games such as *Spore* (Maxis, 2008) and *Little Big Planet* (Media Molecule, 2008) allow the generation of user-created content with few skills. With no cheats easily available on the web, *Call of Cthulhu: Dark Corners of the Earth* seems very assured that its players will be "old school" gamers— prepared to work at getting at the content. That is therefore a brave approach to adaptation, and in some sense illustrates a remarkable faith in the pull of the brand.

But failure within a game also highlights some core features of video games as cybernetic systems with very specific interface rhetorics that key into the way games seem to be especially good at creating the types of affect that work well with horror.

Steve Shaviro (1993) argues that horror cinema exploits the spectator's submission to events. Henri Bergson (1971, 2004) writes that cinematic pleasure is based on the fact that kinetic energy is turned inwards which produces the experience of intensity. A player's contract with a game, particularly action/adventure and shoot-and-survive games, is to act on a situation with a sense of striving to move forward — projecting ourselves, as Barry Atkins says, into the future (2006). Striving and mastery are therefore at the core of games of progression (Juul, 2002). Players must respond to the events seen and heard in a timely and well-judged way. Failure leads to a strangely Freudian conception of death as stasis. In order to play a video game, players must perform very careful, controlled, and managed movements with their hands. We have to reduce down a real action to a symbolic or sometimes synecdochic one (particularly the case with the Wii). When panic sets in, control is diminished — our performance impaired. Claustrophobia, the emblem of horror in video games, is also felt through our ability to act — or more precisely not to act, which further connotes a lack of agency. It is in the act of having to finesse and reduce down precisely our physical actions in response to what we see, hear, expect, and read, that intensity swells — perhaps that is why when our actions are inadequate the compulsion to act large comes, perhaps to throw the controller across the room, or jump and shout. This is all underpinned within the effects of actions seen on screen: our small movements having much larger effects there. Mihaly Csikszentmihalyi (2002) argues that the pleasurable experience of "flow" comes with skill mastery. I would suggest that this model goes someway to showing what is in play in our engagement with video games yet it doesn't quite explain how it is that affective intensity is generated through making diminutive our movements in relation to on screen events; and indeed this small rule of thumb is what distinguishes games from other media.

So is Lovecraft rolling in his grave propelled by the act of his stories having been "remediated" by the demon technology? Perhaps, but *Call of Cthulhu: Dark Corners of the Earth* is in many ways a respectful and careful adaptation that uses aspects of video game media to bring new dimensions to encounters with the Cthulhean; even if the game has bugs and requires fiendish precision and saintly patience. The game is marked out because it bucks certain trends that have become habitual to contemporary game design and indeed popular horror. Instead of the mechanical twitch of the shoot-and-survive format, *Call of Cthulhu* requires the player to develop skills and sharp tactics. These are structural to the game's hermeneutic code, which in other media is generally far more transparent and immediate. The way that games actively resist the player, and the concomitant emotions that arise for the player when they are resisted by the game, has a sublime dimension, arising at times from aporia. The particular nature of resistance and the emotions it solicits is not possible in other media. Such resistance transforms the game — uncannily appropriately as *mise-en-abyme*, into an occult text, that the player must work to decipher. While it might not benefit from the Pirensean visual paradoxes found in the liminal spaces of the *Silent Hill* games, *Call of Cthulhu* plays with other paradoxes that undermine or subvert the conventional rhetorics of games and horror — including the rejection of shoot-and-survive tactics, Manichean sophistry, and the subversion of rhetorics of the investigative gaze, as well as the market-paradox of the game's baseline level of difficulty and resistance. What the game does so well, using the strengths of video game media, is to destabilize any easy sense of agency, eschewing muscular, categoric, sovereignty and making thereby a suitably Cthulthean comment that runs deep into the player's engagement with game and its themes.

Works Cited

Aarseth, Espen (1997), *Cybertext: Perspectives on Ergodic Literature*, Baltimore: John Hopkins.

Atkins, Barry (2006), "What Are We Really Looking at? The Future Orientation of Play," *Games and Culture*. Vol. 1, No. 2, April, pp. 127–140.

Bergson, Henri (2004), *Matter and Memory*, New York: Dover Publications.

_____ (1971), *Time and Free Will*, London and New York: George Allen and Unwin.

Bolter, Jay David and Richard Grusin (2002), *Remediation: Understanding New Media*, Cambridge, MA: MIT Press.

Burke, Edmund (2008 [1958, 1757]), in James T. Boulton (ed.), *Burke: A Philosophical Enquiry into the Sublime and the Beautiful*, London: Routledge.

Caillois, Roger (2001), *Man, Play and Games*, Urbana and Chicago: University Illinois Press.

Csikszentmihalyi, Mihaly (2002), *Flow: The Class Work on How to Achieve Happiness*, London, Sydney, Auckland and Johannesburg: Rider.

Gottlieb, Sidney (2003), *Alfred Hitchcock: Interviews (Conversations with Filmmakers)*, Jackson: University Press of Mississippi.

Joshi, S.T. (2004), *The Evolution of the Weird Tale*, New York: Hippocampus Press.

Juul, Jesper (2002), "The Open and the Closed: Game of emergence and games of progression," in Frans Mäyrä (ed.), *Computer Games and Digital Cultures Conference Proceedings*, Tampere: Tampere University Press, pp. 323–329.

Kawin, Bruce (1984), "The Mummy's Pool," in Barry Keith Grant (ed.), *Planks of Reason: Essays on the Horror Film*, Metuchen and London: Scarecrow Press, pp. 3–20.

Kosofsky, Eve Sedgwick (1986), *The Coherence of Gothic Conventions*, New York and London: Metheun.

Krzywinska, Tanya (2002), "Hands-on Horror," in Geoff King and Tanya Krzywinska (eds.), *ScreenPlay: cinema/videogames/interfaces*, London and New York: Wallflower Press, pp. 206–233.

_____ (2008), "Zombies in Gamespace: Form, Context and Meaning in Zombie-based

Videogames," in Shawn McIntosh and Marc Leverette (eds.), *Zombie Culture*, Lanham, MD: Scarecrow Press, pp. 153–168.

Lovecraft, H.P. (1999), "The Shadow Over Innsmouth (1931)" and "The Call of Cthulhu (1926)," in S.T. Joshi (ed.), *The Call of Cthulhu and Other Weird Stories*, Harmondsworth: Penguin.

Ndlianas, Angela (2005), *Neo-Baroque Aesthetics and Contemporary Entertainment*, Cambridge, MA: MIT Press.

Shaviro, Steve (1993), *The Cinematic Body*, Minneapolis and London: University of Minnesota Press.

Simmer, Aaron (aka Omni) (2005), "Call of Cthulhu: Dark Corners of the Earth," *The Armchaire Empire*, December 10, available online at <http://www.armchairempire.com/Reviews/XBox/call-cthulhu-dark-corners-earth.htm>.

Suits, Bernard (1990), *The Grasshopper: Games, Life and Utopia*, Boston: David R. Godine.

Zizek, Slavoj (1991), *Looking Awry: An Introduction to Jacques Lacan Through Popular Culture*, Cambridge, MA: MIT Press.

About the Contributors

Clive Barker was born in Liverpool, England, where he began his creative career writing, directing and acting for the stage. Since then, he has gone on to pen such bestsellers as *The Books of Blood, Weaveworld, Imajica, The Great and Secret Show, The Thief of Always, Everville, Sacrament, Galilee, Coldheart Canyon,* and the highly acclaimed fantasy series, *Abarat.* As a screenwriter, director and film producer, he is credited with the *Hellraiser* and *Candyman* pictures, as well as *Nightbreed, Lord of Illusions, Gods and Monsters* and *The Midnight Meat Train.* He is the creator of the acclaimed Video Game *Jericho.* Mr. Barker lives in Los Angeles, California.

Inger Ekman received a master of science in computer science degree from the University of Tampere in 2003, after which she worked for several years as a lecturer in hypermedia. She is currently an interaction designer and researcher at the Center for Knowledge and Innovation Research (CKIR), Helsinki School of Economics. She is also pursuing a doctoral degree at the Department of Information Studies and Interactive Media, University of Tampere, investigating sound design for computer games. Inger Ekman has published several essays on game design and sound, such as those in the journal *Computer & Graphics,* as well as numerous conference proceedings. [inger.ekman@uta.fi]

Ewan Kirkland lectures in media and cultural studies at Kingston University, London. Specializing in the textual analysis of horror videogames, he has written on self-reflexivity in *Silent Hill,* the remediation of analogue media in digital games, and the relationship between art and videogame promotional culture. As well as game studies, he also writes on popular cinema, fantasy television and children's culture, having published papers and articles on Robin Williams, romantic comedy film, Disney, *Buffy the Vampire Slayer* and *Battlestar Galactica.* He has published in *Screen, Games and Culture, Convergence: The International Journal of Research into New Media, SCOPE: An Online Journal of Film Studies,* and *The International Journal of Cultural Studies.* Currently, he is working on a study of the representation and construction of whiteness, masculinity and heterosexuality in contemporary popular culture. [kirklanduk@yahoo.co.uk]

Tanya Krzywinska is a professor of screen studies at Brunel University, London. She is the author of several books and many articles on different aspects of videogames, horror and fantasy and is particularly interested in occult fiction and fantasy worlds. She is the co-author of *Tomb Raiders and Space Invaders: Videogames Forms and Meanings* (IB Tauris, 2006), *Sex and the Cinema* (Wallflower, 2006), *A Skin for Dancing in: Witchcraft, Possession and Voodoo in film* (2001), and co-editor of *ScreenPlay: Cinema/Videogames/Interfaces* (Wallflower Press, 2002) and *Videogame/player/text* (MUP, 2007). She convenes a BA, MA and PhD program in the theory and design of digital games at Brunel University, and is president of the Digital Games Research Association. [tanya.krzywinska@brunel.ac.uk]

Petri Lankoski works at the Media Laboratory, University of Art and Design Helsinki, where he teaches and researches game design. His research interests include character-driven game design and game aesthetics. Petri Lankoski has published on game design and roleplaying theory, and edited two books on experience design (titles translated): *Human, Place, and Time* (2001) and *Personal Navigation: Principles for Designing User Interfaces and Experiences* (2002). More information can be found at <http://www.iki.fi/petri.lankoski/>.

Christian McCrea is a writer and lecturer in games and interactivity at Swinburne University of Technology, Melbourne, Australia. His work peers over the fences of art and game culture, looking to complicate some of gaming's own questions using the longer narratives of art practice and history. He has written on the spectatorship of strategic play, dandy game heroes, game ecologies and the aesthetic of bursting bodies in both games and anime. [cmccrea@swin.edu.au]

Simon Niedenthal is an associate professor of interaction design at the School of Arts and Communication, Malmö University, Malmö, Sweden. His areas of research include digital game aesthetics, simulated illumination in games, and design process for games and interaction. His work has been published in such scholarly journals as *Leonardo*, *Game Studies*, and *Cyberpsychology and Behavior*. [simon.niedenthal@mah.se]

Michael Nitsche is an assistant professor at the School of Literature, Communication, and Culture at the Georgia Institute of Technology, where he teaches courses on virtual environments and digital moving images. He heads the Digital World and Image Group, which explores the design, use, and production of virtual spaces, machinima, and the borderlines between games, film, and performance. His work combines theoretical analysis and practical experiments and his collaborations include work with the National Film and Television School in London, Sony Computer Entertainment Europe, Turner Broadcasting, Alcatel Lucent, and others. He is the author of *Video Game Spaces: Image, Play, and Structure in 3D Worlds* (MIT Press, 2008) and has published on game studies, virtual worlds, digital performance, games and film, and machinima. In a former life he was co-author for a commercial videogame, professional improv actor, and dramaturgist. More information can be found at his websites: <http://www.lcc.gatech.edu/~nitsche/>; <http://dwig.lcc.gatech.edu/>; and <http://www.freepixel.org>. [michael.nitsche@lcc.gatech.edu]

Bernard Perron is an associate professor of cinema at the University of Montreal. He has co-edited *The Video Game Theory Reader 1* (Routledge, 2003) and *The Video Game Theory Reader 2* (Routledge, 2008). He has written *Silent Hill: il motore del terrore* (Costa & Nolan, 2006), an analysis of the Silent Hill video game series. He has also edited issues on play for *Intermedialities* (Montreal, 2007), on cinema and cognition for *Cinemas: Journal of Films Studies* (Montreal, 2002), and co-edited one on intermedial practices of montage and configurations of alternation in early cinema for *Cinema & Cie* (Milan, 2007). His research and writings concentrate on editing in early cinema; on narration, cognition, and the ludic dimension of narrative cinema; and on interactive cinema and video game. More information can be found at his website <http://www.ludicine.ca/>. [bernard.perron@umontreal.ca]

Martin Picard is a Ph.D. candidate in comparative literature and film studies and part-time lecturer in the History of Art and Film Studies Department at the University of Montreal. His publications and research interests cover film and digital media, video game culture and theory, and Japanese film and aesthetics. He's currently writing a thesis on the relationship between the aesthetics of video games and cinema. [martinpicard@videotron.ca]

Dan Pinchbeck is a researcher and lecturer at the University of Portsmouth, UK; specializing in first-person gaming, with particular focus on the relationship between game content and player behavior. He is currently part of a European team developing KEEP, a new system that will enable the archiving and emulation of all digital artifacts (with a particular focus on gaming). He recently completed his doctorate on FPS content as a function of gameplay and leads a mod development team creating experimental FPS games, most notably the cult *Half-Life 2* mod *Dear Esther*. A full publications list, links to game downloads and information about all of these projects can be found at <www.thechineseroom.co.uk>. [dan.pinchbeck@port.ac.uk]

Richard Rouse III is a game designer and writer who has worked in computer and video game development for more than a decade. He is currently lead single player designer on an unannounced project at Kaos Studios in New York City. He was creative director and writer on the hit action/horror title *The Suffering* and its sequel, *The Suffering: Ties That Bind*. Rouse has led the design on a number of other games, including *Centipede 3D*, *Damage Incorporated*, and *Odyssey: The Legend of Nemesis,* as well as contributing to the design on *Drakan: The Ancients' Gates*. During a stint as director of game design at Midway Games he consulted on a wide range of next-generation titles, including *Stranglehold*, *Wheelman*, and *This Is Vegas*. He has written about game design for publications including *Game Developer*, *SIGGRAPH Computer Graphics*, *Develop*, *Gamasutra*, and *Inside Mac Games,* and has lectured on game design at numerous conferences, including the Game Developer's Conference and the Electronic Entertainment Expo. Rouse's popular and sizable book about game design and development titled *Game Design: Theory & Practice* was released in an expanded second edition in 2004. More information can be found at his website <http://www.para noidproductions.com>. [rr3@paranoidproductions.com]

Guillaume Roux-Girard is a master's degree student in film studies at the University of Montreal. His research concentrates on sound in horror video games. [guillaume.roux-girard@umontreal.ca]

Laurie N. Taylor is the interim director of the Digital Library Center in the University of Florida's George A. Smathers Libraries. Her articles have appeared in various journals and edited collections, including *Game Studies: The International Journal of Computer Game Research, Media/Culture, Works & Days, Videogames and Art: Intersections and Interactions,* and *The Player's Realm: Studies on the Culture of Video Games and Gaming,* and her writing about games and digital media has also appeared in many popular venues. Her current research includes studies of game and digital media interfaces, methods of digital representation, and issues of the archive. [laurien@ufl.edu]

Carl Therrien is currently pursuing a Ph.D. in semiology at Université du Québec in Montreal. His research focuses on the playful and mediated immersion in fictional worlds, in video games and other media. Major publications include two historical contributions in Mark J. P. Wolf's *The Video Game Explosion: A History from PONG to PlayStation and Beyond* (Greenwood Press, 2007), articles on the methodology of interactive film studies ("»Pointez-et-cliquez ici« Les figures d'interactivité dans le cinéma interactif des premiers temps," in *Lo stile cinematografico,* Forum, 2007), on videogame design ("L'appel de la simulation. Deux approches du design vidéoludique," in *Le game design de jeux vidéo,* L'Harmattan, 2005), and on the playful nature of contemporary cinema ("Cinema under the influence of play," in *Narrativity: How Visual Arts, Cinema and Literature Are Telling the World Today,* Dis Voir, 2006). [carl.therrien@gmail.com]

Matthew Weise is the lead game designer for the Singapore–MIT GAMBIT Game Lab, a lab dedicated to the research and development of video games. There he works with both students and staff on various game development projects that seek to push the medium of games forward by leveraging MIT technology. In the past Matt has worked in experimental games for education and mobile game development. He studied film production at the University of Wisconsin–Milwaukee and got his master's degree from the Massachusetts Institute of Technology in comparative media studies. Matt's writing has appeared in academic conference proceedings such as the *DIGRA Level Up Conference Proceedings* (2003) and such industry publications as *Game Career Guide* (2008). [sajon@mit.edu]

Index

Numbers in **bold italics** indicate pages with illustrations.